The Age of Firearms

A PICTORIAL HISTORY FROM THE INVENTION OF GUNPOWDER TO THE ADVENT OF THE MODERN BREECHLOADER

New and Revised Edition by the Author
Much New Textual and Pictorial Matter

by ROBERT HELD

ONZ'VNA DIB.

Research Assistance and Book Design by

NANCY HELD

Revision edited by

JOSEPH J. SCHROEDER, JR.

PUBLISHED BY THE GUN DIGEST COMPANY, NORTHFIELD, ILLINOIS

T-0068

ABOUT THE AUTHOR

Robert Held, a New Yorker, was born on December 11, 1929. He whiled away the years between then and 1963 by going to sea as a Third Assistant Engineer, attending Columbia University for a degree in Greek, Latin and Classical History, writing historical articles and short stories under his own and assumed names, marrying the very best of wives in the history of wifehood, and keeping up his interest in antique firearms (which began with the present of an old cap-and-ball shotgun from a great-aunt for Christmas, 1939). Since 1963 the Helds live in an ancient rookery composed of an abandoned ninth-century church and the adjacent vicarage and farm house (dating in various parts from A.D. 1000 to about 1600) on a hilltop in the heart of the Chianti wine lands about twenty-two miles south of Florence; there they manage their vineyards and olive groves, continue to write, draw and paint, and to keep up with collecting guns, early Italian wood sculpture and documentary material—books, manuscripts, &c.—pertaining to both these pursuits. Their son Joshua was born there in 1967. Mrs. Held, under her maiden name Nancy Jenkins, designed the layout of THE AGE OF FIREARMS, did all the modern diagrams and drawings (including the widely-copied series on page 93), and shouldered much of the research for antique illustrations.

THE AGE OF FIREARMS, A Pictorial History
Copyright © 1957, 1970 by Robert Held and Nancy Held
Printed in the United States of America

*Second, revised edition published by The Gun Digest Co.,
540 Frontage Rd., Northfield, Illinois 60093, by special
arrangement with Harper & Row, Publishers. All rights reserved.*

Library of Congress catalog and number: 70-90430

ISBN 0-695-80068-X

CONTENTS

A FEW (886) WORDS ABOUT THIS EDITION . . .

In the dozen years since THE AGE OF FIREARMS was first published by Harper & Brothers in November, 1957, the study and collecting of antique arms and armor has gone through a phase of immeasurable expansion all over the world. No need to dwell here on the many plus and minus aspects of this phenomenon—most readers will be only too sadly aware of the chief minus, viz., the catastrophe of supply, demand and prices. By now the very finest specimens have nearly all been swallowed up by public and private *permanent* collections, never to emerge again, sharing place of pride with treasured works of art and science; while the acquisition of good middle-and-up-quality pieces has become the prerogative of few men indeed, and even run-of-the-mill mediocrities are the objects of frenetic steeplechases by panting pursuers brandishing the-devil-may-care-how-many dollars, drachmas, francs, kroner, lire, marks, pesos, pounds, yen . . . and in recent years also rubles. Inevitably, fakes, semi-fakes and "restorations" (three-quarter fakes) abound; inevitably, tastes, quality standards and perspectives have wilted into rather disagreeable decadence everywhere. Rare indeed these days, in Europe, America or Japan, lives the collector with innate sensitivity for the patina, for the historical color and flavor, for the silent, melancholy evocations of any good antique, gun or not; among gun collectors they now seem rarest of all.

But the plus side of the balance, too, is heavily weighted: and without doubt the most impressive of the positives is the wealth of arms-and-armor publications in all languages representing an inordinately high level of scholarship, literateness and dedication. Again, no need to go into this in detail here—many readers will be familiar with the catalogs of the half-dozen booksellers in America and Britain specializing in arms-and-armor literature. Excellent works are available today on every phase, nook, corner and cranny of arms history: from very costly, limited-edition, massive volumes with hundreds of full-color photographs to inexpensive, thin little monographs on some recondite peculiarity, from definitive studies of an entire nation's martial arms to—like the present work—over-all, panoramic surveys.

All this was not so in 1957. Meaningful arms-and-armor books were then limited to a few classics, most of them of the late 19th and early 20th centuries, a half-dozen of immediate pre-war years, and another four or five of the twelve years after. Of survey histories designed, like THE AGE OF FIREARMS, for the collector as well as for the general reader, and drawing on the inexhaustible but rarely-tapped reservoir of antique illustrative material, there were none.

Why pontificate on all this here and now? Definitely not to praise THE AGE OF FIREARMS: rather, to warn the reader about those of its characteristics which may be, and have been, fairly criticized as failings, but may with equal fairness be held up as virtues. Most vulnerable to criticism is the abrupt ending: the book ends with the death through lingering of the muzzleloader and the advent of mass-production arms in the middle 1800's, with barely a nod in the direction of cartridges, breechloaders, the Civil War and all that followed. Why? Because the author's grasp is strong up to the 1840's, falters toward the 1860's and slips away entirely in the 1870's. Moreover, so great are the quantities of semi-modern and modern arms to be taken into account, and so tree-like do their variations and complexities branch out into stems and twigs, that to represent them adequately in a general history would take up a third of the volume. Consequently the author stands squarely by his 1950's decision: rather than do a poor job in an area in which he is not competent, he refers the reader to the bulging cornucopia of specialized works by expert colleagues—a great many of them, but by no means all, listed in the Bibliography— for all the aspects of gun history not covered here; thus the reader is served best. Similarly, it has been asked why more princely and royal "high-art" arms and more atypical eccentricities were not included: because a survey history must present mainly the typical, of course. If THE AGE OF FIREARMS does not include this or that sub-species or variant, it does dedicate the gained space to paintings, woodcuts, etchings and engravings which show the evolution of firearms through, as it were, contemporary eyes. Hence the main scheme of the present edition is that of the 1957 one. The reasons I submit are sound.

Nevertheless, much in this new edition has been changed. Errors have been corrected, many new illustrations have been added, quite a few old illustrations have been replaced by better ones, and long sections of text have been re-written in the light of studies and experiences gathered in the intervening years.

San Pietro a Sillano
Greve in Chianti
Firenze, Italy
January 1st, 1970

To all those readers who have done the author the honor of making the old THE AGE OF FIREARMS one of the three or four most popular and durable works in the field: many, mank thanks! To all those about to read the new one: be pleased by its virtues, be charitable toward its vices, spead many entertaining hours with it, give it away for birthdays, Christmas, First Communions and Bar Mitzvahs, but above all please do not lend it—tell your friends to buy their own.

Cordially,
R. H.

ACKNOWLEDGMENTS

For their kind co-operation, the author is grateful to:

Mr. Peter A. Beford, Beckenham, Kent, England

Mr. Stephen V. Grancsay, Curator-Emeritus of Arms & Armor of the Metropolitan
Museum of Art, New York

Mr. Joel A. Gross, Los Angeles, California

Mr. Thomas E. Hall, Firearms Historian of the Winchester Repeating Arms
Company, New Haven, Connecticut

Sig. Alberto Vincenzo Merli, San Casciano Val di Pesa, Florence, Italy

L'avv. Modesto Palasciano, Bari, Italy

Sig. Walter Tonolino, Brescia, Italy

. . . and especially to Robert Abels of New York, in whose shop the author as a
boy and youth spent so many hundreds of happy days, and to whom he owes a
good measure of the foundations on which this book was built; nor with less
esteem and goodwill to Bernie Day.

The Age of Firearms

A PICTORIAL HISTORY FROM THE INVENTION OF
GUNPOWDER TO THE ADVENT OF THE
MODERN BREECHLOADER

Fig. 1—13th-century armor on the Great Seal of Ottokar, King of Bohemia, 1269.

CHAPTER ONE

Medieval arms and armor—The institution of knighthood and the feudal system—The Black Death and its effect on the fourteenth-century economy—The possible origins of gunpowder and explosives: Classical Antiquity; Marcus Graecus and the LIBER IGNIUM; *China and India; Berthold Schwartz and Roger Bacon; probable development in Moslem North Africa between 900 and 1250* A.D.—*The appearance of the first primitive firearms in the middle of the thirteenth century.*

HEN HENRY III, FOURTH OF THE Plantagenets, expired at the age of sixty-five in the Year of Grace 1272 (to become the first monarch entombed in Westminster), and his son Edward ascended the throne on limbs which had already led to the celebration of his name as Edward Longshanks, the implements of war both in England and on the Continent were but slightly changed in principle from those of Caesar, or for that matter from those of Agamemnon.

Essentially, only tactics and protective armor had changed. The organization of armies into uniformed, disciplined corps of infantry, cavalry, engineers, couriers and rigid officer hierarchies had crumbled with the walls of Rome some 850 years before. Most wars had long since ceased to be instruments of policy. In the Middle Ages, war was more or less an incessant slaughter among the hundreds of potentates both great and petty who ruled over the fragments of a Europe which was then but barely stirring out of the long sleep of nine desolate, sterile centuries. Now, as the world began to waken almost imperceptibly to the bright but still chilly spring of the Renaissance, it was the knights who rode foremost in the lines of battle: anthropoidal tanks, in the year of Edward Longshanks' accession still sheathed in chain mail from crown to ankle, but three or four generations later in sixty pounds and more of articulated steel, astride such massive, pillar-legged beasts that all pretense to mobility and pace was sacrificed to the support of the deadweight burden. Few were the methods of attack and defense which prevailed against this one-ton unit—and they were immemorially ancient. The lance, firmly cradled in the gauntlet and lance rest of a knight in full charge, its hard, sharp point commended to the guidance of the patron saint, might enter a joint in the opponent's armor and do mortal injury; or knock him out of the saddle and send him crashing to the ground. Once unseated, the knight was relatively easy prey, for he was helpless under the encumbrances of his iron, and the foot soldier could lift his visor or gorget and apply the *coup de grâce* with a dagger whose name, the *prie-à-dieu*, requires no further explanation. The great two-handed sword, twenty-five pounds of double-edged blade well over four

feet long, could slice through all but the thickest armor if it was wielded by a good man and struck squarely. Maces, morning stars, battle axes of literally countless shapes and sizes, clubs, hammers and the lesser swords were plied on the theory that the best armor and the staunchest occupant could eventually be knocked into ruin and senselessness if battered long enough and hard enough with heavy enough an object. And if the horse could be killed or crippled, the rider would again come clanking to the ground to find himself once more in the awkward and vulnerable attitude in which we left him barely three sentences ago.

Figs. 2 & 3—Anglo-Norman knights in 13th-century chain mail armor. Left: bas-relief from the tomb of Sir John d'Abernoun (died 1277) in the church of Stoke d'Abernon, Surrey. Right: bas-relief from the tomb of William Longuespée, Earl of Salisbury (died 1226), in the church at Salisbury.

11

But throughout the ages of medieval combat no simple, effective and reliable projectile weapon had been devised to pierce good armor (save chain mail) and to penetrate into a vital organ from any distance greater than a few

Fig. 4—Sling slinging. Triangular box suspended from short end of arm was filled with tons of stones, released suddenly; force of drop brought long arm and attached sling upward violently; sling unhooked itself and released missile at height of arc. Woodcut from the 1511 German translation of the *De Re Militari (Concerning the Military)* of Flavius Vegetius Renatus.

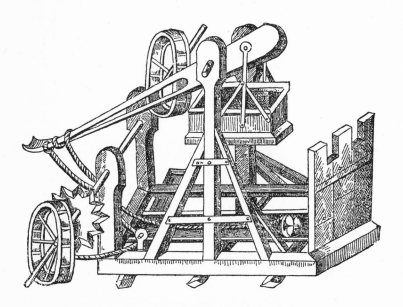

Fig. 5—Siege sling of the 12th to 15th centuries. When weight box was released, long arm jerked attached sling outward and upward to hurl missile. After a miniature in the *Bellifortis* of Konrad Keyser, 1405.

arms' lengths. Spears glanced off, and longbow arrows, so devastating against infantry, fell away harmlessly unless by the merest chance they should happen to enter a visor slit or a joint in the articulations. Only the massive, squat crossbow quarrels, propelled with stunning force by the energy latent in steel or whalebone bows compressed by powerful windlasses or levers, could easily pierce even the best of armor; but the time required for making and loading crossbows, not to mention the years required to train proficient shooters, rendered this genre of weaponry far more useful in leisurely hunting than in frenetic battle. Nor were the great engines of war—the catapults, slings and ballistas—of much avail. Many could hurl hundreds of pounds of boulders or great vats of boiling pitch for three hundred yards and more, or single missiles of twenty-five to fifty pounds for over half a mile. But these were mostly creaking powerhouses constructed of enormous beams, wheels, levers and pulleys which could be moved five miles on a dry day, requiring hours for positioning and half an hour to ready for shooting (Figs. 4 to 6). Their only effective use lay in besieging towns and fortifications.

The infantry was all but defenseless against the charge of knights. Armored lightly, if at all, in a shirt of mail and a helmet, armed with shield or buckler and with sword, halberd, pike, mace or crossbow, the foot soldier could do little but shoot as many arrows into the advancing thunder as possible in the hope of inflicting some hurt, then make a last effort at crippling the horses before being lanced, axed, brained or trampled under a thousand hoofs.

On the institution of knighthood, invincible by any save its own kind and by the darts of chance, rested the enforcement of the social order of the Middle Ages. Its effect on the wretched masses of serfs was to perpetuate their wretchedness, but less so through the exercise of the Divine Right, which sanctioned unspeakable atrocities, than through an inexorable socio-political process: as long as the king, dukes, earls, barons and lords of the demesnes warred with and were warred upon chiefly by mounted ironclads, the serf (although he owed his master fealty and military service in times of turmoil) was of very little account in the military tactics and ambitions of his masters, and consequently even less in the social structure. In war, serfs generally perished in digging mines and tunnels, were expended as draught animals, tended the vats of pitch, cut and fetched the wood, slept among the offal in the stables, ate what dregs the soldiery had left. The serf was in effect a slave, in peace the sower and thresher but never the ultimate reaper of the earth's wealth, a mute beast whose labor was ensured by threat of death and torture, born not to raise children but to breed more of his kind for the intractable system, and to bear on his back the economic burden of a civilization he never knew.

Figs. 9 & 10—Above: Encounter between knights and footmen, 14th to late 15th centuries; woodcut from Thomas Lirar, *Schwäbische Chronik (Chronicle of Swabia)*, Ulm, 1486. Right: Foot soldier of the 12th to mid-14th centuries; after a wall painting in the church at Schwarz-Rheinsdorf, Germany, circa 1150-60.

Fig. 6—*Biffa*, or giant sling, 13th to 16th centuries, in principle the same as Figs. 4 and 5 but vastly larger (note size of men turning spanning winch). Reconstruction by M. Viollet-le-Duc after contemporary descriptions.

Fig. 7—Crossbowmen of the 12th to 14th centuries. Man at left is spanning bow with goat's-foot lever (linkage not shown). After a miniature in the Velislav Bible, Prague, mid-14th century.

Fig. 8—Serfs paying rent in cash and kind, 13th to 15th centuries. Woodcut from Rodericus Zamorensis, *Spiegel des Menschlichen Lebens (Mirror of Human Life)*, Augsburg, 1475.

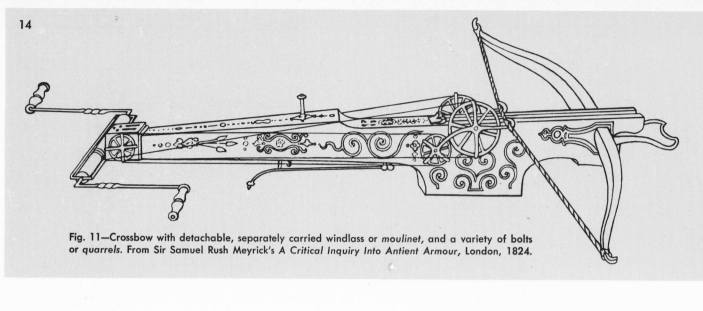

Fig. 11—Crossbow with detachable, separately carried windlass or *moulinet*, and a variety of bolts or *quarrels*. From Sir Samuel Rush Meyrick's *A Critical Inquiry Into Antient Armour*, London, 1824.

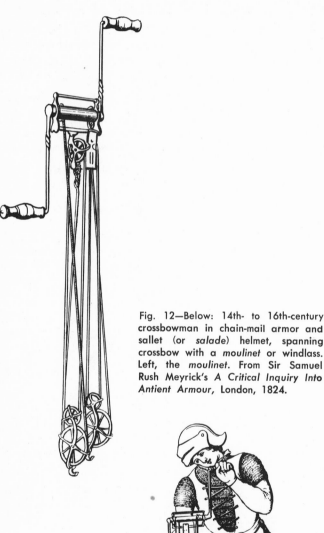

Fig. 12—Below: 14th- to 16th-century crossbowman in chain-mail armor and sallet (or *salade*) helmet, spanning crossbow with a *moulinet* or windlass. Left, the *moulinet*. From Sir Samuel Rush Meyrick's *A Critical Inquiry Into Antient Armour*, London, 1824.

Two new factors insinuated themselves into this stagnant equation in the course of the fourteenth century. One was the great cycle of epidemics known as the Black Death, some of which were bubonic plague. The outbreak of 1347–50 alone left an estimated twenty-five million dead in its swath across Europe, which amounted to about one-quarter of the population. Flaring up again and again, its fearful depredations decimated some nations by as much as two-thirds or three-quarters. One of its aftereffects was the increase in the economic value of each survivor. The demand for labor exceeded the supply on a universal scale for the first time in European history. Gradually, the serf became less expendable, less easily replaceable. His services, further distracted by the beckoning opportunities in the growing renascent cities, had to be bought by an increase of his share in the produce, or to be bound by laws enforced at times with the most savage brutality.

The other factor, coeval with the plague, was far less effective than the plague for more than two centuries after its advent: this, of course, was the use of explosive substances to hurl projectiles out of tubes. But let one point be made clear at once: the argument that vast multitudes of sorely oppressed serfs were seething on the brink of rebellion, requiring only a weapon like a gun to rise up and blast their masters out of armor and existence, is a fable, an absurd oversimplification which survives with astonishing tenacity. The advent of firearms did in fact contribute enormously to the eventual demise of the feudal system, but this was brought about not by serf rebellions but by an indirect and circuitous route which will presently be traced.

Very little is known about the origins of the chemical compositions eventually to become known as gunpowder. History records neither their birth dates nor their cradles. Classical Antiquity did not know them, and consequently had no projectile weapons other than bows and arrows and catapults of various designs. Incendiary mixtures of naphtha, sulphur, oils, pitch, turpentine, tars and the like, loosely known as *Greek fire*, seem to have been known as early as the fifth century before Christ, for their use was nothing new to Thucydides. "The Boeotians," he wrote of the siege of Delium in 424 B.C., the seventh year of the Peloponnesian War (Thucydides, IV, 100), "after having tried other forms of assault . . . captured [Delium] by bringing up a machine made in the following way: having sawed a great wooden beam in half [lengthwise], they hollowed it and fitted it together again like a pipe. Then they hung a cauldron at one end of it from chains and stuck a curved bellows pipe into the cauldron from the beam, which was itself lined with iron." This contrivance was brought up to the wooden section of the walls and by means of "a great bellows" the fiercely burning incendiary mixture in the cauldron was blown through the siphon and the hollow beam; the walls instantly took fire and Delium was captured. Other writers of Antiquity make occasional reference to what were probably similar fire tubes, called *siphons,* but the fact that none of these ever became standard equipment, nor even found frequent application, is ample evidence that their effectiveness must have been trifling.

Over sixteen hundred years passed between Thucydides and the next important reference to violent incendiaries: the LIBER IGNIUM AD COMBURENDOS HOSTES (*The Book of Fires for Consuming the Enemy*), a late twelfth-century manuscript purporting to have been written by one Marcus Graecus. It contains several score recipes for potent incendiaries and weak, slow-burning near-explosives which prescribe the basic ingredients of gunpowder —saltpeter, charcoal and sulphur—but these in such impure states and mixed in such proportions that they would have produced a fierce flare rather than an explosion. Many of the mixtures, it is advised, may be loaded into "small tubes," which, when fired, will "rise into the air with a great whirring noise"—in other words, rockets. Thus it is likely that a workable rocket powder—which is quite unlike gunpowder—may have sent rockets whizzing out of the windows of alchemical laboratories as early as 1150. Not much else can be learned from the LIBER IGNIUM. It appears fairly certain from internal evidence that at least its earliest recipes were translated into Latin from a lost Arabic original of unknown antiquity; that the translator was probably a Spaniard and the translation made between the years 1180 and 1225; that later recipes were added by different hands between 1210 and 1300; and that the alleged author "Marcus Graecus" is either the pen name of the translator or a blind to lend the authority of a classical name to fraudulent additions. Thus the book proves only that an embryonic knowledge of crude mixtures approximating inefficient near-explosives—but *not* gunpowder—existed in the Mohammedan world or Moorish Spain in the one hundred or two hundred years prior to the close of the twelfth century. No records exist to suggest that any of these were ever put to practical use other than as hissing and popping toys.

Much has been written about the use of explosives in China centuries before they assaulted the ears, noses and mortality rates of Europeans. This thesis was probably launched on its widest publication by the first historiographer of firearms and their military uses, Diego Ufano. In his ARTILLERIA, published in Madrid in 1614, he cited letters and reports by Portuguese navigators who arrived in China after the first commercial contact had been made in August, 1517, and who confessed themselves awed by the "wondrous cannons of incredible designs" and "firearms of the most marvellous sorts" which they found in Chinese arsenals. A few of these instruments may indeed have been firearms embellished in Chinese fashion, but the greater number were probably the props and paraphernalia of fireworks which were unfamiliar to the Europeans. Not knowing that scores of Mohammedan and European craftsmen and adventurers had brought gunnery to China over the land route through India in the course of the late thirteenth, fourteenth and fifteenth centuries, the seafaring newcomers thought themselves to be the first Europeans in the polychrome empire and consequently assumed that guns and explosives were the heritage of Chinese antiquity. Other writers, ill informed, nurtured this conclusion from the seventeenth to the early nineteenth centuries, but few were able to vest their works in the prestige of Sir George Staunton, who in 1798 wrote in his EMBASSY TO THE EMPEROR OF CHINA:

> Nitre [saltpeter] is the natural and daily product of China and India, and there accordingly the knowledge of gunpowder seems to be coeval with that of the most distant historic events. Among the Chinese it has been applied at all times to useful purposes, such as blasting rocks and removing great obstructions, and to those of amusement, in making a vast variety of fireworks. It was also used as a defense by undermining the probable passages of an enemy and blowing him up. . . . But its force had not been directed through strong metallic tubes, as it was by Europeans soon after they discovered that composition.

Alas for Sir George and many others (who most likely had all derived their information from sources which ultimately stem from one focal source), there is no evidence whatever to support the contention of the use of gunpowder in China before a date when it could long have been imported from the West via land. No reliable Chinese records exist to show that any guns were known before circa 1350. Very likely China had its own "Marcus Graecus," or rather "Marci Graeci," anonymous putterers among retorts and alembics who discovered incendiary mixtures, primitive rocket fuels and crude near-explosives between the eleventh century and the time of the Portuguese. Perhaps a considerable variety of cascading, sputtering, crackling, popping and even flying fireworks may have vied with the moon for emblazoning the mantle of night over the cherry blossoms and lotus ponds a century or more before the galleons of Emanuel II hove into sight in 1517. But neither gunpowder nor guns antedated the middle of the thirteenth century.

The case of India is similar. When the great philologist Nathaniel Halhed (1751-1830) translated the ancient Gentoo Code from a Persian copy in 1776, he mistakenly rendered as "guns" and "muskets" what had merely been "fire-weapons" in the original Sanskrit, thus suggesting the thesis—echoed by others for a century—that gunpowder and firearms had been in use in India since about 1200 B.C.! But we know now that the development of explosives in India was coextensive with that of China, the two paralleling each other within fifty years.

Among Europeans, a deathless fable perpetuates the image of the German monk Berthold Schwartz, who, according to many writers of the past four centuries, was not only the inventor of gunpowder but of guns as well (Fig. 13). According to some versions he was born in 1175, while others leave him unborn until the early 1400's (when firearms were already firmly and universally established). In fact, however, it is extremely doubtful whether the good Father Berthold ever lived at all. There is no evidence, no birth or baptismal record, tombstone, monastery roll or trustworthy contemporary allusion to show that he did. A tottering case may be advanced that one Konstantin Anklitzen, an early fourteenth-century alchemist monk in one of several possible monasteries in the Black Forest region of Germany, *may* have assumed the monastic name *Bertholdus Niger* (Latin *niger* = German *schwarz*, black) and *may* have been known in the vicinity as Father Berthold Schwartz. But it seems all but certain that *the* Berthold Schwartz is a figment of folklore and myth, an embodiment of many dozens of apothecary and alchemist monks who in the course of the thirteenth century stumbled upon the possibly unholy and certainly startling consequences of mixing charcoal, sulphur, saltpeter and a spark.

Fig. 13—Fanciful "portrait" of Berthold Schwartz; frontispiece in Joseph Furtenbach's *Büchsenmeisterey-Schul (School of the Art of Gunnery)*, Augsburg, 1643. Superscription says: "Portrait of the Venerable and Ingenious Reverend Father called Bertold Schwartz, of the Franciscan Order; Doctor, Alchemist and Inventor of the Noble Art of Gunnery in the Year 1380." Eulogistic quatrain: "See here what time and nature have brought to day through ingenious men: the art of shooting in guns has been born, created out of the nature of fire and vapors of nature."

So far as the Italian peninsula is concerned, the retrospect is even foggier. On one hand, considering that Italy was womb, mother, breast and cradle to most of the appurtenances of Western civilization, it would seem that pre- and early-Renaissance science could and should have produced so simple a substance as gunpowder—how trifling in comparison to an infinity of far more complex, subtle discoveries of Italian empiricism, and how useful for the relentless wars of Guelfs and Ghibellines, for the expansionist aims of Venice, Genoa, Florence, the Papacy, the Hispano-Norman South! On the other hand, no unassailable proof exists that Italians in this regard jumped, as it were, the gun. A dozen early thirteenth-century frescoes here and there—especially in Sicily and Liguria—show the use of mortars or cannons in naval battles and sieges. But the dating in these cases is purely stylistic, subject to dispute, and unsupported by such corroborative evidence as documents or surviving guns of certain vintage.

Where, then, and by whom was gunpowder invented? Barring the discovery of hitherto unknown manuscripts or other evidence, we shall probably never know. Most likely explosive substances compounded of saltpeter, charcoal and sulphur were discovered by accident by many alchemists and apothecaries in many parts of the world between the eleventh and thirteenth centuries, especially in the Mohammedan-Moorish nations which were then preserving the jewels of art, science and human culture from the clutches of a largely barbaric Christendom.

The strongest claimant is the venerable Roger Bacon, late Fellow of Merton College, Oxford, who (unlike Father Schwartz) not only lived without a doubt but contrived to do so for seventy-eight years, from circa 1214 to 1292. To this irrepressible genius belongs the honor, uncontested, of being the first known man to write about true, thunderous, noxious gunpowder. He experimented with it exhaustively and finally arrived at a mixture of saltpeter, charcoal and sulphur in a ratio of 41.2 : 29.4 : 29.4; but the niter and sulphur available to him must have been very impure and the charcoal gritty—a mixture which, although certainly explosive, seems more likely to have issued a youthful growl and a flash rather than the "thunder and lightning" which its creator announced. Bacon set down his formulae at great length in his EPISTOLA DE SECRETIS OPERIBUS ARTIS ET NATURAE (*Treatise Concerning the Secrets of Science and Nature*), written before the year 1249; but this enlightened genius, living some five hundred years before his time, knew all too well the murky ways of our kind and added:

> The common herd is unable to digest scientific facts, which it scorns and misuses to the detriment of the wise. Let not pearls be cast, then, before swine. . . . It is madness to commit a secret to writing unless it be done so that it is unintelligible to the ignorant and just barely intelligible even to the most educated and the wisest.

And accordingly, he enshrined his secrets in riddles and anagrams so that future readers might be able to read all about each experiment except *the* vital ingredient or *the* step, the *sine qua non*. So well did he succeed that it was not until the middle of the eighteenth century that "the most educated and the wisest" contrived to crack his elaborate codes, and many defied all efforts until barely a hundred years ago.

But although Roger Bacon was the first to write about true gunpowder, and very scientifically at that, it cannot be said that he alone invented it. Almost certainly he had access to the LIBER IGNIUM and probably to many less ambitious but similar manuscripts now lost. Taking up where the other experimenters had left off, he probably arrived at his gunpowder purely empirically and on his own; nonetheless, even while he worked, approximately between 1230 and 1248, the first dozen or so firearms in history may have belched out their anger in faraway Spain. That by 1280 they were doing so in considerable numbers—perhaps a hundred or two hundred primitive firepots, stubby iron buckets loaded with powder and crushed rocks and fired by a coal—seems certain. Consequently someone in Moorish Spain or North Africa seems to have paralleled Bacon's efforts, for cultural exchange between Oxford and the Alhambra or Baghdad existed hardly at all, and Bacon's jealously guarded discoveries of the 1240's could not have passed into the Mohammedan world and been there adapted to projectile use within so short a time. Neither this use nor any other save undermining and firecrackers was suggested by Bacon for his powder.

No matter to where the roots of explosives extend, their fruit ripened in mid-thirteenth-century Europe, as pure science at Oxford, as myth breeders in Germany, as rock hurlers in Spain; and the descendants of these last will be the concern of the following 175 pages.

CHAPTER TWO

Firearms probably "invented" through the accidental explosions of laboratory mortars—The first firearms: iron and wooden buckets in thirteenth-century North Africa and Moorish Spain—Their spread throughout Europe—True cannons by 1300—"Crakys of War" of Edward III—Gun expenditures and the Great Wardrobe Accounts of Edward III and Richard II—Petrarch's misgivings—The first battles with firearms—The appearance and effectiveness of the early hand cannons—Their indirect effect on the feudal system—"Holy Water Sprinklers"—The state of firearms in about 1385–1415.

E MAY ENVISION WITH A CONSIDER-able chance of being correct how the invention of guns came about. Hundreds of alchemists, apothecaries and physicians between Baghdad and Manchester in the thirteenth century —mostly in the Moslem world—busied themselves with compounding niter, charcoal and sulphur in iron mortars with iron or stone pestles. The spark, generated by friction or static electricity, was inevitable sooner or later. After several thousand pestles had roared off ceiling bound, it must have occurred to quite a number of fingerless experimenters that perhaps this reaction could be put to less immediately suicidal uses. Thus the very earliest firearms were most likely laboratory mortars cautiously loaded with powder and a round stone, inclined at an angle and fired by a glowing wire thrust through a small hole drilled into the bottom. The results were gratifying: the stone flew upward, traveled in a high arc and fell to ground a few yards away. Both its range and weight were too insignificant to be of any practical use, but if the mortar could be made much larger, and the stone proportionately more massive . . .

Having grown out of such experiments, the first true, specifically designed firearms appeared perhaps as early as 1240 or 1250 in North Africa, many more being almost certainly put to use in the fortifications of Granada and other Moorish centers in Spain before 1275. They seem to have been large rough iron buckets, about the size of an office waste-paper basket, or hardwood buckets reinforced by an iron lining inside and iron hoops around the outside. They were loaded with a pound or two of the crude gunpowder and probably a dozen or so smaller round stones rather than one large one. A small hole in or near the bottom served as a touchhole into which the cannoneer thrust a red-hot wire or live coal. When the smoke of the ensuing eruption had cleared, it was found that the stones had been hurled over the ramparts into the enemy's midst—or approximately in his general direction—in a high, wide arc. Whatever the effectiveness of such machines may have been, their destructiveness could not possibly have equaled that of the mechanically powered catapults and ballistas—but how easy it was to manufacture, transport, position, load and fire the thun-der buckets! And more than one besieging army broke and fled in wild, terrified panic at their smoke, flash and alarum.

By 1300, knowledge of their existence had spread into central and northern Europe and Britain; many ambitious potentates and princes must have procured prototypes to be copied by their own smiths and armorers. The difference between a high-angle mortar and a horizontally firing weapon had come to be appreciated very early in the fourteenth century, and the bucket shape gave way to long tubes which, however crudely forged or cast and however uncertain their effectiveness, were true cannons. More or less primitive examples had found their way into arsenals as far north as Copenhagen, as far east as Kiev, and into the Tower of London by 1330. The tongue of Cicero and Horace had been enriched in Britain by the insinuation of *gunna, -ae,* while on the Continent the classical *tormentum* and *ballista,* hurling machine, were pressed into service as *tormentum pyrium,* fiery hurling machine, *ballista mirabilis,* astounding hurling machine, and *igniferens tubus,* fire-bearing tube.

The etymology of the word *gun* is uncertain. It appears to have been derived from a relative of the Teutonic stem *gun* in such names as *Gunhilde* and *Gundeline,* meaning "war." An account of the arsenal at Windsor Castle of 1330–31 may be cited, which lists *"una magna balista de cornu quae vocatur Domina Gunilda,"* "a large ballista of horn which is called Lady Gun[h]ilda"; but the lady could as well have been a large siege engine with a huge bow made of laminated horn as an iron-lined and iron-hooped horn tube. Whatever the word's genesis, it was in use in English by 1335 or 1340 as *gonne, gounne* and *gunne.* John Barbour asserted in THE BRUCE, written in 1375, that when Edward III attacked the Scots in 1327, he brought along a few "crakys of war"; these were small cannons of perhaps fifteen to thirty pounds weight. "Crakys" is not a plural in *-s* of a singular "craky," as is often supposed, but a plural in *-ys* of the singular *crake,* meaning a crow or raven; so that the "crakys of war," besides being the first reference to guns in British literature, show that already at this early date the naming of guns after birds was in use—a system to survive well into the eighteenth century.

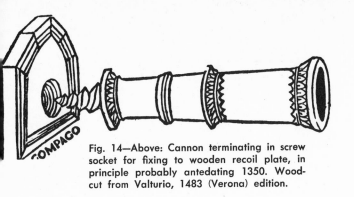

Fig. 14—Above: Cannon terminating in screw socket for fixing to wooden recoil plate, in principle probably antedating 1350. Woodcut from Valturio, 1483 (Verona) edition.

Figs. 15 & 16—"Tormentum" (below), and "ballista" (right), cannons of circa 1330 to 1400. Adaptations of classical Latin *tormentum* and *ballista* (hurling engine, catapult) did not distinguish one type of cannon from any other, were indiscriminately applied to all. Woodcuts from Roberto Valturio, *De l'Arte Militare*, Verona, 1483.

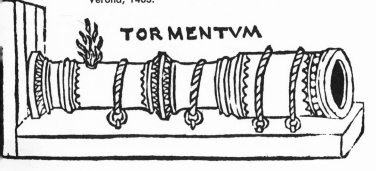

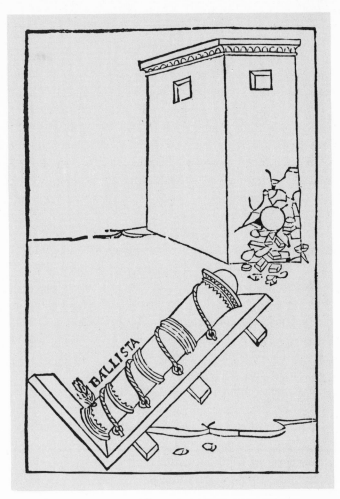

Fig. 17—"A fearsome engine . . . of Arabia . . . for besieging cities," says text accompanying this chimera in the 1483 (Verona) edition of Valturio. Note cannon shooting mammoth arrow. Less vividly sculptured but principally similar engines, designed for psychological more than physical destructiveness, were used in Spain and Italy, probably never in Arabia.

On February 1, 1345, the accounts of the Great Wardrobe of Edward III listed payments for the repair and transport of *"xiii gunnae cum pellotis,"* "13 guns with pellets," for the king's projected expeditions that year, and it may be reasonably supposed that if the guns required repair, they had been in use for some time before and had been damaged by the action of the powder or the elements. Unfortunately this account throws little light on the size of gun or ball. A *pellota* was certainly many times larger than a small-arms bullet developed fifty to one hundred years later, while a translation to "cannon ball" would suggest a sphere of prodigious size probably far in excess of the projectiles fired by Edward's *gunnae*. Many of the early cannons used elsewhere throughout Europe and the Mohammedan world fired huge arrows with sheet-metal fins as "feathers," their shafts being wrapped in leather sheaths to fit tightly into the bore but which dropped off as soon as the arrow had cleared the muzzle (Fig. 17).

The Great Wardrobe accounts for October 1, 1345, listed payments for *"c ribaldos pro passagio regis versus Normandiam,"* "100 ribaldos for the king's campaign against Normandy." *Ribaldos* were the same as the *ribaudequins* with which the Norman fleet for the invasion of England had been equipped in 1338, fully seven years earlier, and known probably even before then; variously they appeared throughout the next four hundred years as *barricadoes*, *orgues* and *Orgelgeschütze* (the last two from their resemblance to organ pipes) in

Spanish, Italian, French and German. They were long and rather slender barrels of iron or brass grouped in rows or tiers on wooden carriages, firing balls perhaps one and a half to two inches in diameter, shot off either individually by touching each touchhole separately with the glowing wire or the coal, or in rapid succession by laying a train of powder across all the touchholes and igniting the train at one end. Used in this latter way, they may be considered the ancestors of the machine gun (Fig. 20).

Fortunately the accounts do leave us records of at least an approximate scale of sizes and prices of artillery after about 1350. "Small guns" ("*gunnae parvae*") weighed 15 to 25 pounds, not counting carriage or cradle; "medium guns" ("*gunnae de pondere medio*") 25 to 50 pounds; "large guns" ("*gunnae magnae*") 50 to 100 pounds; and the "largest guns" ("*gunnae maximae*") between 100 and 300 pounds. Most of these seem to have been made of a cupric alloy simply described as cuprum (perhaps bronze or brass or similar metals) rather than of iron. Prices were computed according to weight. In 1353 the prices paid for a gun ran between three shillings sixpence and four shillings sixpence per sixteen pounds, so that a *gunna parva* of 15 to 25 pounds could not have cost much more than six or seven shillings—at a time when a great crossbow was purchased for sixty-six shillings and eight-pence! On the same scale, a great crossbow was equal in value to nothing less than a *gunna maxima* of some 250 pounds. The new engines were still experimental curiosities in 1340–70 England.

Similar accounts have survived the perils of time in other nations. Many major principalities of the Continent had probably incorporated guns in their military machines some fifteen or twenty years before the English, while others apparently remained unimpressed until the last quarter of the fourteenth century. But in general, there were few Continental cities and royal armories by 1375—in many regions even few manorial and baronial redoubts—which did not have at least two or three dozen heavy guns, while many powerful cities, such as Nuremberg or Worms, probably had two or three hundred. Some of the Italian states were the most precocious. The chronicles of Perugia show that there were no fewer than 497 *bombardi e bombarderi*—"bombards and bombarderos"—in the municipal arsenal in 1364. The Florentine Republic at about the same time boasted over a thousand instruments of assorted shapes, sizes and vintages which were more or less cannons, although over half of them seem to have been retired to the inactive list owing to "great holes of rust, and cracks from unwisely large loads of powder." Even before 1365 the vaults of the Castello Sant' Angelo appear to have bristled with bronze, brass and iron tubes, plus great quantities of shot and powder.

Many battles have been advanced as the first in which firearms were used; but in that era of interminable wars between cities, principalities, duchies, manors, robber barons and mercenary bands, no one battle is recorded as antedating any other in the use of cannons. Without a doubt, iron tubes roared stubby arrows and lead and stone balls at besiegers and besieged in Spain and Italy as early as 1325 not merely as incidental oddities, but as weapons used in deadly earnest, procured at the behest of deliberative commanders. On the other hand, their effectiveness remained insignificant for many decades more. The French chronicler Jean Froissart (1338–1410?), for example, mentions "*kanons*" brought to the field by the English at the battle of Crécy (August 26, 1346); but the issue was contested by nearly fifty thousand French knights, men-at-arms and crossbowmen, *versus* less than a third that number of English men-at-arms, among them five thousand longbowmen. By midnight, these last had annihilated the French army.

In short, cannons appeared with increasing frequency throughout the fourteenth century, here crude, there advanced and formidable. In its closing decade, if they had not yet been developed to surpass the long-range destructiveness of the largest of the mechanical siege engines, they were nonetheless standard equipment in every major campaign and armory: for unlike the mechanical engines, they could deliver wall-smashing blows over short, flat trajectories, while catapults and slings lobbed their missiles in high arcs. And compared to any mechanical engine, cannons were absurdly easy to make and to transport, extremely cheap, and could be positioned and fired twenty and even fifty times for a catapult's one. *Breechloading* mechanisms were in use before 1380 for weapons of moderate calibres—two- to three-inch bores. The top half of the barrel was cut away for about a one-foot section at the rear of the gun; into this opening was fitted a removable, slightly conical breech chamber which looked like a German beer stein. The powder and ball were loaded into this container, which was then replaced into the open breech; turning the handle downward locked it into position. The touchhole was in the breech chamber itself. The only advantage of this system was that the piece could remain in position behind a small gunport or crenelation while being loaded, and the gunner did not have to expose himself to the fire of the enemy. But the art of making closely fitting parts with fine tolerances was beyond the gunfounders of the day, and consequently much compression was lost when the fierce and dangerous gas seepage spewed through the ill-fitting breech closing. By far the greater number of cannons—probably ninety-nine out of one hundred—remained muzzleloaders until about 1870–80.

Philosophy and *belles-lettres* soon took notice of the new force. Petrarch heaved a troubled sigh at the prevalence of cannons in the ninety-ninth *Dialogue* of his DE REMEDIIS UTRIUSQUE FORTUNAE, written in 1366. Thomas Twynne's translation of 1579 (London), PHISICKE AGAINST FORTUNE, renders it thus (*Joy* and *Reason* are debating; italics mine—R.H.):

Joy: I have innumerable engines and artillerie.

Reason: It is a marveyle, but thou hast also pellets of brass which are throwne foorth with terrible noyse and fire. Thou miserable man, was it not ynough to heare the thunder of Immortal God from heaven? O crueltie joyned with pryde! From the earth, also, was sent forth unimitable lightning with thunder, as Virgil sayth, which the madness of men hath counterfeited to do the like: and that which was woont to be throwne out the cloudes is now throwne abroad with . . . a devlysh device, which, as some suppose, was invented by Archimedes at what time Marcellus besieged Syracuse. Howbeit, he devised it to the extent to defend the libertie of his citizens and to avoyde or defend the destruction of his country, which you now use to the subjection or subvertion of free people. *This plague of late was but rare, insomuch as it was behelde with great wonder; but now, as your myndes are apt to learne the worst thyngs, so it is as common as any other kind of munition.*

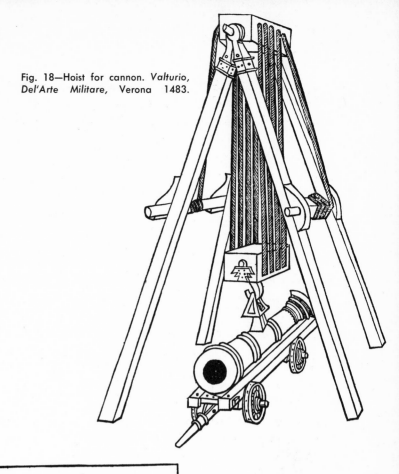

Fig. 18—Hoist for cannon. *Valturio, Del'Arte Militare,* Verona 1483.

Fig. 19—Mobile tower and breastwork with shielded cannon, early 15th century. Woodcut from Valturio, 1483 (Verona) edition.

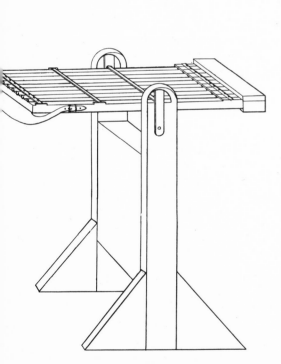

Fig. 20—One frequent arrangement of multiple-barrel cannons, first used in about 1330-40 and continued until the early 19th century; weapon shown dates from about 1400. Owing to their resemblance to organ pipes they were known as *orgues* and *Orgelgeschütze,* or, variously, as *ribaldos, ribaudequins* and *barricados.* Barrels ranged from .75 to over two inches in calibre, were about chest-high.

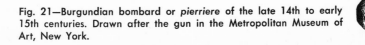

Fig. 21—Burgundian bombard or *pierriere* of the late 14th to early 15th centuries. Drawn after the gun in the Metropolitan Museum of Art, New York.

Figs. 24 & 25—Two carriages for cannons, middle 14th to 16th centuries; these are transport, not shooting carriages. Accompanying text does not explain geometry of carriages with converging wheels. Woodcut from Valturio op. cit.

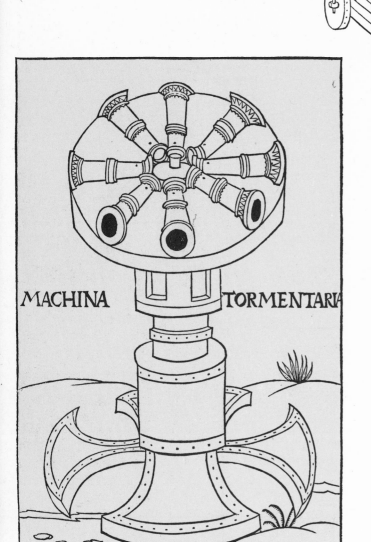

MACHINA TORMENTARIA

Fig. 22—Eight horizontally mounted barrels fired in succession from turntable, probably in use by 1360. Machine is of chest or shoulder height. The firing of all eight barrels at once by stray sparks from the touchhole flash of one must have been a regrettable but not infrequent occurrence. Woodcut from Valturio, 1483 (Verona) edition.

Fig. 23—"Instrument for raising and lowering a cannon from behind." Woodcut from Valturio, 1483 (Verona) edition.

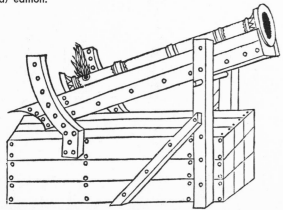

Instrumentum erigendi ponè machinam deprimendique.

Fig. 26—Cannon with pivoted shield to protect gunners; shield closes under own weight, is lifted by pulling on rope (far side of cradle). Flash at touchhole again artist's error. Cannon balls are most likely hewn stone, possibly solid iron. Woodcut from Valturio op. cit.

It must be remembered that the weapons under discussion were still cannons mounted on cradles or carriages, and not small arms fired by one man. We can only conjecture that the first small arms appeared somewhere and at some time in the third quarter of the fourteenth century, although there is slight evidence that in Tuscany and southern Germany they *may* have been known as early as 1340. In the monastery of St. Leonardo in Lecetto, near Siena, a now peeled and faded fresco depicts soldiers clearly shooting small hand-gun tubes about three feet long. These were painted by Paolo del Maestro Neri in 1340–43, and unless the guns are later additions commissioned by a prelate who felt a mission to modernize, they may well be the first, or at least among the very first, small arms in recorded history.

The earliest account of them in Britain appears to be contained in a list of arms delivered by John Halton, Keeper of the Tower, to the Chamberlain of Berwick in 1371. *"Idem computat liberasse,"* Halton entered in his ledgers, *"iii cannones parvos vocatos handgonnes. . . ."* "He furthermore accounts to have turned over three small cannons [or barrels] called handgonnes." Known as *hand cannons* to historians today, these were more or less straight iron tubes welded shut at one end and fitted with a touchhole on top of the barrel at the breech end—small versions of the full-fledged cannons. They were mounted on wooden shafts for holding and steadying during discharge. Some were prolonged at the rear into hollow tubular sockets into which a long wooden pole was fitted and fastened with rivets or strong cross pins, which proceeds clearly from an entry in the Privy Wardrobe for January 20, 1374, and another in 1375, listing expenditures for *"helvyng viii gunnorum et x hachettorum de stauro antiquo ad modum pycoys . . ."* "the stocking of eight guns and ten hatchets from an old pole, *in the manner of pikes"* (Figs. 27 to 29). The bores of these arms rarely if ever exceeded three-quarters of an inch in diameter, although some contemporary illustrations (unreliable in this respect) show weapons of considerably more impressive dimensions (Figs. 31 and 32).

Fig. 30—Warship, by Valturio (date of birth unknown, wrote circa 1458-70, died 1483) suggested for use in his own time. Note cannoneers thrusting *touches* into touchholes, most clearly shown in first or lower cannon on left side of ship. Three hand cannons can be distinguished by their positions and wooden stocks underneath the barrels: (1) last or highest of the guns on extreme right side of main deck, firing sizeable ball behind archer; (2) and (3) on left and right side of tower ramparts; and possibly a fourth (without wooden forestock) on right side of crow's nest. Woodcut from Valturio, op. cit.

Figs. 27-29—Three hand cannon, circa 1375-1450; drawings based on arms appearing in contemporary Italian paintings. Top: crude iron tube, about 22 inches long, stocked *ad modum pycoys* (in the manner of pikes.) Middle: brass barrel, about 24 inches long, terminating in long prong held in socket of pole. Bottom: hand mortar with 12-inch barrel, approximately 1¼-inch bore.

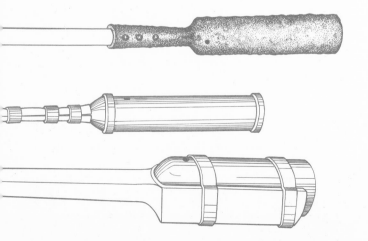

Fig. 31—War car with scythes on axles and harness. Note huge hand cannon. Woodcut from Valturio, op. cit.

The Tower Wardrobe, the Great Wardrobe and the Privy Wardrobe Accounts throw some light on the procedure of loading and firing both cannons and hand cannons. Throughout the second half of the fourteenth and the first quarter of the fifteenth centuries there were entries of payments for "drivells," "tampiones," "touches" and "fyrpannes." The cannoneer first loaded his piece with the desired quantity of powder, using a long sugar-scoop-like ladle in the case of a full-sized, horizontally mounted cannon to place it well into the breech, or simply pouring it into the upturned muzzle of a hand cannon. This he followed by ramming down a *tampion*, a wooden disk to separate powder and ball and to increase the compression, with his *drivell*, or ramrod. Next he rammed the ball on top of the tampion. The balls for cannons in the years between 1350 and 1425 seem to have been mostly hewn stone, and those for hand cannons lead and brass, although iron and bronze ones were certainly not infrequently used in cannons and hand cannons both. Near the cannon or battery of cannons stood a *fyrpanne*, a fire pan or brazier of coals. From these the cannoneer lighted his *touche*, either a short piece of wire or a small torch or faggot; or he may have picked up a live coal with a pair of long tongs. A little powder had been poured into the touchhole to communicate with the propellent charge inside the gun. Into the touchhole the gunner now thrust the touche, the propellent charge went off with a noxious thunderclap, and if the piece had not burst into a thousand fragments and killed whatever fearless souls had tempted its proximity, the ball was on its way. The touche with which a cannon was fired had to be rather long—about two or three feet—because of the fountainous backflash erupting through the touchhole. The glowing wire or fuse was accordingly held in a clamp at the end of an iron rod of the necessary length, a contrivance which by 1500 and perhaps much earlier was called the *linstock* (see Figs. 176 and 226-M). Shakespeare has the Chorus tell how the fleet of HENRY V (Act III) set sail for France, and prays the audience to

Work, work your thoughts and therein see a siege;
Behold the ordenance on their carriages,
With fatal mouths gaping on girded Harfleur.
Suppose the ambassador from the French comes back,
Tells Harry that the king doth offer him
Katherine his daughter, and with her, to dowry,
Some petty and unprofitable dukedoms:
The offer likes it not: and the nimble gunner
With linstock now the devilish cannon touches,
       [Alarum; and the chambers go off]
And down goes all before them!

This was in 1415; but the decisive battle of the campaign, fought at Agincourt on October 25 of the same year, belonged not to the gunners but to the English archers and their invincible longbows, about whom more will be said presently.

If the loading procedure was substantially alike for cannon and hand cannon, firing was not. The hand-cannoneer planted the end of the pole of his gun firmly on or in the ground immediately before shooting, holding the gun at an upward angle with one hand while applying the touche with the other. Alternatively, the pole was passed under the armpit and the touche applied with the other hand, although this stance seems to have been an innovation appearing after the first decade of the fifteenth century. Obviously, such methods of shooting reduced any pretensions to accuracy to nothing more than the most whimsical hope. Contemporary accounts, unfortunately lacking measured distances, give the impression that until about 1410–25 hand cannons were formidable weapons against unarmored enemies at fifty to sixty yards if fired point-blank into an advancing column, and even armor-piercing from ranges of twenty yards or less. Among the few accounts which approximate any degree of explicitness is the report of the siege of Lucca by the Florentines in 1430 written by the Italian historian Pierino Belli. The besiegers had busied themselves for some days with peppering stone balls against the Luccanese walls, shot from cannons and bombards of various potencies; but the walls were made of sterner stuff than the Florentines had reckoned with, and after three of four noisy, sulphurous days the besieged Luccanese regained a good measure of their confidence. They broke forth from the city to make sorties against the Florentines, carrying in their hands, Belli wrote, "a sort of club, about three feet in length, to which they had fastened iron pipes . . . which threw small iron balls by force of fire. The impact meant certain death, *and neither armor nor shield was effective against them.* Not infrequently *a single ball penetrated a file of two or three men. . . .*"

Fig. 32—Two hand cannoneers of 1390-1475. Note the wire *touche* in nearer shooter's hand, evidently quickly withdrawn, after being applied to touchhole, to save hand from flash. Woodcut from the *Rudimentum Noviciorum*, Lübeck, 1475.

Thus firearms, spitting lead, lapidary and finned missiles out of all shapes and sizes of cylinders, with unevenly predictable results, bellowed their way into and through the first quarter of the fifteenth century. Large cannons were rapidly being improved and were well on the way to relegating the catapults and siege engines to the firewood sawyer. But hand cannons, which could not be directed with any degree of nicety deserving the word pointing, let alone be aimed, were still far out of sight in the running with crossbows and of course the English longbow as far as accuracy was concerned. Their chief virtues were that they could pierce armor and that they were easy to manufacture and to supply with projectiles: a bowyer labored some two weeks to make a crossbow, another two to make the windlass, and more than an hour for each bolt or quarrel, while hand cannons could be smithied and welded in half a day and balls could be cast a dozen a minute. By 1390 a troop of hand cannoneers, cheaply equipped and easily maintained, could do considerable damage on a dry, windless day at close ranges. But the crossbow and the longbow shot further (the latter with deadly force against unarmored enemies up to 230 yards if handled by an expert); and while the caprices of Jupiter Pluvius could weaken bows and slacken bowstrings (cf. excerpt from Sir Roger Williams, Par. 2, p. 66), rain and high humidity ruined gunpowder and hand-cannon shooting completely. On the other hand, whatever the failures of hand cannons, there was one overwhelming argument in their favor: more than two thousand gunners might be required to match the effectiveness of only five hundred longbowmen against infantry—but only a few weeks were required to convert raw peasants into passable shooters, while nothing less than an entire lifetime of long hours of daily practice made the archer. Not quite such long and arduous, but nonetheless rigorous years of training made the crossbowman. The consequence was that a feudal lord was likely to eye a healthy young serf not so much as an expendable animal but as a potential soldier. It was this aspect of firearms throughout the late fourteenth and fifteenth centuries, not the mistaken notion of serf rebellions, which contributed strongly to tolling the knell of the feudal system.

Figs. 33 & 34—"Holy water sprinklers"—combinations of multiple-barrel hand cannons and maces. Weapon in photograph has been reposing in the Tower of London for some four centuries, is known as "King Henry VIII's walking stick"; a connoisseur of extravagant wheellocks, king was probably never aware of its existence. Similar thunderbolt in engraving from Sir Samuel Rush Meyrick's A Critical Inquiry Into Antient Armour (London, 1824) has hinged muzzle cover, sliding flashpan covers, belt hook.

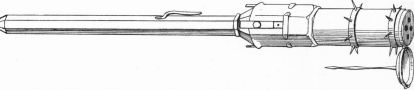

As the fifteenth century began, knights in plate armor could still ride fairly securely. If most hand cannons could pierce armor from point-blank distances, they had not yet grown into efficient, serviceable, long-range armor-piercing gunhood. Certainly they were no novelties in 1400: Chaucer may be supposed to have thought his readers familiar with them when he wrote in THE HOUSE OF FAME in about 1380:

> As swift as pellet out of gonne
> Whan fyr is in the poudre ronne . . .

among many similar references in other works. A new element had introduced itself into the lives of men, but few could have been aware of its enormity. And the institution of armored knighthood had been launched, even if almost imperceptibly, on its path to the museum.

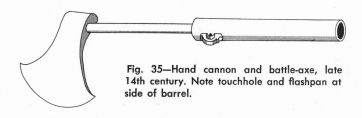

Fig. 35—Hand cannon and battle-axe, late 14th century. Note touchhole and flashpan at side of barrel.

CHAPTER THREE

Disadvantages of hand cannons and culverins, 1400–50—The earliest matchlocks—Slow matches—Armor thickens—Importance of gunners in war at the close of the fifteenth century—The fully developed matchlock—The arquebus—The sear lock—Serpentine powder and corned powder—Bore sizes—Invulnerability by magic—Effectiveness of bullets—The wheellock invented—Rifling—The Landsknechte—*The trigger lock—The caliver and musket—Sir Roger Williams' opinion (1590)—Seven engravings from de Gheyn's* Maniement d'Armes— *The matchlock's obsolescence— Oriental matchlocks.*

Y THE END OF THE FIRST QUARTER of the fifteenth century, it must have occurred to a great many hand cannoneers that their weapons would do better execution among enemies and animals of the forest if there were only a way of aiming. This could of course be done with some measure of success by sighting along the top of the barrel, but since this required supporting the gun with both hands, how was the touche to be applied to the touchhole? Nothing seemed to do save a third hand, which was supplied by the second member of the team, the *incendiarius,* or firer, who fired while the *collineator,* or aimer, aimed. For a time, from about 1430 to about 1460, it was thought expedient to take advantage of this arrangement by enlarging the hand cannons of some of the troops to two-man size, the *collineator* bearing the weight of such a so-called *culverin* or *hand culverin* on his back or shoulders. Culverins were extremely long in relation to their bores, measuring perhaps five or six feet and firing but a .70 or .80 calibre ball—a characteristic reflected in their name which ultimately traces back to Latin *colubrinus,* snakelike. One wonders at the number of unsung *collineatores* who, having aimed and braced themselves for the shot, were propelled off the ramparts backward, hotly pursued by the smoking gun. A method was urgently required whereby one man alone might aim and fire a gun of reasonable proportions.

Accordingly, the first firearms which could be considered crude but nonetheless truly functional guns appeared in the form of the early *matchlocks* in some unknown country at some unknown date in the second quarter of the fifteenth century. As is the case with virtually every solution of a vexing and universal problem, it was probably invented in many places by many men independently of each other; historians have not been able to agree on any date within fifty years, although the preponderance of the evidence suggests that about 1440 may have been the time and Genoa the place, with the gunmakers of other cities across Europe following within the next thirty years.

In its most primitive form, the matchlock was nothing more than a hand cannon with an S-shaped iron arm pivoted on its side near the breech end of the barrel; the bottom half of the arm was longer than the top half so that the weight of the longer section kept it hanging vertically, while its upper end terminated in a clamp or small tube (Fig. 36). There a long fuse was held in place, its glowing tip protruding just beyond the front of the clamp. The radius and inward angle of the upper half were such that when the lower half was pulled backward, the glowing point of the fuse was brought down over and into the powder-filled touchhole. This S-shaped device was called the *serpentine* owing to its obviously ophidian shape. To facilitate quick ignition, the opening of the touchhole was surrounded by a small saucerlike depression or a craterlike circumference. A bit of powder heaped into this rudimentary *flashpan* communicated through the touchhole with the powder inside the barrel; priming powder exposed freely over such a relatively large area—perhaps the size of a penny—was much more likely to be ignited rapidly and certainly by the glowing fuse.

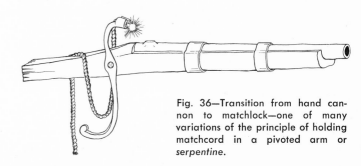

Fig. 36—Transition from hand cannon to matchlock—one of many variations of the principle of holding matchcord in a pivoted arm or serpentine.

The shooter equipped with one of these revolutionary weapons—and they were no less—was at last able to aim and fire. Having loaded his piece more or less in the manner of hand cannons, he primed his gun by heaping a little priming powder into the saucerlike flashpan, taking care to keep the glowing match well away from the powder flask. This accomplished, he fastened the lit end of the match in the serpentine and assumed the aiming stance. The gun was not placed against the shoulder: it was either held free-hand, away from the body, or against the chest if the butt was of the sharply curved type which terminated in a large flat end to distribute the force of the recoil over a wide area (Figs. 41 and 135). Doubtless the use of a forked stick to support the barrel while aiming heavy pieces was already in use in Italy and France as early as 1450. The target having been aligned with what appeared to be the center line of the top of the barrel, nothing remained to be done but to crook the finger about the lower half of the serpentine, pray and pull; all going well, the ball roared off more or less into the vicinity of the target. After a time it was noticed that this system left quite a bit to be desired. A tilt, a joggle or a gust of wind would spill or blow the priming out of the flashpan; the saucer-shaped depression appeared calculated to collect the first drop of rain in the neighborhood; and if the priming were spilled and had to be replaced, the shooter had first to take the glowing fuse out of the serpentine or take the chance of having his powder flask explode in his hand. Assuming, however, the utmost caution in loading and priming, a steady hand thereafter, and a dry and windless day, such weapons probably fired, if not whenever called upon, at least whenever coaxed.

Rapid improvements between 1440 and 1470 brought about startling differences. A century before, touch fuses had probably been nothing more than twisted cords which were easily extinguished by their own imperfections. But soon it had been found that by soaking them in a solution of saltpeter and drying them they could be made to glow evenly and slowly; and in this form they remained among the world's armaments until the end of the seventeenth century under the name of *slow match*, *match cord*, or just lengths of *match*. The fully developed matchlock, as it emerged out of the third quarter of the fifteenth century, was a highly efficient weapon fashioned in conformity to the fruits of empirical observation destined to become in time the science of ballistics. The exteriors of barrels were often milled to exact octagonal flats, or half octagonal and half round, polished to mirror finishes or darkened (to eliminate glare) by any one of several methods of staining iron by artificial oxidation and acids. True gunstocks with deep thumb notches and massive butts gradually replaced the shafts of the hand-cannon era, often lavish with the labors of woodcarver, ivory inlayer, goldsmith and other artisans. To these the barrels were fastened by pins about the thickness of medium finishing nails which passed through holes in the forestock and small eyelets welded to the underside of the barrel. The barrel was closed at the breech end by a deeply threaded *breech-plug*, an inch or two long, which screwed directly into the bore; it was prolonged rearward to a narrow tongue, or *tang*, which was secured to the top of the stock immediately behind the barrel by a long screw.

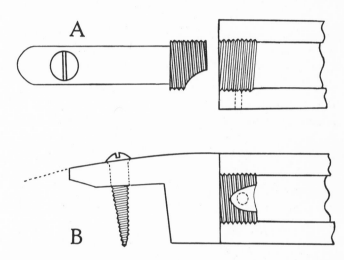

Fig. 37—Simple breech-plug, as it was developed for matchlock arquebuses in the late 15th century and was essentially to remain until about 1830. Top view (A) shows plug unscrewed from cut-away section of breech of barrel; note touchhole in side of barrel and powder notch in plug. Side view (B) shows plug screwed into barrel; touchhole is behind the now closed-up end of the bore, but notch in plug fills up with powder when gun is loaded. This arrangement somewhat reduced recoil, but not nearly so much as was believed (see excerpt from Blome, Par. 3, p. 94). Wood screw through prolonged *tang* holds rear of barrel to stock (indicated by dotted line).

Fig. 38—Municipal foot guards, circa 1450-1500. Only one of the eight men is armed with a hand cannon or an early matchlock, probably because a gunner's dependency on a nearby source of fire, or alternatively, on yards of constantly smoldering matchcord, made matchlocks impractical for squad's police-like prowl duties. Woodcut from the *Revelationes Celestes Sanctae Brigittae*, Lübeck, 1492.

These weapons had the first true *gunlocks*. The flashpan had moved from the top of the barrel to its right side by about 1460–80, where it projected horizontally literally as a small pan, the touchhole communicating into the breech chamber of the barrel. A hinged, sliding cover,

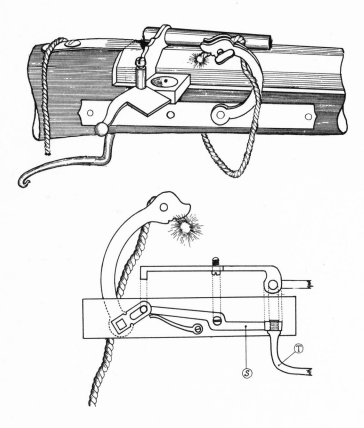

Figs. 39 & 40—Simplified diagram of a typical sear-type matchlock circa 1475-1590. Above: outside view; note tang of breech-plug, match, hinged flashpan cover, flashpan as integral part of barrel, wing nut on serpentine, flash shield and trigger bar. Below: interior mechanism. Trigger bar T is screwed into rear half of the sear S; squeezing trigger bar upward rotates sear about its pivot; downward motion of sear nose, which hooks into buckle of tumbler, depresses tumbler and thereby brings serpentine with glowing match down into flashpan; flat spring returns mechanism to normal position when trigger bar is released.

opened by the shooter immediately prior to firing, protected the priming from spillage, wind and at least the first few drops of rain, while an iron partition, logically enough called the "fyre-shielde" or "fyre-garde" by Tudor writers, rose up behind the flashpan to the top of the barrel to protect the shooter's eyes and face from the violence of the igniting priming. The mechanisms of the locks were simple, but they incorporated three functional parts, two of which, having passed through several evolutionary forms in the next five hundred years, remain in gun mechanisms to the present day, while the third survived into the 1890's. The first was the *sceare*, or in its more common modern spelling, *sear*, the part which releases the firing mechanism when the trigger is pulled; the second was the *tricker* or *trigger*; the third the *tumbler*. The function of these will be seen from Figs. 39 and 40, and since the entire mechanism was little more than one long jointed sear, it was known as a *sear-type matchlock*, or simply a *sear-lock*. Now the shooter could aim with some leisure, then bring the glowing slow match in the serpentine down into the flashpan merely by squeezing the trigger bar upward.

Fig. 41—Elevating siege turret raised by jack-screw, for approaching and rising above besieged ramparts. Note that matchlock is being butted over, not against shoulder (cf. Fig. 135). Woodcut from 1511 German translation of the *De Re Militari (Concerning the Military)* of Flavius Vegetius Renatus.

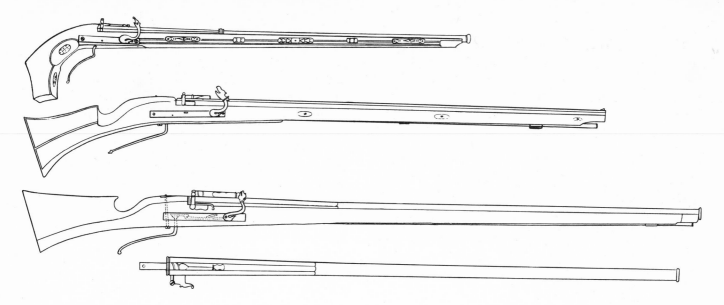

Figs. 42-44—Three sear-type matchlock arquebuses, circa 1480-1560. Top: light German hunting smoothbore; overall length 43 inches, weight 7½ pounds, calibre approximately .58; sharply dropped stock was butted against chest, not shoulder, originally a French feature (cf. excerpt from Sir Roger Williams, *A Briefe Discourse on Warre*, second paragraph, right column, p. 39); barrel is half octagonal, half round. Middle: massive Italian smoothbore of caliver size; overall length 56 inches, weight 10½ pounds, calibre approximately .79; barrel is all octagonal. Bottom: leviathan military piece, probably Spanish prototype of the muskets of 1570-1620; overall length 66 inches, weight almost 19 pounds, calibre approximately .84; such weapons were rested on forked sticks when fired. Insert shows top view of the one-third octagonal, two-thirds round barrel; note tang of breech-plug, match-guide tube, flashpan (closed) which is integral part of barrel rather than of lock. Recoil was tremendous but largely absorbed by inertia of gun's massiveness.

Weights, lengths, calibres, shapes and proportions varied wildly, but for a century and more following their emergence nearly all matchlock long arms were grouped together under the name of *arquebus* and *harquebus*. The term had originated in the German *Haken*, a hook, plus *Büchse*, a gun, to give *Hakenbüchse*, or hook gun. Exactly what the "hook" was is now uncertain, but it was apparently either the serpentine, the curved butt, the thumb notch or the forked stick on which the heaviest pieces were supported. The German *Haken* having been translated into its French equivalent *arque*, and the German *Büchse* having suffered the fate of becoming a mere suffixal *-bus*, the term *arquebus* and its phonetic variants were in use in all languages of the West by 1500. York and Tudor Englishmen accomplished its contortion to *hagbuse, hackbushe, hackbut, harkbutte, hagbut* and the like.

On a dry, not too windy day the effectiveness of arquebuses must have been quite impressive. Truly cylindrical, well-finished bores, loaded with tightly fitting bullets, enabled many of the lighter ones between .60 to .70 calibre to hit a playing card at seventy yards, kill a wild boar at eighty and a deer beyond one hundred. The heavier ones between .70 and .80 calibre could penetrate all but the thickest armor at forty to fifty yards, some at sixty and seventy, and massive forerunners of the musket had no difficulty piercing armor at upward of one hundred yards if fortune should guide the ball to the target at such distances. One of the immediate effects of such feats was that armor was not only made thicker, but that it passed out of the domain of knights and dreadnought warriors to become common—at least partial armor, e.g., breastplates, helmets, brassarts and cuisses—among footmen, travelers, wagon escorts and anyone else whose business required braving the roads and forests aswarm with murderous and, of late, fire-armed robber bands. Nevertheless, armored knighthood in the second half of the fifteenth century was far from obsolete; indeed, the universally increasing prevalence and power of firearms spurred the armorer's art to new levels of efficiency.

Fig. 45—Burgher pricing armor, perhaps a prospective traveler mindful of Fig. 47. Woodcut by Hans Weiditz from Augsburg edition of Cicero's *De Officiis*, 1531; scene could be any time after 1460.

Figs. 46 & 47—Foot travelers of the late 14th and early 15th centuries leaving a wayside inn (left) to brave, and in this case fall prey to, the perils of the roads and forests (right). Woodcut by Hans Weiditz from Augsburg edition of Petrarch, 1539.

But the weight of tactics fell more and more on cannoneers and fire-armed infantry, and by 1450 vast mercenary bands armed with matchlocks began to roam the Continent in search of princely employers. Gunners appeared on battlefields in such increasing numbers with such effect against infantry and armor alike that they bid fair to become the deciding factors of future battles and to hold the sway of tactics once held by knighthood.

Until the middle of the fifteenth century, gunpowder had been ground almost to a floury dust known as *serpentine powder* or just *serpentine*. By about 1400–20 the proportions of the constituents had settled generally to eighty parts of saltpeter, thirteen parts of charcoal and seven parts of sulphur. It was extremely inefficient and required the skill of many years of experience to load and use: for if rammed into the gun too hard, there were no interstices between the near-microscopic grains for the flame to pass through, and the load would then burn and fizzle rather than explode, or not take fire at all; or if rammed too loosely, it would lack compression and belch the projectile for only a few yards. Cannoneers who really knew their business came to be in great demand after about 1450. Almost every large and wealthy French, German and Italian city kept one or two master gunners on the municipal payroll and not only sent them traveling about with escorts to keep up with the latest developments among their colleagues in other places, but supported them in luxury and supplied them with whatever materials they declared necessary for the maintenance of the artillery in the best possible order.

Shakespeare sketched the tribulations of one city cannoneer in Act IV of HENRY VI, Part 1:

SCENE IV.—*France. Before Orleans.*
Enter, on the walls, the Master-Gunner *and his* Boy.

M. Gun. Sirrah, thou know'st how Orleans is besieg'd
and how the English have the suburbs won.
Son. Father, I know; and oft have shot at them,
Howe'er unfortunate I missed my aim.
M. Gun. But now thou shalt not. Be thou rul'd by me:
Chief master-gunner am I of this town;
Something I must do to procure me grace.
The prince's espials have informed me
How the English, in the suburbs close entrenched,
Wont through a secret gate of iron bars
In yonder tower to overpeer the city,
And thence discover how with most advantage
They may vex us with shot or with assault.
To intercept this inconvenience
A piece of ordnance 'gainst it I have plac'd
And fully even these three days have I watched
If I could see them. Now, boy, do thou watch,
For I can stay no longer.
If thou spy'st any, run and bring me word:
And thou shalt find me at the Governor's   [*Exit*]
Son. Father, I warrant you; take you no care; I'll never
trouble you if I may spy them.   [*Exit*]

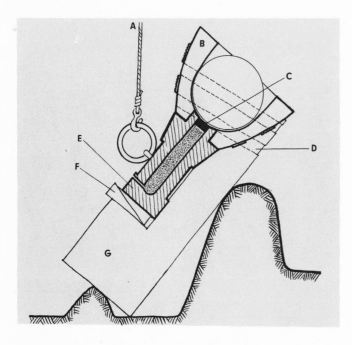

Fig. 47a—Reconstruction of an Italian breech-loading mortar or "bombard" whose breech chamber survives today in the Arms and Armour Collection of Cesta Castle, Republic of San Marino. The mortar (B) was firmly and permanently joined to a wooden caisson (G) by iron hoops (D). The removable breech chamber (E) (shaded part) was loaded with powder and wooden stopper (C), replaced into caisson and locked up against mortar by iron wedges (F). Projectiles were usually stone balls, lobbed in high arcs over the enemy's walls to knock down the wooden defense walls behind. The San Marino breech chamber may date as early as the late 13th century, but similar devices were in use much later, too; nevertheless, artillery had become overwhelmingly muzzle-loading by 1500 because all breech-loading devices then suffered from enormous loss of gas pressure. (Reconstruction by Sig. Giovanni Giorgetti, Director of the Cesta Castle Collection.)

Fig. 48—Matchlock with dragon or chimera serpentine; behind it is side plate from left side of stock, opposite lock, which acts as washer for screw holding lock to stock. Engraving from Meyrick's *A Critical Inquiry Into Antient Armour*, London, 1824.

To come back to serpentine gunpowder. In addition to its badly workable consistency, it had the vexing and unfailing caprice of separating into layers according to the specific gravities of the constituents when joggled over the potholed roads in the lumbering supply wagons. The sulphur, being the heaviest, fell to the bottom after an hour or two of transport, the saltpeter forming the middle layer and the charcoal coming out on top. Swirling clouds of noxious and highly explosive dust followed in the wake of the wagon trains, nothing but a nearby fire being required to accelerate the train and a goodly section of the army to the ultimate of destinations. It was necessary to remix the ingredients at the site of the shooting, a process which again yielded copious clouds of deadly dust. To remedy the first of these ills, the ingredients were transported separately, but this still required mixing at the battery (see Fig. 49). And serpentine left such thick deposits of fouling in the barrels that after half a dozen shots loading became difficult, and after another eight or ten the barrels had to be thoroughly decaked and scrubbed. The solution of this problem—one which may have been thought of in Nuremberg as early as 1410—was the wet incorporation of the ingredients. These were ground together in a mortar or stamping mill

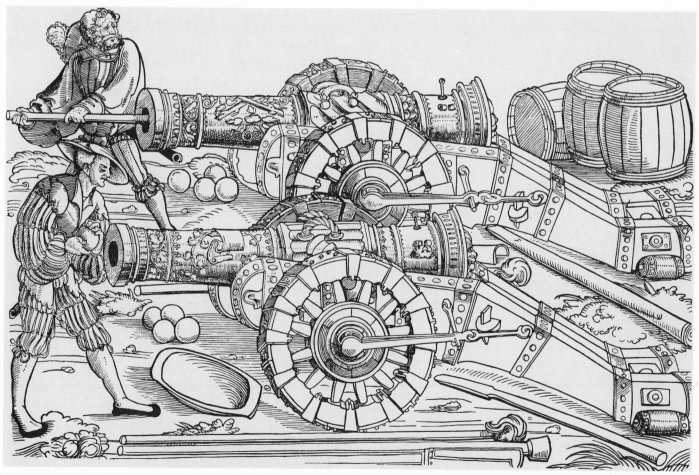

Fig. 49—Cannoneers, first half of 16th century. Serpentine gunpowder used for artillery was weak, inefficient and fouling, gave off huge gaseous clouds of highly explosive dust when transported. Ingredients —sulphur, charcoal, saltpeter—were therefore carried separately in three barrels (right background), were mixed in shallow mixing trough before loading (left foreground). Note cleaning swab, rammer, mixing paddle, long-handled scoop for placing powder far down the barrel into breech chamber. Touchholes of both guns are stopped up during loading to keep out stray sparks from any nearby brazier. Woodcut by Erhardt Schoen (fl. 1514-50).

while alcohol and water were added to make a moist paste. Urine was considered an excellent medium, a wine drinker's urine being better than a beer drinker's, and a wine-drinking bishop's best of all (this last commodity having been at times collected at the source and dispensed as a token of episcopal favor to the fortunate community). The mixture was then dried almost completely, but not quite, and pressed into cakes which were fragmented into grains in rolling or stamping mills; alternatively, the paste was forced through sieves, and the resulting "worms," when dry, were gently crushed to grains. These were then sifted, the coarsest cannon powder being then composed of grains about the size of corn kernels,

the finest like fine sand (Figs. 52 and 108). The final product was called *corned powder*. The first to write of it was Konrad von Schöngau in his FEUERBUCH (*Book of Fire*) in 1429. Its advantages were that it did not separate, made little or no dust in transport, was much less fouling, much less vulnerable to atmospheric moisture, and vastly more efficient and powerful than serpentine powder. But this last virtue proved to be double-edged: it was so efficient that when tried in cannons it blew them to fragments after a few shots, sometimes on the first (unfortunate effects which further aggravated the scarcity of good gunners), while lesser charges, which did not burst the cannon, failed to give the necessary

Figs. 50 & 51—Above: distillation of sulphur. Below: purification of saltpeter. Woodcuts from Swiss edition of Georgius Agricola, *De Re Metallica (Concerning Mining)*, Phillipp Bech translation, *Vom Bergwerk*, Basel, 1557.

Fig. 52—Hand-powered powder stamping mill, similar to most between circa 1500 and 1750. Four mortar cavities were filled with cakes of virtually dry, barely moist incorporated mixture; as crank, flywheel and cylinder were turned, cams lifted and dropped vertical stamping pestles (cf. Fig. 108). Engraving from Joseph Furtenbach, *Mannhaffter Kunst-Spiegel (Mirror of the Manly Arts)*, Augsburg, 1663.

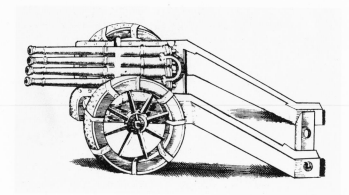

Fig. 53—Four-barreled cannon, early 17th century. Engraving from Robert Norton, *The Gunner, Shewing the Whole Practice of Artillery,* London, 1628.

establishing how many balls of pure lead of any arbitrarily selected diameter were required to make up one pound. For example, balls of such a size that five of them weighed exactly one pound would always measure .983 inches each in diameter, 10-to-the-pound measured .786 inches, 41-to-the-pound .484 inches, 210-to-the-pound .280 inches, and so on. A shooter now requiring bullets of .762 calibre would ask for that size of which eleven weighed a pound and he would be fairly sure of getting what he wanted within a negligible margin of error. The number of balls per pound had become known as the *bore number* by 1540, having remained until then expressed merely as so-many-to-the-pound. The gun barrel which accommodated them was of course called the same: a *12-bore gun* fired bullets of twelve to the pound, or .747 inches, which was consequently the diameter of its bore. This system remained in use until about 1850, and it is still used today (with certain standardizing modifications) to express the diameter of shotgun barrels, save that the term *gauge* has now largely replaced *bore*.

range and momentum. It was not until the late sixteenth and early seventeenth centuries that metallurgy progressed to cannons which could withstand the shocklike pressures generated by the pounds of corned powder required to hurl cannon balls. Consequently serpentine powder, for all its failings, had to be continued for use in cannons for another two centuries. Slowly, however, the use of corned powder in arquebuses spread throughout Europe, arriving in England probably before 1480, for the barrels of small arms were much stronger in relation to the trifling quantities of powder required—between half an ounce and an ounce and a half—than cannon barrels were in relation to several pounds.

A new problem followed in the wake of the new armaments, viz., the chaos of sizes of barrel diameters and bullets. A shooter in 1485 might have a piece requiring a .76 calibre ball—76/100 of an inch in diameter—but how was he to find one? If he was a Nuremberger he would ask for one measuring about .83 of a Franconian *Zoll*— but the Franconian *Zoll* was not used anywhere save in Franconia, and if the shooter happened to be hunting in the Black Forest, he would find upon inquiry in Freiburg that the Badian *Zoll* was only about 7/8 of a *Zoll* in Nuremberg, but larger by a tenth than the same Badian *Zoll* used in Karlsruhe, and maddeningly elusive through a dozen different centimeter equivalents. City, duchy, principality, kingdom and commune had each its own unit of measurement which was likely to vary by a quarter from one village to the next. Happily, a better system was available in politically homogeneous England. It was relatively easy for the king to ordain that a certain arbitrary weight be the official pound; brass or iron masses weighing exactly this amount could not only be sent about the domain fairly easily, but copied and standardized to very fine approximations since a good balance would record at least 1/100 of an ounce and therefore 1/1600 of a pound or even closer. The weight of a pound having been standardized throughout the kingdom, the sizes of bullets could now be measured quite closely by

Fig. 54—Siege of a city. Woodcut by Albrecht Dürer, ca. 1500.

**Keyn ding hilfft fur den zeytling todt
Darumb dienent got frrwe vnd spot**

Fig. 55—Death admonishes soldier in woodcut by Albrecht Dürer, dated 1510; illustration from poem *Keyn ding hilfft fur den zeytling todt—Darumb dienent got frrwe vnd spot (There is no help for certain death—Therefore serve God early and late)*.

Whatever death and mayhem the fifteenth-century arquebuses could mete out in war, their initial success as military weapons owed less to the actual physical destruction than to the psychological destruction which followed in its wake. Rank terror of hell and all its ministers gripped the illiterate, ignorant men and the all but equally illiterate, ignorant captains and princes in that age when devils and demons lurked abroad in every place at every hour. A crossbow quarrel or an arrow flew with the aid of feathers; so did angels. Consequently it could be proved with irrefutable logic that a quarrel or an arrow was essentially a good, if not an angelic object. It acquired virtue or wickedness depending on the use to which it was put. Such missiles, once discharged, were subject to no control whatever save the will of God as it pleased His infinite wisdom to direct or divert them. Bullets, on the other hand, presented quite another story. They were launched by fire, brimstone and stench; consequently a bullet was essentially a diabolical, if not actually a hell-made object. It was wicked by nature, and although of course it was within God's power to alter its

path, it had become clear by 1475 that (a) He chose to do so less frequently than hitherto with arrows, or (b) that the invisible imp astride it could direct it to dodge the beams or rays of God's will. Furthermore, the struggle between God and Satan was a ferocious and incessant one, and who could tell but that the latter had gained at least a momentary victory by having sent up to earth these machines which in turn sent down so many new arrivals? In all, it was safer to enter an *entente cordiale* with both parties. As early as 1480 it was possible to acquire invulnerability against bullets by observing magic rituals and carrying magic amulets, such as crucifixes mounted on phallic medallions, pentagrams, cabalistic formulae, saintly and diabolical icons of an infinite variety, and of course innumerable forms of the ubiquitous mandrake root. Traveling gypsies and young scholars, Till Eulenspiegels and Dr. Faustuses by the hundreds, grew rich in peddling bullet-proofing talismans in the camps of armies. German muster rolls of the time began to show the first of countless subsequent entries such as "Johannes Schmidt, Q.D.I.G.," an abbreviation for "*qui dicetur impenetrabilis glandibus*" or "*quem dicunt impenetrabilem [esse] glandibus*," "who is said to be impenetrable by bullets." Physicians, quack and genuine (the difference was a tenuous one), prepared and sold astrological tables of anatomy showing when the various parts of the body were most favored by the heavenly signs and therefore least likely to sustain injury in battle.

Figs. 56 & 57—Left: The influence of the zodiac on 15th-century human anatomy: throughout the year the various members were least likely to sustain injury or illness as the sun entered the indicated constellations. Horoscope-like charts were sold to soldiers by shrewd quacks according to the buyer's birthdate, or if unknown (most often the case), according to the day of his patron or namesake saint. Woodcut from Blaubirer's *Calendar*, 1477. Below: "Male and female mandrake roots," according to the *Hortus Sanitatis (Garden of Health)*, Augsburg, 1486; anthropoidally shaped roots could be carved into human effigies, were the *sine qua non* in most invulnerability potions.

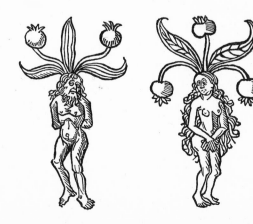

It is not difficult to understand why bullets were vested in such a miasma of hellishness. Arrows could often be removed from flesh wounds without too much difficulty; the wound was usually a fairly neatly sliced hole which could be washed out (Fig. 58). The mortality rate from infection was of course enormous, but with luck one might have a sporting chance to survive a flesh wound inflicted by blade or arrow. Furthermore, arrows striking long bones generally broke them in clean fractures, and not infrequently were deflected altogether. Bullets, however, unholy pills of hell, were terrifying in their sulphurous stench and thunder even when they missed and instead went overhead so that one could hear the accompanying demon scream and whistle to chill the blood. But when they hit, they did not cut or drill flesh: they mashed; they did not glance off bones or break them cleanly: they shattered them beyond hope of repair. Vermin from garments and hair, bits of cloth, layers of filth from the very infrequently washed skin and other purulent intrusions were ground into the flesh by the bullet's path and *sealed* into the wound. Probing for a bullet introduced more fetid and infectious matter into a wound already acrawl with half the bacteria of Europe, the other half biding their time on the surgeon's instruments (Figs. 59 to 61). The mortality rate from even the simplest bullet-inflicted flesh wounds was such that a shot through the buttocks, besides being awkward to explain, must have been very nearly as deadly as a shot in a vital organ, or for that matter as the slightest graze.

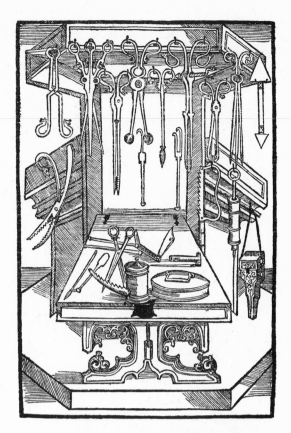

Fig. 59—Surgical instruments; woodcut from H. Brunschwig, *Chirurgia (Surgery)*, Strassburg, 1497.

Figs. 60 & 61—Above: field surgeon's tent behind the lines. Below: field surgeon's kit and other medical paraphernalia. Woodcuts from Theophrastus Paracelsus, *Drei Bücher von Wunden und Schäden (Three Books on Wounds and Injuries)*, Frankfurt-a.-M., 1563.

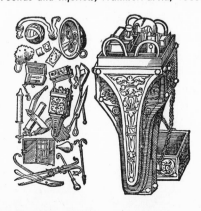

Fig. 58—Removal of an arrow. Woodcut from H. Gersdorf, *Wundartzenei (Wound Therapy)*, Strassburg, 1528.

Fig. 62—Armored car, late 15th to middle 16th centuries, manned by officer and matchlock squad. Woodcut from 1511 German translation of *De Re Militari (Concerning the Military)* of Flavius Vegetius Renatus.

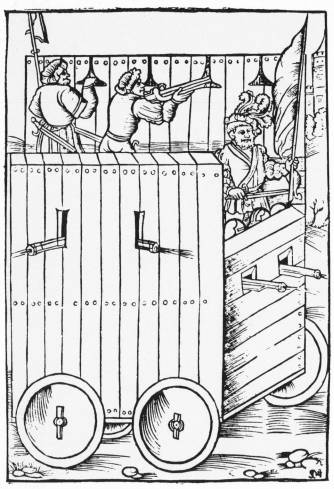

Two inventions appeared at the end of the fifteenth and the beginning of the sixteenth centuries which were to have a profound effect on the future of firearms, and indeed, of the world. One was the remarkable contrivance known as the *wheellock*, probably first developed (perhaps as household tinder-lighters) in Lombardy-Veneto in the late 1400's and subsequently perfected in the early 1500's in Nuremberg, Prague, and Brescia. But this engine ushered in such a vast new phase of firearms history that we shall pass it by here and devote our full attention to it in succeeding chapters.

The other invention was *rifling*. Since the days of the Pharaohs it had been known that arrows feathered somewhat obliquely would spin about their axes and could be made to fly farther and more truly than those which did not spin. Legend has it that one Kaspar Köllner of Vienna in about 1496–99, or alternatively one August Kotter of Nuremberg in about 1520, was the first to apply this principle to bullets. As early as 1460, however, there were arquebuses whose bores were grooved with eight, ten or more perfectly *straight* grooves, spiraling not at all, nor were such barrels infrequent fully 100 to 125 years later. Straight grooves had of course no effect on the motion of the bullet; and it may therefore be safely surmised that these were carbon-accumulating grooves. Although corned powder fouled much less than serpentine powder, it nevertheless still caked the bore with a deposit

of carbon after each shot so that ramming the ball down became progressively more difficult and accuracy fell off sharply. But by cutting straight grooves into the bore and allowing these to fill up with the sooty fouling, the number of shots which might be fired before cleaning became imperative could be greatly increased. Long before 1510 some gunmakers appear to have reasoned that the inevitable scrubbing could be delayed even further if the grooves were made longer than the barrel itself in order to collect more carbon still, which could be done by the simple expedient of cutting them spirally, making, say, one or one and a half turns in the length of the bore.

Whether this or conscious imitation of spinning arrows led to rifling is uncertain, although the carbon-accumulating groove theory seems more likely. Whichever way, the first few shots fired from spirally grooved barrels must have proved hair-raising experiences for the experimenters: what black art had they innocently stumbled upon? For the ball found its mark at nearly twice the range that even the most abandoned optimist might have dared to hope! The playing card was plugged at one hundred yards—where hitherto it had been a feat for sharp eyes and steady hands to hit the deer-sized target in some part! The Bavarian necromancer Moretius (Herman Moritz) found the explanation in 1522: a bullet fired from a rifled barrel flew true because no devil could remain astride a spinning object, as witness the rotating heavenly spheres (devil-free) and the stationary earth (devil-infested). Until Benjamin Robins read his paper OBSERVATIONS ON THE NATURE AND ADVANTAGES OF RIFLED BARREL PIECES before the Royal Society in 1747, no one understood the simple physics of a spinning projectile (which will be noted in Chapter X).

Whatever the origins of rifling, empirical or fortuitous, it was certainly known by 1475. The Turin armory had at least one rifled iron gun in 1476; and a *Schützenbrief*—a broadside advertising a shooting match—of Eichstaedt in the summer of 1477 invited arquebusiers to compete at a range of 200 meters—219 yards—a feat which is impossible for smoothbored barrels but plausible for rifles even of that age. An inventory taken in the Nuremberg fortress in 1479 refers to "*iv tubi cum rugis per cochleas bullantibus,*" or roughly "four tubes with ridges performing spirals,"—very likely four rifled barrels. Certainly by 1525 rifles of the finest quality were made throughout Europe, especially in Germany. Smoothbores, however, remained in the great majority. For one thing, a rifle could not be used with bird shot, for the spiral grooves would of course scatter the pellets in a whirling maelstrom, while a smoothbore was equally suitable for shot and ball even if the ball was only half as accurate at half the range. For another, if a rifle could send sure death to deer and bear at 150 to 200 yards, it was also very hard to load. The ball had to fill the grooves in order to grip them firmly and to prevent gas seepage around it through the grooves; therefore its diameter had to be that of the bore between two opposite grooves, not that between two opposite elevations, or as they are technically known, *lands.* This required hammering the ball down the barrel with an iron ramrod and generous blows of a wooden mallet, a laborious and lengthy procedure wholly unsuited for the heat of battle and slow to find acceptance among hunters. How this problem was solved in time will also be seen in Chapter X.

Rapidly now the military complexion of the Continent began to change. The roving bands of mercenaries of the fifteenth century evolved into a new sort of professional soldiery in the form of the *Landsknechte,* or as they soon became known in other tongues, the *lansquenets, lanz-chinetti* and other variants. It is uncertain whether the word was originally *Lanz-knecht,* lance-servant, or *Lands-knecht,* servant of the country. Roaming in hordes numbering from a few hundred to more than ten thousand, these armies consisted of the most abandoned savages in Christendom. The men were loyal only to their elected captains, who arranged contracts with kings, princes, cities, bishops, anyone in need of the service of an army, the terms of pay being usually ·a small wage payable semiannually plus the right to anywhere from 50 to 90 per cent of the plunder looted from sacked cities. The internal discipline of each band was remarkably rigid: the leader's authority was enforced through elaborate structures of officer hierarchies, provosts, courts-martial and executioners who dealt swiftly and severely with infractors of the regimental laws and traditions. In times of peace, or at least during intervals between employment, these mobs lived off the land, extorting and plundering the luxuries and necessities of life from the terrified peasantry. But such depredations were nothing compared to the atrocities beyond all belief which they perpetrated during the Thirty Years' War of 1618–48 (cf. p 84). Their legacy of murder, arson, syphilis, bastardy and desolation was branded so deeply into the tissue of communities upon which they descended that thick scars remain to this day.

In general, the prevalence of firearms by the end of the first half of the sixteenth century was such that Pierino Belli (1502–1575) in his DE RE MILITARI ET BELLO TRACTATUS (*Treatise on War and the Military*), published in Venice in 1563, burst out bitterly:

> And inasmuch as it was ordered by the law of the Church that Christians should use in their wars no darts or catapults (in order to reduce as far as possible the number of engines of destruction and death), and the prohibition was enforced under pain of anathema, this might be listed among the soldiers' privileges, since they were the first and in fact the only ones to reap advantage from this law.
>
> But today regard is so far lacking for this rule that firearms of a thousand kinds are the most common and popular implements of war, as if too few avenues of death had been discovered in the course of the centuries, had not the generation of our fathers, rivalling God with his lightning, invented this means whereby even at a single stroke men are sent to perdition by the hundreds.

Fig. 63—Arquebusier with spring-driven matchlock. Unfinished left hand was probably continued in adjoining block, which may have shown horse being led by reins. Woodcut by Niklas Stoer (fl. 1532-62).

Fig. 64 —— *Landsknecht* drummer. Anonymous woodcut, circa 1525-40.

Fig. 65—*Landsknecht* arquebusier loading arquebus. Five small containers or "cartridges" hanging from bandolier hold measured quantities of powder for one shot each (cf. Figs. 72 to 78); powder horn behind hip holds either more coarse propellent powder or finely ground priming powder. Gun has lock on left side because woodcut is mirror image of drawing after which it was cut. Note that soldier's right thigh is bare, probably a regimental fashion. Woodcut by Sebald Beham (born ca. 1498, died ca. 1549).

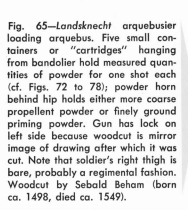

Fig. 66—The firemaster of a mercenary regiment; his task was to supply fire where needed—to braziers and matchcords, cooking fires, sacked towns. Woodcut by Erhardt Schoen (fl. 1514-50).

Fig. 67—Peasants with matchlock arquebuses out fowling in wintertime; engraving by Hans Bol (1534-1593), from *Venationis, Piscationis et Avicupii Typii (Scenes of Hunting, Fishing and Birding)*, published 1580-88, probably Amsterdam (see also Figs. 94 & 138). Similarity of setting and style to Stradanus' engraving in Fig. 135 reflects Stradanus' influence on engravers of such genre scenes.

Other forms of matchlocks appeared in the closing years of the fifteenth century. In these the serpentine was activated by a flat spring, either outside or inside the lockplate; it was held erect by a sear, the nose of which receded inward when the trigger was squeezed or a button was pushed on the side of the stock so that serpentine and match were driven downward into the priming by the force of the spring pressing on the tumbler, or on the tail of the Serpentine (e.g., Fig. 63). Such locks came into common use in abundant varieties of mechanical detail between about 1480 and 1540, notably in Germany, but thereafter they lost favor and yielded to the sear-type lock.

In the second half of the sixteenth century the matchlock arquebus underwent considerable alteration, although by then the wheellock had replaced it almost everywhere as the weapon of men of means. Sometime before 1580 the flashpan became a part of the lock rather than of the barrel, and the unwieldy and dangerous trigger bar was replaced by an essentially modern trigger, to be pulled by the index finger, its interior section acting as a lever which raised the rear of the sear as had the older screwed-in trigger bars. To guard against accidental discharge it was surrounded by a broad brass or iron loop, a *trigger guard*. When in 1631 Charles I appointed a select committee of "gunmakers, armorers, pikemakers, bandolleer-makers and the like artists, being the skillfullest and prime workmen of this land" to super-vise the manufacture and procurement of arms for the national militia, the *Table of Gun Makers' Rates* established by the august assembly (cf. p. 87) included

For a match-tricker lock compleat......... £ – / 1/0
For a handle or guard of a tricker........ £ – / –/6
For furnishing and setting of a tricker lock in place of a sceare lock, with handle, tricker and tricker pynnes.................. £ – / 2/6

The catch-all term *arquebus* became more and more confined to a rather light-weight hunting gun, whether rifled or smooth, while two new words were introduced together with two new, or at least two newly defined, weapons. One was the *caliver*, a weapon sporting a barrel of some 39 to 44 inches in length, weighing with stock some 10 to 12 pounds and firing a 10- or 11-bore ball (approximately .76 to .79 calibre). It was fired without a forked rest stick, but many toyed with the outer limits of massiveness and recoil which one man alone might reasonably be expected to support and endure. Its name, if one is to believe the account in Sir Samuel Meyrick's A CRITICAL INQUIRY INTO ANTIENT ARMOUR (London, 1824), was derived in the 1560's from the French *une arquebuse du calibre de Monsieur le Prince,* "an arquebus of the calibre of the prince," or of the guns of the prince's own regiment; it was soon corrupted to *arquebuse calibre* and eventually merely to *caliver*. (The word *calibre* itself traces its ancestry either to the Arabic *q'alib*, a mould, or to Latin *qua libra*, of what weight?). Rapidly calivers became all-around service and household guns.

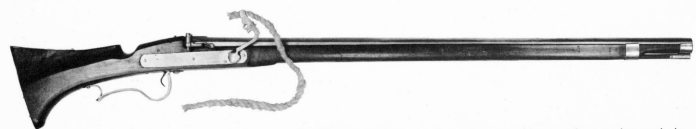

Fig. 68—Large Austrian matchlock caliver, possibly a cut-down musket, made between 1580 and 1620; 53½ inches in overall length. .79 calibre. (In the collection of Mr. Thomas E. Hall, New Haven, Connecticut.)

The other new weapon was one which the Italians had called a *moschetto*, or "sparrow-hawk." Probably introduced by the infamous Duke of Alva (1508–82) in his campaigns of horror during the Spanish subjugation of the Netherlands (1565–81), it was not long before it had arrived via France (as a *mousquet*) in England, where it became in short order a *mousquit, muskitt* and eventually a *musket*. Firing a 9- to 6-bore ball (apprximately .80 to .92 calibre) out of a 45- to 55-inch barrel, this 14- to 20-pound terror was designed to send its missile smashing accurately through whatever armor it might encounter up to 125 yards, and to stop in his tracks by sheer impact whatever man or beast it might hit at ranges well over 200 yards. But what the musket gained in power it lost in all pretense to maneuverability. The musketeer carried (as did the arquebusier and the caliveer) small wooden cylindrical containers or *cartridges* suspended from his bandoleer, each filled with a measured quantity of powder for one shot, sometimes also with a bullet. Preloaded cartridges of paper, complete with ball and powder and tied at both ends, which were bitten open by the shooter immediately before loading, were known before 1550; Leonardo da Vinci had suggested them about seventy years earlier (Fig. 71). In 1590, Sir John Smyth, fellow war horse of Sir Roger Williams, wrote familiarly of "cartages with which [musketeers] charge theyr peeces both with poudre and ball at 1 time"; while Whitehorne in 1560 described "bagges of linen or paper with powder and shotte" for cannons. In addition, the large flask of coarse propellent powder, the small flask of fine priming powder, the leather bullet pouch and half a dozen four-foot lengths of slow match all hung from the musketeer's belts and buckles. Burdened by the weight of the prodigious weapon, he had further not only to negotiate the forked stick, but to hold the burning slow match (lit at both ends in the event one would be extinguished) between his fingers whenever loading, marching, standing at ease—in short, whenever it was not clamped into the serpentine just before shooting. The loading procedure consisted of cumbrous gymnastics with the gun, the rest, the ammunition and the perilous match cord, as the selected seven of Jacob de Gheyn's famous 116 engravings will testify (Figs. 72 to 78); it was a nimble musketeer who could fire two shots in three minutes. Yet let the virtue of the weapon be attested by Sir Roger Williams, who published his BRIEFE DISCOURSE ON WARRE in London in 1590:

TO PROOVE MUSKETIERS THE BEST SMALL SHOT THAT EVER WERE INVENTED

In my judgement five hundred Muskets are better than 1000 Calivers, or any other such shot, and are to be valued from that rate unto the greatest number. My reasons are thus: The Musket spoyles horse or man thirtie score off [200–220 yards] if the powder bee anything good and the bearer of any judgment. If armed [armored] men give the charge, few or any of them carrie Armes of the proofe of the Musket being delivered within ten or twelve score [few or none of them will be wearing armor which is proof against the Musket being fired from 70 to 100 yards]. If any greate troupes of horse or foote offers to force them [the musketeers] with multitudes of smaller shot, they [the musketeers] may discharge four, five or six bullets being delivered in volley, the which pearceth al they strike, unless the enemie be so heavily armed as of new [be armored especially in the new type of bullet-proof steel], the which they are not unless it be some 100 of a thousand at the most of either horse or foot. By that reckoning, 100 Muskets are to bee valued unto 200 Calivers or more. The Çalivers [i.e., the shooters and advocates of calivers] may say they will discharge two shot for one [of a musket], but cannot denie but that one Musket doth more hurt than two Calivers shot, farre or nere and better cheape; although the Musket spend a pound of powder in 8 or 12 shot, yet considering the wages and expenses of two to one, the Musket is better cheape and farre more serviceable. Some think the Musket cannot march farre in day or night or continue long without rest by reason of their weight, nor skirmish so nimble nor so often by reason of their length, weight and sore recoyling. Armed [armored] men are heavier loaden than the Musketiers and more cumbersome in carriage; lightlie no great troupe marches ten miles without resting, bee it but a little at everie stand and neere the enemie. The Musketiers are suffered to quit their weight, leaving their Muskets in their rests [forked sticks]: the armed [armored] men will not be suffered to disarme themselves in their march, let them stand ever so often, if they bee within five houres march of an Enemie anything equal of either horse or foote. By that reason they [the musketeers] have a little advantage. . . .

Touching on their often discharging, nimbleness and profite, I answered before. For recoyling there is no hurt if they [the muskets] be streight stocked after the Spanish manner. For their weight [i.e., power] and sure shooting, the Muskets have advantage on all the other small shot by reason they shoot in their rests. True it is, were they stocked crooked after the French manner, to be discharged on the breast, fewe or none could abide their recoyling by reason of their great charges of powder; but being discharged from the shoulder after the Spanish manner, with the thumbe betwixt the stocke and the face, there is neither daunger nor hurt if the shooter have any discretion, especiallie not to overload their peeces, and take heede that the bullets ioyne close to the powder. . . .

Touching light skirmishes, unles it be to some purpose, none uses them unless it be rawe men or light headed that delights to heare the peeces cracke. . . .

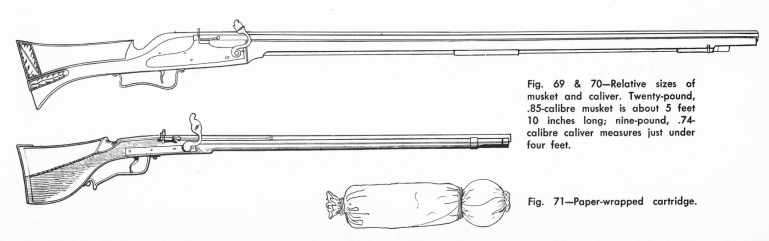

Fig. 69 & 70—Relative sizes of musket and caliver. Twenty-pound, .85-calibre musket is about 5 feet 10 inches long; nine-pound, .74-calibre caliver measures just under four feet.

Fig. 71—Paper-wrapped cartridge.

Fig. 72-78—Seven of the 116 engravings in Jacob de Gheyn's *Le Mainiement d'Armes, d'Arquebuses, Mousquetz et Piques (The Management of Arms, Arquebuses, Muskets and Pikes)*, commissioned by Maurice, Prince of Orange, in about 1606 and published in Amsterdam in 1608. *Le Mainiement* remained the classic of musketry exercise until the matchlock was replaced by the flintlock some seventy or eighty years later; the engravings were plagiarized in dozens and perhaps hundreds of manuals of arms. In the first of the selected engravings (left), the musketeer stands at ease with his elephantine musket and its forked rest stick; the two glowing ends of the slowmatch, in accordance with approved practice, protrude between the fingers of his left hand. About two dozen wooden cartridges, or powder containers, hang from his bandolier. In addition, he carries spare lengths of match, a small flask for priming powder, a bullet pouch and a rapier.

Fig. 72—Musketeer at rest (note that equipment, clothing and men vary in all the engravings). Loading procedure began when . . . →

Fig. 75— . . . rammed it down with the ramrod until he felt it seated firmly on top of the powder. After returning the rod . . . →

Fig. 76— . . . he primed the flashpan with fine powder from the small priming flask, taking utmost care with the match. Finally . . . →

Fig. 73— . . . musketeer seized a powder-filled wooden cartridge on his leather bandoleer and opened it with his thumb. Next . . . →

Fig. 74— . . . he poured its contents into the barrel, took a bullet from his pouch, started it into the muzzle with his thumb, and . . .

Fig. 77— . . . he rested the musket in the forked stick, blew the ashes off the match and clamped it into the serpentine, and . . . →

Fig. 78— . . . assumed the aiming stance. Constantly adjusting the protruding end of the match, he was ready for the command "Fire!"

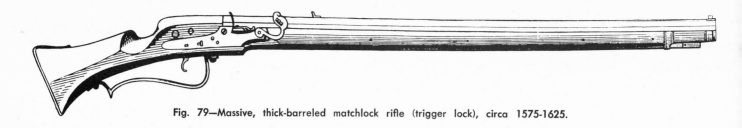

Fig. 79—Massive, thick-barreled matchlock rifle (trigger lock), circa 1575-1625.

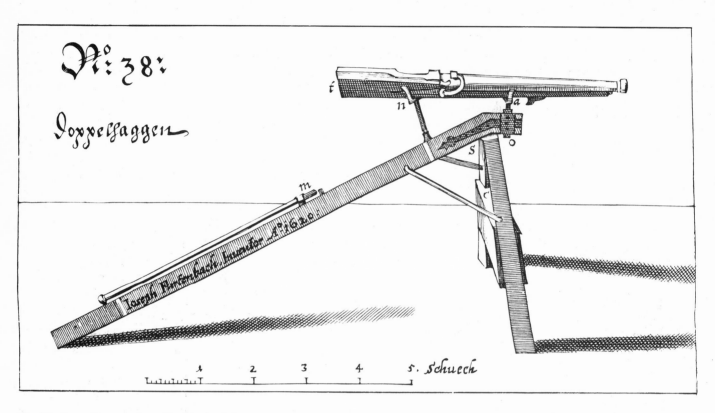

Fig. 80—*Doppelhaggen,* i.e., "double hook," says Fig. No. 38 in Joseph Furtenbach's *Büchsenmeisterey-Schul (School of the Art of Gunnery),* Augsburg, 1643. Here "double hook" means an arquebus of double size (-haggen is variant spelling of *Haken,* i.e., hook, as in *Hakenbüchse* or arquebus); such terminology was arbitrary, varied from place to place and author to author. Weapons such as these were in effect small matchlock cannons, fired about 1¼-inch balls with armor-piercing power beyond 300 yards, but were inaccurate and impractical save as defenses mounted on fortified ramparts. Diagonal brace is inscribed with the claim "Ioseph Furtenbach Inventor A⁰ 1620," which at best could be truthfully applied only to minor improvements in the construction of the carriage. When gun was removed from cradle and fired from rampart, small projection under forestock in front of letter *a* was hooked over wall to anchor it.

Fig. 81—Engraving from J. J. von Wallhausen, *Art Militaire au Cheval (The Art of Mounted Warfare),* Frankfurt-a.-M., 1616, one of a series used to illustrate the relative strengths of three-quarter-armored lancers versus musketeers. Musketeer has the advantage if he can hit charging rider or rider's horse with his one and only shot; if he misses, he is helpless prey for the rider's lance.

Fig. 82—German matchlock ten-shot revolver, circa 1490-1530. Cylinder was rotated manually; when top chamber was aligned with barrel, spring on top of barrel snapped into small hole in front end of cylinder. Each flashpan had sliding cover (uppermost one is shown open), but often stray sparks must have ignited a chain reaction of all ten chambers. Rare weapon was in a famous private collection in Nuremberg, Germany, when engraving was cut for *Quellen zur Geschichte der Feuerwaffen (Source Material for the History of Firearms)*, published in Leipzig by the Nuremberg Germanic Museum in 1872, but has since dropped from sight.

Sir Roger's panegyric notwithstanding, the great musket eventually declined in favor among the commanders of later days until the armies thus equipped were few by 1650; or, more accurately, it should be said that the musket shrank steadily down to caliver size and even smaller until it arrived at the proportions of the weapon called a "musket" in the second half of the seventeenth century and ever after. Guns of such less prodigious sizes were found more practical after all for field service. By 1670, too, wheellocks, miquelet locks, snaphaunces and early flintlocks had made the matchlock all but obsolete, although it survived well into the eighteenth century among some sections of the peasantry and banditry because of its cheapness and simplicity. Before 1680 matchlocks had become historic driftwood in Europe, but they enjoyed a better fate in Asia.

Early in the sixteenth century—legend, wrongly, makes it about 1580-90—the Japanese were introduced to matchlocks by the Dutch and Portuguese traders who called from time to time in the imperial islands. At once the inhabitants set out to adapt and improve the new import, reducing it to an austere but very graceful simplicity of line and function. The mechanism of the Japanese matchlock was spring driven with a forward-falling serpentine; nearly always lock, spring, serpentine, trigger and flashpan were made of brass, while the barrels were of brass, bronze or iron (Figs. 87 to 90). Japanese gunmakers were among the few anywhere who ever made and evidently managed to sell matchlock pistols—weapons which, if the reader will reflect a moment, were such astounding monuments to uselessness that European makers despaired of trying. Only a few Polish ones—and these from the late eighteenth century—survive to testify that only on the primitive eastern periphery of Europe were they ever made in any quantity, however modest. But Japanese matchlock pistols are not infrequent, and Japanese matchlocks remained largely unchanged in form and mechanism until the 1860's, when, after Perry's "opening" of the Empire to the West, the Japanese arms industry converted within five years from matchlock to percussion cap and soon after to metallic-cartridge breech-loading repeaters; there was never a transition period.

The Chinese never developed a small-arms industry to speak of. Hand cannons were used as late as 1900 and probably still are today in some nooks of some provinces. Such matchlocks as were made closely adhered to the Japanese patterns, but for the most part guns were imported from Korea and Japan.

In India and the Near East, however, matchlocks of characteristic shapes and styles (Figs. 83 to 86) reached considerable stages of perfection, though few of them could compete with the fine products of Japan. Experts in Indian armaments distinguish three and possibly four main types of matchlock long arms, each peculiar to a vast region. Matchlocks survived in India into the present century and many thousands are still in use.

Figs. 83-86—Four Indian matchlocks; serpentines protrude through slits on top of stocks. Right: cylinder and lock of South Indian revolving smoothbore military weapon, circa 1800; in the Tower of London. Below: three smoothbore "muskets," circa 1750-1800, two with touchhole prickers attached by short chains.

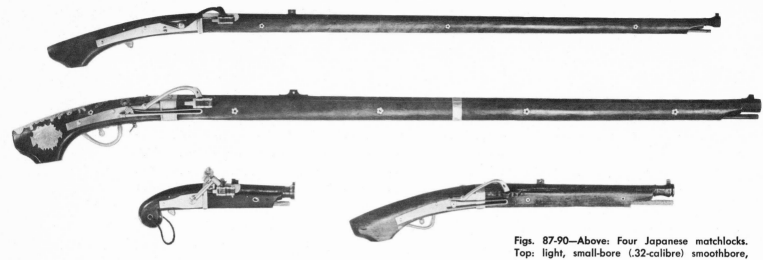

Figs. 87-90—Above: Four Japanese matchlocks. Top: light, small-bore (.32-calibre) smoothbore, 47¼ inches overall length, intended for rabbits, squirrels, other small game. When serpentine is cocked, tail slides down over beveled nose of sear, which protrudes through lockplate and holds serpentine erect; pulling trigger causes sear to recede inward, releases serpentine to be snapped into flashpan by mainspring inside lock. Middle: medium-sized. 51-calibre smoothbore, 52½ inches in overall length; sear works as in gun above but mainspring is on outside of lockplate. Bottom: two smoothbore pistols; smaller one is .54 calibre, 11¼ inches long; larger one is .50 calibre, 23 inches. Serpentines of Japanese matchlocks terminated in small tubes or U-shaped ferrules rather than in vise clamps, could be used either with matchcords or bits of frayed tinder (such as in the first pistol) set aglow immediately before shooting.

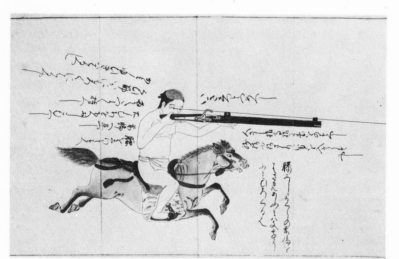

Figs. 91-93—Three watercolors from the manuscript The Book of Firearms, written by Nagasawa Shagetzuna in 1612 (now in the Spencer Collection of the New York Public Library). Apparently Japanese shooters could shoot from all possible and several impossible bodily attitudes.

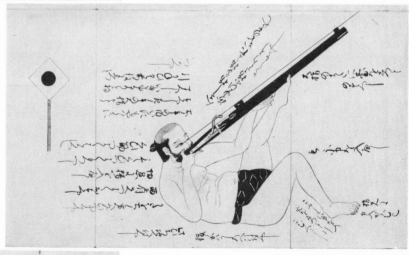

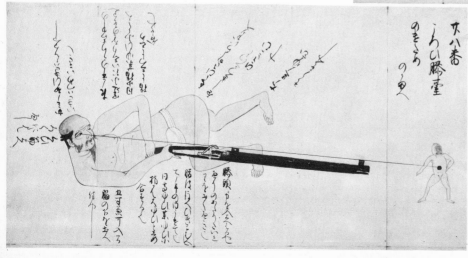

CHAPTER FOUR

Failures of the matchlock—The ancestry of the wheellock: invented by Leonardo da Vinci?—The wheellock of circa 1520 and after: how it worked—The main types—Their performance and reliability—Wheellock drawbacks—The scarcity of good gunsmiths—Matchlock-wheellock combinations, double locks, revolvers—Art in firearms—Charles V, King of Spain and Holy Roman Emperor—Pistols—A bitter ballad—Pierino Belli—High cost of wheellocks—Sir Roger Williams' opinion —The remarkable privies of Albrecht V—Henry VIII and Tudor guns—Guns vs. longbows—Parliament and the first gun laws—How to make hail shot—Shakespeare—Sir John's awkward dilemma; Mr. Ford a scofflaw?—A colorful inventory.

T HOWEVER MANY PACES THE MAMmoth matchlock musket may have "spoyled horse and man," and whatever untold myriads of birds and beasts the arquebus may have precipitated to their succulent destinies on roasting spits and serving platters, the faults inherent in the matchlock ignition system rendered these weapons useless except under the most favorable circumstances. The hunter or soldier was obliged, as has been noted, to carry about long coils of smoldering slow match which grew shorter with every passing minute; hours, and therefore yards of match, might be spent while prowling through the fields and woods in search of game, or in military life while awaiting action. The bear having been spied, no fast shot was possible, for the match had first to be blown free of ash and clamped into the serpentine; likely as not the bear had in the meantime come to view his future with suspicion and was well into the neighboring duchy by the time the fumbling nimrod was ready to let fly. The soldier awaiting the order to fire had to keep adjusting the match so that just the right length protruded, for should the glowing point burn into the clamp it would of course be smothered and go out. One way of overcoming these problems was to prepare for the unexpected shot by carrying the gun with just an inch or two of *unlit* match or a little dry tinder in the serpentine; this could then be set aglow by touching it quickly with the slow match directly upon seeing the deer or hearing the captain's order, and for a few seconds—until the glow reached the clamp —the gun was ready to fire (cf. Fig. 89). But this saved only seconds at the very best, for it still took time to stub the lit end of the match cord against the unlit tinder and to blow the latter brightly aglow. The effects of rain on a matchlock are too obvious to require discussion (at the battle of Uddevalla in Sweden in 1677, to name only one, rain put an end to all hopes and preparations for firing and the issue was settled by the bloody clangor of *armes blanches*). Then, many an animal and many an army was warned of what lurked in the bushes when the wind brought the smell of glowing match; and at night the red dots of a musketeer ambuscade could be seen half an hour's march away if the terrain was right (i.e., wrong). What was needed was a system for igniting the priming which would generate its own fire when required.

Vel plumbo eiecto flämis, vel cuspido seua *Dentatos capiunt celsis in montibus apros.*

ig. 94—"Either the lead hurled by fire or the cruel spear point kills the erce-tusked boars high in the mountains"—a fair prose rendering of the erse "Vel plumbo eiecto flammis, vel cuspido saeva / Dentatos capiunt celsis montibus apros" captioning engraving by Hans Bol (1534-1593) from 'enationis, Piscationis et Avicupii Typii (Scenes of Hunting, Fishing and Birdg), published between 1580 and 1588, probably in Amsterdam. Horseman is firing while hunter kneeling in foreground is either fumbling with matchcord or attending to the mechanism of a wheellock. If guns are matchlocks, theatrical tableau would clearly underscore their awkwardness: while shooters reload and fumble, the fate of the unfortunate wretch in left foreground will be up to the spearmen and the dogs, acting under the spirited encouragement contributed by the fellow in the upper left.

Fig. 95—If at first you don't succeed . . . Engraving from J. J. von Wallhausen, *Ritterkunst (Art of Knighthood)*, Frankfurt-a.-M., 1616.

Fig. 96—Cut-away diagrams of containers for carrying lit matchcord in rain and for protecting clothing from scorch. Notation inside left box says "Ioseph Furtenbach, Inventor, Ao. 1626"; accompanying text in his *Büchsenmeisterey-Schul (School of the Art of Gunnery)*, Augsburg, 1643, prophesied modestly: "That prince or general who . . . will first supply my inventions to all his troops will surely conquer the Turks—yea, the world, for with them his army will be invincible."

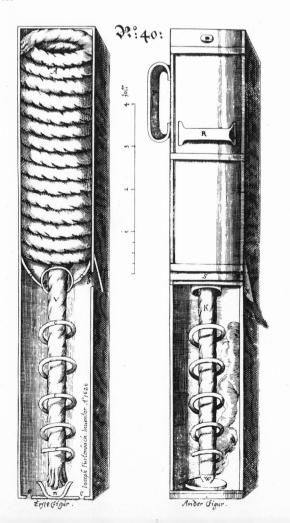

Since time immemorial man had been making fire by striking the glassy, opaque quartz called *flint*, or any of the metallic sulfides called *pyrites*, against a piece of hard iron so that the ensuing sparks set fire to some dry tinder placed beneath. It would seem that nothing would have been simpler than to imitate the action of human hands mechanically for a gunlock—a snapping arm with a flake of flint or pyrites to strike a piece of steel, the ensuing sparks to fall into the flashpan and priming powder beneath. But as so often, the complex invention preceded the simple one, to be slowly developed to what is minimally functional, and such a device was to remain unknown until about the 1540's. Instead, there appeared a mechanism in the north of Italy toward the close of the 15th century which was astounding no less for the effective results it achieved than for the mechanical labyrinth through which it achieved them. This was the *wheellock*.

Its ancestry was inconspicuous and brief, unless we count the first flint-and-pyrites fire strikers of Pleistocene prehistory. Sometime between 1450 and 1500 a few contrivances called *"monk's guns"* appeared here and there, although evidently in small numbers (Fig. 97). Here a piece of pyrites was screwed between two vise jaws at the end of a curved spring arm so that the quartz was pressed down firmly on a long flat rasp which rested in the bottom of a trough which served as a flashpan. This last was filled with priming powder, covering the rasp; when the rasp was pulled backward quickly by its handle, it scraped against the pyrites, sparks issued, the priming ignited and the fire flashed through the touchhole to fire the shot.

Broadly speaking, the wheellock employed the same basic principle, save that the straight-pull rasp was replaced by a spring-driven serrated wheel. The first known representations of it (naturally in very elementary form) are two drawings by Leonardo da Vinci in IL CODICE ATLANTICO, datable between 1483-85 (Fig. 98). But a

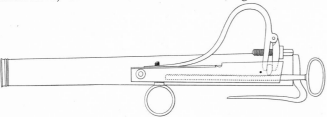

Fig. 97—A so-called "monk's gun." Priming powder was heaped on rasp in bottom of flashpan-like trough; spring arm pressed piece of pyrites against rasp; when rasp was pulled backward, ensuing sparks ignited priming, priming ignited main charge in barrel through touchhole. Such weapons, primitive ancestors of the wheellock, were known probably as early as 1400 but were very rare. Note belt hook.

great deal of debate goes on as to whether da Vinci had (a) invented these devices on his own, perhaps for submission to Ludovico Sforza, Duke of Milano, for the use of his armorer Gentile de' Borri; (b) had sketched for possible future gunlock use a kind of household tinder-lighter in general use in Lombardy; (c) had seen such actual gunlocks somewhere and had jotted down their mechanics in his notes. But in spite of bits of evidence here, a couple of indices there, that can be adduced to support any one of these possibilities, the whole business is shrouded in mystery and complicated by contradictions. It would seem, though, that (c) is the most likely, for the existence of primitive wheellock guns in Genoa, Milan and Venice in the 1480's has long been suspected and seems a bit more probable (though far from certain) nowadays in the light of recent researches.

Be this as it may, there is no doubt that wheellocks were late-15th-century Italian in origin. Then they spread into the world at large, especially into Germany, where they struck remarkably firm roots in Nuremberg . . . or so a time-honored tradition would have it, and there is nothing to contradict it. Certainly the earliest true, rather than perfected, and quantitatively quite abundant surviving specimens are Nurembergese of 1510-20, about coeval with Italian versions apparently made in Brescia and Bologna but—it seems—in lesser numbers.

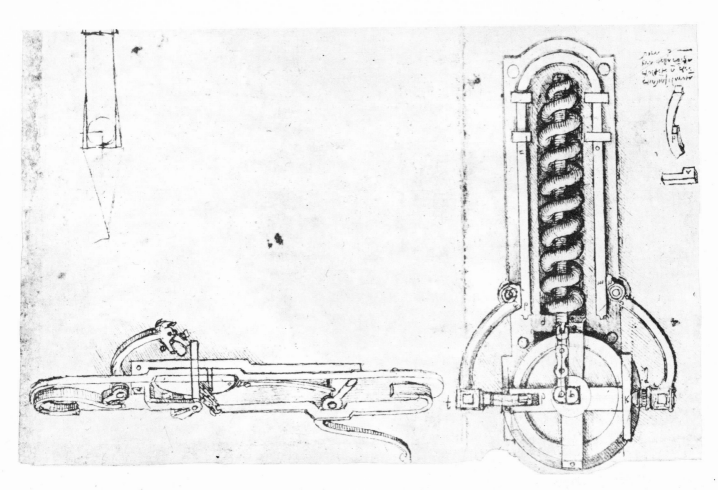

Fig. 98—Two wheellock mechanisms by Leonardo da Vinci, probably sketched between 1480 and 1485. Device in lower left is a gunlock; three-dimensional view is from above, showing inside; upper half of wheel is cut away to show axis, slightly recessed lockplate and sear (long bar on outside of lockplate). Save for external sear and internal feather-spring, design is similar to the wheellocks appearing in Nuremberg in about 1515-20 (cf. Fig. 99). Machine at right is a general-purpose fire striker. Wheel was to be wound counter-clockwise, thereby winding chain about axis and compressing coil-spring; arm at left caught wheel in wound position. Arm on right held pyrites, was pressed against wheel by force of large U-spring on arm's spur behind pivot. When catch was released, wheel spun against pyrites, ensuing sparks fell on and ignited tinder or other combustible placed beneath.

To shoot a wheellock, the gunner first loaded the barrel by ramming down powder and ball with the ramrod, just as in matchlocks. Then he took his *spanner*—a small wrench—fitted it over the winding lug R (Fig. 99) of the *wheel* and wound the wheel clockwise for about a three-quarter turn until it "caught" in wound-up position. The edge or periphery of the broad, thick wheel had sharp grooves and serrations; its top intruded slightly *into* the flashpan, which had a pierced bottom to admit it. Next he opened the flashpan by pushing the cover L forward with his thumb, primed the flashpan with a little finely ground powder, and pushed the button D which caused the cover to snap back again and cover the priming. Since the wheel intruded into the flashpan, the priming powder actually covered the intruding edge. Now the *doghead*, the swinging arm which held a piece of pyrites screwed between its vise jaws, was swung down over the flashpan so that the pyrites rested on the flashpan cover. The *feather-spring* E exerted an upward tension on the spur C of the doghead so that the pyrites did not merely lie on the flashpan cover, but was pressed down on it. The gun was now loaded and primed and ready to shoot.

Pulling the trigger released the wheel to spin for one lightning-fast three-quarter turn. The flashpan cover snapped open automatically an instant after the wheel had begun to spin, the pyrites dropped down into the flashpan, contacted the serrated edge of the spinning wheel, sparks issued, the priming was ignited, its fire flashed through the touchhole into the barrel and the shot went off. The trigger pull and the split-second *brrrt* of the wheel were followed so quickly by the shot that all three seemed almost, but not quite, simultaneous. The lapse of time was so brief that it was only barely perceptible. Fig. 99 will explain the mechanics of all these functions in detail for the mechanically-minded.

An effective safety was provided by keeping the doghead swung away from the flashpan (e.g., Figs. 100 and 101), for if the trigger were then accidentally jostled and the wheel released to spin, no sparks, and therefore no shot, could possible ensue. But in such an event the flashpan cover would still be opened automatically and the priming spilled, with the consequent necessity of winding the wheel and priming all over again. By about 1525 there had appeared the additional safety device of a small hook (best shown in Figs. 100, 110 and 118) which pinioned an eyelet on the sear through the lockplate so that if the trigger were now pulled, the wheel could not be released to spin.

Fig. 99—Outside, inside and top views of a typical wheellock.

Diag. I: Doghead B holds piece of pyrites A in vise jaws; doghead may be swung manually into position shown, or back to lie on feather-spring E (dotted arrow 1). Feather-spring exerts upward force on spur C of doghead, thus pressing pyrites down on closed flashpan cover L. Wheel S is wound by spanner wrench which fits over winding lug R (cf. Fig. 116). Lock is shown primed and spanned, ready for firing.

Diags. II & III: Mechanism is shown before priming and spanning. Shooter first swings doghead back to lie on feather spring. Then he spans wheel S in clockwise motion, i.e., counter-clockwise as seen from inside. Spanning winds bicycle-chain-like links J about spindle I, draws up and compresses lower arm of mainspring K. When small hole G on inner surface of wheel aligns with hole H in lockplate, beveled nose Q of primary sear V, pivoted on screw T, snaps into it under force of searspring U. As nose snaps into hole, rear arm of sear snaps outward (dotted arrow 2); simultaneously, searspring U exerts force on toe of secondary sear X, pivoted on screw W, causing secondary sear X to snap forward so that its notch Xa engages primary sear's notch Va (dotted arrow 3); when both sears have been so engaged, beveled nose Q of primary sear is firmly held in small hole G on inner surface of wheel, and wheel is locked in wound-up position. Shooter now fills flashpan M with priming powder; powder lies on and around top periphery P of wheel, which projects through pierced bottom of flashpan. Next, shooter presses button D (Diag.I) on outside of lockplate; this pushes inward on spring-catch F (Diag.II) which holds flashpan cover lever O drawn backward against force of spring N; thus, when button D on lockplate is pressed, flashpan cover lever O is freed to be snapped forward by spring N and to snap flashpan cover L over flashpan M. After flashpan has been primed and snapped shut, shooter swings doghead into position shown in Diag. I. Gun is now ready for shooting. The trigger (not shown except in Diag. I), when pulled, forces secondary sear X backward (dotted arrow 4), disengaging its notch from the notch of the primary sear (shown disengaged in Diag. III). Beveled nose Q of the primary sear at once slips out of small hole G on inner surface of wheel; wheel, under force of mainspring K pulling down on chain J, makes rapid three-quarters or seven-eighths turn. Spindle I spins with wheel; its eccentric cam knocks against flashpan cover lever O (which rests against spindle when flashpan is closed), and in pushing lever backward opens flashpan. Pyrites in doghead drops down into flashpan and priming under force of feather-spring E (Diag. I) and contacts spinning wheel; sparks issue, priming ignites and shot goes off. In spite of complicated mechanics, good wheellocks fired so instantaneously that trigger pull and shot were virtually simultaneous.

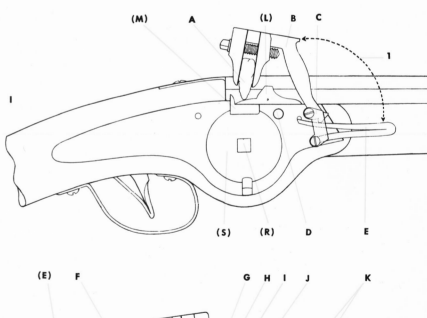

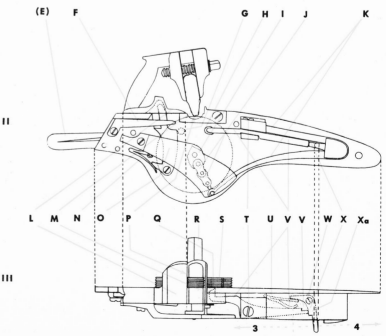

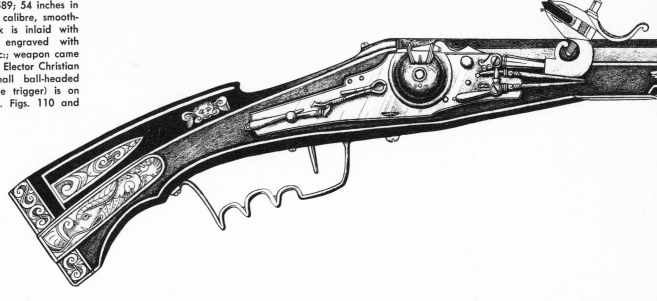

Now for the first time a gun could be loaded and primed, then left standing in a wardrobe, or carried about in pockets and saddle holsters in war or on the hunt, ready to shoot on an instant's notice. Four basic forms of this machine developed in the half century following its invention:

—those in which an *uncovered* wheel was on the *outside* of the lockplate. e.g., Figs. 99 (note Diag. III) and 111;

—those in which a *covered* or *housed* wheel was on the outside of the lockplate, e.g., Figs. 100 and 103;

—those with wholly *internal* wheels, such as Figs. 143 and 145;

—and the *Tschinke*, in which an uncovered wheel and much of the mechanism were on the outside (Fig. 101).

How well any of these worked depended of course on factors such as quality of workmanship, care in loading and priming, granulation and quality of the powder (especially the priming), condition of the pyrites, and so on. All these being favorable, a good, reasonably clean wheel-lock could be expected to give fire forty-nine out of fifty times; unfortunately many of them were very often not favorable. Wheellocks were subject to all sorts of maladies. The weakest point was the pyrites, an extremely friable substance which was likely to crumble or shatter if it projected too far from the jaws of the dog-head or if it had a fault or fissure. Its fire-striking qualities varied greatly from place to place throughout Europe. Carbon from the priming and abraded pyrites grit filled the serrations of the wheel in the course of a day's shooting, eventually clogging the entire wheel housing and choking the wheel beyond operation. This problem was obviated by the uncovered-outside-type of wheel, but not without creating the new menaces of breakage, torn clothing and cut fingers, and of showers of burning priming being hurled like pinwheel sparks onto the shooter's hand, clothes and horse, or worse, into the neck of the powder flask. Although locks with internal wheels prevented such pyrotechnics and were the least vulnerable to damage, fouling eventually accumulated not only around the wheel but on the interior mechanism, and the works ground to a halt unless the lock was removed and decarbonized after some thirty-five or forty shots. The graceful, delicate but powerful *Tschinke*, which appeared in northern Germany and the Baltic provinces toward the end of the sixteenth century (Fig. 101), was extremely easy to keep clean because its mainspring, chain drive and spindle were all on the outside; on the other hand, these not only caught and tore clothing, but were so vulnerable that careless handling—let alone dropping—could, and usually did, spell ruin.

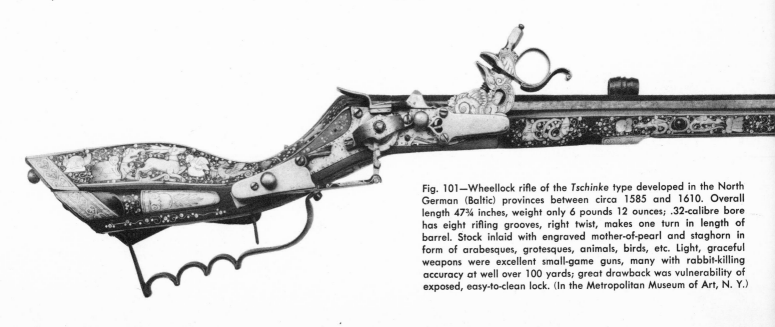

Fig. 101—Wheellock rifle of the *Tschinke* type developed in the North German (Baltic) provinces between circa 1585 and 1610. Overall length 47¾ inches, weight only 6 pounds 12 ounces; .32-calibre bore has eight rifling grooves, right twist, makes one turn in length of barrel. Stock inlaid with engraved mother-of-pearl and staghorn in form of arabesques, grotesques, animals, birds, etc. Light, graceful weapons were excellent small-game guns, many with rabbit-killing accuracy at well over 100 yards; great drawback was vulnerability of exposed, easy-to-clean lock. (In the Metropolitan Museum of Art, N. Y.)

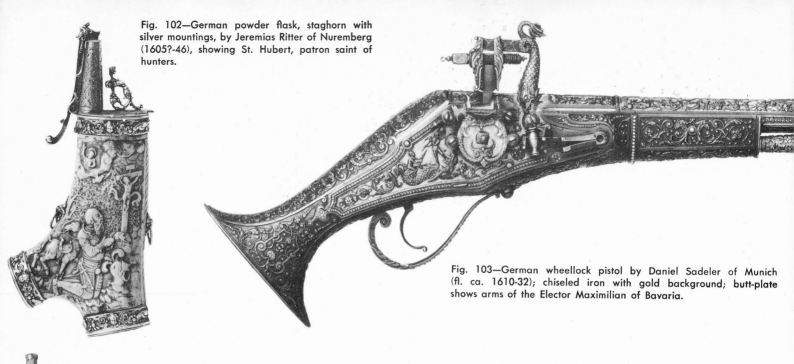

Fig. 102—German powder flask, staghorn with silver mountings, by Jeremias Ritter of Nuremberg (1605?-46), showing St. Hubert, patron saint of hunters.

Fig. 103—German wheellock pistol by Daniel Sadeler of Munich (fl. ca. 1610-32); chiseled iron with gold background; butt-plate shows arms of the Elector Maximilian of Bavaria.

Fig. 104—Left margin: French carbine-and-pistol convertible, middle 17th century. The butt, characteristically Spanish in shape, unscrews at break marked by silver bands; front half of barrel unscrews at break visible as a thin line immediately above tip of short ramrod. With butt and front of barrel removed, 42-inch carbine becomes 19-inch pistol.

Furthermore, should the shooter of a wheellock lose his spanner, the gun was useless until another could be procured. Before 1550, therefore, the spanner-and-powder-flask combinations (Fig. 105) had become popular; and in the absence of contemporary accounts, one wonders how many hunters crawled through the bushes on all fours searching now not only for the lost spanner but for the ammunition as well.

But in spite of all these ifs, ands, and maybes, wheellocks were the most rapid-firing and unfailing gunlocks in the history of firearms until the advent of chemical percussion systems in the early nineteenth century, exception being made for British flintlocks in their final phase—say, 1795-1825. Except for these, no ignition system ever fired with such an imperceptible lapse between trigger-pull and shot (measured in a few milliseconds), nor went off so faithfully in the vilest weather (short of downpours that wet the priming), nor kept their priming in the pan so tightly even in rough-and-tumble knocking about in saddle holsters and traveling trunks, nor offered quite so positive a "safety" against accidental discharge. Only two really significant drawbacks militated against their universal application and in favor of other, competitive systems: One, wheellocks were necessarily quite large; and Two, the manufacture of even a relatively simple one was a hide-

ously expensive process requiring weeks of labor of the most expert craftsmen, for every screw, nut, bolt, wheel, sear, lockplate and others of the thirty-five to fifty components of such a mechanism—all of which had to fit with watchlike precision—entered the gunmaker's shop as bars of pig iron and scraps of steel which could take shape only by patient and skillful application of the smelting furnace and of a hundred different tools through a thousand stages of gradual, hand-wrought progress. Save only for the coil-spring clocks and pocket watches invented by Peter Hähnlein of Nuremberg at about the same time (between 1500 and 1510), wheellocks were the first automatons in history in the modern mechanical sense. And save again the timepieces, no machines had hitherto approximated the compactness, efficiency, durability, ingenuity and burnished perfection required of and usually delivered by them—virtues which had furthermore to be bound by a matrix of staunch ruggedness not required of clocks and watches. Since even an outwardly simple but mechanically sound hunting arquebus (the word was applied to wheellocks as well as to matchlocks) with relatively plain or only conventionally carved stocks cost in mid-sixteenth-century Vienna, Munich and Paris the equivalent of $300–$650 in

Fig. 105—Combination powder flask, double-headed spanner and screwdriver; by Daniel Sadeler of Munich, ca. 1625. Compare Fig. 144.

present-day buying power, none but the most prosperous of the bourgeois class and the nobility could afford either such weapons or the leisure to give them employment; and those who could afford them at all lost no sleep over the worry of the extra hundred or two guilders or florins or whatever which were involved in commissioning the best gunsmith in the province and in paying for the best materials. Thus it is not difficult to understand that while there were a good number of wheellocks which were only competently made, there were extremely few bad ones.

Furthermore, repair of a matchlock could be undertaken by the next village blacksmith if he was at all clever, but should a wheellock break during the hunt, nothing could be done until a master gunsmith could be found to mend it. There were few master gunsmiths skillful in the making of wheellocks before 1560, and none at all in the nearest village; repairs, consequently, often meant sending the piece back to its maker, who (if it was any good) was most likely in Nuremberg, Munich, Lübeck, Brescia, Milan, Paris or in one of a few other great centers or communes. Although the English gunsmiths were destined to become the undisputed masters of the art after the first quarter of the eighteenth century, it seems almost certain that not a man in all of Albion could make a passably good wheellock before 1650—when wheellocks were already obsolescent if not obsolete—and hardly anyone who could repair one before 1600.

Fig. 106-108—Gunsmith, stockmaker and powdermaker; three engravings from Christoff Weigel, *Abbildung der gemein-nützlichen Haupt-Staende (Depictions of the Most Important Communally Useful Occupations)*, Augsburg, 1698.

Right: In gunsmith's shop, worker in background is rifling a barrel with a long T-handled rifling tool. Master gunsmith in foreground is clamping a new barrel blank into vise while assistant behind crankwheel is beginning to turn horizontal fine-boring drill. On wall hang, from left to right, a pistol barrel, a wheellock, a small wheellock pistol, a large wheellock pistol, a bow-strung wire saw, a wood clamp, a matchlock, a large wheellock and a combination matchlock-wheellock arquebus. On bench is foreground are two stocks, a snaphaunce or flintlock pistol, a rasp, a wheellock pistol and a pistol barrel or tool.

Lower left: The stockmaker puts the finishing touches on the underside of a stock while apprentice in background brings in more rough-hewn blanks and journeyman works at bench.

Lower right: Two journeymen powdermakers sift grains of stamped corned powder through screens while master powdermaker rakes through the troughs from which the various grades or granulations of sifted powder will be loaded into leather sacks or barrels. Powder-stamping mill in background is powered by waterwheel (cf. Fig. 52).

Throughout the sixteenth century, in all lands, there were those who knew that nothing would *ever* replace the matchlock, there being no possibility of improvement upon this ultimate of weapons, least of all by foolish contraptions with wheels and jaws and chains like an Archimedean nightmare. Thus many matchlocks continued to be made even for the well-to-do, until toward the end of the century the last few of these sagacious prophets had been laid to rest. Many other prudent but less crotchety hunters, however, viewed the wheellock's ills with a more sober eye and resorted to a number of measures which actually served to circumvent rather than to cure them. For the conservative the most obvious was to add a matchlock serpentine so that in the event of misfortune the hunt might proceed at least as well as it had prior to the new contrivance's invention; such combinations (Figs. 109 and 110) were not wholly extinct as late as 1640. A double lock, the priming of each connecting through its own touchhole into one loading, was hailed as the weapon beyond improvement by those who could afford it; while others, troubled most by memories of the pyrites shattering when a wild boar had come charging with lowered razor tusks, or some similar graying experience, had their gunsmiths make them a one-lock gun with two dogheads, the auxiliary to be used in the event of disaster befalling the pyrites in the other (Fig. 111).

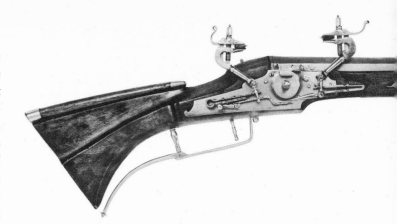

Fig. 111—Elegant design of sweeping lines marks this splendidly functional early 17th-century wheellock arquebus with two dogheads.

Fig. 110—Diagram of a wheel-and-match combination lock, circa 1550-1600, essentially identical to lock of the Archduke Ferdinand's arquebus in Fig. 109. Matchlock serpentine is here turned back, but when in use it would be turned forward until its foot came to rest on sear protruding through lockplate (seen as small rectangle); when trigger is pulled, sear recedes and spring acting on spur drives serpentine into flashpan. Note wheellock safety catch with pointed prong, here turned back and held in place by spring above it; when turned to "safe" position (dotted line), prong engages and locks small eyelet of the secondary sear protruding through lockplate (hidden under rear section of serpentine spring).

Fig. 109—Wheellock arquebus with auxiliary matchlock serpentine, one of the hunting weapons of Ferdinand, Archduke of Tyrolia, circa 1560. Serpentine has own mainspring and sear (cf. Fig. 110). Stock is inlaid with engraved staghorn and ivory showing Homeric scenes, hunting scenes, nudes and floral motifs; barrel is chiseled with foliation. For the 1st shot, the matchlock serpentine was lowered unlit into the flashpan, and the gun was fired by wheellock. This lit the match, and the hunt or war could then progress for dozens of shots by matchlock, obviating the necessity of winding the wheel and also saving 90 per cent of wear and tear on the wheellock. (In the Metropolitan Museum of Art, New York)

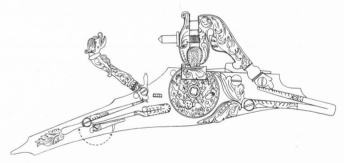

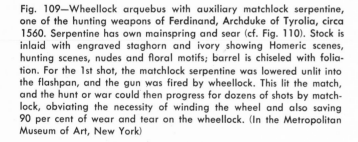

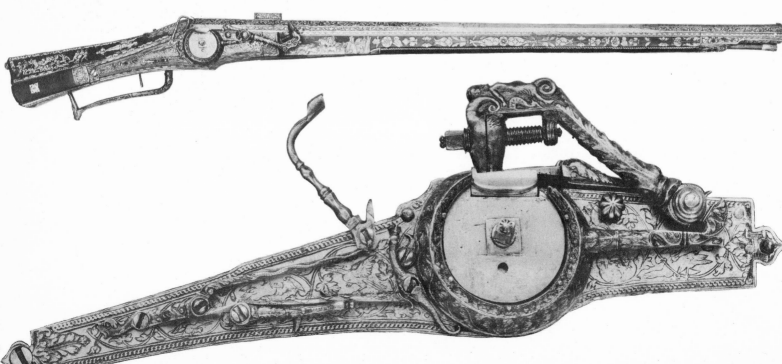

Double-barreled wheellocks were nowhere unusual (Figs. 115 and 130). And the manually-turned revolvers (Fig. 112) held out the promise of shooting several times without reloading but probably failed at times to distinguish between several shots in succession and several shots at once owing to imperfectly fitting flashpan covers; stray sparks from the top chamber must often have fired all the others, and if such a regrettable *malheur* did not kill the shooter, it surely mutilated his hands beyond resemblance to anything human. All these panaceas, however, became less frequent as the sixteenth century passed into the seventeenth. New manufacturing methods enabled gunsmiths to mill the parts to finer, more closely fitting tolerances, so that by 1560–80 wheellocks showed fewer tendencies to erratic temperaments, becoming progressively more reliable.

Fig. 112—German seven-shot revolving wheellock carbine, circa 1620. Nose on spring on top of barrel engages holes in front of cylinder to align chamber with barrel. Compare Fig. 82. (In the Tower of London)

Kings, nobles and the richest among the commoners were naturally the most demanding customers of the best gunsmiths. From the very earliest, man had decorated his weapons, some barbarously, others tastefully, here simply, there profusely; but never in all of history before or since had weapons inspired such artistry as gunmakers now lavished on wheellocks for these clients. Under the aegis of the *Zeitgeist*, Mars was wed to Muse for a prolific union; the breath of the Renaissance blew freshly among firearms as everywhere else. Constellations of arabesques, incredibly detailed panoramas of men and monsters, took form in the bits of wood, ivory, mother-of-pearl and bone of the inlayer. From the gold- and silversmith's wire coils and casting molds blossomed Gardens of Eden; Scylla in cold steel emerged from under the steel carver's chisel to clutch pyrites in golden fangs, while Charybdis, fresh from the engraver's bench and etcher's bath, yawned horribly to bare the priming powder. Pious saints in bas-relief lent the protection of their effigies to hunter and soldier; imperial and regal arms and heraldic devices proclaimed the owner. Motifs without end in all media varied in a kaleidoscope of classical mythology, Chris-

tianity, Old and New Testament, the demonaic, abstractions; nor was the obscene overlooked. It was not infrequent for such weapons to require but a few weeks for the manufacture of the lock and the barrel blank, which were then subjected to months or even years of ornamentation, while other artisans busied themselves with the stock which was to bed them.

Charles V, Holy Roman Emperor and King of Spain (1500–58, reigned 1519–56), was the embodiment of all gunsmiths' dreams. His predilection for fine private arms was insatiable, his purse munificent to the point of folly for those who could keep him delighted (he once paid the equivalent of about $33,000 to a Vienna gunsmith for a matched set of two pistols, a rifle and a bird gun). Since he was Emperor of Germany as well as King of Spain, he was free to transplant the seeds of the gunmaking arts from the former to the latter. According to the Spanish gunsmith-author Isidor Solér, who in 1795 published his COMPENDIO HISTORICO DE LOS ARCABUCEROS DE MADRID (*A Historical Compendium of the Gunmakers of Madrid*), Charles had found two fertile seeds named Simon and Peter Markhardt, brothers and master gunsmiths of Augsburg, in 1530. He lured them to Madrid by offering them the posts of Imperial Gun Fabricators at annual salaries which in the good Augsburgers' eyes must have approximated those of archangels. Planted in Iberian soil as Simon and Pedro Marquarte, they thrived, taught apprentices, spread the German ways of wheellock-making throughout Spain (until about 1580 most Spanish guns were purely German in character), and may in short be said to have founded gunsmithing in that peninsula.

Fig. 113—Left side of the butt of a French wheellock hunting rifle, circa 1600. Engraved staghorn and ivory inlaid in walnut. (In the Metropolitan Museum of Art, New York)

Fig. 114—Charles V, 1500-58, King of Spain 1516-56, Holy Roman Emperor 1519-56, among other things magnanimous patron of gunsmiths, occasional gunmaking hobbyist. Woodcut shows him at about age 40.

Fig. 115—Over-and-under double-barreled wheellock pistol made by Peter Pech of Munich for the Emperor Charles V in about 1540, and the fifty-nine separate parts of the lock. (In the Metropolitan Museum of Art, New York)

Charles V himself from time to time was wont to make his ancestors in Hapsburg tombs sit upright when he donned work clothes and imperiled the holy imperial fingers by plying file and hammer in the Marquarte workshops. Unfortunately history does not record his aptitudes, nor whether a wheel serrated by a chisel in majestic hands struck more majestic fire. To the rejoicing of dungeons full of heretics and Protestants, under whom he was fond of striking a lot of fires, but to the lament of gunmakers, he retired to a monastery in 1556 and died two years later, leaving many a shot unfired; which was just as well.

For obvious reasons, not all or even most wheellocks were as resplendent as the ones described. It was of course the aesthetic value of the beautiful ones which rescued them in later centuries from the rapacity of rust in forgotten nooks of armories and cellars, the fate of most obsolete weapons (which accounts for the rarity of hand cannons and the infrequency of matchlocks). There were also the fairly plain wheellocks, and although their cost was high, their values were strictly functional; when after years of service senescence at last rendered them useless they were cast aside—by then usually for the new snaphaunces and flintlocks.

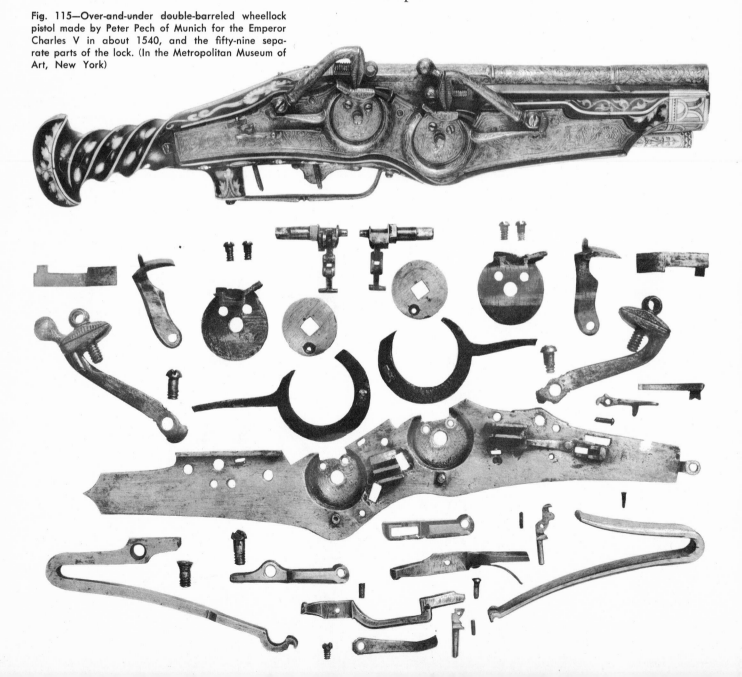

Fig. 117—French wheellock dag, one of a pair, circa 1600. Contrary
to a common belief among collectors, wooden ball-butts *never* served
as bludgeons if shooter had missed and was forced into hand-to-hand
combat—they were doweled to the stocks in quite fragile a way, served
to give better purchase to heavily gloved hands. Reddish wood stock is
inlaid with engraved ivory plaques showing Renaissance foliate motifs
and Roman soldiers; barrel is deeply chiseled and gilded with foliage,
fruit, chimerae and figures from classical allegories. (In the Metropolitan Museum of Art, New York)

The application of the wheellock to one-hand guns which could be carried in pockets and saddle bags followed directly on its invention. By about 1540, such small guns were known in Italy as *pistolette* and in French as *pistolets*, seemingly from the Latin *pistolese*, of or pertaining to the Tuscan city of Pistoia—a neologism drawn from 16th-century Italian "un'arma pistolese" or "pistoiese," with the diminutive *-etta;* and this is a fairly good clue to where pistols may first have been made. But nothing whatever is known about the etymology of the word *dag* or *dagge*, which by 1535 in English and to some extent in German had come to mean any massive, heavy, powerful pistol. No matter whence, pistols, or as they were known before about 1570, pistolets, leaped brightly into popularity. Doubtless at once the mortality rate among travelers and dwellers in lonely places dropped as sharply

as it rose among highwaymen and vagabonds. Men past the prime of youth, no longer able to lay on with the sword as once perhaps they had been, and especially ladies, were now in a position to meet the cutthroat and the rapist on more than equal terms. Even when villains were firearmed (and by 1542 some of them were to such an extent that a drastic Act of Parliament was vitally urgent) it was one thing to swoop down on a traveling coach in anticipation of resistance with swords, quite another if the passengers and the coachmen might be expected to open fire at thirty yards. Ultimately, of course, violence begat violence, and if portable firearms offered a measure of personal protection, the situation was soon equalized not only by offering the same measure to evildoers but by increasing their advantage of surprise.

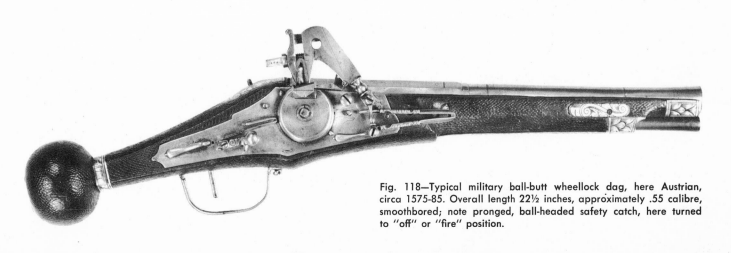

Fig. 118—Typical military ball-butt wheellock dag, here Austrian,
circa 1575-85. Overall length 22½ inches, approximately .55 calibre,
smoothbored; note pronged, ball-headed safety catch, here turned
to "off" or "fire" position.

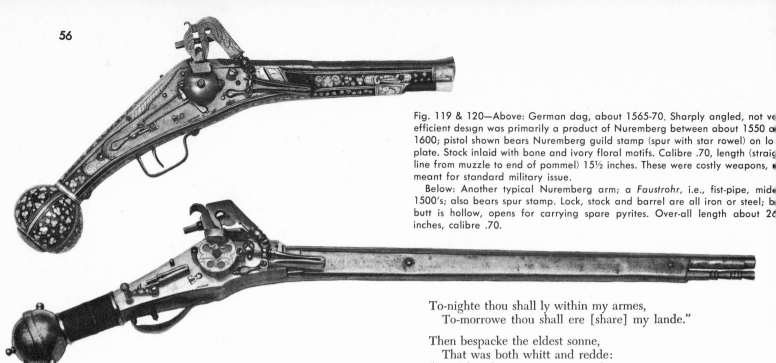

Fig. 119 & 120—Above: German dag, about 1565-70. Sharply angled, not ve efficient design was primarily a product of Nuremberg between about 1550 a 1600; pistol shown bears Nuremberg guild stamp (spur with star rowel) on lo plate. Stock inlaid with bone and ivory floral motifs. Calibre .70, length (straig line from muzzle to end of pommel) 15½ inches. These were costly weapons, meant for standard military issue.

Below: Another typical Nuremberg arm; a *Faustrohr*, i.e., fist-pipe, midd 1500's; also bears spur stamp. Lock, stock and barrel are all iron or steel; b butt is hollow, opens for carrying spare pyrites. Over-all length about 2(inches, calibre .70.

Among the earliest references to pistols in English or any other literature is the account of the plight of poor Lady Forbes of Towie, commemorated as Lady Hamleton of Crecrynbroghe in the Scottish ballad "Captain Car," datable about 1553. Sir John Forbes, master of the castle Towie, had ridden out with his men, leaving Lady Forbes, their three young sons and about 24 servants and relatives in charge. Upon hearing of this, a renegade named Car set out to plunder the castle. When he approached, according to the ballad,

> The ladie she leand on her castle-wall
>   She loked vpp and downe;
> There was she ware of an host of men
>   Come riding to the towne.
>
> "Se yow, my meri men all,
>   And se yow what I see?
> Yonder I see a host of men,
>   I muse who they be."
>
> She thought he had ben her wed lord
>   As he comd riding home;
> Then was it traitur Captain Car,
>   The lord of Ester-towne.
>
> They wer no soner at supper sett,
>   Then after said the grace,
> Than Captaine Car and all his men
>   Wer light aboute the place.
>
> "Gyve ouer thi howsee, thou lady gay,
>   And I will make thee a bande [agreement]

> To-nighte thou shall ly within my armes,
>   To-morrowe thou shall ere [share] my lande."
>
> Then bespacke the eldest sonne,
>   That was both whitt and redde:
> "O mother dere, geve ouer your howsee,
>   Or elles we shalbe deade."
>
> "I will not geve ouer my hous," she saithe,
>   "Not for feare of my lyffe;
> It shalbe talked throughout the land,
>   The slaughter of a wyffe.
>
> "Fetch me my pestilett
>   And charge me my gonne,
> That I may shott at yonder bloddy butcher,
>   The lord of Easter-towne."
>
> Styfly vpon her wall she stode
>   And lett the pellettes flee;
> But then she myst the blody bucher,
>   And she slew other three.
>
> "I will not geve ouer my hous," she saithe,
>   "Netheir for lord nor lowne [loon; i.e., scoundrel];
> Nor yet for traitour Captaine Care,
>   The lord of Easter-towne."

Alas, poor Lady Forbes! She had not enough pellets, gonnes and pestiletts in the house—wicked Captain Car set fire to the castle (probably with fire arrows such as in Fig. 121) and she, her children and all her kin and servants, numbering in all about twenty-seven, perished horribly. Lady Forbes's *gonne* may have been anything from a wheellock or matchlock arquebus to a swivel-mounted wall cannon, while her *pestilett* (pistolet, of course) had necessarily to be a wheellock similar to any among the chronologically correct ones shown in this chapter; it would naturally have been imported.

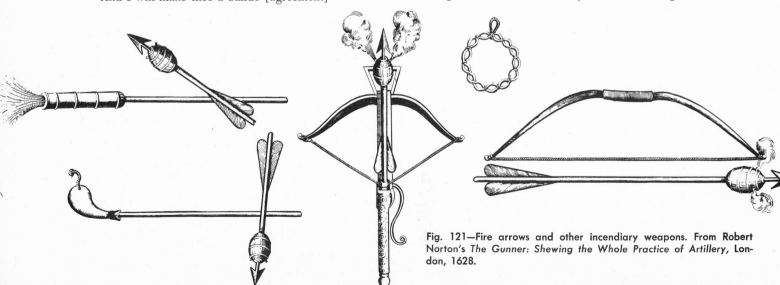

Fig. 121—Fire arrows and other incendiary weapons. From Robert Norton's *The Gunner: Shewing the Whole Practice of Artillery*, London, 1628.

If, then, wheellocks proved so effective, and if they obviated the headaches of the matchlock, why was this latter to remain the mainstay of the military for 180 to 200 years after the wheellock was invented? Simply because of the matchlock's cheapness and the ruinous cost of the wheellock. Few rulers or captains were able or willing to arm any significant number of troops with such treasury depleters. For example, in 1580 the Duke of Tuscany would have had to pay the equivalent of $200 in present-day buying power for a simple but serviceable smooth-bore wheellock musket such as Fig. 129, and $300 for a pair of horseman's pistols such as Figs. 120, 123 and 124; add to this $20 per man for powder flasks, pyrites, spanners, cleaning brushes, holsters, grease and other necessities. These amounts are correct within 15 per cent either way. Assume that each gun might have been expected to require the service of a gunsmith once a year and each servicing took an average of two hours; this, even in the case of small palace armies, would have kept quite a few

gunsmiths busy. No experienced master gunsmith worked cheaply—by 1580 that trade was universally among the most lucrative, the others being, characteristically enough, in Germany watch- and clockmaking and armoring, in Italy landscape gardening and mosaic in-laying, and in England, where there were still few gunsmiths, shipwrighting, printing and bookbinding. Thus, allowing $20,000 for repairs, the total cost of maintaining three thousand wheellock musketeers and two thousand mounted pistoleers would have been about $1.2 million, give or take 20 per cent, for their weapons alone, not counting the basic expenses for subsistence and quarters, armor, horses, gear, powder, shot, wages, etc. Matchlocks, on the other hand, would hardly have cost more than $75 per musket and $55 per caliver, and hardly anything for repairs, for a total of only $335,000 for three thousand musketeers and two thousand caliveers, including flasks and two slow matches a day for every man—about one quarter of the wheellock total!

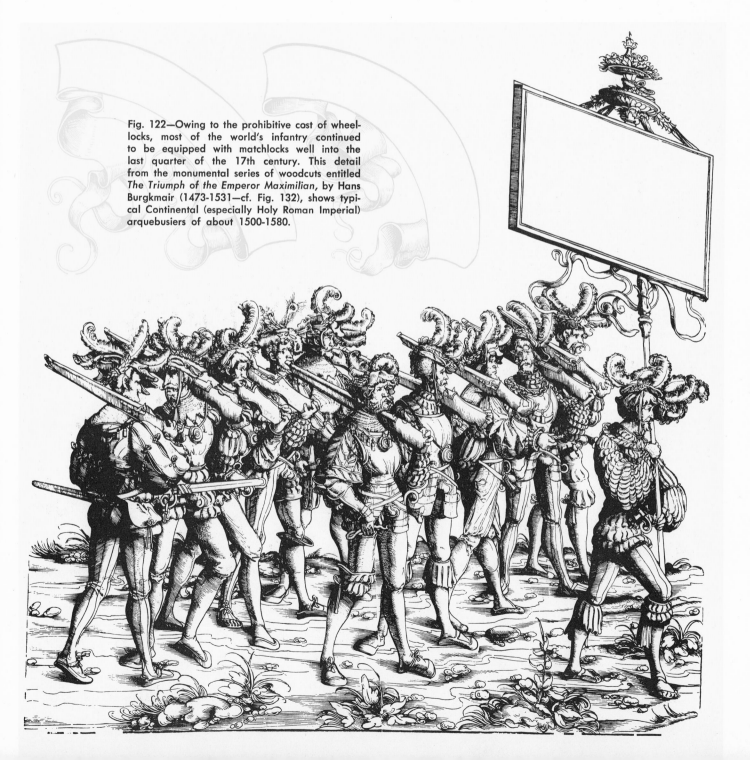

Fig. 122—Owing to the prohibitive cost of wheellocks, most of the world's infantry continued to be equipped with matchlocks well into the last quarter of the 17th century. This detail from the monumental series of woodcuts entitled *The Triumph of the Emperor Maximilian*, by Hans Burgkmair (1473-1531—cf. Fig. 132), shows typical Continental (especially Holy Roman Imperial) arquebusiers of about 1500-1580.

Fig. 123—Three-quarter armored pistoleers and lancers, the "Rutters" in Sir Roger Williams' *Briefe Discourse on Warre* (below). Engravings from J. J. von Wallhausen, *Art Militaire au Cheval (The Art of Mounted Warfare)*, Frankfurt-a.-M., 1616. See also Fig. 125.

Such economy, on the other hand, sacrificed the tactical and even strategic advantages offered by several thousand armored horsemen who could charge, fire two, three or even four shots from pistols and carbines, wheel out of the enemy's range, reload, charge again, and so on. Done in relays, one-third charging, one-third wheeling, one-third reloading, a fast and murderous fire could be delivered against nearly any military unit. The disadvantage was that the effective accurate range of a typical pistol was about 20 yards, the effective unaimed range (at which it could still kill if fired into the midst of the opposing ranks) about 50 to 80 yards; carbines were serviceable for respectively 70 to 120 yards; but by then both pistoleer and carbineer were far within the lethal range of the enemy's calivers and muskets. Furthermore, the lance, if well presented by a few thousand staunch mounted lancers, was still a formidable weapon, especially useful for riding down pistoleers after these had fired and wheeled about for the reloading retreat. Sir Roger Williams, whose opinion concerning muskets we already know, had this to say in his BRIEFE DISCOURSE ON WARRE, published in 1590 (note the references to the misfiring of pistols due to loading difficulties in the heat of combat; italics in original):

Considering the resolute charge done with the might of their horses, the Launtiers [lancers] are more terrible and make a farre better shew either in Muster or Battaile. For example, the *Almaines* [Germans], during the time they carried Launces, carried a farre greater reputation than they do now being pistolers named *Rutters* [corruption of German *Ritter*, knight, or *Reiter*, horseman]. The most Chiefes or Souldiers of accompt are armed at the proofe of the pistoll [are armored to withstand pistol shots]. If the leaders commaund their troupes to spoyle horses, the Launces are more sure, for divers pistols faile to go off; if they do, they must be charged with discretion. Being overcharged it shakes in a mans hand so that often it touches neither man nor horse; if the charge bee too little it pierceth nothing to speak of. True it is, being pickt and chosen, the pistolers murther more . . . but I was often in their companie when they ranne away, three from one Launtier both in great troupes and small. . . . Without a doubt, the Pistoll discharged hard by, well charged and with iudgement, murthers more than the Launce; [but] out of a hundred pistolers, twentie nor scarce tenne at the most doo neither charge pistoll nor enter a squadron as they should, but commonlie and lightly alwaies they discharge their pistols eight and five score off [fifty-five to thirty-five yards, not close enough for effective shooting], and so wheele about; at which turnes the Launtiers charge them in the sides, be they well conducted. . . . The Launtiers have or ought to have one pistol at the least.

Gardes-du-corps of affluent potentates, rarely numbering more than a few dozen men, were armed with wheellocks from time to time, notably in Italy and southern Germany. A few favorite regiments were supplied with them for the delight of their masters, although in 1580 uniformed national armies were still unknown; the business of war was still being trafficked for the most part by the captains of the mercenary bands of the *Landsknecht* types. Wheellocks remained essentially private weapons, the supreme example having been set by Albrecht V, Duke of Bavaria (1528–79), called "The Magnanimous"

("*Der Grossmütige*"), who was so inordinately fond of shooting that all the ducal privies in the palace were at the ends of long corridors; paper bull's-eyes hung at the opposite ends and racks of loaded wheellocks stood ready within arm's length of every convenience.

In general, rulers provided wheellocks for those companies which could use them well enough to justify the expense. Mercenaries, whose source of pay and supply was plunder, stole them from the burning homes of well-to-do burghers in sacked cities. But really fine guns, both pistols and long arms, soon wound up on the gaming tables after the drunken victory celebrations; and since rich and craftily sober captains could outlast nearly the whole company for cash and stakes, the weapons mostly reverted to the ownership of the leaders; and as the leaders (or those who survived) grew in time into solid elderly citizens, many ennobled, the best guns followed them into retirement and domesticity.

Fig. 124—German pear-butt wheellock pistol, one of a pair; 1590-1610. Walnut stock has profuse ivory in- and overlays engraved with flowers, leaves, fruit, animals, masks and arabesques. In tasteful contrast, lock, barrel and trigger-guard are absolutely plain. Lock is the type diagrammed in Fig. 99. Over-all length 22 in.; calibre .55. (Tonolini Collection, Brescia, Italy)

Fig. 125—Three-quarter armor and accoutrements of the "Rutters," i.e., *Reiter* or *cavaliers* in Fig. 123. Left half: front view of armor, surrounded by: helmets with upper visor open (left) and both visors open (right); gorget (between helmets); left and right brassarts or armpieces; inner and outer breastplates; and the rapier, naked and in scabbard. Rider's plumed helmet has both visors closed. In addition to elements enumerated, rider wears gauntlets, articulated lobster cuisses, kneepieces, leather boots with turned-down lace stockings (no armor beneath) and spurs. Lance with hourglass grip (center) is broken to fit into rectangle. Right half: rear view of armor (note unarmored cloth trousers) surrounded by: pistol in saddle pipe (note spanner, bullet pouch and powder flask); drawn pistol; backplate; tasse (tasse is worn hooked over prong on backplate, as shown in figure); saddle (note lance cup on right stirrup); and lance with leather thong. Engraving from J. J. von Wallhausen, *Art Militaire au Cheval (The Art of Mounted Warfare)*, Frankfurt-a.-M., 1616.

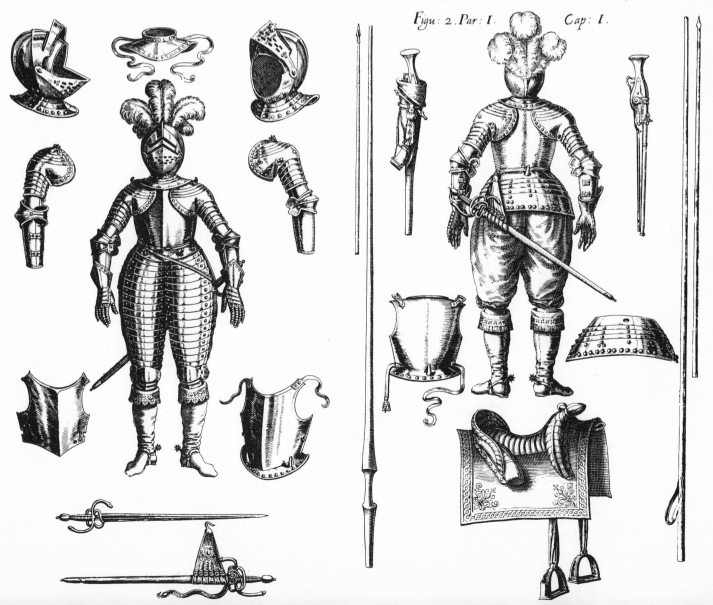

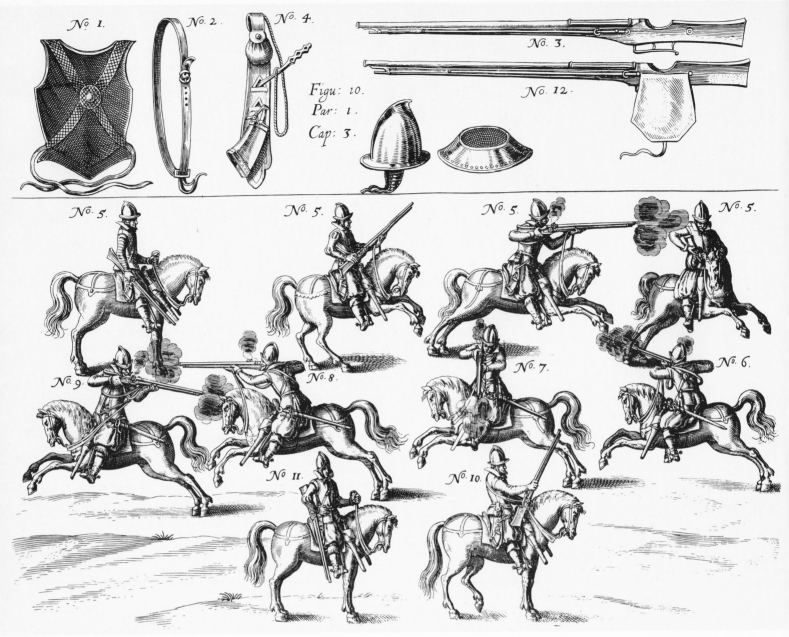

Fig. 126—Carabineers of circa 1590-1640 in various maneuvers, and, above them, their accouterments: No. 1, breastplate; No. 2, carbine belt; No. 4, *sacoche* with bullet pouch, spanner and powder horn; Nos. 3 and 12, carbines (note "rider," the attaching ring free to slide along bar on left side of guns to permit bringing muzzle down to hip height for loading in saddle; and leather apron to protect primed lock from rain); and, not numbered, morion helmet and gorget. Every rider also carries two pistols in saddle pipes. From J. J. von Wallhausen, *Art Militaire au Cheval (The Art of Mounted Warfare)*, Frankfurt-a.-M., 1616.

Fig. 127—Right: Flat powder horn with brass mountings, engraved with St. George and the dragon; German, dated 1593. Cowhorns were softened by heat and steam, pressed flat and allowed to harden.

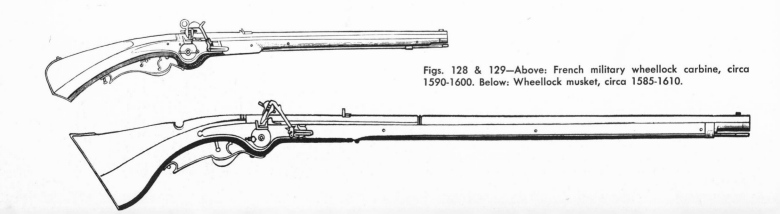

Figs. 128 & 129—Above: French military wheellock carbine, circa 1590-1600. Below: Wheellock musket, circa 1585-1610.

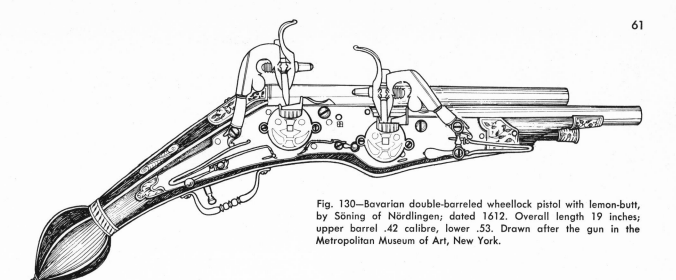

Fig. 130—Bavarian double-barreled wheellock pistol with lemon-butt, by Söning of Nördlingen; dated 1612. Overall length 19 inches; upper barrel .42 calibre, lower .53. Drawn after the gun in the Metropolitan Museum of Art, New York.

While such developments were afoot on the Continent, all England was growing ever more astir as the first trembling run of the sap of commerce and empire (to boil over in the heyday of the first Elizabeth) rose in the veins of a body politick ministered to since 1485 by the prosaic, capable, hard-working realist Henry VII. His death in 1509 bequeathed the throne to his eighteen-year-old son, second of the Tudors, eighth (and last) of the Henrys, England's and the Reformation's answer to the Hapsburgs' Charles V. Only one facet of this brilliant if brutal personality concerns our narrative directly: no sooner had the boy king's already ample seat warmed the pillow of St. Edward's chair than he vaulted from it, so to speak, into the cellars to inspect the state of the royal armories in all his castles and redoubts. An adolescent, he was fired by visions of heroic deeds and vast armies with shiny arms abristle awaiting his royal nod; and it took some adroit coddling on the part of Parliament and more mature ministers to prevent his giving it until early manhood had infused his fiery genius with cold reason and crafty political skill. His delight in hawking, hunting, shooting and fine guns, however, grew apace with his other precocious appetites, far outdistancing that of his Hispanic colleague. By 1520 the adult Henry VIII had become, and was to remain until the day of his death in 1547, not only the founder of the Royal Navy (firearmed to sink the Spanish into his daughter's ocean), but also a munificent patron of sporting-gun makers. All his fine personal guns were of course imported from France, Germany and Italy. Of special interest are the *breechloaders* which were delivered to his gun rooms in considerable numbers, some made perhaps after designs of his own suggestion (Fig. 131). These gained in vogue among his courtiers and lords for a time, though more by force of snobbery and royal example than from any degree of serviceable utility. Not until the eighteenth century were

gunsmiths able to overcome the problems of gas seepage and even deadly backfires at the breech to make such weapons efficient, save by breech blocks and locking mechanisms which required so much labor that their cost was prohibitive. Even with these some gas pressure was lost, and the only advantage gained was that a rifle—not a smoothbore—could be loaded at the breech with an oversized ball to ensure its following the rifling grooves. But there was little game in England for long-range rifle hunting. Tudor gentlemen, aquiver now and then with British sporting spirit, coursed the deer *par force*—i.e., they ran them to death with hound and horse, which inspiring pastime was not to be adulterated by the new German fashion of simply shooting them with guns. But even in Germany and other big-game-hunting countries, breechloaders, odd to say, remained exceedingly rare until about a hundred years ago.

For the most part, guns were used in early Tudor England by the poorer classes of rustics who depended on wild fowl and venison for at least such a measure of their sustenance as was required to keep body and soul on speaking terms during the winter months. The fact that the fowling piece, although not by that name, was already in use by 1525, and probably a quarter of a century earlier, proceeds clearly from the royal patent granted by Henry VIII to the overseers of the Guild of St. George (now the Honourable Artillery Company of London) by which they and their successors were licensed, "without hys speciall warrant," to

exercyse themselves in shoting with the long-bowe, crosse-bowe and hand-gonne, at all manner of markes and buttes, and at the gayme of popynjaye, and at al other gaym or gaymes, as at foule or fowles, as well in the Cittie of London and Sub-urbs as in all other places wheresoever within the realme of England, Yrelande, Calice [Calais], and the Marches of Wayles, and elsewhere within the kyng's Dominions, his forests, chayses and parkes . . .

Fig. 131—Left: Close-up of breech of a breech-loading wheellock arquebus made in Germany for Henry VIII of England (reigned 1509-47); the lock has been removed better to show breech opening. After ball and powder have been loaded into breech chamber in front of opening, hinged breechblock is closed, then locked by pushing bolt handle (projecting from top of open block) forward, which slides locking bolt into notch in side of barrel at front of opening. (In the Tower of London)

Fig. 132—Alpine hunting with crossbows. Woodcut by Jost Amman, 1568. Compare Fig. 290.

Fig. 133—Below: Underside of a German hunting crossbow, mid-16th century. Bow is of blued steel, stock of polished deerhorn carved in white relief against green-dyed background; underside shows death of Lucretia (top) and Judith with head of Holofernes (bottom). This crossbow, like many, was spanned with a *cranequin*, an internal jack-and-gear arrangement with an external lever, rather than with a *moulinet* (Figs. 11 and 12) or a goat's-foot lever (Fig. 7). Crossbow weighs 8 lbs. 14 oz., winder 5 lbs. 3 oz.; hunter burdened with about 14 pounds was not able to deliver a fraction as accurate, long and powerful a shot as from a good rifle of similar weight. By 1560-70, crossbows were rapidly becoming pure sporting implements as rifles replaced them in professional, or food-supply, hunting; by 1600 they had virtually passed from the military scene. (In the Metropolitan Museum of Art, New York)

Nearly all the guns in the hands of lower classes were matchlocks or even hand cannons and culverins, and since it was impossible to shoot flying game with such engines, nearly all fowling with guns must have been done by creeping up on unwary birds on ponds and branches, much in the manner shown in Fig. 135. Thus more hard-working people ate better than their fathers and grandfathers had; but all medallions must have a reverse to the obverse, and the reverse of this fair aspect was that the parks and deer reserves of king and lord as well as the holdings of the lesser landowners were being poached until wildlife and the sporting life of the rich was threatened with extinction. This was alarming enough, but in England a greater calamity—indeed, a national crisis—soon made its repercussions echo through Parliament and palace: for gunshooting was leading to the abandon of hunting with the longbow, so that the councilors of the realm were haunted by the specter of an England without a reserve of citizen archers. Such alarm was, in fact, quite justified, for it must be remembered that the longbow, uniquely the weapon of the English, had hitherto proved vastly more effective against England's enemies than any kind of "hand-gonne" (save rifles, the drawbacks of which for military use have already been noted briefly, and which anyhow no one in early Tudor England knew how to make). But the longbow's terror lay rooted in virtually daily exercise and practice from boyhood into advanced middle years—nothing less could steel a man to send a warhead flight arrow three hundred yards and more unaimed into the enemy ranks, or aimed and murderously accurate beyond a hundred. Naturally, a generation of Englishmen habituated into physical decadence by the use of guns and crossbows would make a flabby sort of safeguard for the king's dominions—not sinewed by the sort of stuff their forefathers had brought to tell at Agincourt and Crécy. What the king's dominions might have gained by a safeguard of citizen arquebusiers was not yet understood in England. As early as 1508, therefore, the twenty-third and last year of the reign of Henry VII, an Act of Parliament forbade the use of guns and crossbows without royal pat-

ent or special license. But soon it became clear that it was one thing to forbid a man to load his family's dinner table by an easy means, and quite another to keep him from doing so; Dick Hawkins and his Sunday goose were not so easily parted. When, therefore, during the next three years the English fens and forests continued to reverberate more and more with the roar of lead and powder, and more and more longbows warped and cracked forgotten in the chimney corner's warmth, a new act set the scofflaws to a sterner task: it demanded in 1511, the second year of the reign of Henry VIII, that every Englishman under the age of forty provide himself with bow and arrows and practice daily at the butts, under pain of heavy fines. The success of this was as conspicuous as that of its predecessor. Four more years—and, it may safely be surmised, a great many more deer, ducks, geese, quail, pheasants, warped longbows and barrels of unrestrainedly expended gunpowder—passed into the stream of history. A number of royal proclamations, admonishing all good loving subjects to obey the law, passed with them.

Fig. 134—Right: Crude matchlock gun, late 1400's or early 1500's. General-purpose "hand-gonne" is typical of thousands used by rustics in pursuit of fowl and beasts.

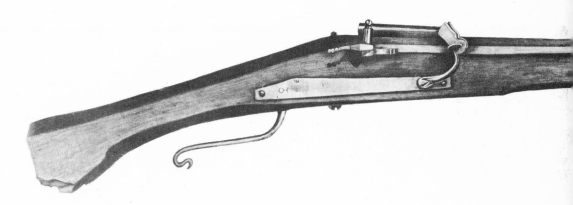

Fig. 135—Common folk hunting ducks in wintery landscape with matchlock birding pieces similar to Fig. 134. Hunter shooting in center is resting the butt of his gun over, not against his shoulder (cf. Fig. 41); man stalking in foreground wears large flask for propellent powder, small horn for priming. Iambic hexameter caption says: *Sic fluvialis Anas capitur cane, fulminis ictu / Dum percussus obit, pennasque in flumine spargit*— "Thus the duck on the river, struck by the bolt of fire, is captured by the hound while she dies and drapes her wings in the stream." Engraving from Jan van der Straet (alias Stradanus), *Venationes Ferarum, Avium, Piscium (The Hunt of Beasts, Birds and Fish)*, Antwerp, 1566; book is among the earliest to describe and depict firearms in hunting, probably the first to show birding- or fowling-pieces (cf. Figs. 67, 94 and 138).

Fig. 136—Left side of butt of a wheellock rifle, another example of the Munich team of gunmaker Daniel Sadeler (fl. ca. 1610-32) and stockmaker Hieronymus Borstorffer. See Figs. 144 and 146. (In the Metropolitan Museum of Art, New York)

At last, in 1515, king and council had enough of playing, and now charged Parliament with spelling out the Law in deadly earnest. Thus was passed that year AN ACTE AVOIDYNG SHOTING IN CROSSBOWES AND GONNES (6 Hen.VIII.c.13), which decreed that:

> Where the Kings Subjects daily delite them selfs in shoting of Crosbowes wherby shoting in long bowes is the lesse used, and diverse good statutes for reformacion of the same have been made and had, And that notwithstanding, many and diverse not regarding nor fearing the penalties of the said estatutes daily shote in Crosbowes and hand gonnes whereby the Kings dere [and those of] other Lords of his Realme ar distroid and shalbe daily more and more onlesse remedie therfor be provided; Wherefore be it ordeyned and enactid by auctoritie of this present parliament that no person hensforth shote in any Crosbowe or hand gonne upon payne of forfeiture of the same bowe and gonne onlesse he or others to his use, or to the use of his Wife, have lands and tenents, fees, annuyties or other profits to the yerely value of CCC marks [1 mark = 13s. 4d., 300 marks = £ 200], And for every tyme so shooting in Crosbowe or hand gonne [shall] forfaite x li. [£ 10] for every tyme so offending; and that it shall be lefull [lawful] for every of the Kings Subjects to sease and take any suche Crossbowe or gonne and to retayn them to his own use, and that every man that will [pursue another man carrying an illegal crossbow or gun] shall have of the penaltie of x li. the one moytie [half] and the king the other moytie; And that noman after the fest of Whitsontid next coming kepe in his house nor elliswhere any Crossbowe or hand gonne upon payne of imprisonment and to forfeit to our Soveraign Lord the King x li., onles that he or other to his use have lands and tenents to the yerely value of CCC marks as is above said. . . .

This strategy was shrewd: the £ 200 yearly income qualification for owning or shooting guns in effect disqualified the entire population of England (which was about 4.8 or 5 million in 1515) save the nobles and perhaps 350,000 merchants and country squires, representing in all some 7 per cent of the total. But those who could qualify were satisfied, the more so since the law empowered them to seize any gun or crossbow from any unqualified subject, keep it, and receive half of the fine if the wretch were convicted. The qualified were happy, the rest were unhappy but also unfirearmed, and for a time all went well. Of course the law's aim was as much or more the insurance of a class monopoly on shooting as it was the perpetuation of longbow practice, but if viewed knowledgeably in relation to the vast complicated matrix of its time, it was not "tyrannical" (as our twentieth-century egalitarian prejudices may make it seem) but in fact a wise outgrowth of the world's most efficient and enlightened judicial system.

Fig. 137—Walnut stock of a light German wheellock arquebus, inlaid with engraved staghorn; circa 1550-75. Gun is .40 calibre, 34 inches in overall length.

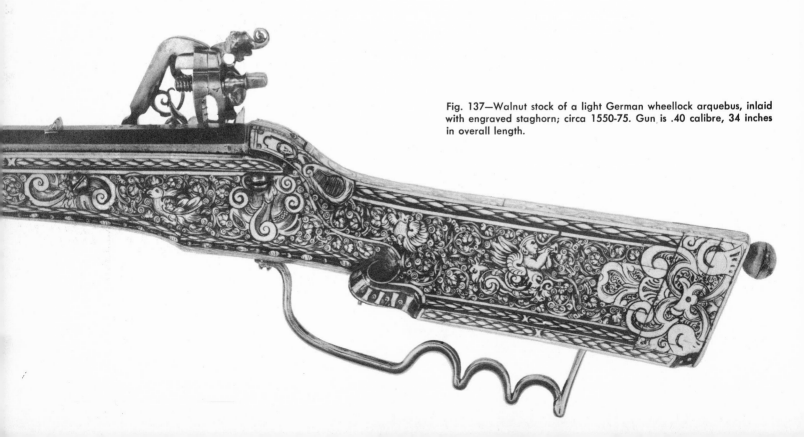

Sic fluuialis Anas ignito fulminis ictu   *Aut Canibus capitur, longeq; volante sagitta.*

Fig. 138—"Thus the duck on the river is killed by the fiery blow of lightning, or by the hounds and the long flying arrow"—a prose translation of the Latin verse "*Sic fluvialis Anas ignito fulminis ictu / Aut Canibus capitur, longeque volante sagitta*" beneath engraving by Hans Bol (1534-1593) from *Venationis, Piscationis et Avicupii Typii (Scenes of Hunting, Fishing and Birding),* Amsterdam[?], ca. 1580-88 (cf. Fig. 94). Note wader in foreground with arquebus slung over his back, man spanning crossbow next to shooter, and shooter on island.

During the next twenty-five years, however, enforcement became gradually more difficult and finally impossible owing to a new and frightful social menace: firearmed robbers and cutthroats by the thousands had come to roam the highways and the countryside, so that in turn farmers and travelers with modest incomes—less than £200 a year—were compelled to firearm themselves illegally in self-defense. By 1540 all efforts at enforcement had dissolved in chaos. A new, realistic, unequivocal law was needed which would not only regulate the ownership of firearms and make them accessible to the poorer squires with only £100 a year (which would still leave 90 per cent of the population disqualified), but which would provide for hunting licenses, hunting seasons, special cases such as gunsmiths, gun dealers and servants carrying their masters' guns on orders, and prohibit, save in very rare exceptional circumstances, the carrying of pistols. This was accomplished by Parliament in 1542 with the enactment of the famous 33 Hen.VIII.c.6, which began:

> WHERE in the Parliament . . . sondrie holsome and lawdable Acts, Statutes and ordynances [were] made and ordayned for the avoydinge and eschewinge of shotinge in Crosbows and Handguns, since the makinge of whiche . . . diverse malicious and evill disposed persons not only presumynge wilfullye and obstynatlye the violation and breach of the said [acts], but also of their malicious and evill disposed myndes and purposes have wilfully and shamefully commytted, perpetrated and done diverse detestable and shamefull murthers, roberies, felonyes, ryotts and routes with Crosbowes, lyttle shorte handguns and little hagbutts [arquebuses], to the great perill and contynuall feare and daunger of the Kings most lovinge subjects . . . [And whereas] Keepers of Forests, Chases and Parks aswell as . . . Commons and diverse Gentlemen, Yeomen and Servingmen nowe of late have layde aparte the good and laudable exercise of the longe bowe, whiche alwayes heretofore hathe bene the suretie, saveguarde and contynuall defense of this Realme of Englande and an inestimable dread and terror to the Enemyes of the same . . . [And whereas] nowe of late the saide evill disposed persons have used and yet doe daylie use to ride and go in the Kings highe Wayes and elswhere, having with them Crosbowes and little handguns ready furnished with Quarrel, Gunpowder, fyer & touche, to the great perill and feare of the Kings most loving Subjects: FOR REFORMACION WHEREOF be it enacted, ordeyned and established by the King our Soveraigne Lorde, the Lords spirituall and temporall and by the Commons in this present Parliament assembled and by auctoritie of the same . . . that noe person or persons of what [ever] estate or degree he or they be, except he or they in their owne right or in the right of his or their wyeffs . . . have landes, tenents, fees, annuyties or Offices to the yerely value of one hundred pounds, from or after the last daye of June next comynge [June 30, 1542] shall shote in any Crosbow, handgun, hagbutt or demy hake [small arquebus], or use to kepe in his or their houses or elsewhere any Crosbowe, handgun, hagbutt or demy hake in any manner otherwise than ys hereafter in this present Acte declared, uppon payne to forfeyt for everie tyme that he or they so offend contrarie to this Acte tenne poundes.

Among all its other provisions, this statute established the world's first officially issued hunting licenses. Hunting of any game, whether fowl or beast, was strictly forbidden to *all* classes save by special royal license. But this could be obtained—provided of course that the applicant could meet the £100 per annum qualification—by paying £20 in the King's Courts of Chancery as a *recognisance,* in effect a refundable deposit or bond as a warranty for compliance with the laws of game, guns, property and trespass; it was rendered forfeit by a conviction. Any license which did not state specifically what kind of game the holder was permitted to shoot was null and void.

66

But the most interesting index to the changing times was that although the new law deplored the neglect of "the good and laudable exercise of the longbow," it nonetheless not only encouraged the qualified to "shote at buttes and banks of earth" for target practice, but also all dwellers near the seacoast and the Scottish border, of whatever class or income, to own and exercise with guns. Thus at last, in 1542, Crown and Parliament conceded tacitly *de jure* that firearms had eclipsed the value of citizen archers *de facto*. Even the still doubtful traditionalists were persuaded by the loss of Calais in 1558, and by the fate of the English soldiers in the pay of the Netherlands—many of them archers—when a dozen years later English arrows were pitted against Spanish muskets. Sir Roger Williams drew on thirty years' experience when he wrote in 1590 in his BRIEFE DISCOURSE ON WARRE:

TO PROOVE BOW-MEN THE WORST SHOT USED IN THESE DAIES.

Touching bow-men, I perswade my selfe 500 musketers are more servicable than 1500 bow men, from that rate to the greatest numbers in al manner of services. My reasons are thus: among 5000 bowmen you shall not finde 1000 good Archers, I meane to shoot strong shootes; let them be in the field 3 to 4 monthes, hardlie finde of 5000 scarce 500 able to make anie strong shootes. In defending or assailing anie trenches, lightly they must discover [expose] themselves to make fair shootes, where the other shot [the enemy's muskets and calivers] spoyle them by reason they discover nothing of themselves unlesse it be a little through small holes. Few or none doo anie great hurt 12 or 14 score off [eighty-five to one hundred yards]. They are not to be compared unto the other shootes [firearms] to line battels or to march. . . .

Besides, the munition that belongs unto bow men are not so commonly found in all places, especially arrowes, as powder is unto the other shot. Also time and ill weather weakeneth the bowes as well as the men. In our antient wars, our enemies used crossbowes and such shoots; few or anie at all had the use of the long bowes as we had, whereof none could compare with us for shot. But God forbid we should trie our bowes with their Muskets and Calivers without the like shot to answer them. . . .

Fig. 139—Portable breastwork of wooden beams protects French "Calivers," who "discover nothing of themselves unlesse it be a little through small holes." Engraving from Jean Appier-Hanzelet, *La Pyrotechnie,* Pont-à-Mousson, 1630.

But to return to civilian life. Gradually the 33 Hen.VIII, too, fell into disuse. Soon only the £100 qualification was enforced, but it must be remembered that there were also dozens of other game and land laws—some harking back to the days of King Alfred—which circumscribed the hunter's and the fowler's every step and motion. These and the principle of qualification remained in effect in one form or another until the early twentieth century, having been modified or reiterated by a dozen statutes and thousands of judicial decisions in the intervening centuries. In Elizabethan England, bird and deer shooting flourished nonetheless, laws or no laws, as innumerable poachers and unqualified, unlicensed rustics went shooting for food and profit. Hundreds of thousands of qualified and licensed farmers, squires and tradesmen shot for food and amusement; and a small number in the highest circles of the social hierarchy—King Henry, Drake and Essex among them—occasionally went shooting with very good, beautiful and expensive imported wheellocks, but not very often because shooting was not yet considered a respectable sport, let alone a noble or royal one. Gentlefolk mainly still coursed the deer with hounds, and generally left birds alone. Middle- and lower-class shooting, however, was conducted with such enthusiasm that already in 1549, the second year of the reign of Edward VI—scarcely seven years since the enactment of the 33 Hen.VIII.c.6—a new law was required to proclaim sternly that there had grown

muche idlenesse and . . . such a liberty [that] not only dwelling-houses, dove-cotes and churches are dailie damaged by the abuse . . . but also there is growne a customable manner of shoting of hayle-shot [i.e., bird-shot pellets] whereby an infinite sort of fowle is killed and much gayme thereby distroyed, to the benefitt of no man; whereby also the [original intention of the 33 Hen.VIII of rearing a citizen reserve of shooters by allowing shooting at butts and banks of earth] is defrauded, for . . . the use of hayle-shot utterlie distroyeth the certainty of shotynge which in warres is much requisite: BEE IT THEREFORE INACTED that noe person under the degree of Lord in Parliament shall henceforth shote in any handgunne within any citie or towne at any fowle or other mark, upon anie church, house or dove-cote, [and] neither shal any person shote in any place any hayl-shot or any more pellets than one at a tyme, upon payne of . . . tenne pounds [or three months' imprisonment].

The point was well taken that shooting with birdshot reduced marksmanship to nothing compared to the skill required for hitting a flying bird with a ball, so that now shot was imperiling the prowess of citizen gunners as guns had once imperiled that of citizen archers. But though well taken, the point was not well received, and the prohibition against shot was of no avail whatever. Dick Hawkins and his hopes for Sunday goose were now more firmly welded than ever.

Fig. 140—German matchlock hunting arquebus, smoothbore, circa 1560-85; probably once belonged to a noble in the court of Elizabeth I. Only an extreme conservative would have used a matchlock at this late date. Ivory inlay of scrollwork and foliage surrounds Adam and Eve, serpent, forbidden tree. Stock is walnut. (In the Tower of London)

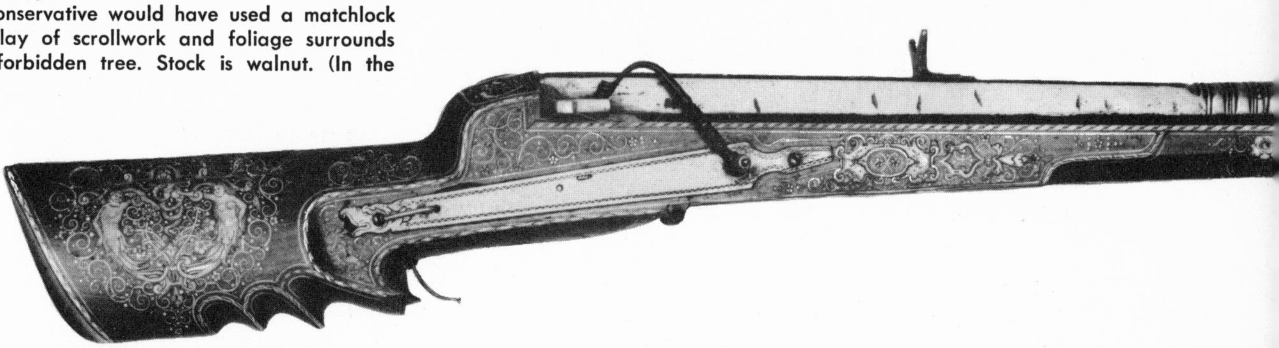

Between circa 1520 and 1570, shotmaking in England as well as on the Continent consisted of cutting up a sheet of lead into small squares or cubes, then rolling these about for hours in a barrel to wear down the edges and corners. Anywhere from twenty to two hundred of these confetti were loaded into the gun for one shot, then sprayed hopefully at a bird thirty yards distant with but a few reaching it and most scattering every which way. In the last quarter of the sixteenth century, however, an inefficient but workable method for making *round* shot came into universal use (Fig. 141). Richard Blome's description of it in THE GENTLEMAN'S RECREATION, although published in 1686, was admittedly copied from "an extreamly antient recipie":

Let your Shot be well cast and round, without Tails hanging on, which in the Flight gathereth Wind and by Consequence Flieth not so far. As to the sizes it must be according to the Fowl or Birds you design to kill, but not too great, for then it flies thin and scattering; nor yet too small, for then it is of small force; for the Fowl will Fly away with it, as having neither strength nor weight to enter far to their prejudice.

Now forasmuch as Shot can't be had in all places answerable to your desired size, and for that the making is so easie and cheap, it will be convenient to lay down some Directions for the making of the same.

Being provided with Lead (let it be old or new, it matters not), Melt it down in an Iron Vessel, keeping it always stirring with an Iron Ladle, which should have a Lip or Notch in the Brim for the better convenient pouring it out, and be sure to take off all the Dross and Filth that swims on the top: And when it is so hot that it appears of a Greenish colour, strewn upon it as much of the Powder of Auripigmentum [yellow arsenic] as will lye upon a Shilling (provided there be about ten or twelve pound of Lead), and then stir the Lead well and the Auripigmentum will flame; then take out a little of the Lead in the Ladle for an essay, and cause it to drop out into a Glass of Water, and if the Drops prove round and without Tails, there is enough Auripigmentum in it, and the temper of the heat is as it ought to be; but if the Drops be not round and with Tails, then add more of the said Auripigmentum, and augment the heat until it be well.

Then take a Copper or Brass Plate of about the size of a Trencher, or bigger or lesser as you think fit, with a Concavity in the middle, about three or four Inches in Diameter, wherein must be made forty or fifty holes of several sizes, to what you would have your Shot to be; this concave bottom should be thin, but the Brim thick, the better to retain the heat. This Plate should be placed on two Bars or over an Iron Frame, over a Tub or Pail of Fair Water, about four inches from the Water. Then with your Ladle take off your Lead and pour it gently on the Plate, on which should be burning Coals to keep it hot, for the Lead will find its passage through the Coals into the Water, and fall in round Drops; when the Coals are out or dead, put on more, and so continue pouring the Lead until you have finished what you intend. If the Lead stop the Plate, and yet is not too cool, give the Plate a little knock and it will drop again.

Your chief care is that the Lead be in good Condition, as not too cold, or too hot, for if too hot it will drop cracky, and if too cold it will stop the holes; therefore as near as you can observe the temper of the heat, and you will have a good round Shot without Tails.

Fig. 141—Making birdshot in the late 16th to middle 18th centuries. Molten lead is poured through coals in trencher, which is pierced with holes corresponding to desired size of pellets; drops of lead fall into bowl of water below. On wall hang two ladles, two trenchers with holes of different sizes, three lead-cutters and several bars of lead (draped over a peg). Woodcut from Vita Bonfadini, *La Caccia Dell' Arcobugio (Hunting with the Arquebus)*, Venice, 1691.

It was not until the middle of the eighteenth century that anyone thought of the obvious method for making small shot, which is to pour the lead through a screen with perforations of the desired size, then to allow it to fall from a third-story window or from a higher *shot tower* into a box below so that the equal air pressure all around each drop will cool and harden it during its fall as a nearly perfect sphere.

Shakespeare confirms the outbursts of shooting sport enjoyed from time to time by Tudor gentlemen. In the second scene of the fourth act of THE MERRY WIVES OF WINDSOR the would-be lover Sir John Falstaff desperately seeks a place to hide before the return of Mr. Ford and his friends (as Mrs. Ford had assured him, "He's abirding, sweet Sir John"). Panicky, Falstaff cries:

> *Fal.* No, I'll come no more i' the basket. May I not go out ere he come?
> *Mrs. Page.* Alas, three of Master Ford's brothers watch the door with pistols, that none shall issue out; otherwise you might slip away ere he come. But what make you here?
> *Fal.* What shall I do? I'll creep up into the chimney!

> *Mrs. Ford.* There they always use to discharge their birding-pieces.

May we infer from Mr. Ford's brothers' making free with pistols in broad public daylight that they felt quite safe from the blunt and wobbly teeth of the law? Probably we may. THE MERRY WIVES was written between 1590 and 1600, when the 33 Hen.VIII was about fifty-seven years old and the 2 Edw.VI about fifty. In the two generations since their passage, prosperity and firearms had found a still greater sphere among the English, and consequently the already ancient and often contradictory *corpus juris* governing hunting, hawking and shooting became increasingly more ill defined. Mr. Ford had certainly paid the £20 recognizance for a license to shoot, but his peculiar manner of unloading his piece up the chimney was almost surely not standard practice but rather his (or Shakespeare's) own. Surely it must have been preferable to use a *worm*, a small corkscrew-like ramrod attachment, rather than to clean the eruption of soot which was certain to cascade down the chimney by the Ford method.

Fig. 142—Wheellock pistol by Felix Weeder of Zurich, dated 1630. Stock is inlaid with gold horsemen, hounds, rabbits, foliage, Scottish thistle, English rose, Irish shamrock; barrel is half gilded. Magnificent weapon once belonged to Charles I of England. (In the Metropolitan Museum of Art, New York)

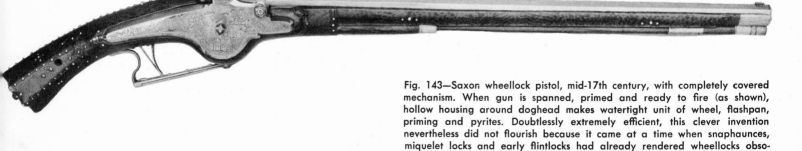

Fig. 143—Saxon wheellock pistol, mid-17th century, with completely covered mechanism. When gun is spanned, primed and ready to fire (as shown), hollow housing around doghead makes watertight unit of wheel, flashpan, priming and pyrites. Doubtlessly extremely efficient, this clever invention nevertheless did not flourish because it came at a time when snaphaunces, miquelet locks and early flintlocks had already rendered wheellocks obsolescent if not obsolete.

Fig. 146—In right margin: plaques of walnut inlaid in rifle stock of polished white deerhorn. See lock in Fig. 144, butt in Fig. 136.

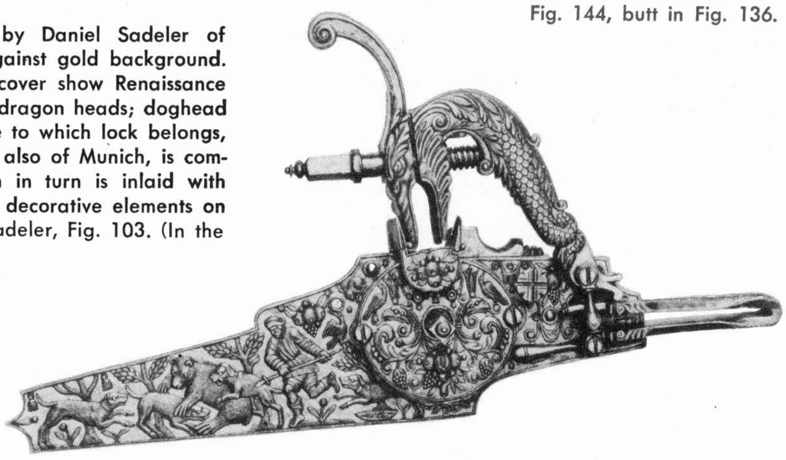

Fig. 144—Lock of the rifle in Fig. 136, by Daniel Sadeler of Munich (fl. ca. 1610-32), black iron relief against gold background. Plate shows bear hunt; flashpan and wheel-cover show Renaissance motifs of scrollwork, foliage, fruit, birds and dragon heads; doghead in form of sea monster. The stock of the rifle to which lock belongs, made by stockmaker Hieronymus Borstorffer, also of Munich, is completely overlaid with white deerhorn, which in turn is inlaid with walnut plaques; three of these are shown as decorative elements on p. 69 (Fig. 146). See also pistol by Daniel Sadeler, Fig. 103. (In the Metropolitan Museum of Art, New York)

Inventories of the arms in all the royal arsenals were taken upon the death of Henry VIII in 1547. Perhaps nothing can sum up the wheellock century, the status of such (imported) guns in England and the image of a patron king of gunmakers to better advantage than this colorful inventory taken at Greenwich Castle:

ITEM, one chamber pece black [one blue-steel breech-loader], the stocke of redde woode set with bone worke, with a fier locke [wheellock] in a case of crymson vellet.

ITEM, one longe white·[bright steel] pece with a fier locke.

ITEM, one longe pece graven and guilte [gilded], with a stocke of redde woode set with white bone, and a fier locke, in a case of lether.

ITEM, two chamber peces [breechloaders] guilt and graven, with a fier locke in a stocke of yellow.

ITEM, one guilte chamber pece parcell [partially] guilt, with a redde stocke, with a fier locke in a case of purple vellet.

ITEM, one lytle short pece for a horseman of damaskine work [Damascus or damascened steel], the stocke of woode and bone, set with a chamber [a breech-loading pistol?].

ITEM, one dagge with two peeces in one stock [a double-barreled dag].

ITEM, two blacke swordes in a case of lether, and two letle daggers garnished with silver, parcell guilte and emaled [enameled or embossed with a raised pattern], with knyves and bodkyns.

ITEM, c Italion peces [100 Italian pieces], and every one hys moulde [bullet mould], flaske, touch boxe [priming-powder flask], and matche.

ITEM, one horne for gonne-powder, garnished with silver.

ITEM, iii grete flaskes covered with vellet, and three lytle touche boxes.

ITEM, ii longe small cofers [cases] for gonnes.

ITEM, a white tacke [i.e., dag, pistol] with fier locke graven, and all the stocke white bone; a great flaske varnished and paynted; a touche box of iron graven and gilded.

ITEM, ii tackes after the fashion of a dagger, with fier lockes vernished, with redde stockes, shethes covered with blacke vellet, garnished with silver and guilt, with purses [bullet pouches], flaskes and touche boxes of black vellet garnished with iron guilte.

ITEM, two tackes hafted like a knyff with fier locks, and doble lockes, a pece; th'one graven parcell guilte and tother vernyshed; with two purses, two flaskes and two touche-boxes of black vellet, th'one garnished with iron and guilt.

Fig. 145—Wheellock with internal wheel and shielded doghead by Antonius Zurschenthaler of Munich (fl. 1690-1730). Lockplate shows Salome dancing before Herod, Herodias and court; shield of doghead shows the beheading of St. John, servant with platter waiting for head. (In the Metropolitan Museum of Art, New York)

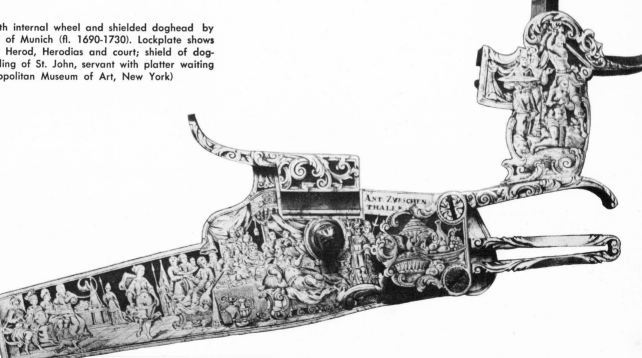

CHAPTER FIVE

Chicken thieves and gunlocks—The snaphaunce—A snapping rooster or a snapping dog?—The distinguishing features of a snaphaunce—Its cost compared to wheellocks, matchlocks—Distances in late sixteenth-century Europe—The miquelet lock—Origin of its name—Going off half-cocked—Some of the miquelet's virtues and failings—The South Italian miquelet —National characteristics in gunnery—English social climate of 1580–1660 in respect to guns—The coming flintlock.

NY READER WHO IS IN THE HABIT OF stealing Dutch chickens will have no difficulty in sympathizing with the professional embarrassment confronting Dutch chicken thieves in the late sixteenth century. These, known at the time—in the singular—as a *Schnapphans*, (Snatching Jack), or as a *Schnapphahn* (Snatch-the-rooster), were in urgent need of some serviceable guns; but wheellocks were far too costly, and one really cannot climb fences stealthily and crawl into a chicken coop with one's hands full of glowing slow match. Even if the farmer did not see it, the dogs and the hens would smell it and raise a furor.

Fig. 147—Two *schnapphanses* with one schnapped *hahn* (here more of a goose) and one impedient matchlock musket. Engraving by Abraham Bosse, Antwerp, ca. 1630. (Courtesy of Lucien Goldschmidt, New York)

It has often been written that one or several ingenious *Schnapphahns,* or *Schnapphanses,* driven by professional necessity and poverty, were the first to devise a simple gunlock in which the action of human hands was imitated mechanically: where a piece of *flint* held in the jaws of a *cock* struck against a piece of steel to issue sparks. Perhaps so. The only certain thing is that such a lock appeared sometime in the late fifth or sixth decade of the sixteenth century in the Netherlands, and that from the day of its invention it has been known by the name of *snaphaunce lock,* or variously as a *snaphance, snaphans, schnapphahn* or *schnapphans.*

The alternative to the chicken-thief etymology (and in the author's opinion, by far the more credible) is that the action of the cock so resembled a pecking chicken that the Dutch and Flemish not only called the lock a *Schnapp-hahn,* which could mean "pecking rooster" as well as "snatch-the-rooster," but that from this comes the very word *cock* for such a gun part. It is called *cock* (rooster) in English, Dutch, German and the Scandinavian countries, but to the speakers of the Romance languages, for reasons of their own, it looked like a dog, being in Italian *cane,* Spanish *cano* and in French *chien.* In old letters and military tracts written in Latin, such zoology depended on the native language of the writer, being either a *gallus* or a *canis,* save in the case of purists who prefered *retinaculum pyritae,* fire-stone holder.

In its earliest form the snaphaunce in the Netherlands looked much like Figs. 148 and 149. The S-shaped cock holding the flint was drawn backward (in the direction of the arrow) until its tail came below the beveled nose of the sear which protruded through the lockplate; the flashpan was much like the flashpan of a wheellock save that it had no pierced bottom. A sliding cover was closed manually after priming but opened, when the trigger was pulled and the cock snapped, by a plunger connected to the cock or to the tumbler. The lock in Fig. 150, which is dated 1598, clearly shows this as well as the overall mechanism. Where the doghead was in wheellocks now was fastened a swinging arm which, exactly as a doghead, could be swung manually either to lie horizontally on the featherspring or up and backward to come down over the flashpan. It terminated in a flat or very slightly curved piece of steel called the *battery.** When the arm was

* The battery is sometimes also called the *frizzen* and the *steel.* Throughout the seventeenth and eighteenth centuries, however, *battery,* as well as *hammer* and *hen,* were the terms most frequently applied to this part of flintlocks, miquelet locks and snaphaunces. For this reason *battery* has been used throughout this book.

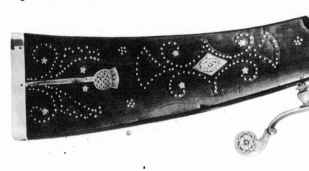

Fig. 148—Scottish snaphaunce gun with Scottish adaptation of the Dutch-type lock, from the armory of Louis XIII of France (1601-43, reigned 1610-43); probably a present from Charles I of England when he was Prince of Wales. Elaborate, sturdy lock, virtually identical to the one in Fig. 150, is dated 1614. (In the Tower of London)

swung over the flashpan, the battery was presented as a piece of steel for the flint to strike, held in position with considerable firmness by the action of the feather spring on the spur of the arm, just as a wheellock doghead was pressed down on the flashpan cover. When the trigger was pulled, the nose of the sear receded into the lockplate, the cock snapped forward, the flint struck against the battery, the battery was knocked up and away from the flashpan by the impact, sparks rained into the flashpan, the flash of the priming burned through the touchhole and the main charge went off. The buffer fastened to the outside of the lockplate arrested the fall of the cock. Such snaphaunces (Figs. 148 to 150) are usually called the *Dutch type*.

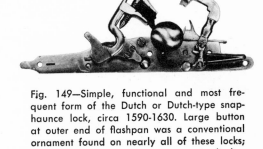

Fig. 149—Simple, functional and most frequent form of the Dutch or Dutch-type snaphaunce lock, circa 1590-1630. Large button at outer end of flashpan was a conventional ornament found on nearly all of these locks; flashpan behind it is a narrow semi-cylinder.

In Italy, especially in Tuscany and Emilia, a similar device appeared at about the same time—say, 1550-1560—but it was to evolve along quite different stylistic lines. By about 1630 it had developed into the elegant, sophisti-

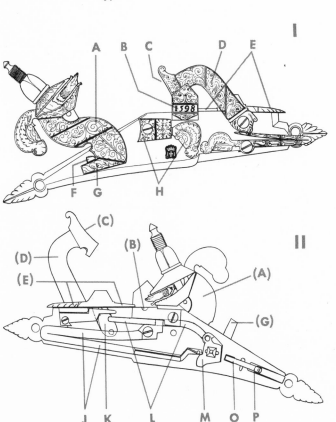

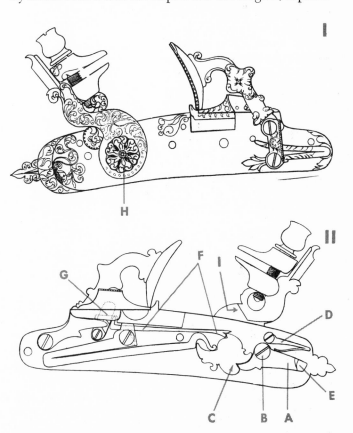

Fig. 150—Outside and inside of a Scottish snaphaunce lock, dated 1598. When cock A is cocked, tail G slides below beveled nose F of sear O, which then snaps out and holds cock cocked. When trigger is pulled, its internal section pulls backward on rear arm P of sear O, thereby pulls nose F inward. Mainspring J, acting downward on tumbler M, snaps cock forward; flint strikes battery C and knocks battery arm D up and away from flashpan B. Simultaneously plunger L, which connects tumbler M to flashpan cover lever K, snaps flashpan cover E open. Sparks are hurled into the now exposed priming in flashpan B; priming ignites and fires shot. Buffer H arrests fall of cock. A loaded and primed snaphaunce was carried cocked but with the battery arm up, as shown in lower diagram, so that accidental snap of cock could not strike sparks.

Fig. 151—Outside and inside of an Italian snaphaunce lock, circa 1630-1730. Besides obvious differences in shape and proportions between Italian and Scottish or Dutch-type snaphaunces, Italian locks had mechanical features of their own or in common with true flintlocks. In inside view, note that sear A pivots vertically on horizontal screw B and engages notch in tumbler C (searspring D snaps it into notch). When trigger is pulled, its internal section pushes up on sear's rear arm E, thereby lowering the nose out of the tumbler notch and releasing cock to snap. Plunger F connects tumbler to flashpan cover lever G so that when trigger is pulled the flashpan snaps open simultaneously with cock's snap (cf. Fig. 150-II, shown snapped and open). Fall of cock of Italian snaphaunces is arrested by the shoulder I on cock's inner surface, which strikes top edge of lockplate.

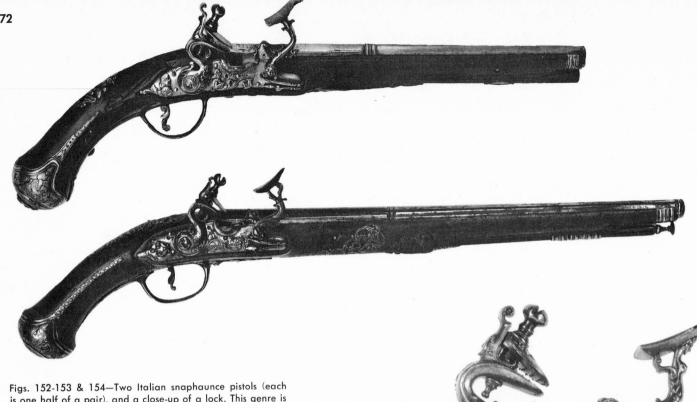

Figs. 152-153 & 154—Two Italian snaphaunce pistols (each is one half of a pair), and a close-up of a lock. This genre is generally called "Brescian," but in fact has nothing to do with that city or its school of gunmaking. Rather, it is a style characteristic of Tuscany and Emilia, and it changed so little between about 1670 and 1820 that dating requires considerable experience. Here the upper weapon is of 1790-1810, the lower about 1725-40, and the detached lock about 1680. (Tonolini Collection, Brescia, Italy)

cated *Italian snaphaunce,* incorporating three features which made it mechanically a close relative of the true flintlock. These were (Fig. 151, Diag. II): first, the wholly internal sear; secondly, the shouldered cock, in which the shoulder I arrested the fall of the cock when it struck the top edge of the lockplate (cf. cock in Fig. 242(3)); and thirdly the square axis of cock and tumbler which was an integral part of the tumbler, not of the cock, and passed outward through a round hole in the lockplate and through a square hole in the cock; the cock was held firmly over it by the screw H, which was screwed on from the outside into a threaded hole in the end of the axis (cf. tumbler in Fig. 243(17)).

Fig. 155—Italian (Brescian) snaphaunce pistol lock, 1679; gilded reliefs of chiseled scrollwork, foliage, bird, hound, hare, cherubs' faces, grotesque masks and sea monsters are set against deeply blued steel background. Knob of vise screw on cock has been broken off. (In the Metropolitan Museum of Art, New York)

All snaphaunces, no matter of what type, nationality or vintage, had these features in common, by which they may be distinguished from flintlocks or miquelet locks (which will be taken up directly):

—the battery was always at the end of a hinged arm which could be rotated manually and which did not serve as a flashpan cover;

— and the flashpan cover was always a separate sliding piece, nearly always opened automatically by a plunger driven by the action of the snapping cock.

Snaphaunces offered no improvement in performance over wheellocks. Indeed, wheellocks survived well into the eighteenth century because they grew ever more excellent between 1600 and 1700, and *no* gunlock before 1810 ever fired with the imperceptible rapidity of a fine late-period wheellock. The snaphaunce's biggest virtues were efficiency and cheapness: in Rotterdam in 1615 a good snaphaunce cost about one-fourth of the price of a good wheellock—and to most gun users, the wheellock's *slightly* faster ignition was not worth the difference. Moreover, flint, unlike pyrites, is not at all friable, and a good snaphaunce could be counted on to yield copious showers of sparks as long as the flint had a sharp edge, which is to say for about twenty shots; then the flint had to be changed. There was no worry about a fouled and choked wheel housing or chain drive, so that firing could be kept up more or less indefinitely without cleaning the lock if only the touchhole were pricked clean and the flashpan brushed free of carbon from time to time. Finally, not only was the initial cost of the new system much less than that of the older, but its comparatively few, simple parts were relatively easy and inexpensive to maintain and to repair.

In spite of all these advantages, however snaphaunces had little opportunity to realize the future which at first had seemed to be theirs. They were still much more expensive than the tried-and-true matchlocks, an argument which, as we have seen, weighed heavily in the considerations of princes and ministers of exchequers. Every army in the world between 1580–1650 was equipped almost exclusively with matchlock calivers and muskets; hundreds of thousands, in time millions of these had been bought, paid for and stacked in hundreds of arsenals and armories. Had the Landgrave of Hessen, for example, decided to re-equip his five thousand men with snaphaunces, he would have had to start with a deficit of some $50,000 worth of scrapped match*locks* (the barrels and stocks would of course have been kept and the lock recesses recarved to accommodate the new invention). In addition, the cost of five thousand new snaphaunce locks and their installation would have amounted to enormous sums in the budgets of the time—far too much for nothing more important than new gunlocks. The old matchlock, although awkward and inefficient, did after all shoot. So many millions had to be spent for the maintenance of the military already that councilors of state were not eager to appropriate still another fortune for a convenient but not absolutely essential modernization. Thus, with the exception of pistols, the snaphaunce never got an appreciable foothold in the military armaments of the late sixteenth and early seventeenth centuries.

Parenthetically it may be mentioned here that neither gunlocks nor any new invention, school of thought, artistic movement or other innovation spread very fast in these times. There were few roads, and such as there were teemed with murderers, became ribbons of axle-deep mud in spring and turned into glaciers of snow and ice in winter. There was as yet no such thing as scheduled or public transportation. The rich traveled in their own coaches with armed escort; others rode horseback; the poor (95 per cent of the population) walked. Under the most ideal conditions, Nuremberg lay fourteen hazardous, bone-rattling days north of Venice by wagon. Eighteen days was good sailing time from Venice to Alexandria across the pirate-infested Adriatic and Mediterranean. A fast courier could bring news from Paris to Buckingham Palace in just a little over two days if he forswore sleep for a day and a half between Paris and Calais, but normal traveling time over the same route was three days. The sea route from Portsmouth to Naples could be covered, with luck, in a month—if storms and virulent fevers didn't decimate passengers and crew, if pirates didn't slaughter or sell all into slavery, or if the Inquisition didn't capture and burn the Protestants aboard. To a journeyman gunsmith, Rotterdam was three footsore weeks from Bremen and over six from Nuremberg. The Italian boot from Milan to Reggio was twenty-one days long by coach and two months long by foot—with chances of survival getting poorer and poorer with every bend in the road south of Benevento. Understandably enough, life was parochial when a hundred-mile journey was fraught with vastly greater perils than a trip around the world today. Ninety-nine out of a hundred souls died in the towns and villages in which they were born and never ventured more than twenty miles out of it in all their lives. The city a hundred miles away was a mysterious other world from which occasional sojourners brought tantalizing trickles of incredible tales of great cathedrals, palaces and countless citizens (rarely more than sixty thousand, most often fewer than twenty thousand). For most good farmers, bakers and candlestick makers the other side of the mountain was as close as the other side of the moon. Rhenish Gothic architecture was unknown fifty leagues away; Regensburger sausages were unheard of in Cologne; the manufacture of Venetian glass was inimitably the monopoly of that republic. The world was a complex sea of islands of peculiar native skills, traditions, customs, morals, religions, tongues, fashions and islands within islands, with not many routes of communion among them.

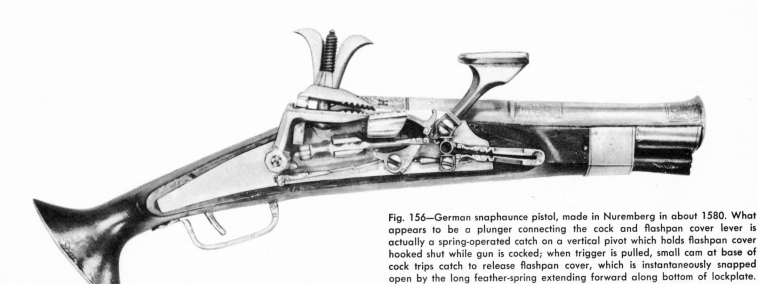

Fig. 156—German snaphaunce pistol, made in Nuremberg in about 1580. What appears to be a plunger connecting the cock and flashpan cover lever is actually a spring-operated catch on a vertical pivot which holds flashpan cover hooked shut while gun is cocked; when trigger is pulled, small cam at base of cock trips catch to release flashpan cover, which is instantaneously snapped open by the long feather-spring extending forward along bottom of lockplate. Complex machine was the only native German version of the snaphaunce ever to develop—Germans preferred wheellocks. (In the Tower of London)

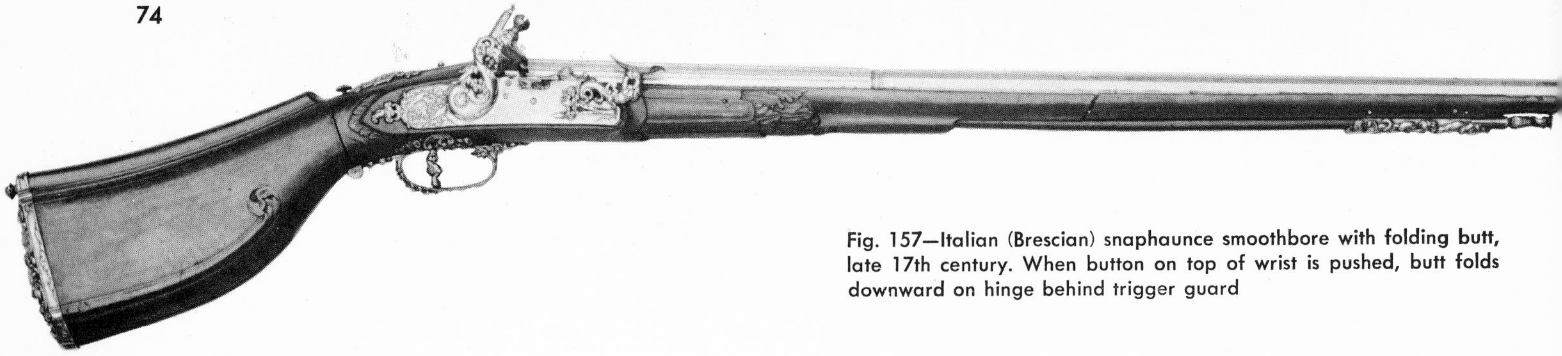

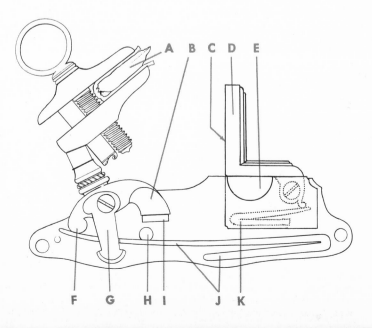

Fig. 157—Italian (Brescian) snaphaunce smoothbore with folding butt, late 17th century. When button on top of wrist is pushed, butt folds downward on hinge behind trigger guard

The subjects of the present history were merely tiles of this mosaic. No doubt details of the new gun ignition system invented in Holland, and samples of it, were passed along the trade routes within months to interested princes and worldly cosmopolites who lived on the plateaus of leisure and affluence. But there the avenues of exchange stopped; and it is therefore not surprising that the same device should be a marvel of novelty in a French hamlet or a Bavarian village twenty-five years later, or that while Sir Francis Drake may have brought dozens of fine Dutch snaphaunces to London from his 1587 Cadiz expedition, the mechanism was hardly if at all known in Sanlúcar or Frontera just thirty-odd miles north of Cadiz.

On the other hand, something was known in Cadiz—or, at any rate, in some part of Spain—which was not known in London in 1587: the *miquelet lock*. This was an engine of utmost importance in firearms history for it formed the last link between all earlier ignition systems and the true flintlock which was to dominate firearms for two whole centuries from 1630 on.

The miquelet, in the simplest terms, was a snapping lock like a snaphaunce but refined by the revolutionary feature of having the battery combined with the flashpan cover in one L-shaped piece hinged at the toe, the upright section being struck by the flint and the horizontal forming the flashpan cover.

To shoot a miquelet lock, the shooter first cocked it until the quadrant-like foot of the cock came to rest on the nose of the secondary sear; this was the *half-cock* position, and no amount of pressure on the trigger could release the cock to snap. Next he flipped the L-shaped flashpan cover up and open, primed the flashpan and flipped the cover shut again. The feather-spring exerted tension on a small spur under the hinge of the flashpan cover so that it was kept firmly pressed down over the flashpan, or, when the shooter's hand or the snapping cock had opened it halfway, would be snapped all the way open. The gun was now primed and the cock safely on half-cock so that it could be carried about without the danger of accidental discharge. To fire it, nothing remained but to cock it to *full-cock* and pull the trigger. Under the force of the mainspring the cock snapped forward, the flint struck the upright battery, its impact knocked the flashpan cover open about halfway and the feather-spring flipped it open the rest of the way, the priming was instantly bared to the plentiful shower of hot sparks, the priming ignited, the flash flashed, etc., etc. But at times a worn or defective gunlock *did* snap out of half cock while being carried about, an always unexpected and usually disastrous occurrence commemorated in the saying "to go off half-cocked." The diagram in Fig. 158 will explain its workings in detail.

The miquelet's origins are now obscure. Isidor Solèr wrote flatly in 1795 that it had been invented in Madrid by the son of Simon Markhardt (cf. p. 53), Simon, Jr., in the reign of Philip II (1527–98, reigned 1556–98). This can outrightly be said to be wrong. No one man "invented" this device any more than one man "invented" gunpowder or the matchlock, although Simon, Jr. may have *improved* it in the late sixteenth century.

Fig. 158—Simple diagram of the outside of a typical Spanish miquelet lock (see also Fig. 159). When lock is cocked, as shown, foot B of the cock rests on the rectangular nose I of the primary sear, which protrudes through the lockplate. When trigger is pulled, sear nose recedes inward and cock is snapped forward by the force of mainspring J acting on spur F. The flint A strikes face of battery C, which is an integral part of the L-shaped flashpan cover D; impact knocks pan cover open, shower of sparks is hurled into the flashpan E, priming ignites and shot goes off instantaneously. Feather-spring K and hinge of flashpan cover are drawn in dotted lines because they are behind boxlike protective shield (cf. Fig. 159). When flashpan is closed, feather-spring holds cover pressed down tightly over it; when cover has been knocked open past halfway mark by the striking flint, the feather-spring snaps it all the way open. Below the rectangular primary sear nose protrudes the circular button-like secondary sear nose H. When foot of cock is brought to rest on this, gun is half-cocked; mushroom shape of secondary sear nose prevents it from receding inward while foot of cock rests on it, consequently also locks trigger so that it cannot be pulled. Inner edge of mainspring, i.e., edge against lockplate, has crescent-shaped indentation to allow secondary sear nose to snap out and foot of cock to pass down between spring and lockplate. When gun is fully cocked and trigger is pulled, secondary sear nose recedes inward slightly ahead of rectangular primary sear so that the foot of the snapping cock will not catch on it. The bridle G merely serves to steady cock's pivot or axis screw.

Fig. 159—Spanish miquelet lock, circa 1635. The lock is half-cocked, i.e., the foot of the cock is resting on the round nose of the secondary sear (visible below the mainspring); the inner edge of the mainspring, i.e., the edge against the lockplate, is recessed in a crescent to accommodate the secondary sear and to allow the downward motion of the foot of the cock between the spring and the lockplate. Note the rectangular nose of the primary sear, which will snap out when lock is cocked and foot of cock has risen above it.

From the craggy Pyrenees comes, so to speak, a more mountainous thesis. Throughout the sixteenth century the northern regions of Aragon and Catalonia had been kept in a lively state of tumult by a fraternity of assassins who were called, or who called themselves, *los Miqueletes* or *Miguletes,* "the Little Michaels" (one form being the diminutive of Spanish *Miquel,* Michael, the other of Catalan *Miguel*). These, like their less sanguinary colleagues in iniquity, the Schnapphanses in the faraway Province of the Netherlands, found matchlocks unsuited to the exercise of their profession but could neither afford nor steal enough wheellocks to equip themselves decently. As in the case of the snaphaunce lock, legend has it that the miquelet lock was born when some very clever Little Michael designed it as a boon for his companions, who put it to use with such success at once that it was soon rumored about among the frightened citizenry as "the new gunlock of the miqueletes."

This fanciful tale is a myth. The term *miquelet lock* was unknown before the early nineteenth century; writers and inventories before circa 1810, in Spanish as well as in other languages, refer to it merely as "the Spanish lock," "the snap lock" or by the catch-all "fire-lock" (which was also used for a wheellock, snaphaunce and flintlock). There is no evidence to show that the *miqueletes* (who really did exist) had anything whatever to do with either the invention or the adoption of the mechanism.

In 1689 Louis XIV hired some three thousand nominally French *miqueletes* on the French side of the mountains as a mercenary army, who probably were armed with miquelet-lock guns; but by then the miquelet was the standard lock used on virtually every gun made in Spain and it was in considerable use in the districts on the French side of the border; nothing, therefore, would have been in any way peculiar about such equipment to lead to its identification by the name of these troops.

Similarly, the British armies in Spain during the War of the Spanish Succession (1701–13) found nothing but miquelet locks among all of the Spanish forces, so that again the arms of the *miqueletes* would have attracted no particular attention.

Not until the year 1808 do we strike etymological pay dirt. In that year the British under Wellington embarked on the Peninsular Campaigns to drive Napoleon out of Spain. Long since reduced to relatively honest living, the *miqueletes* were by then nothing more than a body of lightly armed soldiers used chiefly for escort duty. Although the miquelet lock was still *the* ignition system for almost all Spanish pistols and private sporting weapons, the military muskets of most Spanish regiments were now flintlocks after the French, Prussian and British patterns. Only the *miqueletes* were issued *fusils,* or lightweight muskets, with miquelet locks instead of true flintlocks. There and then the identification was made by the French and British who in 1805–13, some 230 years after the lock's invention, originated the name by which it has been known ever since but never had been before. Barring only a possible but unlikely traveling Frenchman or Englishman who may have affixed the tag as early as 1795 or even 1790, this is how the name originated. Both the Catalan and Spanish spellings survive, respectively *migulet* and *miquelet,* but the latter is by far more frequent. Both the anglicized pronunciation *mee'-k^{wu}-let* and the gallicized *mee'-k^{eh}-lay* are in use.

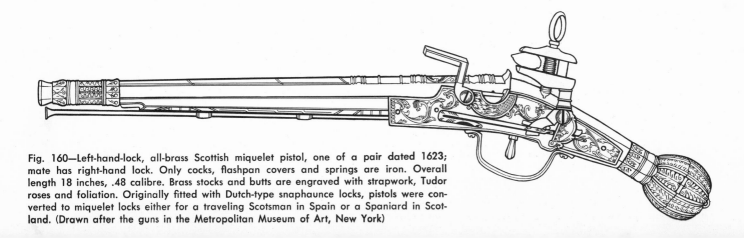

Fig. 160—Left-hand-lock, all-brass Scottish miquelet pistol, one of a pair dated 1623; mate has right-hand lock. Only cocks, flashpan covers and springs are iron. Overall length 18 inches, .48 calibre. Brass stocks and butts are engraved with strapwork, Tudor roses and foliation. Originally fitted with Dutch-type snaphaunce locks, pistols were converted to miquelet locks either for a traveling Scotsman in Spain or a Spaniard in Scotland. (Drawn after the guns in the Metropolitan Museum of Art, New York)

Fig. 161—Characteristic shape of the so-called *Ripoll pistols*, named after Ripoll, Catalonia, Spain's most active gunmaking center next to Madrid and Barcelona. Many pistols of this genre had completely brass- or silver-sheathed stocks, often chiseled in large, bold, involuted scrollwork patterns; they were most popular between about 1650 and 1725, but the traditional shape did not die out entirely until some 75 years ago. Lengths ran from 9 to 14 inches, calibres from .50 to .65. Although clumsy-looking, Ripoll pistols have surprisingly well-balanced and comfortable "feel" in the shooter's hand.

But there is no doubt whatever that the miquelet lock is Spanish in origin, having appeared first in about 1560, perhaps even a little earlier. It remained the hallmark of Spanish guns throughout the seventeenth, eighteenth and early nineteenth centuries, even long after the rest of the world had turned to flintlocks first of the French and Italian, then of the British styles. By 1620 it had emerged substantially as it was to remain for all its long life.

The very longevity of the miquelet lock—some 250 years—may be taken as testimony to its excellence: a poor device would have yielded to better sometime in the course of two and a half centuries. When better *did* come along in the form of the late eighteenth- and early nineteenth-century English flintlocks, the Spanish nevertheless continued to cling to their (by then also greatly refined) miquelet locks, owing partly to stubborn tradition and partly to the fact that no one in the world, not even the master craftsmen of Madrid, Ripoll and Barcelona could make guns like Knox, Bond, Egg, Manton, Tate *et al.* of London.

The miquelet's advantages over the snaphaunce will become obvious on a moment's thought: the simple efficiency of the L-shaped battery-and-flashpan-cover combination was not only much sturdier than the long, easily loosened snaphaunce battery arm, but it eliminated the costly and not 100 per cent reliable sliding, automatically opening flashpan cover. The powerful, short, choppy, nearly vertical scrape which the flint delivered against the battery ensured a fountain of sparks hurled directly into the flashpan. It was easily possible to get as many as 150 successive fires out of a good miquelet lock without a single miss, provided one observed the elementary rules of using high-quality, knife-sharp flints and fine priming powder, and pricking the touchhole every fourth or fifth shot. No other snaplock could equal a well-made

miquelet for reliability until the advent of the British flintlock masterpieces of 1760-1825. The large ring atop the jaw screw—an almost invariable feature of miquelet locks—made for easier changing and tightening of the flint than in snaphaunces and flintlocks, whose slotted screws required the use of a screwdriver. The external mainspring, although vulnerable to damage, saved recessing even more deeply the stock in what was already its weakest place.

Essentially only one major variation of the miquelet developed in its 250 years of life. The type until now discussed was strictly native Spanish, and is hence known to collectors, shrewdly enough, as the *Spanish miquelet lock*. In about 1625 there appeared somewhere in Italy a variant type distinguished from the Spanish in that the mainspring, instead of pushing upward on a spur at the rear of the cock's base, pulled downward on a spur on its front, where in the Spanish lock there was the quadrant-like foot. The sear noses of these *Southern Italian miquelet locks* projected through the lockplate behind, not in front of the cock, engaging a spur or notch on the cock's heel where in the Spanish lock the mainspring spur was located (Figs. 165 to 166a). Why this variant is known as a "southern" Italian lock in Anglo-American collecting jargon is not really clear to anyone. There is as little foundation in fact for this geographic qualification as there is for the "Kentucky" in Kentucky rifles (of which more in due time). Indeed, in Bourbon, i.e., southern Italy, the Spanish-type miquelet lock was by far the most common; while the "southern" lock was made most generally in Rome, Tuscany, Lombardy and the Veneto (that is, in the center and north). But by now the term seems permanently established in English-language collectordom. Italian collectors chuckle at it.

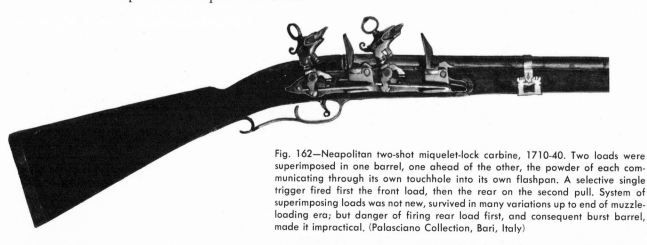

Fig. 162—Neapolitan two-shot miquelet-lock carbine, 1710-40. Two loads were superimposed in one barrel, one ahead of the other, the powder of each communicating through its own touchhole into its own flashpan. A selective single trigger fired first the front load, then the rear on the second pull. System of superimposing loads was not new, survived in many variations up to end of muzzle-loading era; but danger of firing rear load first, and consequent burst barrel, made it impractical. (Palasciano Collection, Bari, Italy)

Fig. 163—Small Italian (Brescian) miquelet pistol lock, pierced and chiseled iron, circa 1620; shown in actual size (3¼ inches long).

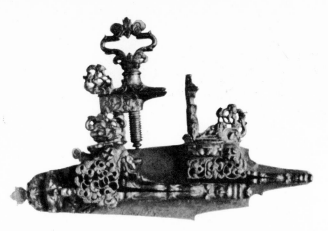

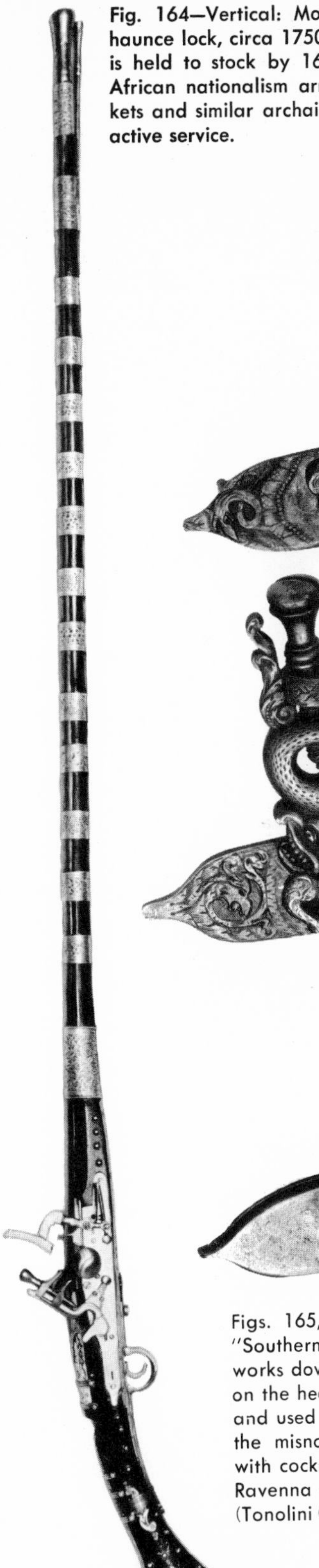

Fig. 164—Vertical: Moorish fishtail "musket" with large Dutch-type snaphaunce lock, circa 1750-1800. Overall length 63½ inches, .59 calibre. Barrel is held to stock by 16 silver filigree bands. In an age of surging North African nationalism armed with jet aircraft and heavy tanks, fishtail muskets and similar archaic weapons are nonetheless still very much in deadly, active service.

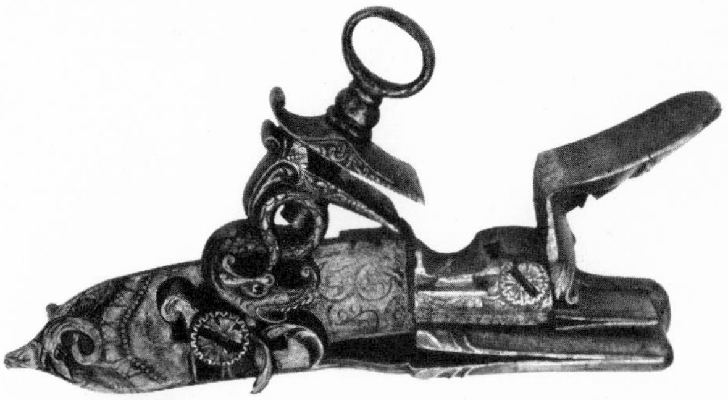

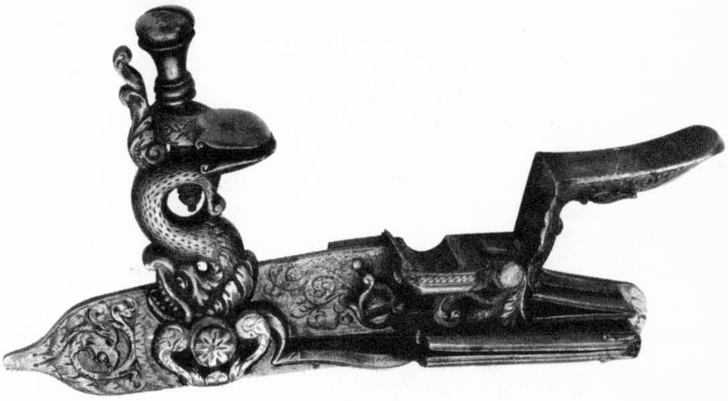

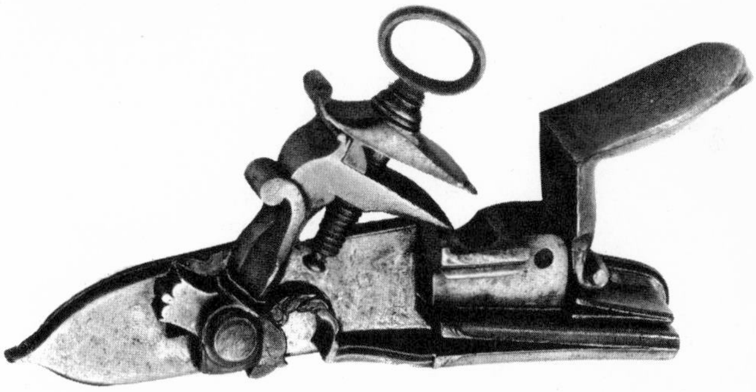

Figs. 165, 166 & 166a—Three specimens of the so-called "Southern Italian" miquelet lock in which the mainspring works downward on the toe of the cock rather than upward on the heel. "Southern Italian" miquelets were in fact made and used mainly from Rome on up to Venice and Milan, but the misnomer persists. Two ornate examples shown here, with cocks in form of sea monsters, may have been made in Ravenna around 1650; simple one is Umbrian, about 1800. (Tonolini Collection, Brescia)

Both the snaphaunce and the miquelet lock found wide use in many parts of the world in the seventeenth century. The bailiwicks of the Dutch-type snaphaunces were mainly the Netherlands, Flanders, Scotland, parts of Denmark and Sweden, and nearly all of North Africa and the Near East, including virtually the whole vast Ottoman Empire, save for Persia and Arabia. The highly sophisticated Italian snaphaunce was popular, but not exclusively so, in Italy as well as among the rich of almost every nation as an exceptional item of cost and quality, its value lying mainly in further distinguishing its owner by conspicuous consumption. Whoever spoke Spanish and could muster the money for gentlemanly sport shot Spanish miquelets; so did Persians and Arabs. Needless to say, there were broad areas of overlap. The Germans seem to have considered both snaphaunces and miquelets an affront to the German genius for employing a complicated means when a simple one was at hand, and nothing was to pry German trigger fingers away from the *Gemütlichkeit* of wheellock hunting until the beginning and even the middle of the eighteenth century. Equally characteristically, the German wheellocks for the most part continued to be made with traditional and distinctive pride and conscientiousness. The French gunsmiths in 1580–1620 were busy refining existing types of guns both mechanically and aesthetically; their great contribution to firearms was just in the offing in 1620.

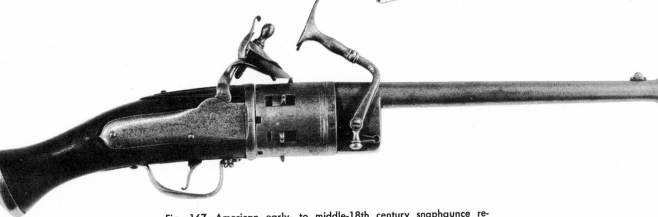

Fig. 167—American early- to middle-18th century snaphaunce revolver, marked J. PIM of BOSTONNE *fecit;* well-executed piece is probably unique among American firearms made before the War of Independence. (In the collection of the Winchester Repeating Arms Company)

But the English, the only people to have achieved a stable, enlightened, prosperous society (compared to any other of the age), whose law-abiding, orderly lives provided endless opportunities for the exercise of sports which were cherished by all classes from king to freeholder, had in 1620 not yet learned to make any guns worth mentioning save clumsy matchlock calivers and muskets and assorted cannons. Paradoxically, this owed to the very nature of the British way of life. After Bosworth Field in 1485, England enjoyed a peace and an absence of mercenary troops or even standing armies utterly unknown on the Continent. Wars were fought (mainly overseas) by the king's own militia of Englishmen trained in small groups in their home counties, not by hired foreign cutthroats who lived off and terrorized the land, and consequently there was neither the demand nor the dissemination of firearms which attended the mercenary system. Wild predators—wolves, bears, boars—so deadly and plentiful on the Continent, had been all but exterminated before Elizabeth I's reign (1558-1603) was half over; such deer as remained were reserved quarry for the monarch and great lords, while in the vast Continental mountains and forests they and much other big game thrived in abundance. Until about 1650, bird and rabbit shooting was considered an idle pastime, not yet (but very soon to be) a serious sport for gentlemen. Though the king's highways were perilous, they were havens of security compared to those, say, of the German states. One body of law, statutory and judge-made, enforced by one homogeneous and on the whole efficient structure of the king's sheriff's, bailiffs, beadles, justices of the peace, courts, jails, nooses and axes, obtained in Cornwall no less than in Northumberland and Kent.

Already in Henry VIII's time there was a large middle class, newly risen and growing by leaps in the succeeding generations, without parallel in numbers and social and political power on the Continent. These *nouveaux riches,* then and there as always and everywhere, wore imported goods as badges of social rank, no matter how the item might measure up to the domestic product. Even a nearly bankrupt young baronet or a lawyer with a modest income (£100-a-year-plus) went shooting (if he ever did so at all) with the finest German, French, Italian or Spanish gun he could buy, beg or borrow, not because one shot better than the other but because it was almost exactly like the one with which the Duke of Gloucester had been seen at Windsor on Wednesday last. These conventions prevailing through Tudor and early Stuart times among most of those enfranchised by law to shoot, no native gunmaking industry was given a chance to bloom until the British middle class had found the same measure of self-reliance in its own fashions and foibles that marked its unshakable faith in the rightness of "our king and our laws and our ships on the ocean, the Protestant Cause and old London's commotion." How they did, and wrought the climax of firearms history, will proceed from the sections of this account which are to follow.

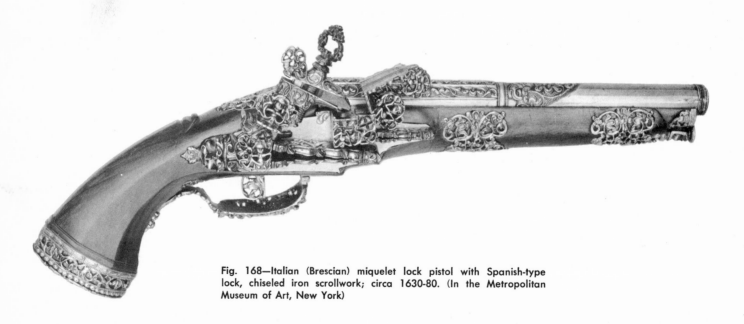

Fig. 168—Italian (Brescian) miquelet lock pistol with Spanish-type lock, chiseled iron scrollwork; circa 1630-80. (In the Metropolitan Museum of Art, New York)

CHAPTER SIX

The first flintlocks: Jacobean locks—Fowling a lowly trade—Gentlemen shoot for occasional practice, not sport—Gervase Markham—Mechanical problems—A rebellion of fowlers under one Oliver Cromwell—The TABLE OF GUN MAKERS' RATES, 1631—The true flintlock appears in France in about 1630—The Thirty Years' War and the Civil Wars—Royalist and Parliamentarian arms procurement problems—Sporting instinct vs. military discipline—A repeating breech-loading magazine rifle—An ingenious revolver—The Restoration and the import of new sporting fashions—Three new weapons emerge.

OTH THE L-SHAPED FLASHPAN-cover-and-battery combination of the miquelet lock and the wholly interior snapping mechanism of the snaphaunce were by themselves mechanical ingenuities of the first order. They are to be ranked with those monumental simplifications which succeeding ages think of, when they think of them at all, as self-evident commonplaces which required no invention but have simply always been; the swinging axle tree, the coilspring, the equestrian chest harness, the door hinge and many others are all in their company. But both suffered from the failings of the complete gunlocks of which they were parts: the snaphaunce from the fragility of its spiny battery arm, the miquelet from the fragility of its exterior mainspring and slender-stemmed cock. What was required next was a combination of the best features of each: a gunlock with the durable innards of the snaphaunce and the efficient L-shaped flashpan cover of the miquelet. Not, of course, that either of these features had yet come to have any more than a scant approximation of the potential efficiency which craftsmanship and experience were eventually to give them—but they had already proved themselves so serviceable on their respective mechanisms that their merger into one was inevitable.

But just where and when this inevitability was first consumated remains an unanswerable question. Public and private collections throughout Europe contain primitive gunlocks of about 1540-1600 in a bewildering variety of shapes and functions which do essentially combine the best of the snaphaunce with the best of the miquelet to become ancestors, more or less distant, of true flintlocks. Yet the difficulty—in many cases the impossibility—of placing these geographically, or of dating them any closer than plus-or minus twenty years (often enough plus-or-minus fifty), reduces most of the traditional histories on this subject to so much stardust in the love for one's own dearest theory.

Curiously enough, however, even if many archetypal quasi- and pseudo-flintlocks sprouted up between Moscow and Lisbon, between Oslo and Brindisi, throughout the second half of the seventeenth century, there does seem to be plausible reason to believe that English gunsmiths were the first systematically to exploit a clumsy but work-

able and fairly uniform, native version of these on a large commercial scale. If it would be absurd to suppose that proto-flintlocks were "first used" in Britain, it does appear fair to say that sometime between 1600 and 1620 the so-called *English lock* or *Jacobean flintlock* found wider acceptance there than any similar device elsewhere, probably spreading outward from London. Certainly by 1630 a large number of arms (muskets, fowling pieces, pistols) with these locks seem to have found their way throughout the Isles. When Scotsmen marched to the border in 1638 to resist the policies of Charles I, and their boots beat the first distant thunder of the Civil Wars, they—that is, *even They*, from the farthest wilds of semi-barbarism—carried (in addition to the vastly greater numbers of matchlock muskets and calivers) military long arms and very likely even pistols fitted with the new fire-striker.

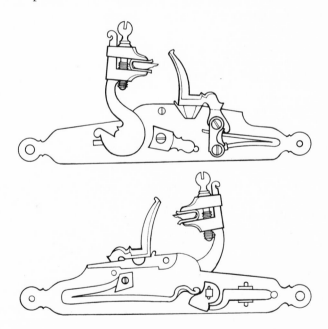

Fig. 169—Outside and inside views of so-called "Jacobean" or "English" flintlock, early 17th century. Flashpan cover and battery are one integral L-shaped unit. Cock is held at half-cock when sear engages tumbler as shown in inside view. A nose also protrudes from sear outward through the lockplate and holds cock fully cocked by snapping out over top of tail (cf. Figs. 149 and 150). Buffer affixed to outside of lockplate arrests fall of cock. Jacobean flintlocks, the earliest of all flintlocks, were potentially tremendous improvements over snaphaunce and miquelet locks because of L-shaped flashpan cover, but were usually poorly made, clumsy and unreliable.

But the new system made a much noisier splash in the pond of civil use than in the stormy seas of war. In 1610 and after, the £100-per-year qualification of the 33 Hen.VIII.c.6. was still enforced with vigor, and it remained a legal club to be wielded by any more fortunate subject when whim or spite set his wrath against an offending pauper. Jeremy Bentham (1748–1832) summed up the legal situation acidly after 250 years of it in 1792 in TRUTH VS. ASHHURST; OR, LAW AS IT IS, CONTRASTED WITH WHAT IT IS SAID TO BE:

> I sow corn [wheat]; partridges eat it, and if I attempt to defend myself against partridges, I am fined or sent to jail; all for fear that a great man, who is above sowing corn, should be in want of partridges.

Englishmen of all those rural classes whose lands, whether free-held or rented, did not yield adequate support for their families (which is to say 50 per cent of rural England) went shooting in the face of all risks to augment the food supply, although shooting in turn still only augmented the ancient ways of catching birds in, on and with nets, snares, lime rods, intoxicating baits, etc. But the fowling piece gained rapidly in popularity and usefulness in Jacobean and Caroline times. Not that guns could be considered as having been a panacea for rural poverty, but undeniably fowling pieces in the hands of poor country folk early proved that they could not only provide rich nutriments, but in so doing also free a greater portion of the land produce for sale in town.

From the prolific pen of Gervase Markham (1568?–1637), who undertook to write bustling, windy handbooks and manuals on all the household activities known to man and woman, flowed in 1621 a long dissertation on fowling entitled HUNGER'S PREVENTION, OR, THE WHOLE ARTE OF FOWLING BY WATER AND LAND. Hardly anything could serve better than the stark realism of this title to illustrate that birding in Jacobean England was still largely a vulgar trade, unthinkable to the upper classes as anything but an occasional pastime of target practice, assuredly not as a sport to which gentlemen might earnestly devote their precious leisure. Markham's attention to firearms is scant. His advice that "the best Fowling Pieces are five Foot and a half or six Foot long, with an indifferent Bore under Harquebus," may be read along with more illuminating divulgences in Fig. 170. "An indifferent Bore under Harquebus" was really an utterly meaningless specification; if an [h]arquebus was some civil or military weapon of specific calibre to Gervase Markham, such knowledge was highly individual and is wholly lost to us. Probably the guns Markham had in mind were such as Fig. 171, their bores varying from No. 20, or .63 calibre, to No. 9, or .80 calibre, depending on the use for which they were intended, e.g., woodcock and other small-bird shooting, cluster shooting, duck shooting or shooting flying. The fact that this last-mentioned art was so difficult as to be virtually impossible with the clumsy pieces of the time contributed heavily to sporting gentlemen's disdain of fowling: for the only effectual shots were those in which the shooter crept up on the roosting beast until its startled eye was scarcely farther from the muzzle than the shooter's from the breech. Alternative methods called for as large a gun as possible, loaded with as much powder and shot as dictated solely by the limits of the barrel's endurance, discharged from the closest range approachable into the largest flocks accessible.

Of the Stalking Horse and Fowling piece.

THE best Fowling Pieces are five Foot and half or six Foot long, with an indifferent Bore under Harquebuss, pound your best sort of Powder, and let your Shot be well siz'd, and not too big; for then it scatters too much: And if too small it has not weight nor strength sufficient to do execution on a large Fowl. In Shooting observe always to Shoto with the Wind if possible, and rather behind the Fowl or side-ways, than full in their Faces ; and observe you

shelter your self behind a Hedge, Bank, Tree, or any thing else that may keep you from the sight of the Fowl; and be sure to have your Dog at your Heels, and at good Command, not to stir after you have Shot, till you bid him ; but sometimes the Fowls are so shy, there's no getting a-near them, without a Stalking Horse, which must be some old Jade train'd up for that purpose, who will gently and as you will, walk along with you, but for want of such a live Horse you may cut out the resemblance of one in Canvas, or Match Paper, pasted together a sufficient bredth and length, with Ears, Legs and Tail, and all the Parts proportionable, which you must Paint to the lively Colour of a Horse, and something like Grass at his Nose, and his Head being stooping as Grazing, and you may do this either stuft or flat, but the latter is more easie to carry ; there are other things that are used for shelter in this case, as in woody Places, a Bush in Marshes and Rivers, Bents or Rushes, or such things as grow there: But these being unusual to Motion, you must move them very slowly, or else the Birds will take flight and be gone.

To take Birds or Rabits.

TAke seed of Letice, Popy, Henbane and Hemlock, or some of them will do, boil them in Dregs of Wine, and then boil some Wheat in it, and strow where they come and it will make them drunk, for Rabits use Oates.

Fig. 170—Advice on hunting in Gervase Markham's *Hunger's Prevention, or the Whole Arte of Fowling by Water and Land*, London, 1621.

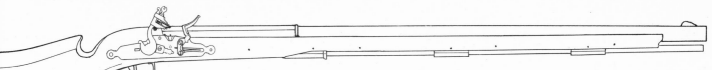

Fig. 171—Typical leviathan Jacobean-lock fowling piece, circa 1620-1660, "five Foot and a half or six Foot long, with an indifferent Bore under Harquebus"—i.e., somewhere between .63 and .80 calibre.

Fig. 172—Snaphaunce trap guns for bird shooting. Weapons are set in ground by spearlike prongs, aimed at tied-down bait, and concealed by a cover of leaves and branches. Shooter stands good distance away, pulls trigger with long string. Engraving by Giuseppe Maria Mitelli (1634-1718) is one of a series on birding used in many late 17th- to late 18th-century hunting books (cf. Fig. 261). One such German publication of 1797 advises the shooter to lead the string into his nice warm kitchen, sit by the window with a pot of coffee, and "go hunting in *Gemütlichkeit*."

Fortunately for a good many birds, the ignition of Jacobean locks was slow, a very perceptible lapse of time passing between trigger pull and the shot arriving at the spot where the flying quarry had just been. This delay was owing to two simple circumstances: first, the locks were poorly designed and usually badly made; secondly, the English makers of Jacobean locks, unlike their Spanish miquelet-making brethren, had not yet mastered the delicate balance of the force of the mainspring (which drove the cock) against that of the feather-spring, nor the fine points of adjustment of leverages which rendered miquelet locks and the later true flintlocks so excellent. Thus, when the flint struck the battery of a Jacobean lock, it met too little or too great resistance, the flashpan cover snapped open too lightly or too stiffly and not quite fast enough for instantaneous or nearly instantaneous fire, and the shooter had to allow for the resulting time lapse by aiming well ahead of the flying bird. And the ignition was

so vexingly capricious, firing now fast, now slowly (the difference being measured in fractions of a second), that with none but the best-made locks could one ever arrive at a satisfactory working distance by which to "lead" the bird; not infrequently, too-furiously or too-gently snapping cocks would produce no ignition at all. Indeed, the importance of the balance of these spring forces was a constant care throughout the flintlock era. Thomas Johnson's explanation in THE SHOOTER'S GUIDE is entirely applicable to the locks of the period under discussion, although he wrote and published this extremely readable and informative little work in London in 1816, about two centuries later, at the geographical and chronological zenith of the true flintlock in its ultimate state of perfection (when reading this, or any of the other seventeenth- and eighteenth-century writers to be encountered hereafter, one must constantly remember that the term *hammer* did *not* mean the cock, as it does in modern usage, but always and exclusively *the flashpan cover and the battery*):

It is of the utmost consequence to the excellence of a lock that the springs be proportioned to each other: if, for instance, the main-spring be very strong and the hammer-spring weak, the cock will be liable to be broken for want of sufficient resistance to its stroke; on the other hand, if the hammer-spring be stiff and the main-spring weak, the cock has not sufficient force to drive back the hammer; and, in both cases, the collision between the flint and the steel is too slight to produce the necessary fire. The face of the hammer also may be too hard or too soft: if too hard, the flint will make scarcely any impression upon it, and the sparks will be few and small; if too soft, the flint will cut into the hammer at every stroke, whilst the sparks will also be few in number, and of a dull-red colour. When the strength of the springs, and the temper of the hammer, are in their due degree, the sparks will be numerous, brilliant, and accompanied with a whizzing sound.

To explain these differences, it will be necessary to observe, that the sparks produced by the collision of flint and steel are particles of the metal driven off in a strongly-heated state, and which, falling among the powder, kindle it instantly. By snapping a gun or pistol over a sheet of white paper, we may collect these sparks; and, by submitting them to a microscope, demonstrate the truth of this assertion. If the sparks are brilliant, and accompanied with a whizzing sound, we shall find the particles collected on the paper to be little globules of steel; which were not only melted, but have actually undergone a considerable degree of vitrification from the intensity of the heat excited by the collision. When the face of the hammer is too hard, the particles which the flint strikes off are so small, that they are cooled before they fall into the pan; and when the hammer is too soft, the particles driven off are so large as not to be sufficiently heated to kindle the powder.

For my own part, I prefer a lock, the springs of which are rather strong than otherwise, on account of its being less liable to *miss fire*. It is true, it will wear the flints much faster; but the expense of these is too trifling to merit consideration.

In the Eastern Counties—Lincolnshire, Norfolk, Cambridgeshire, Huntingdonshire and part of Northamptonshire—wildfowling was practiced with joyous, even professional abandon in the early seventeenth century owing to peculiarly favorable natural causes. Vast areas of land in these regions were good grazing ground in the summer and fall, but turned to boggy fens and marshlands in winter and spring. Then the countryside became host to endless clouds of wildfowl in search of more clement homes than their native Scandinavia and Scotland. Since the days of King Harold's archers, the local inhabitants as well as outsider hunters had plucked their bounties of feathered fruit from the heavy boughs of this Britannic Eden. In time the privilege had come to be regarded as an inalienable right, which, although nowhere written down or even explicitly stated, was deeply rooted. Then catastrophe struck in 1634: King Charles I granted a royal charter to the 4th Earl of Bedford for the drainage and reclamation of the marshlands. The first canals constructed near Ely were destroyed by irate fowlers. Compensation was demanded of the Crown according to the traditions of the right of eminent domain, but leadership was urgently required to channel the outraged emotions into seeking recourse in the courts and in political action.

In Ely dwelt a gentleman farmer named Oliver Cromwell, moderately prosperous, of medium stature and reddish complexion, deeply devout and stern but not yet excessively intolerant. Already he had given proof of his eloquence and the forcefulness of his personality when six years earlier, in 1628, he had been elected to Parliament and had been so outspoken in his denunciation of "popery" that the ill-starred Charles had dismissed him. Now, in the crisis of the fowlers' rights, it was inevitable that he should assume the reins. His organizing led to wide enlistment of popular sympathy, and although it proved futile for the moment, it heralded his rapidly growing fame as a leader and a champion of the people's rights. The Earl of Bedford and the courtiers generally dubbed him derisively "Lord of the Fens." He remained on his farm until again sent to Parliament for Cambridge in 1640, after which his tryst with history was held on a greater stage.

Soon Cromwell's attention was to be diverted from fowling pieces to the procurement of military small arms. In the time immediately before the Civil Wars, these were still predominantly matchlock calivers and muskets, although the term *caliver* began to grow less frequent after the first quarter of the century and *musket* was ever more commonly applied to caliver-sized weapons and to a whole panoply of lesser guns which Sir Roger Williams would have lumped together as "smaller shoots." The standard service matchlock musket had come to be fitted with a new-style, well-proportioned lock and stock more than less in the form of a modern gunstock. Its bore was standardized at No. 10, or .786 calibre, but it was loaded with the regulation 12-bore ball, or .747 calibre, the missile being thus about 1/24 inch smaller than the diameter of the bore. This facilitated loading, but the stormy windage of gasses which escaped around the ball upon firing enormously reduced the compression, and therefore the velocity and energy of the bullet. Moreover, the ball "chattered" in its course down the barrel, i.e., it ricocheted up and down, left and right, from one side of the bore to the other, finally leaving the muzzle at whatever angle the last bounce might prompt (Fig. 173). Even if such a final deflection was slight, being measured in seconds rather than minutes or degrees of angle, it was sufficient to make the standard regulation service shot fired with standard regulation service ammunition fly whimsically wild of a man-sized target at any range beyond 50 yards, although such a gun loaded with a *tightly* fitting ball could perform surprisingly well above 120.

Fig. 173—Simple diagram of an undersized ball "chattering" along the inside of a smoothbore barrel when fired. Ball bounced erratically left, right, up and down in hundreds of stuttering ricochets (here simplified to eight), finally left muzzle at any unpredictable angle. Simultaneously a great part of the pressure of the expanding gases generated by the burning powder was lost as "blow-by" by escaping through space between ball and barrel. The resulting inaccuracy could be very largely obviated by wrapping ball in thin patch of leather or cloth before loading, but this required more time and was therefore not used for loading military muskets in battle when rapidity of fire in unaimed volleys, not accuracy, was the determining factor.

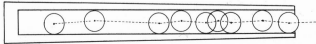

In France, meanwhile, that remarkable device which has been alluded to on several occasions in this chronicle was born: the true *flintlock*. It will hardly be necessary to expound again the obscurity attending the nativity of such inventions. If any one man first constructed it, his name has gone gurgling down the drain of mortality. Customarily the date 1630 is accepted as approximating the time when the first true flintlocks were seen in the vicinity of Paris, although no arms historians would insist that it could not have been 1625 or 1635.

The true flintlock differed from the miquelet lock and the snaphaunce in that it employed a wholly interior mechanism and a one-piece L-shaped flashpan cover and battery, just as did the Jacobean flintlock. Beyond this, its distinctive features were those of refinement. The cock was arrested at the terminus of its fall by a shoulder on its inner side which struck against the top edge of the lockplate, as has already been seen in the case of the Italian snaphaunce (Fig. 151, Diag. II), instead of being stopped by a buffer like those on Dutch-type snaphaunces or Jacobean locks. The cock itself was fashioned in the gooseneck shape in which it was to survive for two centuries, being later only made more elegant in the sweep of its proportions. The sear, rather than protruding

through the lockplate to catch the rear of the cock, now was pivoted vertically on a horizontal screw and engaged successively two notches in the tumbler inside the lock (Fig. 174, inside view). The first was the half-cock notch, or in the jargon of the flintlock age, the *half-bent*; it was cut so deep that once the nose of the sear had snapped into it, pressure on the trigger could not release it. The second notch held the cock at full-cock, the nose of the sear there being easily forced out by the trigger. The flashpan cover and battery (or, as already noted, the *hammer* in the language of 1600–1840) was pivoted on its hinge so that it served more readily the proper balance between yielding to the flint too easily and too stiffly.

Between circa 1610 and 1650 there were many locks which incorporated features both of the older English archetype (e.g., a protruding sear, a buffer) and the new French design. Some had horizontally acting sears which, however, did not protrude through the plate but engaged the tumbler more or less as shown in Fig. 175; others varied in shapes and proportions. It is not possible to show here *all* the variants of gunlocks of the snapping-flint variety which cropped up locally here and there before the general features of the true flintlock had been all but universally accepted by the middle of the century.

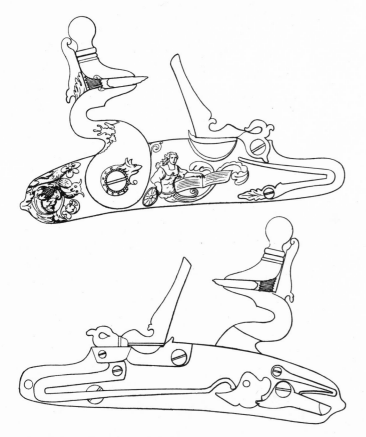

Fig. 174—Outside and inside views of a true flintlock in its earliest form, second and third quarters of the 17th century. Besides obvious differences in shape and proportions, true flintlock differed from Jacobean flintlock (Fig. 169) in having a wholly internal mechanism. The sear pivots on a horizontal screw like the sear of an Italian snaphaunce (Fig. 151), but, unlike Italian snaphaunce, engages successively two notches in the tumbler. First notch, called the *half-bent* in the flintlock era, held cock at half-cock (as shown in inside view), was cut so deep that nose of sear could not be pulled out by accidental pressure on the trigger. Second notch held cock fully cocked, released it when trigger was pulled and its internal section pushed up on rear arm of sear. See Figs. 242 & 243 for details.

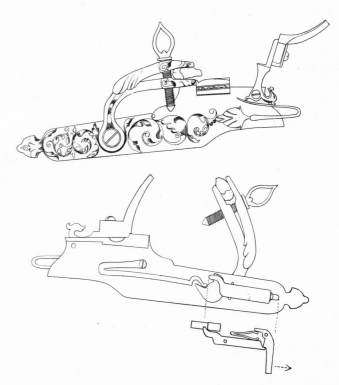

Fig. 175—Outside and inside view of a so-called "Baltic" flintlock, made in small quantities in the German Baltic provinces in second and third quarters of the 17th century. Not only was shape of lockplate adapted from wheellocks, but internal mechanism, as shown in inside view and top view insert below it, employed primary and secondary sears which engaged each other exactly as did the sears of wheellocks (Fig. 99). Guns with such locks tended to drift eastward into Poland and Russia as true, Western-style flintlocks replaced them between circa 1650 and 1675; now extremely rare in antique shops or collections west of the Oder River, many splendid examples survive in Russian and East European museums.

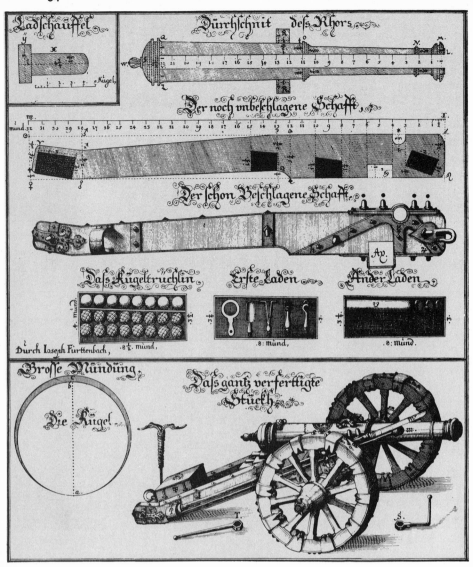

Fig. 176—Engraved plate from Joseph Furtenbach, *Mannhaffter Kunst-Spiegel (Mirror of the Manly Arts)*, Augsburg, 1663, showing construction of mid-17th-century 12-pounder cannon (cf. Fig. 229). First of the three rectangular containers in bottom row of upper section of plate is a cross-section of a cylindrical (actually truncated conical) cannon ball trough containing eight solid balls and sixteen explosive fragmentation grenades. Other two rectangles are removable drawers or compartments which fit into iron-lined chest shown at end of cannon carriage in lower section (note double-headed linstock standing behind it). First drawer contains various cleaning and loading implements, second one powder measures. Beneath cannon in lower section lie two giant wrenches for tightening up nuts and bolts loosened by four or five rounds of fire. Loading scoop and rammer are held in clamps along nearer side of carriage. Circular insert shows relationship of ball diameter to bore.

The new French flint device, if well-executed, proved much more reliable and faster-firing than any gunlock known, save of course the best-made wheellocks, which, as has been noted (p. 72), grew constantly better—and constantly more prohibitively priced. At the time of the flintlock's invention, mankind had again contrived to maneuver itself into two catastrophes: one, the outbreak of the Civil Wars in England in 1642; the other, the Thirty Years' War of 1618–48 in Germany, and the consequent paralysis of European civilization. One might think that no time would have proved more advantageous to the adoption of a new firearm than one in which war raged through the Holy Roman Empire and the nation whose global might was in ascent. But not so. Military matchlocks had prevailed by the hundreds of thousands at the outbreak of the Thirty Years' War. Once Germany was aflame and the resources of the Empire had been mobilized, there was no time for experimentation, and when by 1625 the customary establishments of communal life had began to dissolve in the acid of blood and hunger, there were few gunsmiths to replace even the worn-out old matchlocks. By the end of the fifteenth or seventeenth year of the war—1633 or 1635—such craftsmen as continued to serve the demands of either side were barely given time to repair decrepit old weapons before these were shunted back into active service. In Eng-

land in 1642–49 the situation was not nearly so desperate, the war not a fraction so frightful. But then, neither were English gunsmiths nearly so numerous nor more than a fraction so skillful as the German ones, and the procurement of arms was therefore almost as much of a problem to the king and to Cromwell as it was to Wallenstein and to Gustav Adolf. The service muskets, augmented by such private arms as either side could buy, commandeer or plunder, were the weapons of the day, and gunsmiths were kept at their benches repairing whatever pieces had not garnered irreparable glory.

Furthermore, sporting came to an end in Germany in 1620, in England twenty-two years later. The realities of the times left little occasion for the waste of lead on animals. True, in Germany the *Landsknecht* armies which rolled over the land in seemingly endless seesaw plagues plundered, killed and devastated fields, crops, gardens, yards, barns, stables, horses, cattle, poultry, houses and inhabitants, so that by the end of the fifth year, hunting (with such weapons as remained to their owners) had become a matter of survival. But after the twentieth year, when there were neither any weapons nor any game left, the famines and the terror and the brute anguish of hopelessness had reduced humanity to a point where parents ate their children and children picked over the battlefields for unspoiled, edible corpses. In England, where the war for all its savagery was a tempest in a tea-pot compared to such conditions, most able-bodied men were busy lending at least some service to whichever side, Parliamentarian or Royalist, was able to persuade or catch them. At the outbreak of the war the Royalists had a decided advantage: their leaders were the upper-caste aristocrats and the wealthiest landed proprietors, many with military experience, who naturally pressed into service their parkkeepers and gamekeepers (already familiar with guns) and the host of their tenants and dependents. The better arms, too, and most of the arsenals were in Royalist hands, while even before 1642 Cromwell had procured at his own expense the arms for two companies from whatever sources he had been able to obtain them. When war became obviously inevitable in 1642, one of his first acts was to seize the arsenal at Cambridgeshire to prevent the arms and valuables stored there from fall-ing into Royalist hands. The Parliamentarian forces had mostly to be recruited among such motley crews of un-disciplined, untrained and illiterate souls as would rally, or could be forced to rally, to a cause they understood vaguely if at all and which shook the foundations of the order they had learned to accept as the *status imutabilis* for twenty generations and more. The first to follow the "Lord of the Fens" were his grateful friends, the grazers and fowlers of the eastern counties. Out of such as these, Hampden, Fairfax, Ireton and Cromwell built the cele-brated New Model Army, its cavalry at the start largely raw farm youths, its musketry in part disaffected fowlers, its officers mostly dour Puritan squires—but all fused to The Cause in the furnace of fanaticism. Soon irresistible, invincible, they slashed a bloody swath from Marston Moor to Naseby, from Dunbar on to rulership via victory at Worcester.

Fig. 179—Above: Hand grenade with time fuse and rope for hurling. Engraving from Robert Norton, *The Gunner, Shewing the Whole Practice of Artillery*, London, 1628.

Figs. 177 & 178—Two graphic battle scenes in the Thirty Years' War. Matchlock, wheel-lock, dags and muskets are pictured by the artist. Johann Wilhelm Baur, *Don Paolo Giordano*, Rome, 1636.

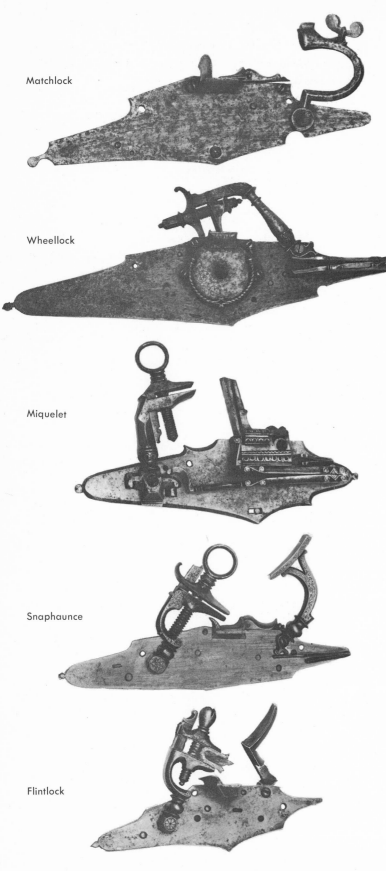

Matchlock

Wheellock

Miquelet

Snaphaunce

Flintlock

Figs. 180a-180e: These five gunlocks exemplify the mystery shrouding the evolution of miquelet-, snaphaunce and flintlocks. All are Brescian (note typical Brescian-form lockplate), but similar lots can be equally well selected from the armaments of any other nationality. All fall into the 70 years between 1550 and 1620 (the matchlock may be earlier). But are they contemporaries, all in use pretty much at the same time as accepted and functional mechanisms, or do they succeed and supersede each other as new developments over the predecessor? There is no way of knowing, no conclusive method of dating. Traditional firearms history would place the small prototypal flintlock (with an internal frizzen spring!) into the early 1600's, the snaphaunce into the 1580's and the miquelet about ten years earlier. But recent studies suggest that the three basic varieties of snapping locks were in use coevally with wheellocks and matchlocks by 1550, or 1570 at the latest. (Tonolini Collection, Brescia)

If, then, sporting and peaceful fowling of the larder-stocking variety ceased in these tumultuous years, there was soon rampant a new fashion of sport which so devastated the wildlife of England that it never fully recovered. Thousands of Englishmen hitherto barred by law or poverty from the execution of living creatures now found themselves armed and free to indulge in this exhilarating pleasure, confined only by the limits of their powder flasks and bullet pouches. To be sure, the service matchlock musket was not an ideal sporting piece, but it bid fair to kill the deer in the parks of Royalist landowners at well upward of a hundred yards if loaded tightly, and the lads of the embattled forces counted themselves among those mortals tempted beyond the limits of endurance. A regulation ball cut into two or three dozen pieces was found to serve tolerably well against perched fowl at twenty to thirty yards. By 1649 (the Civil Wars having come to a head, so to speak, with the execution of the king on January 30) this diversion had been dampened by more stringent disciplinary measures; but with the invasion of Scotland in 1650 it broke out anew. Thus it became necessary to issue standing orders enjoining the soldiers from bolting out of marching order in pursuit of rabbits, "carrying fowling-pieces charg'd, and keeping grey-hounds" when in garrison or bivouac.

Immediately prior to the war, say in 1635–40, a *few* English gunsmiths of considerable account had begun to make pieces of a quality and ingenuity comparable to the products of the Continent. This does not in any way contradict the earlier observation that on the whole the gunmaking art in Britain in the first half of the seventeenth century was predominantly something rather less than brilliant. In these times it was not yet customary for most English gunsmiths to sign their names to their work, which leaves us in the dark about who excelled or failed in what sort of labors. Thomas Addis, J. Barker, Harman Barne, John Dafte, H. Crips, Nathaniel Edens, Thomas Parkins, John Pill, Guy Nevins, John Norcott and John Watson, all of London, as well as Recktor of Broughton, are about the sum of the names which have come down to us as belonging to Caroline times. Most of these were no more than unimaginative makers of service arms and adequate but in no way distinguished private guns and pistols. While there *were* some good native products—indeed, a few very fine ones—those of Harman Barne (worked ca. 1635–65) and John Dafte (worked ca. 1640–85) tower far above all others. Barne was capable of contriving a repeating six-shot breech-loading magazine rifle in which powder, balls and priming were contained in compartments of a hollow butt (cf. Fig. 191). An astounding mechanism opened the breech, loaded powder and ball, closed the breech, primed the pan, closed the flashpan and cocked the cock in one full turn of a lever, which formed the trigger guard, and its return to starting position. But needless to say, the skill required to make such a mechanical jabberwocky was so rare as to be probably unique, consigning all hopes of ever seeing it in practical production to the pit of vain ambitions. From the bench of John Dafte came a clever snaphaunce revolving six-shot cavalry carbine which may very likely date from the years immediately before or during the wars and almost certainly antedates the Restoration in 1660 (Fig. 181). It now reposes in the Wadsworth Atheneum in Hartford, Connecticut, among other effects of its last owner-collector, Samuel Colt, having been brought to the American Colonies perhaps as early as 1680 and probably not after 1740. From the illustration and the description of its mechanism in the caption it will be seen that this revolver, like its wheellock ancestor (Fig. 112) and all its descendant live-spark ignition revolvers, still presented the catastrophic danger of stray sparks firing all chambers at once.

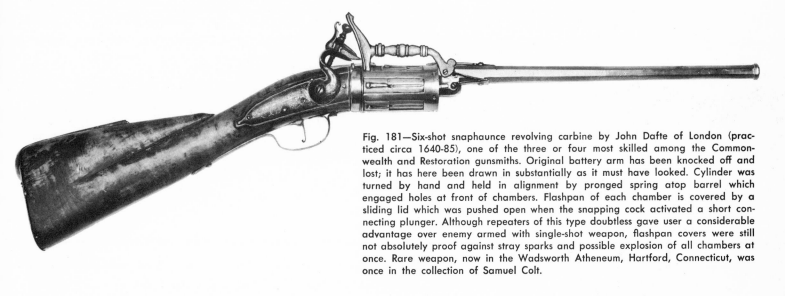

Fig. 181—Six-shot snaphaunce revolving carbine by John Dafte of London (practiced circa 1640-85), one of the three or four most skilled among the Commonwealth and Restoration gunsmiths. Original battery arm has been knocked off and lost; it has here been drawn in substantially as it must have looked. Cylinder was turned by hand and held in alignment by pronged spring atop barrel which engaged holes at front of chambers. Flashpan of each chamber is covered by a sliding lid which was pushed open when the snapping cock activated a short connecting plunger. Although repeaters of this type doubtless gave user a considerable advantage over enemy armed with single-shot weapon, flashpan covers were still not absolutely proof against stray sparks and possible explosion of all chambers at once. Rare weapon, now in the Wadsworth Atheneum, Hartford, Connecticut, was once in the collection of Samuel Colt.

THE GUN MAKERS' RATES

		£ s. d.
[1]	For a new musket with mould, worm, and scouwrer	—/15/ 6
[2]	For a new wolnut-tree stock for a musket, plated at the butt end with iron	—/ 2/ 6
[3]	For a musket stock of beech plated at the butt end with iron	—/ 1/ 8
[4]	For a match-tricker lock compleat	—/ 1/ 0
[5]	For a whole worke consisting of the pan, cover of the pan, the scutchion [flash-fence or fire-shield; cf. Fig. 39], and the screw pynn	
[6]	For a stick [ramrod], worme, sockit, scowrer and bone [the bone tip of the ramrod]	—/ 1/ 0
[7]	For a handle or guard of a tricker	—/—/ 6
[8]	For a new cock fitted	—/—/ 8
[9]	For a new breech [breech-plug]	—/ 1/ 0
[10]	For furnishing a setting of a tricker lock in place of a sceare lock, with a handle, tricker, and tricker pynnes..	—/ 2/ 6
[11]	For a new touch hole screwed [à bushing inserted in a corroded and reamed-out touchhole]	—/—/10
[12]	For a new barrel of a musket, only forged and bored [not fine-finished on the outside], fower foote in length, the bore according to the bullet of ten in the pound standing, and twelve roweling	—/ 8/ 0
[13]	For making clean and new russetting of a musket [i.e., cleaning and browning the barrel with artificial oxidation]	—/—/ 4

		£ s. d.
[14]	For a musket rest	—/—/10
[15]	For making clean a square fyled musket white [polishing down to the shiny steel a musket with an octagonal barrel]	—/ 1/ 8
[16]	For the yearly dressing and keeping clean a musket that needs not new russetting, with the furniture [trigger guard, counter plate, butt plate, etc.] and rest	—/—/10
[17]	For powder and shot for proving every musket	—/—/—
[18]	For stamping [with the official proof mark] every musket proved and allowed	—/—/—
[19]	For a new bandalier with twelve charges, a prymer, a pryming wyre, a bullet bag, and a strap or belt of two inches in breadth	—/ 2/ 6
[20]	For a pair of firelock. pistols [wheel-locks], furnished with a key [spanner], mould, scowrer, worm, flask, and cases of leather, of length and boar according to the allowance of the counsel of war	3/ 0/ 0
[21]	For a pair of horsemans pistols furnished with snaphaunces, mouldes, worms, scowrer, flask, charger and cases	2/ 0/ 0
[22]	For a harquebuze with a firelock and belte, swivell, flask, key, moulde, worme and scowrer	1/16/ 0
[23]	For a carbine with a snaphaunce, belt, swivel and flask &c. as aforesaid	1/ 0/ 0

Fig. 182—*The Gun Makers' Rates,* as established by a Royal Select Committee in 1631.

Fig. 183—Top: Cross section of cannon made of thin inner copper lining, ringed with longitudinal iron bars and tightly wound about with hemp cord; invented in the 1630's. Bottom: Leather cannon invented by Swedish general Baron Wurmbrandt in 1627 and used by Gustav Adolph's army; thin inner copper lining was wound about with hemp, then covered with layers of wet, raw leather which contracted and hardened. Drawn after G. Schreiber, *Büchsenmeister-Diskurs (Master Gunner's Discourse)*, Brieg, 1662.

The Art of Gunnery.

CHAP. 15.
How to make excellent good match to give fire to any Ordnance, &c.

TAke cords made of hemp thats not very fine, or of toe, which is better, although it will sooner consume, and let every cord be so big as a mans little finger; this done, boil the said cords in strong lie, ashes, and a little Saltpeter till all the lie be wasted.

CHAP. 16.
How to make an Engine to finde what proportion of strength one kinde of powder is in comparison of other powder.

THe lid of this Engine is made to rise up in a straight line, and is as big as the box, and also hollow; on each side of the lid or cover, is a small hole for a wyre to pass through, and on one of the pillars of the Engine are little pieces of brass, or steel, so fitted that they may rise with a touch, and give way to the rising of the lid, and so soon as it is past, will hold it there, and will not suffer it to pass back.

The use of this Engine.

Take about one dram of such a sort of powder as you esteem to be the best of all others, and put it into the box, after it is covered with the lid, at the touch-hole, which is in the bottom of the box, fire it with a red hot wyre, being first primed with powder dust; then observe how high and to what division it ascends, which being noted down, take just so much powder of a courser sort, and try that in like maner as you did the former; then by noting up to what degree it ascendeth to, you may perceive the just difference between your best and worst powder; and by the same order of any other sort, as you shall desire to know its strength, and have occasion to use.

But in the next Chapter, I shall describe some other ways, because every man cannot come by a good instrument to try the just strength of any powder.

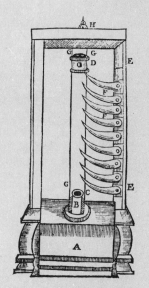

A The foot whereon the Engine standeth.
B The powder box, which hath too small wyres passing from each side to the top, to keep steddy the lid in its motion.
D The lid, which hath also two holes on each side for the wyres to pass through
E The side of the Engine, which is divided, on which is placed at every division, one of those Pieces to slide up and catch the lid.
FF The form of these catches, being either of steel or brass.
CG The too wyres that guide the box lid, and must be put into a little piece of brass, at the top, which may be screwed higher or lower at pleasure, for the better straightning of the same.
H The screw which straightneth those wyres, placed on the top.

Fig. 184—Instructions for making "good match to give fire to any Ordnance, &c," and "an Engine to finde what proportion of strength one kinde of powder is in comparison of another powder." From Nathaniel Nye, *Art of Gunnery*, London, 1647.

One other facet of pre-Commonwealth English firearms which deserves attention is the prevalence of rifles in the war. It is difficult to account for this satisfactorily: for although Henry VIII had rifles, even breechloaders, more than a century before, these were imports for aristocratic pleasures, and the fashions of hunting English wildlife had never really required the use of anything but shot and smoothbore guns. Yet accounts are not rare of "screw'd guns," or rifles, being used with deadly effect by both Parliamentarian and Royalist snipers. From this it may be inferred that many more gamekeepers had been using rifles before the war than a survey of English hunting would lead one to suspect. Perhaps a small percentage of these were English made, but since there has not yet come to light any evidence to show that the run of Jacobean and Caroline makers were capable of such things, it must be supposed that most were German and other wheellocks, probably chiefly of the Bavarian hunting rifle styles then in use for big-game shooting in most of central Europe.

From these considerations of the events in Germany and Britain between 1618 and 1650, it will proceed fairly clearly that the flintlock, upon its invention circa 1630, could thrive in effect only in France, Italy and the Netherlands. Spain was growing ever more enamored of its miquelet lock. The colonists in New England and New Amsterdam were for the most part too poor to replace the matchlock calivers and muskets which they had brought, even snaphaunces having been rare in America before 1650 (there were, of course, a few). The Netherlands not being rich in game, nor its burghers much inclined to pursue such as there was, no demand prompted gunsmiths to adopt, experiment with and perfect a foreign innovation on any large scale. Italians of exuberance and means shot birds, big game and each other with the snaphaunces which their gunsmiths had brought to the ultimate pitch of perfection attainable in this device, but not even in Italy did military matchlocks generally yield to flint firelocks until the last quarter of the century. This left France, her growing wealth and power concentrated in a near-feudal coterie of nobles possessed of enormous estates running over with fowl and beasts. The zenith was yet to come when the five-year-old Louis XIV, the future Sun King, acceded to the throne in 1643 under the guardianship of his mother, Anne of Austria. Here, then, the flintlock was given its start in life and it grew precociously. Both great men and small took to it for the needs of field and battle. By 1660 it had virtually expelled the wheellock and the snaphaunce from Gallic soil, and about 1660–68 Louis XIV was the first powerful monarch—probably the first monarch of any kind—to equip five full regiments with crude but operable military versions of it.

Fig. 185—Bomb with time fuse and eighty or ninety sharp spikes was hurled by ropes or catapult, clung fast to wooden gates, drawbridges or fortifications and blew them to splinters. Engraving from Jean Appier-Hanzelet, *La Pyrotechnie*, Pont-à-Mousson, 1630.

Fig. 186—Two incendiary bombs which could be hurled mechanically or shot from cannons. Bombs, fired by time fuses, were constructed to shatter on impact, spread fiercely flaming incendiary mixture. From Jean Appier-Hanzelet, *La Pyrotechnie*, Pont-à-Mousson, 1630.

Fig. 187 — Combination cannon - and - infantry - charger. Four or five men seized handles along tailpiece, wheeled spiked shrapnel-thrower into enemy ranks at full run. Engraving from Robert Norton, *The Gunner, Shewing the Whole Practice of Artillery*, London, 1628.

Fig. 188—Booby trap in the form of a fake traveling trunk and beer barrel, ostensibly "abandoned" by retreating army; pursuers fell upon it, sought to open trunk lid or lift barrel, thereby triggered snaphaunce-like detonating device and enough powder and shrapnel to slaughter every man within thirty feet. Engraving from Jean Appier-Hanzelet, *La Pyrotechnie*, Pont-à-Mousson, 1630.

In England, it was not until the Restoration of the monarchy with the return of Charles II in 1660 that either the flintlock or firearms generally began to be made there with uniform and widespread skill. From 1649 to 1660, during the ever-souring Cromwell's (and his son's) grim and pious suppression of anything which might expose the people to the perils of pleasure or laughter, there was not only no sport afield but no young cavaliers and landed hotspurs into whose province such delights would naturally have fallen. But at last the king returned, and with him all his polished, arrogant and sophisticated train. Theaters, bear baitings, cockpits, ale houses reopened, dances, musicales and water festivals filled the nights with noise and fireworks, torchlight parades lit the streets and set fire to a few houses now and then, the illegitimacy rate tripled, orange girls and fried-fish wives peddled refreshments to the merry audiences at hangings and beheadings—England was alive again. And with the returning exiles came thousands of French sporting flintlocks of the very best quality. Even more radical and enduring was another import: the fashion of field shooting for gentlemen, which almost immediately upon the return ran like a shiver through all the classes from king to yeoman. What had been a trade for laborers and a condescending means of practice for the gentry scarcely twenty years earlier was now, under French impetus, launched on its way like wildfire to become not merely a sport, not just a maniacal fashion, but among the sporting set a semi-religious cult to endure for a century and three-quarters. The British gunsmiths learned fast, and as they had been sluggards before, they became leaders almost overnight. By 1665 three distinct new weapons of the very best design and workmanship had appeared:

—the English Restoration flintlock fowling piece, the first of a lineage which was to end in the early nineteenth century as the consummate example of gunsmithing;

—the English screw-barrel flintlock pistol, the first of a lineage to end 150 years later in the finest single-shot pistols ever known;

—and the English coaching blunderbuss, which was not to outlive its usefulness in post coaches and accounting offices, aboard the great men-o'-war and under feather-beds until long after Waterloo.

Flintlock arms were to be so interwoven in the expanding world which now entered a new chapter in its history that to follow their course we must do the same in ours.

Fig. 189—Woodcut from a broadside announcing the Peace of Münster, 1648, ending Thirty Years' War.

FASHIONS AND CUSTOMS OF ENGLISH life in the social spheres and on the household level had bobbed like corks on the high and low tides of royal prerogative; and the tides left in their wake much that was new, and swept away much that was old. Guns were but minutiae in the complex overall picture, and yet it would be difficult to find any other single group of implements which were more speedily caught up and more indicative of the changes in the day-to-day English scene, excepting perhaps costumes and furniture.

The importations of the French sport of shooting flying and French flintlock fowling pieces had followed at once in the paths of the Stuarts restored. Charles himself now set the pace for the new field sport. Thus began in England what might be called the *courtier phase* of English sporting shooting, for it spread from the ribald king and the courtly entourage which had returned with him from exile to the jubilant cavaliers who had welcomed him home, and thence to the higher strata of the landed nobility. The demand for fine fowling pieces skyrocketed, although in the courtier phase, which lasted until about 1670, it was mainly for imported French and Italian arms. But English gunmakers were not slow to grasp their golden opportunity: they examined the work of the competition, and by 1665 they were able to turn out as good a product as any of the better makers of the Continent, although the day when they would surpass or even match the *best* Continental masters had not yet arrived.

Fig. 190—Silver sideplate (or "screwholder" for long screws which ran through gun transversely, held lock to stock) of a high-quality French fowling piece, circa 1660-80.

Soon the matter of *proof firing* came to be an issue of general public safety, for although the better imported guns were proved by reputable makers who signed their work with pride, the laws of France, Italy and Germany made no such task incumbent upon them. As a result, the holds of ships disgorged in the English ports many thousands of shoddy or questionable pieces which could be relied upon to blow off the shooter's hands and face sometime between the first and the hundredth shot.

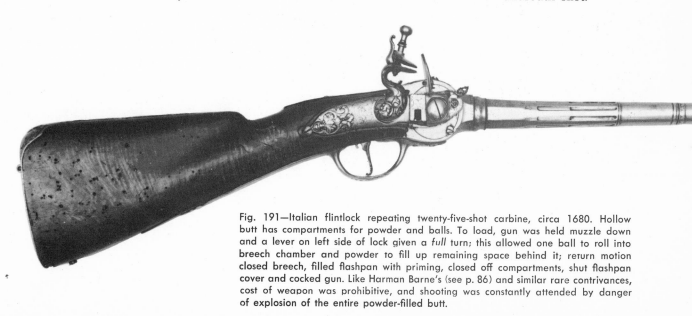

Fig. 191—Italian flintlock repeating twenty-five-shot carbine, circa 1680. Hollow butt has compartments for powder and balls. To load, gun was held muzzle down and a lever on left side of lock given a *full* turn; this allowed one ball to roll into breech chamber and powder to fill up remaining space behind it; return motion closed breech, filled flashpan with priming, closed off compartments, shut flashpan cover and cocked gun. Like Harman Barne's (see p. 86) and similar rare contrivances, cost of weapon was prohibitive, and shooting was constantly attended by danger of explosion of the entire powder-filled butt.

Fig. 192—Top: A typical first-quality English Restoration-style fowling piece, 63 inches over all, and, bottom, one of its Continental ancestors, a fine 65-inch Dutch piece.

The ebullient Samuel Pepys, ever loath to lack in worldly appurtenances befitting a major functionary of administration, had acquired a medium-quality French fowling piece in 1667, and on the evening of March 29 took it with him to the Bull Head Tavern to parade it before his friends. There he met (italics mine—R.H.)

one Truelocke, the famous gunsmith, that is a mighty ingenious man, and he did take my gun to pieces, and made me understand the secrets thereof; and upon the whole did find it a very good piece of work, and truely wrought, *but for certain not a thing to be used with much safety; and he do find that this very gun was never yet shot off.*

One might reasonably expect the owner of such an unproved potential dynamite stick to go steaming back to the seller upon this revelation, pound his fist on the counter and demand immediate justice. Not so Mr. Pepys —nor a good many other gentlemen who had merely bought their modish firelocks to be abreast of high society, but who in this seventh year of the Restoration did not yet entertain the faintest intention of putting them to more strenuous use than as insignia of rank. For Mr. Pepys was "mightily satisfied with it and him, and the sight of so much curiosity of this kind." (It is hardly necessary to comment on the singular magnificence of the name Truelocke for a gunsmith. His first name was Edmund, and he was one of the first British makers of fine guns, having practiced circa 1660–80.)

The proof-firing of gun barrels had been entrusted to the Gunmakers' Company of London in 1637, along with the right of searching for and seizing firearms within ten miles of the city which were deemed unproved and dangerous. The chaos of the Civil Wars, the uncertainty of the Commonwealth and the political corruption of early Restoration years had made enforcement largely a

macabre joke. The death and multilation rate had steadily risen, the victims having been largely lower-class fowlers and near paupers until about 1670, since up to the Restoration they had been the principal shooters, while in the courtier phase of sporting shooting from 1660 to 1670 most sporting gentlemen and nobles were still safe with their fine French pieces of the sort proved by the makers. But the situation took an alarming turn when in the early 1670's the shrapnel of bursting barrels began to take its frightful toll in the bluer blood and whiter flesh of peers and gentry who—like Mr. Pepys—had made incautious purchases in their haste to share in the everspreading fashion. Moreover, exploding musket barrels in the army killed and maimed a soldier or two every month, an annoyance to officers and an expense to the Exchequer. Something had to be done. In 1672 a new charter was granted to the Gunmakers' Company, under the terms of which the sale of unproved barrels was prohibited in all of England, the standard of the proof being set by the Company. This consisted of loading every barrel with double the amount of powder required for a heavy charge and with a tightly fitting ball. An entire "run" of manufacture, up to a hundred and even more barrels, could be tested by laying them on wooden tiers, aimed at sandbags, and firing them by a train of powder running across the touchholes of all. The first test was made when the barrel had been bored in the rough; if it passed the requirements set up by the Gunmakers' Company (i.e., if it showed no damage from the proof load), it was stamped with the letter V for Viewed, surmounted by a crown. The second test came after the fine boring and consisted of the same strenuous loading. If the barrel passed again, it was stamped with the letters G.P. for Gunmakers' Proof, again beneath a crown (Fig. 193). The barrel was then deemed safe for sale and use (cf. items 17 and 18 of *The Gun Makers' Rates*, Fig. 182).

1637

Fig. 193—London proof marks for 1637, 1672 and 1702 (greatly enlarged). Barrels were stamped "V" (for "Viewed") after first test, "GP" (for "Gunmakers' Proof") after second.

1672

1702

Fig. 193a—North-Italian silver mounted flintlock pistol, probably Brescian; early 18th century. (Tonolini Collection, Brescia)

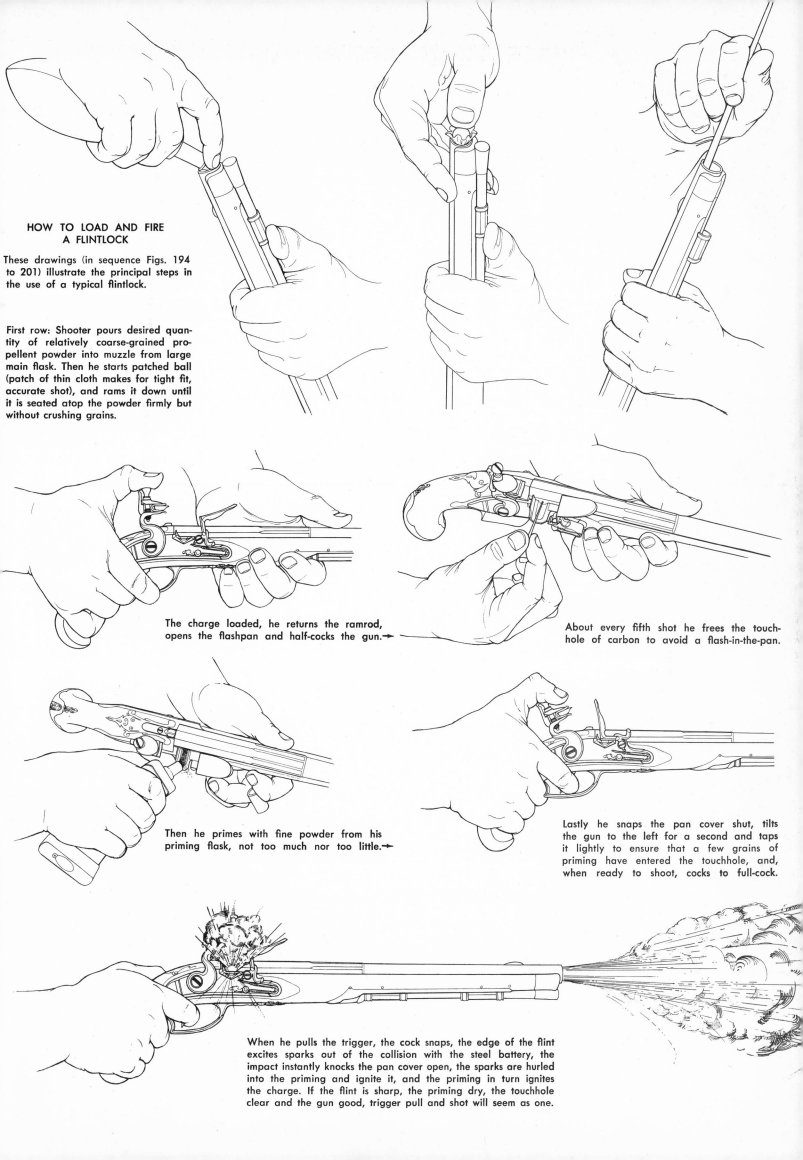

HOW TO LOAD AND FIRE A FLINTLOCK

These drawings (in sequence Figs. 194 to 201) illustrate the principal steps in the use of a typical flintlock.

First row: Shooter pours desired quantity of relatively coarse-grained propellent powder into muzzle from large main flask. Then he starts patched ball (patch of thin cloth makes for tight fit, accurate shot), and rams it down until it is seated atop the powder firmly but without crushing grains.

The charge loaded, he returns the ramrod, opens the flashpan and half-cocks the gun.→

About every fifth shot he frees the touchhole of carbon to avoid a flash-in-the-pan.

Then he primes with fine powder from his priming flask, not too much nor too little.→

Lastly he snaps the pan cover shut, tilts the gun to the left for a second and taps it lightly to ensure that a few grains of priming have entered the touchhole, and, when ready to shoot, cocks to full-cock.

When he pulls the trigger, the cock snaps, the edge of the flint excites sparks out of the collision with the steel battery, the impact instantly knocks the pan cover open, the sparks are hurled into the priming and ignite it, and the priming in turn ignites the charge. If the flint is sharp, the priming dry, the touchhole clear and the gun good, trigger pull and shot will seem as one.

It was not long before the courtier phase of sporting shooting had passed into what may be called the *squire* phase. By 1685, it had become a genteel, modish sport among the rural nobility and the rich landed gentry, who now spent many leisure hours afield blasting away decorously at whatever flew or perched within range. The Restoration climate of boisterous elegance had transformed an English yeoman's vile pursuit of nourishment into an English gentleman's festooned pursuit of happiness. Nothing could serve better literally to epitomize this metamorphosis than the fortunes of a book called THE GENTLEMAN'S RECREATION. When one Nicholas Cox had first published it in 1677 *"In Four Parts, Viz., Hunting, Hawking, Fowling, Fishing,"* it said nothing about shooting save a straight plagiarism of Gervase Markham's

thirteen-line advice of half a century before (Fig. 170); much else was plagiarized from Markham. Then, in 1686, one Richard Blome edited it (or plagiarized it, depending how one looks at it), rewrote large parts, added a long section on shooting, and included it as the second part of a new, elegant, fashionable volume which he called THE GENTLEMAN'S RECREATION, *In Two Parts, The First Being an Encyclopedia of the Arts & Sciences.* The Encyclopedia concerned itself with such patrician topics as Rhetoric, Grammar, Astronomy, Music, Poetry, Greek Drama, Mathematics, Ethics and others which all gentlemen would have done well to master. Such were the circles into which the times (and Richard Blome) had elevated shooting, about which now was said (see also p. 67):

To the Honourable Thomas Fairfax Esq? eldest Son of ye Rt Honbl Henry Lord Fairfax of Denton in York-shire. This Plate is humbly Dedicated by Richard Blome.

Fig. 202—Engraving from Richard Blome's 1686 re-edition of Nicholas Cox's 1677 edition of *The Gentleman's Recreation.* Gentlemen are here shooting flying from horseback, a practice which lost vogue and died out in the early 18th century. Servants muster dogs, pick up dead game, and (background) hand loaded guns to masters.

The Birding or Fowling-Piece is of great use to those that are expert therein. And to be well accommodated therewith, every Fowler ought to have them of several sorts and sizes suitable to the Game he designs to kill. For small Birds [a gun] with a small Bore, about four Foot or four Foot and an half long in the Barrel, is sufficient; for Wild-fowl, as Ducks, Herns, Wild-Geese and the like, the Barrel ought to be about six Foot long, with an indifferent Bore under the size of a Musket [under approximately .76 calibre].

And for the choosing of the Barrel, observe these Directions: Let it be well Polished and smooth within, and the Bore all of a bigness, which you may try by putting in a piece of Paste-board or Board cut of the exact roundness of the top, which gently put [ram] down to the Touch-hole; and if you find it goes down well and even without stops or sliping, you may judge it Even-bored.

Let the Bridge-Pin [breech-pin; i.e., breech-plug] be something above [in front of] the Touch-hole, only with a Notch in the Bridge-Pin, to let down a little Powder; and if so, then the Gun will not Recoil, which it doth when the Bridge-Pin is below the Touch-hole [cf. Figs. 37 & 242(9)].

For your Locks, choose those that are well filed with true work; let the Springs be neither too strong nor too weak; for if too weak it will not strike Fire in raw Sleety-Weather; and if too strong it will shake your hand in going off. Let the Hammer [battery] be very well hardened, and pliable to go down to the Pan with a quick motion. Now for your trying [the cock], move it gently to the Lock; and if it goes without any jerks, in a good circular motion, it is well made.

For the Stocks, Walnut-Tree or Ash are very good for use; but the Maple is the finest, and the best for Ornament. . . .

It is not enough to be well provided with a good Fowling Piece, but your great care must be to keep it in good Order, and for that purpose observe these few directions: Keep it always in a Case either of Wood or Cloth, in a dry place, for the Damp spoils and rusts it. Let your Lock be kept always clean and oyled, that the Cock, Hammer, and all the parts may be of a nimble Motion upon drawing the Trigger. Also a good Flint is of necessary use; and indeed the Fowler ought to be provided with several in his Bag, for fear of any disaster of the other. The Barrel must also be always kept clean; for if foul, it never carrieth true; besides 'tis subject to recoyl, which is dangerous; and it will occasion that oft times it flashes in the Pan a good while before it goeth off, by which means the Fowl are alarmed, and so escape, with several more ill Conveniences that may attend.

You must also be well acquainted with the condition of the Gun, whether it be apt to scatter, or carry the Shot round within compass, that you may load her accordingly; for if you shoot at a Flock of great Fowl, then the Shot must be large, and there must be more Powder and less Shot; and if you shoot at a single Bird, then less Powder and more Shot; for the former will scatter, and the latter fly close and compact.

Directions about Shooting

In Shooting, whether the Game be Flying, or on the Ground, on a Tree or Hedge, always (as near as you can) endeavour to Shoot with the Wind, and not against it; and rather sideways or behind the Fowl than in their Faces; and not at a single Fowl if you can compass more within your Level; and if on a Tree, Hedge, or the Ground, seek the convenientest shelter you can of Hedge, Bank, Tree, or the like, to be absconded from the Fowls seeing you, which is very offensive to them; and being within Shot, and a fair Mark, lose no time but let fly.

Shooting Flying

It is now the Mode to Shoot Flying, as being by experience found the best and surest way; for when your Game is on the Wing it is more exposed to danger; for if but one Shot [i.e., one pellet] hits any part of its Wings so expanded, it will occasion its fall, although not to kill it, so that your Spaniel will soon be its Victor; and if well disciplined to the Sport, bring it to you.

For your better instructions herein, I shall lay down some few Directions: The Gun most proper for this sport should be about four Foot and a half long in the Barrel and of a pretty wide Bore, something under a Musket. You should have your Gun always Cock't in readiness, with your Thumb over the Cock for fear of its going off contrary to your intention; so that when you meet with any Game, you must be quick, and having got an aim to your mind, let fly with all Expedition.

Some are of Opinion that you must Shoot something before the Fowl, otherwise it will be past before the Shot can come to it; but that is a vulgar Error; for no Game can fly so quick but that the Shot will meet it; for the Shot flyeth as wide as about the compass of a Bushel, if rightly ordered in the Charging. [Blome is in error; it is necessary to aim ahead of the bird even today, was all the more so with a flintlock.] Yet I am of the Opinion, if the Game flyeth as it were over your Head, that 'tis best to Aim at the Head; and if it flieth from you, to Aim as it were under its Belly. And 'tis found best to let the Game fly a little past you before you let fly, for thereby the Shot will the better enter the Body. . . .

To the modern shooter, the feat of shooting flying with a four to four and a half foot barrel would seem difficult beyond all hope of success. Yet it was done, and one must bow to still another vindication of the tedious homily that practice makes perfect. It was to be a long time before barrels were shortened to less unwieldy lengths, for these were not merely a fashion or groundless whim: the charge of extremely coarse powder had time to burn more completely and to generate maximum efficiency while the load traveled down the long tube; as a consequence, long-barreled guns shot harder, further and more accurately.

Rain was the flintlock's nemesis: the small flash shield, or lip, which rose from the rear edge of the flashpan of most guns of 1660–1750 was essential to deflect the priming flash from a straight line into the shooter's eyes; but it also guided any drop of water running down the battery infallibly into the flashpan. Throughout the eighteenth century more or less successful efforts were made to waterproof flashpans, but only after about 1780 were locks constructed so that they might be exposed to a moderate downpour for some minutes and still fire. Strong gusts of wind, too, proved inimical to shooting: the sparks were *hurled*, not merely dropped into the flashpan only if the lock snapped with lightning speed and a minimum of friction; only thus could the priming be ignited in strong wind before it was blown off the pan. But until about 1770–80, the maximum wind for even a well-made lock was about 32–38 m.p.h., called No. 6 and "strong" on the Beaufort Scale (officially described as "whole trees in motion; inconvenience felt in walking against the wind"). If the priming was not ignited on the first snap, it was of course blown off in such weather; then repriming involved crouching and shielding the flashpan and the nozzle of the priming flask with one's coat. How the caprices of weather ended days of field shooting may be learned from the 5th and 6th stanzas of PTERYPLEGIA on p. 128. But the perversity of inanimate objects was recorded in the following pearl of journalism in a surprisingly literate sporting manual of unknown authorship published in London in August, 1699 (italics mine—R.H.):

How ceaselessly constant Tragedy followeth ever in the Paths of Sport you may learn from the following Example, which but shortly befell Mr. ——, ESQR, of N——shire, who had gone ashooting with divers Pistolls, to Exercise his Aim at Marks and Butts, of a Morning when golden PHOEBUS and calm ZEPHYRUS had conspir'd to render the Climate friendly and favourable to such Enterprise. But about Two o'Clock after Noon, a suddain and dreadful Storm arose, *with high-pitched Rain, and a Wind which quite bent tall Trees, and broke Branches and Seadlings, and threatened bold to blow Mr. —— and the two serving-men which accompany'd him from the Field.* With much Labour they sought to make theyr Way to a nearby Shelter, but Mr. ——, ill humored by such Discomfiture, and by the Rains spoiling his Lace, was moved to fling a loaded Pistol to the Ground, which he had carried in his hand some time, *so that it was all drizzle cover'd wet and thought spoiled for fire;* but striking the Ground made the Cock snap from Half-bent [half-cock], and albeit the Pistol *struck the Ground inverted Upside-down, and Water and Blow notwithstanding, yet it went off,* and the Ball fortunately miss'd Mr. ——, but hit a serving-boy's Leg, the which it shatter'd, but skillful Surgeons were able to mend, and the boy is growing daily more recover'd, Mr. —— having maintained him at his Wages during his Time of Incapacity. . . .

The generous Mr. —— was likely to be more careful in the future, even though the gods had thoughtfully channeled the pain of his experience into the limb of a mere domestic. It may be mentioned here *en passant* that an excellent way of testing the speed of a flintlock's ignition was to try firing it upside down. If it was well made, and as Mr. Blome had advised, the cock and flash-pan cover were "pliable to go down to the Pan with a quick motion," it would fire before the priming had time to fall off the flashpan after the cock had knocked the cover open (for proof, see Fig. 312).

Fig. 203—Gentlemen amusing themselves with an afternoon of pistol shooting. Detail from a French sporting print, circa 1703-1705.

But the sporting gun was only one of the several forms of firearms which were to find wide use in the second half of the seventeenth century, not only in England but on the Continent as well. Until the advent of the true flint-lock in about 1630, pistols, as has been marked, were mainly expensive wheellocks whose use was confined to a small class, or snaphaunces and miquelets which, though often extremely effective, do not appear to have been made in very great numbers before about 1640. English gunsmiths before the Civil Wars had made various forms of hand guns fitted with Jacobean flintlocks, but these were mostly not distinguished by any greater degree of competence than the indifferent long arms of

the same time (cf. Items 20 and 21, *The Gun Makers' Rates,* Fig. 182). But when the wars began in 1642, it appeared obvious from the outset that superior cavalry would very likely be a major, if not deciding factor, which was another way of saying that carbines, and above all pistols—the only firearms suitable for mounted use—had suddenly come to be of utmost importance in the nation's greatest hour of crisis. Overnight they became the objects of fierce scrambles for possession by both Royalist and Parliamentarian forces. Here the Parliamentarians had a decided advantage: for though the Royalists might have the better raw material for an army, and thousands of matchlock service muskets could be procured by timely seizures of the many county arsenals, gunsmithing was carried on almost exclusively in London, the staunchest stronghold of Parliamentarian sentiment, and consequently the production of pistols flowed directly from the London workbenches into the saddle pipes of Roundhead riders. When in 1643 a fund of £240 for the equipping of a company of musketeers was offered to Cromwell (then a colonel), he was able to answer in a letter dated August 2:

> I approve of the business . . . only I desire you that your Foot-company may be turned into a Troop of Horse: which will indeed (by Gods blessing) far more advauntage the Cause than two or three companies of foot: especially if your Men be honest, godly men, which by all means I desire. . . . Therefore my advice is that you employ your twelve-score Pounds to buy Pistolls and Saddles, and I will provide four-score horses. . . .

For the most part, the pistols used must have been crude, massive Jacobean-type flintlock pistols of about No. 26 to 20 bore (approximately .56 to .63 calibre).

Among the other pistols of the Civil Wars were doubtlessly many snaphaunces, of both English and Continental manufacture (notably Dutch), and such fine imported private weapons as may have been the rightful or wrongful property of individual officers and men.

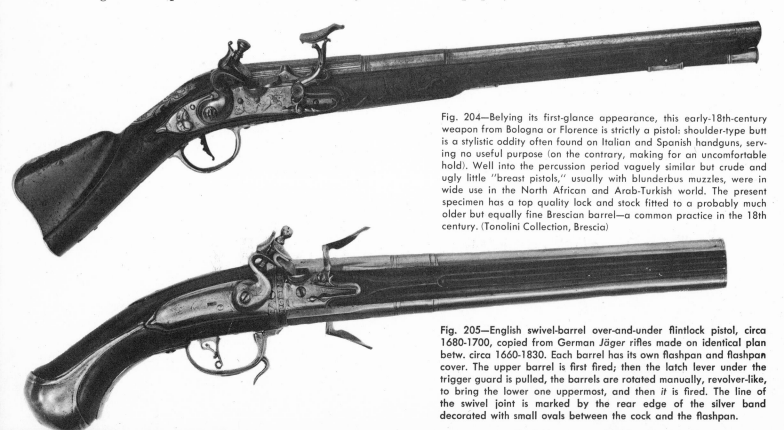

Fig. 204—Belying its first-glance appearance, this early-18th-century weapon from Bologna or Florence is strictly a pistol: shoulder-type butt is a stylistic oddity often found on Italian and Spanish handguns, serving no useful purpose (on the contrary, making for an uncomfortable hold). Well into the percussion period vaguely similar but crude and ugly little "breast pistols," usually with blunderbus muzzles, were in wide use in the North African and Arab-Turkish world. The present specimen has a top quality lock and stock fitted to a probably much older but equally fine Brescian barrel—a common practice in the 18th century. (Tonolini Collection, Brescia)

Fig. 205—English swivel-barrel over-and-under flintlock pistol, circa 1680-1700, copied from German *Jäger* rifles made on identical plan betw. circa 1660-1830. Each barrel has its own flashpan and flashpan cover. The upper barrel is first fired; then the latch lever under the trigger guard is pulled, the barrels are rotated manually, revolver-like, to bring the lower one uppermost, and then *it* is fired. The line of the swivel joint is marked by the rear edge of the silver band decorated with small ovals between the cock and the flashpan.

Yet shortly before the wars, let us say in about 1635–40, a few of the best gunsmiths—doubtless the same whose names are listed on p. 86 in connection with early long-arms—had made the first few hundred pistols of a type which, though well known on the continent, but there neglected, was destined to remain a peculiarly British feature for well over a century and a half: this was the *screw-barrel* or *cannon-barrel* pistol, in which the barrel (without any forestock underneath it) was screwed onto a short breech chamber, as diagrammed in Fig. 206. For loading, the barrel (which derived its alternate name from being tapered and ringed about the muzzle like a miniature cannon) was unscrewed, the breech chamber filled with powder while held vertically with its open end pointing upward, the ball laid into the shallow spherical cup at its end, and the barrel lastly screwed into place again. In many such pistols intended for cavalry use the barrel was joined to the breech or stock by a short chain or a rod-and-swivel to forestall the incommodious disaster of finding oneself left in the heat of battle with the rear half of a primed and loaded pistol while the barrel disappeared somewhere under hoof. Such breech-loading actually consumed considerably more time than muzzle-loading with a ramrod, but it made possible the use of extremely tightly fitting balls rather than the loose ones which convenience dictated for use in muzzleloaders. As a consequence, the ball in a screw-barrel pistol showed no tendency to "chatter" along its course down the barrel when fired (cf. Fig. 173), and there was none of the gas seepage around it which so drastically reduced the efficiency of the conventional muzzleloader. Furthermore, the tight fit and great initial friction of the ball accomplished in the short length of a pistol barrel what we have earlier marked as having been the object of the extreme lengths of fowling-piece barrels: the coarse pow-

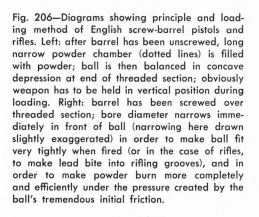
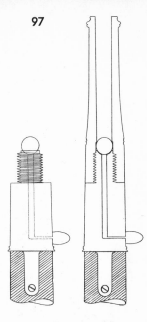

Fig. 206—Diagrams showing principle and loading method of English screw-barrel pistols and rifles. Left: after barrel has been unscrewed, long narrow powder chamber (dotted lines) is filled with powder; ball is then balanced in concave depression at end of threaded section; obviously weapon has to be held in vertical position during loading. Right: barrel has been screwed over threaded section; bore diameter narrows immediately in front of ball (narrowing here drawn slightly exaggerated) in order to make ball fit very tightly when fired (or in the case of rifles, to make lead bite into rifling grooves), and in order to make powder burn more completely and efficiently under the pressure created by the ball's tremendous initial friction.

der had time to burn completely and to generate maximum pressures. All these conspired to make screw-barrel pistols shoot harder and more accurately than muzzle-loaders, and the fact that they could arrive at these ends with short barrels made them ideally suited for use as pocket pistols. When in addition to these virtues such weapons had the further one of being rifled, their accuracy could be nothing less than astounding. Robert Plot records in his HISTORY OF STAFFORDSHIRE one supreme example. On September 13, 1643, the Royal Army paused at Stafford, and Prince Rupert, ever pleased to impress on others his skill with pistols, fired at the weathercock atop the steeple of St. Mary's church with a rifled screw-barrel pistol, the distance from where he stood having been some hundred-odd feet. When the ball neatly pierced the weathercock's head, the Prince's uncle, King Charles, declared that such a shot could only be a matter of luck—whereupon the Prince at once drew his other pistol and pierced the figure's tail.

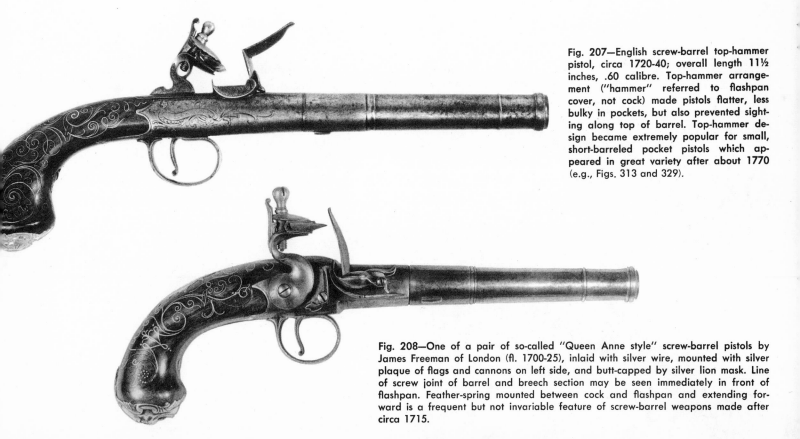

Fig. 207—English screw-barrel top-hammer pistol, circa 1720-40; overall length 11½ inches, .60 calibre. Top-hammer arrangement ("hammer" referred to flashpan cover, not cock) made pistols flatter, less bulky in pockets, but also prevented sighting along top of barrel. Top-hammer design became extremely popular for small, short-barreled pocket pistols which appeared in great variety after about 1770 (e.g., Figs. 313 and 329).

Fig. 208—One of a pair of so-called "Queen Anne style" screw-barrel pistols by James Freeman of London (fl. 1700-25), inlaid with silver wire, mounted with silver plaque of flags and cannons on left side, and butt-capped by silver lion mask. Line of screw joint of barrel and breech section may be seen immediately in front of flashpan. Feather-spring mounted between cock and flashpan and extending forward is a frequent but not invariable feature of screw-barrel weapons made after circa 1715.

Finally, the power of the larger among these weapons was such that at twenty yards the shot penetrated the stoutest breastplate worn, for although such armor was intended to be "pistol-proof," it was designed only to withstand the much less potent performances of typical, crude military muzzleloaders. But muzzleloaders of all qualities remained nonetheless more common in England throughout the seventeenth and eighteenth centuries than screw-barrel pistols, for the breechloaders were much more difficult to make and therefore much more expensive; and for general personal-protection use, the advantages of a breechloader over a good muzzleloader fitted with a patched ball were considerably diminished by the breechloader's slow and fumbling loading procedure.

The same tastes and purses of the returning exiles which had introduced the French fowling pieces into England at the time of the Restoration had also brought thousands of French, German and Italian pistols, most of which were extremely good guns (although all muzzleloaders), and many of which represented the finest workmanship of their native countries. Again the English makers were quick to adopt the best features of these, but they had little to fear from the competition: for while the magnificent weapons of the Continent were often masterpieces of the traditional native genius, beyond the hope of foreigners to equal, many of the English pistols, though simple, came out victorious in most contests of performance. But as sporting shooting had been the concomitant of the import of long arms, so a more sinister one had arrived with the pistols—the French predilection for settling quarrels by murdering the opponent in "affairs of honor." Throughout the seventeenth century, these had become so popular among the French aristocrats and chevaliers that the supply of officers and lush taxpayers was seriously threatened. Richelieu, Mazarin and Louis XIV himself decreed the severest penalties for the victors, and should they survive, for the losers; hanging, hanging by the feet and decapitation in that position, death by impaling on a wooden stake were all tried as deterrents. But these notwithstanding, the deaths in duels rose to more than a thousand in some years. The most trivial, inane misunderstanding, a slip of the tongue, a careless glance could mean precipitous death.

Fig. 209—Above: Ornamentation around the tang of a French 17th-century barrel. See Figs. 211 and 211a.

Fig. 210—Left and below: Pair of Dutch flintlock pistols by Leonard Graeff, circa 1725. All-ivory stocks are silver mounted, terminate in sculptured heads wearing silver helmets; all other stock ornamentations are silver. Barrels are profusely and delicately etched, chiseled and gilded in foliate and classical motifs. (In the Metropolitan Museum of Art, New York)

Until about the middle of the century, most duels had been fought with rapiers. The challenger, usually an expert swordsman by the laws of survival of the fittest, and a belligerent, bloodthirsty bully, would demand satisfaction for some real or imagined offense; the challenged, often a very poor swordsman, had the choice of accepting or of being hounded out of his regiment or social sphere as a coward—or of being skewered in a dark alley on his way home by the challenger and his friends. The living archetypes of such gilded images as Dumas's *Three Musketeers* were in fact unwashed, unscrupulous and illiterate toughs; and Cyrano de Bergerac (1619–55) was a psychotic killer who would have daggered Edmond Rostand with a chuckle. In 1685 an anonymous book was published in London entitled THE LAWS OF HONOUR: OR AN ACCOUNT OF THE SUPPRESSION OF DUELS IN FRANCE. In it was quoted "A Circulatory Letter of the Gentlemen Governors of the Hospital of Paris to the Governors of Other Hospitals of France," which had been written and circulated in 1657. This document contained one of the earliest references to the use of guns in dueling: "The Preparatives . . . are but Instruments for perishing: there are carried [to the dueling fields] Swords, Daggers, Knives and of late Pistols or other Firearms. . . ."

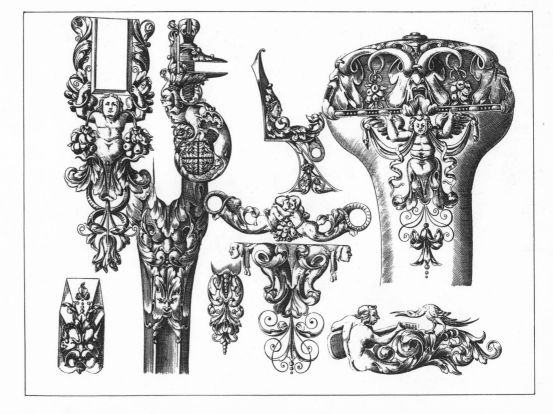

Fig. 211 & 211a—Two pages and excerpted details of gun ornamentation patterns engraved by C. Jaquinet (fl. 1657) for Parisian gunsmiths Thuraine and Hollanaaise, published circa 1660. Well-to-do customers selected designs from these and other samples (usually bound as books or kept in portfolios), returned three or four months later to call (and pay dearly) for finished order.

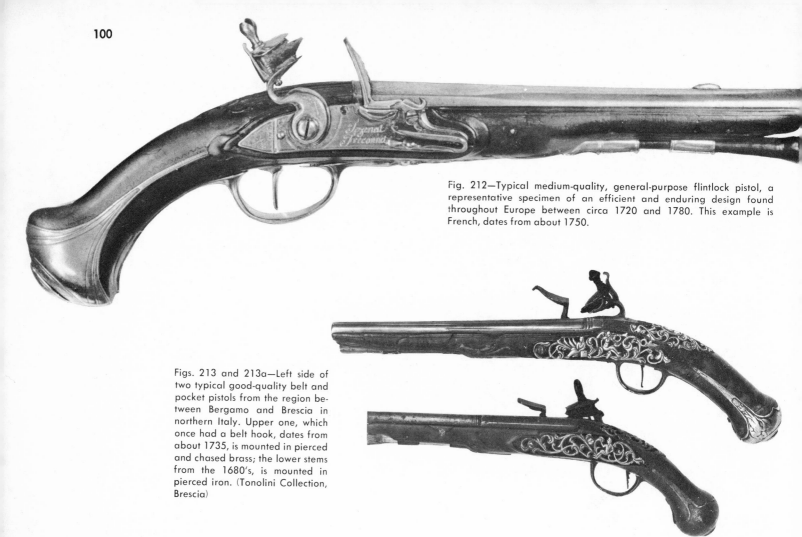

Fig. 212—Typical medium-quality, general-purpose flintlock pistol, a representative specimen of an efficient and enduring design found throughout Europe between circa 1720 and 1780. This example is French, dates from about 1750.

Figs. 213 and 213a—Left side of two typical good-quality belt and pocket pistols from the region between Bergamo and Brescia in northern Italy. Upper one, which once had a belt hook, dates from about 1735, is mounted in pierced and chased brass; the lower stems from the 1680's, is mounted in pierced iron. (Tonolini Collection, Brescia)

Fig. 214—Left: One of a pair of German pistol barrels, first half of 17th century; iron, engraved and inlaid, and sculptured in gilded bas-relief showing Hermes, Perseus, Venus and Eros among Renaissance decorative motifs. (In the Metropolitan Museum of Art, N.Y.)

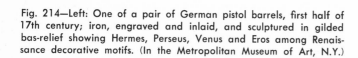

Fig. 215—Detail of a late 18th-century German flintlock pistol.

While dueling did not strike root in England to the depth it had in France, it nonetheless became a diverting pastime among cavaliers, officers and other gentlemen who were in a position to buy immunity from the law after having thrilled to the hunt of the ultimate game. The rapier alone was at first the vogue, but toward the reign of William and Mary (1689–1702), pistols began to accompany it since their use imposed no tiresome strain on choleric warriors save the contraction of an eyelid and an index finger. As yet there had developed none of the somber ritual of seconds, physicians and codes of conduct which were to mark the century following 1750. The combatants merely met in some suitable and secret place, armed with a pistol in one hand and a sword in the other, came to prearranged positions (usually thirty to fifty feet apart), aimed, fired, and if both missed, went at it with *armes blanches*. Like sporting shooting, dueling spread from the higher classes downward until by 1700–10 it was not infrequent—though neither common—among minor officers and young hotbloods with more wealth than wit. One of the earliest printed accounts of such a folly was an anonymous elegaic pamphlet published in 1711 which described the death of one Sir Chomley Deering in that same year. Its naïve, untutored style, virile if bald, conveys such genuine melancholy that it is here reprinted *in toto* (italics in original):

Fig. 216—Title page of *Sir Chomley Deering* (London, 1711).

An Account of the *Life* and *Character* of of Sir *Chomley Deering*, Bar. and Knight of the Shire for the County of *Kent* in the prefent Parliament; who was Unfortunately Shot in a Duel on *Wednefday* Morning the 9th of *May*, by his own Friend and Kinfman, Col. *Thornhill.* With the true Relation of their falling out, and the manner of their Fighting; as alfo the Expreffions of Sorrow that pafs'd between them afterwards. Together with a new *ELEGY* on his Death.

London, Printed by *J. Read*, near *Fleet-ftreet*, 1711.

AN ACCOUNT OF THE LIFE AND CHARACTER OF
CHOMLEY DEERING, BARONET, &C.

The following Relation is a Melancholly Instance of the sad Effects of Wine and Passion, which was so predominant, that on the slightest Occasion it produc'd an irreconcileable Quarrel between Two of the most intimate Friends; who, having not leisure to cool, ran violently into a Course they were sure both of them to repent, upon the least Mature Consideration.

Their intimacy was so great, that they were seldom asunder, either in Town or Country, and the Friendship they profess'd for one another was hardly equal'd; yet having Drank to an immoderate Pitch, it turn'd all this Stream of Fondness into Fury and Dislike: They were of a sudden become the most violent Enemies in Nature, breathing nothing but the Death and Destruction of each other; and as soon as they had satisfied a wretched Passion of Rage and Revenge, their Eyes and Senses were then in a true light, and Grief and Repentance were the Fatal Consequences thereof.

There was a Dying Man reflecting on the Rashness of what he had done, how trifling and how vain had been the Dispute that occasion'd his Death. He had then also the number *of his Sins to recollect, and a Dying Pardon to ask of God; besides, in that unspeakable Hurry and Confusion of Mind, a Mournful and Tender Family to remember, to think of parting with his dear Children when he had scarce Life to give them his Blessing.*

The other, stain'd with the Guilt of Murder, nay even that of his own dear Friend and constant Companion, his Hands imbru'd in his Blood; the dread of Heavenly Vengeance and the Laws of Man, contriving to fly, but unresolv'd whether; and at last severly touch'd with the sence of his Condition, ready to become his own Murderer too.

But I shall now come to a Narrative of this rash and unfortunate Accident, as near as can be collected from the best Accounts.

It seems there was a Club kept every Week at *Hampton-Court*, of several Gentlemen of good Account, of which was the Deceased Sir *Chomley Deering*, and Mr. *Thornhill.* Being at this Club on *Friday* Night last, they drank very hard, and in the heighth of Wine there arose Discourse of a certain L——, being a particular Friend of Sir *Cholmley Deering*, and to his Interest he ow'd a good part of his Election; so upon other high Words, Sir *Cholmney* was provok'd to throw a Glass of Wine at Mr. *Thornhill*, and afterwards to strike him in the face with a Bottle, and using other violences, but in the heat of Wine, having drank very hard.

Mr. *Thornhill* then left the Company, and came to Town, and reflecting on his Usage, began to consider that he cou'd not put it up with Honour; and therefore forgetting all former Friendship, resolv'd to Challenge Sir *Chomley*, which he accordingly did, at Sword and Pistol.

Sir *Chomley* recovering from the Fumes of Wine, and considering what he had done to his Friend, seem'd extreamly sorry for it; and therefore propos'd an accommodation of the Matter, it being begun in Drink; and as we hear, went to Mr. *Thornhill's* Lodgings to endeavour to prevent its coming to the last Extremity. But Mr. *Thornhill* seem'd inexorable, and would not be satisfied any way but by Fighting; and therefore on *Tuesday* Night last, sending his utmost result to Sir *Chomley*, the next Morning at Seven was appointed for the Duel, with Sword and Pistol, and to meet in the *Park* and retire to *Tuttle-Fields*.

According they came there a little before Eight and walk'd to the *Alms-Houses* on the farther side of the Fields, and there under some Trees prepar'd for their Encounter. They each drew a Pistol, and coming up to one another Embrac'd, and then falling back some Paces, came fairly up to one another, Presented so that their Pistoles near Touch'd, and fir'd so together that it can hardly be told which Pistol went off first; but 'tis suppos'd that Mr. *Thornhill's* did, and wounding Sir *Cholmley* on the Breast near his Heart, [at] which he instantly Drop'd.

There was a Person belonging to *Chelsea* Hospital that stood and saw it; and likewise a Woman from the Houses, who being very near when she saw Sir *Cholmley Deering* fall, came running to him, and ask'd him if he was hurt; but finding him make no answer, and that he cou'd not speak, she run after Mr. *Thornhill*, and cry'd out, *Stop him, stop him, he has Murder'd a Gentleman;* and being an unweildy Person, he could not make his escape; so that when the Woman had seen him secur'd, [she] came back to Sir *Chomley* and rais'd his Head from the Ground; but he said to her, *Good Woman let me lie down again, for I am not able to sit up:* So that then she sat on the Ground, and took his Head in her Lap, where he lay till help came to fetch him away, carrying him to the next adjacent House, where Surgeons were immediately fetch'd, and his

Wounds Drest, but presently found to be Mortal. As for saying Sir *Chomley* had no Pistols, it is a Mistake, for there was found two Brace of Pistols loaded, and he had besides loose Balls in his Coat Pocket.

His Friend Mr. *Thornhill,* being secur'd was brought to him before he Dy'd, and he embrac'd and forgave him freely; who exprest the greatest Anguish imaginable to see him in that Condition, there being no hopes of saving his Life.

But above all, he desir'd his Children might be fetch'd to him, and seem'd very impatient and uneasie till they came; when with the utmost Sorrow of a dying Father, he Blessed and took his leave of them.

The next Care, and which indeed was the greatest, was the Care of his Soul; desiring to receive the Sacrament before he Died, which he had administered to him; and about Two a Clock expir'd.

He was a Person of a competent Estate in *Kent,* near *Wye,* and had likewise other Land in *Cornwal.* He serv'd his Country often in *Parliament,* and for the most part was a Member for *Saltas* in *Cornwal;* but his Interest prevailing in the last Election, being visibly supported by the L—— he vindicated, was chose Knight of the Shire for *Kent,* where he made his Election serve. He was a Man heartily in the Interest of his Country, and a Friend to the Church.

An *ELEGY* on the Unfortunate Death of Sir Chomley Deering, Bar[t.]

What double Grief the Consequence attends
Th' unhappy Fate of two such loving Friends?
What cause but Wine and Passion cou'd excite
Two Brothers to inexorable Spight,
That nothing cou'd their furious Rage allay
Till they had vented it a Bloody Way?
Where Heav'n its Justice seems to vindicate,
In punishing their Madness at this Rate:
The Provocation which they justly gave,
Cou'd only such a sad Example have.
Yet, *DEERING,* to thy Death we pity owe,
Thou by thy Friend was Kill'd, not by thy Foe.
Oh sudden Change! Oh sad Vicissitude!
How oft do's Fate our Earthy Hopes delude?
What is there sure beneath the Firmament?
Or what is constant here to give content?
What Truth is in the Mortal Life of Man
Whose Life at most is but a measur'd Span?
But thine was shorten'd in thy Vig'rous age
By the most sad Effects of blinded Rage,
Which neither Love nor Reason cou'd asswage.
Nor is thy Friend, with Life, less punish'd here,
Who ne'er can hold one Moment of it dear:
For if the Law in Favour shou'd it grant,
A quiet Conscience he will always want;
Wretched on Earth he'll still bewail his Friend,
And will that Life he saves in Mourning End.
A Sad Example may it be to all,
How Friends together into Passion fall.

The EPITAPH

Reader, this Epitaph with Grief attend:
Here lies the Man that perish'd by his Friend:
He to no Enemy resign'd his Breath,
But from his Bosom-Friend receiv'd his Death.
Of which, as all Men justly shou'd lament,
This stands to be a lasting Monument.

One type of gun remains whose beginnings must be traced before we leave the seventeenth century: that seeming hybrid between a trumpet and a small church-bell known as the *blunderbuss.* Probably Dutch in origin, such guns appear to have been first made in the second decade of the seventeenth century on the theory that if a muzzle were to flare like a funnel, a load of buckshot would necessarily have to scatter in a fearsome swath of destruction in a very wide arc. The word itself is an English corruption of Dutch *Donder,* thunder, plus the same *Büchse,* gun, which had already been reduced to a mere *-bus* in *arquebus,* to yield *blunderbuss* from what had originally been *Donderbüchse.* Blunderbusses continued to be used in civil and military life until just a little more than a hundred years ago. For some mysterious reasons, they seem to be associated in the popular imagination with a number of myths which prove durable sources of hilarity to cartoonists and visitors of antique shops. Specifically, these are:

—that blunderbusses were loaded with handfuls of rusty nails, bits of broken glass, rocks, old door knobs, garbage, anything;

—that upon the trigger being pulled, this cargo erupted Vesuvius-like in an enormous cone of ruin which demolished all within its compass;

—that the Pilgrims landed on Plymouth Rock, disembarked, fell upon the aborigines, slew turkeys, built Boston and marched to and from church with cavernous blunderbusses ever on their shoulders.

None of these bears any kinship to fact. For one thing, blunderbusses, whether gaping like Fig. 220 or merely politely yawning like Fig. 219, were *never* loaded with anything but powder, a wad, a counted or measured quantity of musket balls, pistol balls, buckshot or birdshot, and another wad to keep these in and moisture out. They were *never* loaded with assorted fragments of rusty junk—if any such piece had become wedged crosswise in the barrel during firing, with the full force of the exploding charge behind it, the barrel would have burst like a bomb with frightful consequences to the shooter. Round, smooth pebbles *may* at times have been used in cases of dire emergency, but the irregular shapes of these would have sent them fluttering off every which way like cinders a dozen yards beyond the muzzles of long arms, even less in the case of blunderbuss pistols.

Even when correctly loaded, blunderbusses did not scatter their loads very dramatically, many not even appreciably. The reason for this is quite simple: the load traveled down the straight, or parallel part of the bore up to the point where the flare began—and kept right on going in a close-knit cluster as though there were no flare at all. Obviously the mere presence of a wide muzzle could not exercise any magic power on the load to pull it apart. Such scattering as there was naturally varied according to bore, length of barrel, point of be-

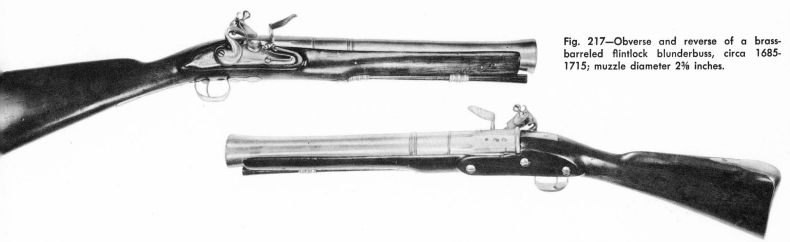

Fig. 217—Obverse and reverse of a brass-barreled flintlock blunderbuss, circa 1685-1715; muzzle diameter 2⅜ inches.

ginning of the flare, quantity of powder and of shot and kind of shot, etc.; but, in general, the dispersion was rarely much more than the pattern of any big-bore duck gun, and often less. All seventeenth- to nineteenth-century references bear this out, and twentieth-century experiments confirm it. Gunsmiths of the blunderbuss centuries surely knew it, and most shooters must have known it. Why, then, did the actually non-scattering or only moderately scattering bell-mouths remain household fixtures in farmhouses, lonely dwelling places, traveling coaches, inns, post coaches and post offices, and dozens of other places where their alleged but largely chimerical proper-

ties were relied upon in times of peril? Probably because the comparatively thick, massive barrels could be loaded with considerably greater charges than sawed-off fowling pieces and muskets, so that they could be made to drive a shot load much *harder* for the initial fifteen to twenty-five yards, albeit at the sacrifice of accuracy. Thus they had considerable value in cutting down the rigging of grappled enemy ships, and enormous blunderbusses with brass barrels (better to resist the corrosive effects of salty sea spray) were regulation arms until long after Trafalgar (1805). But effective aiming along a flaring barrel was of course impossible.

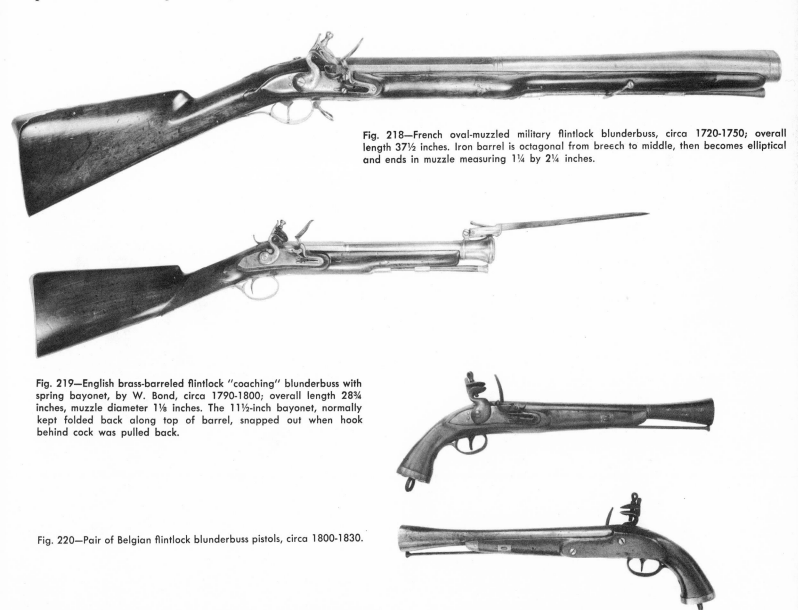

Fig. 218—French oval-muzzled military flintlock blunderbuss, circa 1720-1750; overall length 37½ inches. Iron barrel is octagonal from breech to middle, then becomes elliptical and ends in muzzle measuring 1¼ by 2¼ inches.

Fig. 219—English brass-barreled flintlock "coaching" blunderbuss with spring bayonet, by W. Bond, circa 1790-1800; overall length 28¾ inches, muzzle diameter 1⅛ inches. The 11½-inch bayonet, normally kept folded back along top of barrel, snapped out when hook behind cock was pulled back.

Fig. 220—Pair of Belgian flintlock blunderbuss pistols, circa 1800-1830.

The most frightful employment of blunderbusses was point blank from close range, such as in Fig. 221; but probably the most frequent one was psychological: even if one knew that the gaping funnel pointed at one's head from sixty feet away would almost certainly miss, the suggestion that it would *not* must nevertheless have been an overwhelming deterrent to experimentation. And a two-inch muzzle suddenly emerging from a coach window and thrust directly under one's nose doubtless proved unsettling even to the most veteran highwayman.

As to the Pilgrims, this error has found sustenance in innumerable book illustrations and dime-store prints until barely a generation ago. Usually these showed a maidenly John Alden being asked to speak for himself, while a Valkyrie of a Priscilla has taken the precaution of leaning an elephantine blunderbuss against her spinning wheel toward the event of his attempting flight. The fact is that there were hardly any blunderbusses in the American Colonies before the War of Independence, and not many more thereafter save naval ones. Blunderbusses would have been of very little use in the American wilderness. The original 102 Pilgrim Fathers brought standard matchlock service muskets in 1620, and perhaps such few snaphaunces as they might have been able to afford. Their followers during the next sixty or seventy years brought mostly, although not solely, more matchlock muskets. Good fowling pieces and pistols were useful in the struggle for survival; later on flintlock muskets, and those indestructible "all-around" field guns which would do equally good execution against deer at one hundred yards with a patched ball as against pheasants at forty with shot, could be found two or three in every household. But not unaimable, point-blank thunder funnels.

The Murder of THOMAS THYNN Esq in Pall-Mall

Fig. 221—The murder of Thomas Thynn in London in 1681 is probably history's most celebrated infamy perpetrated with a blunderbuss. Thynn was a professional scoundrel and a favorite courtier of Charles II. In late 1680, Mrs. Thynn had suffered outrage, although rather co-operatively, at the hands of German Count Königsmark, a professional swindler and intriguer. An affair flourished, but the lady protested that it would look reprehensible if she were to run off with another while her husband was still alive, suggesting demurely, however, that this obstacle was not necessarily beyond remedy. Königsmark's remedy, administered by hired professionals under the leadership of renegade "Captain" Christopher Uratz on Sunday evening, February 12, as Thynn's carriage entered Pall Mall from St. James Street, is recorded together with this engraving in Charles Johnson's A General History of the Lives and Adventures of the Most Famous Highwaymen, Murderers, Street-Robbers, &c. (London, 1736). While two killers covered the coachmen with pistols, a third shot Thynn through the open window "with a Blunderbuss, which mortify'd him after such a barbarous manner that Mr. Hobbs, an eminent Chyrurgeon, found in his Body four bullets which had torn into his Guts, wounded his Liver, and Stomach, and Gall, broke one Rib, and wounded the great Bone below; of which Wounds he dyed." The killers were apprehended and hanged.

CHAPTER EIGHT

The influence of military on civil arms—The adoption of flintlocks in the reign of James II—The Glorious Revolution—King William's desperate need for flintlocks—The influence of civil weapons on the military—The end of armor—The bayonet—The Brown Bess—The Duke of Marlborough and the War of the Spanish Succession—New infantry tactics—The use of cartridges in the United States Army in 1779—The virtues, longevity and vices of the Brown Bess—Conditions of eighteenth-century military life—Military punishments—Sanitary conditions of the rococo—Old uniform prints.

I T IS OFTEN THOUGHT THAT THE design of sporting arms has always been strongly influenced by the military weapons of the day. This, in fact, is only very rarely the case. The requirements of military firearms are not only far removed, but often opposite to those of civil arms, so that it has almost always been impossible to reconcile the two with satisfactory results. For example, a fine wheellock rifle might kill with accuracy at well beyond two hundred yards, while a smoothbore wheellock musket, such as there were, could not hit a man with certainty beyond one hundred yards at the most. But the rifle required an extremely involved loading procedure which took more than two minutes to complete, for which the hunter had leisure, while a nimble musketeer might discharge five shots in the same time with his loosely fitting, easily rammed bullets when rapidity of fire was the crucial factor. From the military point of view, a flintlock was still satisfactory if it missed fire three times out of ten, for this meant that in a volley fired by a thousand men there would still be seven hundred shots. For tactical purposes, the three hundred which were lost as misfires or flashes-in-the-pan were not worth the expenditure which would have been necessary to buy locks of such quality that they would miss fire only three times in a hundred. And as has been marked elsewhere in some detail, matchlocks were considered adequate for battles until almost the end of the seventeenth century because the alternatives were simply too expensive. The military idea of efficiency and optimal design was always far below what a private sportsman demanded of his gun.

Upon the restoration of Charles II in 1660, the Commonwealth army was disbanded, its arms were put up in storage, and the king's militia was so reduced that in 1685 it numbered scarcely more than eight thousand men. The foot soldiers—about five thousand—were all equipped with the venerable matchlocks which had served well enough while the enemy had shot back with nothing better, but which now could no longer be relied upon for the defense of the realm. Until the reign of James II, only one military unit had been exclusively supplied with flintlocks, and these only of a light type known as *fusils* or *fusees* owing to their close resemblance to a kind of French woodcock gun to which the English cavaliers in exile had attached the French word *fusil*, a generic term which actually meant any non-military sporting gun. This unit was the North British Fusilers, formed in 1678, the first of many minor instances of an obvious and official influence of civil arms design on the military.

Fig. 222—"Capt. Henry Morgan before Panama wh. he took from the Spaniards." Sir Henry Morgan (1635?-1688), British buccaneer and privateer, is shown with a rapier, a brace of pistols (presumably large-calibre, silver-butted French or Italian flintlocks), and what appears to be a carved and inlaid flintlock of light-weight *fusil* or *fusee* proportions. Engraving from Charles Johnson's *A General History of the Lives and Adventures of the Most Famous Highwaymen, Murderers, Street-Robbers, &c.*, London, 1736.

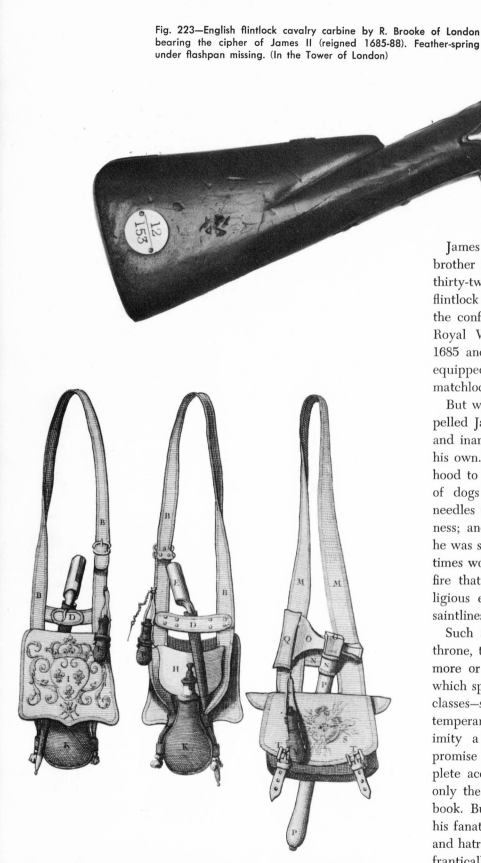

Fig. 223—English flintlock cavalry carbine by R. Brooke of London bearing the cipher of James II (reigned 1685-88). Feather-spring under flashpan missing. (In the Tower of London)

Fig. 224—Left and middle: front and back views of French infantry soldier's *cartouchière*, or cartridge pouch, late 17th to middle 18th centuries. Main pouch, covered by flap brilliantly embroidered with Bourbon device, contained paper-wrapped cartridges (see Fig. 234), spare flints, musket balls, screwdriver. Note large flask for propellent powder (used after cartridges had been spent), small flask for priming, touchhole pricker on short chain, bayonet in leather scabbard. Right: grenadier's *sacoche*; medium-sized pistol flask hangs in front; note axe instead of bayonet. Mule-ear flaps on pouch cover telescope or surveyor's theodolite. Engraving from Surirey de Saint-Rémy, *Mémoires d'Artillerie*, Paris, 1697.

James II, upon his ascent following the death of his brother in 1685, increased the standing army to about thirty-two thousand men and ordered the adoption of flintlock muskets with all the dispatch possible within the confines of appropriated funds. The Royal and the Royal Welsh Fusiliers, commissioned respectively in 1685 and 1688, were two of such completely flintlock-equipped regiments, while the others jettisoned their matchlocks as quickly as the new replacements arrived.

But whatever compels men to be what they are compelled James II to be a comsummation of all the vices and inanities of Stuart fame, plus a diseased cruelty of his own. It had been a favorite pastime since his childhood to attend tortures; he delighted in the vivisection of dogs and cats; he blinded canaries with red-hot needles that they might sing more beautifully in blindness; and toward the end of his life, exiled in France, he was seized by an equal measure of masochism and at times would so mortify his flesh with whips, knives and fire that he often lost consciousness in agony and religious ecstasy, and expired in 1701 in the repute of saintliness.

Such a man was doomed to fare ill on the British throne, the more so as one of a family which was still more or less on probation. The solid British citizenry which spoke through Parliament, as well as the working classes—so far as these mattered—were not inclined by temperament or by past experience to view with equanimity a monarch whose eccentricities held out the promise of eclipsing the worst of his father. The complete accounts of his royal blunders would exceed not only the scope but the physical volume of the present book. But the immediate roots of his downfall lay in his fanatic determination to flout the near-explosive fear and hatred among virtually all Englishmen for what was frantically (and politically) execrated as "sinful, monstrous popery." Thus, when he sought to ensure a Roman Catholic succession to the throne, he precipitated the end of the ancient concepts of monarchy with such rapidity that all was over before most people fully grasped what had begun. On June 30, 1688, seven Parliamentary leaders of the Whig and Tory parties sent an invitation to Prince William of Orange in the Nether-lands, husband of James's Protestant daughter Mary, to cross the Channel and accede as a constitutional monarch. On November 5, William and his army landed at Torbay. Most of the civil population rallied to his banner; many officers and generals of the army—Marlborough among them—went over to him, while the rank-and-file was left leaderless and torn apart by violently conflicting loyalties. On December 11, James fled to France. Four months later, on April 11, 1689, William of Orange and Mary Stuart were crowned as William III and Mary II of Eng-land. So ended the "Glorious Revolution," that swift, bloodless earthquake of history which founded the con-stitutional principle that an English monarch reigns but does not rule, and that he is accountable to the will of his subjects.

But William had also acceded to troubles which were to test all his great gifts of diplomacy and leadership. Until now the leader of that coalition of two-thirds of Europe determined to halt Louis XIV and the hegemony of France's power, William had now to reckon not only with the old wrath of Louis but of Louis's cousin, the exiled James. Louis, as has been observed earlier, had already equipped many regiments with modern flintlocks, and in 1690 his vast army stood poised in France and Flanders awaiting only the vessels and the nod to invade England itself. William was therefore sorely pressed to complete his predecessor's program of changing over from match-locks to flintlocks with utmost haste. His demands, how-ever, far exceeded the supply, although not only every gunsmith in London had been contracted to deliver vir-tually his entire output in the form of muskets, but of late the iron workers of Birmingham as well had been hurriedly taught enough about gunmaking to turn out passable, if not conspicuously good or handsome, military guns. With the crisis growing daily more desperate, and the campaigns in Flanders and Ireland consuming vaster supplies than were being produced, William was forced to buy whatever weapons he could from the gunmakers of Italy, Germany, Austria, Scandinavia and whatever other countries or principalities Louis could not pressure into clamping an embargo on arms for England. Thus there accumulated in England an assortment of muskets which had no feature in common save the approx-imately No. 12 bore (about .75 calibre) and an unfor-tunate tendency to fall apart under the effort of shoot-ing. Further, nearly all of these items were built along the lines, lengths and weights of matchlock muskets and calivers. Such proportions had been serviceable enough for the old weapons, which, owing to the live match, could be fired only within very narrowly circumscribed angles and attitudes; but they totally prevented the poten-tial freedom of motion, tactical maneuvers and rapidity of fire offered by the flintlock if properly designed.

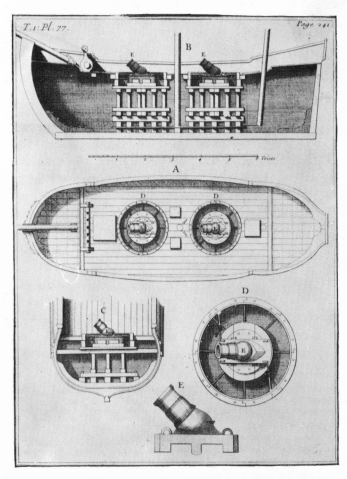

Fig. 225—Two engraved plates from Surirey de Saint-Rémy, *Mémoires d'Artillerie* (Paris, 1697), showing overall view and structural details of a mortar ship; vessel was little more than a floating platform for two enormous mortars. Crew, consisting of a master, three sailors and four gunners, sailed swiftly up to coastal objectives protected by high fortifications or situated atop high coastal cliffs, let loose a bombard-ment of explosive mortar balls lobbed up in high arcs. Mortars pivoted in their bases like huge ball joints.

Therefore, from about 1691 on, considerable caution was exercised before signing further foreign contracts, and the Gunmakers' Company was charged with the supervision of future procurements to ensure that these should conform to such standards as would make them as uniform and as serviceable as the circumstances allowed. The outcome of this inevitably had to be that the representatives of the Company would naturally turn to designs which they had long been developing for their sporting clients. Accordingly, they fitted minimally heavy musket barrels on stocks which, although redesigned to survive the rougher life in the army, were shaped by long experience into the form best suited to the arrangement of arms, limbs, eyes, muscles and other members of the human anatomy involved in shooting. Thus the ancestors of the yet unborn *Brown Bess* began to trickle into the ranks, still comparatively clumsy pillars to be sure, but nevertheless much closer to the light, slender, essentially modern proportions of the best fowling pieces than to the opposite extreme of the rhinocerean matchlock dimensions. These newcomers were on the whole much superior to their French counterparts, especially in that vastly important respect which it has been the object of the last few paragraphs to trace: for with their sensible proportions they enabled the British to march further and faster than the French, and to deliver volleys at the rate of five for the enemy's four. The attempts of Louis and James were frustrated, in Ireland as well as in Flanders, and the adoption of the redesigned flintlock musket was as much responsible for this as in later ages the superior fighter aircraft were for saving the realm and civilization itself.

More important as indices to a historical process were the adoption of the *socket bayonet* and the elimination of the last remnants of armor. The bayonet had been known since about 1580 in the form of a sword or dagger with a wooden handle which was plugged *into* the muzzle of the gun instead of being fastened *around* it by a sleeve or *socket* (Fig. 227). This allowed only tactics in which the troops would fire, plug in their bayonets, charge, unplug the bayonets, load, fire, plug in the bayonets, &c., &c. If the gun should ever be discharged while the bayonet was in the muzzle, the barrel almost inevitably had to burst. Furthermore, the old matchlocks had been far too clumsy for bayonet thrusting, while one need hardly mention the awkwardness of the plugging and unplugging while the soldiers' hands were encumbered by coils of glowing slow match. Until about 1690 it had been found far more effective to let the musketeers and other shooters do the shooting, and leave the charg-

ing and the thrusting to the pikemen, halberdiers and lancers. Bayonets had thus never been considered serviceable weapons until their redesign at the close of the seventeenth century, when an unknown Frenchman thought of attaching them by a tubular socket which fitted around the barrel. Now muskets could be loaded and fired with bayonets mounted, while the new flintlocks themselves, being light and free of glowing matchcords, offered new maneuverability. The new withering rate of three and even four volleys a minute often so devastated the enemy ranks that a bayonet charge could end the business and at times precipitate what is called a great victory. Armor, however, was clearly an impossible impediment to such mobility; consequently it vanished from the infantry within a decade, and after 1700 only the cuirassiers, dragoons and a few other cavalry services continued to be clad even in breastplates. The end of the four-hundred-year path to the museum had been reached.

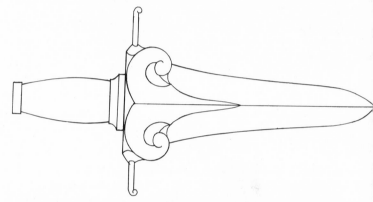

Fig. 227—Broad, massive plug bayonet, circa 1600-75. Round wooden handle was plugged directly into muzzle of gun, had to be removed and reinserted before and after every shot.

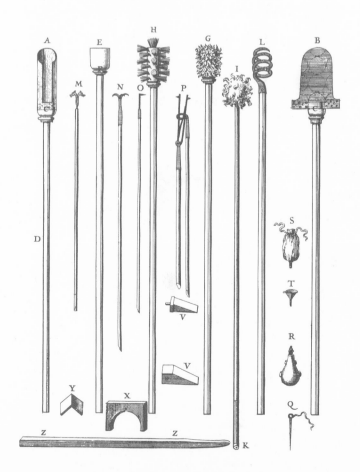

Fig. 226—Cannon-servicing implements; engraved plate from Surirey de Saint-Rémy, *Mémoires d'Artillerie*, Paris, 1697. A—scoop for loading powder (cf. Fig. 49); B—same scoop, showing sheet metal unrolled (cf. Fig. 176); E—rammer; H, G and I—barrel brush and mops; L—worm; M—linstock; N, O and P—hooks for withdrawing cannon balls with fuse holes; Q—touchhole pricker; R—priming powder flask; S—leather grease bag with nozzle for forcing grease between friction areas; T—funnel for filling touchhole with priming; U and V—chocks for elevating barrel and chocking wheels; X, Y and Z—miscellaneous chocks, supports and lever.

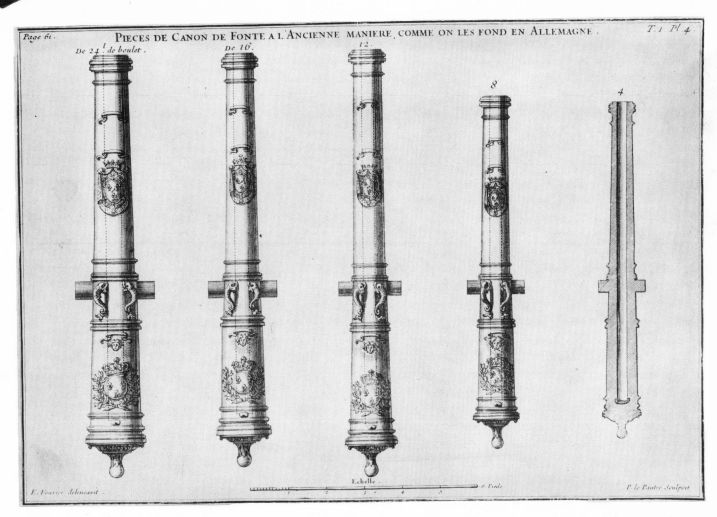

Fig. 228—A pessimist's weapon: combination of flintlock carbine and battle-axe. Now in the Tower of London, it was probably among the foreign arms accumulated in England during King William's policy of overseas purchase in 1689-91.

Fig. 229—17th-century cannons, "cast in the old styles, as they are made in Germany." According to given scale, 24-pounder (i.e., a cannon of such a calibre that a solid iron sphere to fit it would weigh 24 pounds) at extreme left is about 8½ feet long. Sizes of 16-, 12-, 8- and 4-pounders may be judged by comparison. From Surirey de Saint-Rémy, *Mémoires d'Artillerie*, Paris, 1697.

Upon his accession in 1689, William had found an army which had not appreciably changed since the days of Sir Roger Williams a century before, its matchlocks and mounted pole-arms bearers harking more to the late Middle Ages than to the imminent eighteenth century. Before his death in 1702, he had seen his efforts to change all this bear fruit as the foundation of the modern British army, if by "modern" we mean a standing force of uniformed regulars trained in the use of the new-style musket and the bayonet by the discipline of endless drilling, and officered by a pyramid which relayed the orders from Whitehall to the squadron sergeant.

When, therefore, the War of the Spanish Succession (1701–13) found the British allied with Austria and the Netherlands against France and Bavaria, the oppor-

tunity was ready made for John Churchill, then Earl of Marlborough (1650–1722), to build on these foundations the army which established Britain, not France, as the dominant power in Europe, and incidentally won British control of the Mediterranean for future ages by the capture of Gibraltar in 1704. But if the muskets of King William's reign had been radical improvements over the matchlocks of James and Charles, they nonetheless presented a sorry scene of mediocrity compared to the startling designs submitted to Marlborough by the gunmakers of England in the opening years of the war. Out of these fast grew the weapon described officially then and thenceforth as the *Tower Musket* (from the Tower of London arsenal stamp on the lock plate), or as *Her Majesty's Musket* (our history having now passed the death of William and the succession of his sister-in-law Queen Anne in 1702). Upon its having been mass produced, however, and issued to the troops, it became known unofficially almost at once as *Brown Bess,* for reasons which must remain among the secrets of soldiers who have long since returned to dust. Its barrel was browned by the customary pickling process in order to protect against rust and to eliminate glare, but so had most barrels been since the end of the sixteenth century (cf. "russeting" in Items 13, 15 and 16 of *The Gun Makers' Rates,* Fig. 182). Moreover, the brown finish soon wore off in use and cleaning, so that few barrels retained their original finishes after a few years of service. It has been suggested that it was named after a bevy of Spanish camp followers of swarthy complexions and temperaments so volatile as to remind the men of the qualities of their new weapon, but while this theory may offer a measure of piquancy, it must be deemed apocryphal for want of evidence. Whatever the Brown Bess's genealogy, it set out directly to impress its virtues on the unfortunate enemy conscripts sent to test them, and it succeeded so well that Frenchmen soon spoke in awe of *"la Besse bruine"* and the Bavarians of *"die braune Liesl,"* the latter having evidently been informed that "Bess" was the popular English nickname of Elizabeth.

As issued first and in ever-greater numbers from their adoption and evolution into permanency between 1703 and 1712 to the Peace of Utrecht in 1713, Brown Besses had the characteristic stocks, long wrists and sharply dropped butts which were to remain their hallmarks for all their life (Figs. 230 to 232). They weighed about ten pounds, which, as any soldier or ex-soldier can testify, is about the upper limit which can be endured on a long march along with a full field pack. Their barrels measured forty-six inches, round for the entire length and somewhat tapered; the breech ended in a few narrow, raised ornamental bands or rings. The stock was walnut stained to a reddish brown, which, however, did not differ sufficiently from the color of most private and many earlier service weapons to account for the adjectival epithet to Bess's name. The mountings—a massive butt plate, an escutcheon on the wrist, a sideplate and four ramrod thimbles—were almost invariably brass. Usually there was some stylized carving of scrollwork on the wrist immediately behind the breech and around the tang. In overall length the Brown Bess measured some sixty-two inches.

Bess's lock was a vast improvement over any yet seen on any service arm. It was a *bridle lock,* or one in which a small flat plate, or *bridle,* served as a bearing to keep the tumbler in perfectly vertical rotation and to prevent its being pressed against the inside of the lockplate by the pressure of the mainspring (Fig. 233-B). The friction between the lockplate and a tumbler forced out of alignment by the mainspring in locks *without* a bridle could impede the force of the snapping cock sufficiently to render the action so weak that it would often fail to open the flashpan cover completely. In such a case, the sparks would be few and cool (cf. excerpt from Johnson, p. 82), and such as there were could reach the priming not at all or only by odd chance. A misfire was then all but inevitable. With the bridle, however, this hazard was virtually eliminated. Moreover, the Brown Besses of about 1725 and after had the further refinement of a steel strap which ran from the outer edge of the flashpan to the screw about which the flashpan cover rotated, so that the screw was now anchored at both ends and could not be bent by constant use to impede the motion of the cover or to jam it altogether (Fig. 233-A). Both these refinements had been employed on the better-quality sporting arms of both England and the Continent since about 1680, but it was not until about 1720 that they were found as standard members of even fair- and medium-quality guns which made any pretense whatever to being well-made. The features of bridle and flashpan-screw bearing were of enormous consequence in the history of firearms. A lock without them wore quickly, made the cover fit askew on the pan when the screw had become bent in the slightest, and therefore spilled the priming, fired slowly and missed fire perhaps as much as once in seven shots owing to the weakness of the snap described before. A lock *with* both these additions, however, could be expected to give service to the great-grandchildren of the original owner if given reasonable care. It fired quickly, and even without the further boons of a roller bearing on the battery spring and a swivel on the tumbler, which appeared in about 1770 and will be taken up presently, it could be counted on to misfire fewer times than once in twenty-five or even fifty, depending on quality of workmanship and materials.

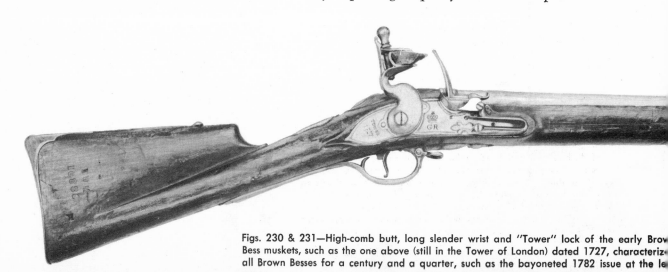

Figs. 230 & 231—High-comb butt, long slender wrist and "Tower" lock of the early Brown Bess muskets, such as the one above (still in the Tower of London) dated 1727, characterize all Brown Besses for a century and a quarter, such as the bayoneted 1782 issue at the le

Fig. 232—Brown Bess or "Tower" lock, here not stamped "Tower" but with maker's name (Grice, who was capable of better—cf. Fig. 300) and the date 1756. Crown and cipher "GR" *(Georgius Rex)* between cock and flashpan remained unchanged throughout reigns of all four Georges and the Regency (1714 to 1830), without addition at any time of particular George's ordinal number (e.g., never "G II R"); this often makes dating difficult. Crown-and-arrow stamp beneath flashpan indicates government ownership. Probably more than 10 million such locks were made in the 130-odd years of Brown Bess service issues; they were used not only on muskets but on pistols, blunderbusses, rifles and even on cannons; millions found their way into civilian use, and very many thousands, perhaps millions, drifted into gunsmiths' shops far outside the British Empire (e.g., Fig. 235).

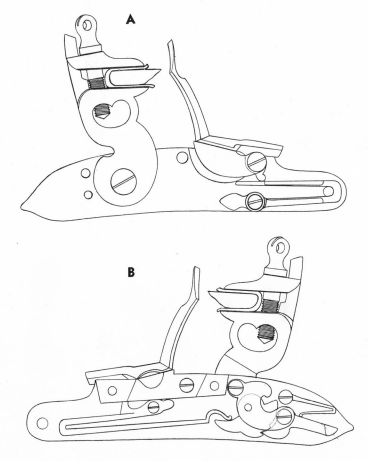

Fig. 233—Outside and inside views of a flintlock with a flashpan cover bridle and a tumbler bridle (here a French cavalry carbine lock of the Napoleonic era). Diagr. A: Bridge, or bridle, extending from front of flashpan around head of hinge screw serves to hold screw anchored not only where it threads into lockplate but also around head; screw thus cannot be bent, and flashpan cover continues to swing about it smoothly. Diagr. B: Crescent-shaped bridle over tumbler similarly anchors head of screw about which sear pivots, and keeps tumbler perfectly vertical against inside of lockplate; tumbler thus cannot be bent, keeps cock snapping smoothly and quickly. All well-made locks after about 1740 had bridles. See also Figs. 242 and 243. Double-neck cocks for heavy-duty military service became frequent after about 1790.

But the Brown Bess's most peculiar talent lay in turning a vice into a virtue. We have noted earlier that the standard matchlock service musket of Caroline and Cromwellian times took a ball 1/24 of an inch smaller than its No. 11 bore barrel, with a resulting "blow-by" and "chatter" (Fig. 173) which reduced its shooting to a fraction of the potential power and accuracy, but which also facilitated rapid-fire loading. In the case of the Brown Bess, the No. 11 bore, which measured about .76 inches in diameter, was loaded with a 14-bore ball measuring about .71 inches, a difference of no less than 1/20 of an inch! The effect of such a gap was that loading was reduced to a minimum effort, the bullet falling down a clean barrel freely if dropped into it and the ramrod being really required only to seat it firmly on top of the powder, or to ram it down after the barrel had become fouled. Thus it was possible to train men to fire six shots a minute, tapering off to five and finally four as fatigue took its toll. Such rate of fire was murderous in the infantry tactics of the day, when two opposing armies would draw up within a hundred yards of each other or less, and fire until the survivors of one side stood deeper in blood, shrieks and corpses than the other. The loss of all accuracy beyond seventy-five or eighty-five yards (against a man-sized target) owing to the use of a ball 1/20 of an inch smaller than the bore was of no consequence as long as two thousand men could be made to send ten thousand balls a minute into the mass of the enemy column (which after the third volley was anyhow totally obscured by an impenetrable smoke screen). It made no difference whatever which man was hit if only the fire could be kept up with untiring fury to slay them all eventually. If the enemy's muskets were loaded with balls which shot more accurately, but only twice or three times a minute, which was the case with most of Britain's enemies until 1815 (save for the Americans, whose regular infantry used mostly Brown Besses themselves), then the battle was only a formality of counting the dead and wounded. Almost always many more of the enemy than British were represented in these fearful statistics. It was these new tactics which the Earl of Marlborough introduced, and proved by winning signal victories for his country in Spain, France, the Netherlands and Bavaria, and a dukedom, a palace, a park and £10,000 a year for himself. It is a fact that he was one of the extremely few generals in history who never lost a battle.

When, however, the occasion demanded shooting with less abandon, the Brown Bess could rise to it. Loaded with a tightly fitting ball, it could make the shot tell with deadly impact and fair-to-good accuracy at a deer-sized target at 120 yards and more.

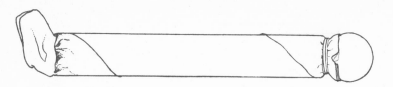

Fig. 234—Typical paper-wrapped cartridge of the flintlock era. Soldier tore off end with his teeth before priming and loading.

The soldiers' ammunition consisted of paper cartridges, i.e., paper cylinders of the diameter of the bore, which contained powder and ball for one shot and were tied or folded at the ends (Figs. 71 and 234). How these were loaded may be learned from Sects. V-XII of Baron von Steuben's REGULATIONS FOR THE DISCIPLINE OF THE TROOPS OF THE UNITED STATES, published in Philadelphia in 1779 (numbers in brackets refer to corresponding soldier's number in Fig. 236):

V.
Half-cock—Firelock! One motion.
Half-bend the cock, briskly bringing down the elbow to the butt of the *firelock* [3].

VI.
Handle—Cartridge! One motion.
Bring your right hand short round to your pouch, [*small figure at right of 2, or upper insert between 3 and 4*], slapping it hard, seize the cartridge, and bring it with a quick motion to your mouth, bite the top off down to the powder, covering it instantly with your thumb, and bring the hand as low as the chin, with the elbow down [4].

VII.
Prime! One motion.
Shake the powder into the pan [*insert right of 4*], and covering the cartridge again, place the three last fingers behind the hammer [flashpan cover], with the elbow up.

VIII.
Shut—Pan! Two motions.
1st. Shut your pan briskly, bringing down the elbow to the butt of the firelock, holding the cartridge fast in your hand.
2d. Turn the piece nimbly around before you to the loading position, with the lock to the front, and the muzzle at the height of the chin, bringing the right hand up under the muzzle; both feet being kept fast in this motion.

IX.
Charge with Cartridge! Two motions.
1st. Turn up your hand and put the cartridge into the muzzle, shaking the powder into the barrel.
2d. Turning the stock a little towards you, place your right hand closed, with a quick and strong motion, upon the butt of the rammer [upon the tip of the ramrod], the thumb upwards, and the elbow down [5].

X.
Draw—Rammer! Two motions.
1st. Draw your rammer with a quick motion half out, seizing it instantly at the muzzle back-handed.
2d. Draw it quite out, turn it, and enter it into the muzzle [6].

XI.
Ram down—Cartridge! One motion.
Ram the cartridge well down the barrel, and instantly recovering and seizing the rammer back-handed by the middle, draw it quite out, turn it, and enter it as far as the lower pipe, placing at the same time the edge of the hand on the butt-end of the rammer, with the fingers extended.

XII.
Return—Rammer! One motion.
Thrust the rammer home [7], and instantly bring up the piece with the left hand to the shoulder, seizing it at the same time with the right hand under the cock, keeping the left hand at the swell, and turning the body square to the front [8]. . . .

In all exercises in detail, the men will use a piece of wood, instead of a flint; and each soldier should have six pieces of wood, in the form of cartridges, which the serjeant must see taken out of the pieces when the exercise is finished.

When the company exercises with powder, the captain will inspect the company, and see that all the cartridges not used are returned.

But the Brown Besses' effectiveness did not rest solely on rapidity of fire. By about 1710 the socket bayonet was in use in most European armies. Improved since its first appearance, it was now affixed by engaging a small stud near the muzzle in a zig-zag slot in the socket; a quick twist and a turn of the locking ring, and it was firmly mounted, ready for instant use without impairing the soldier's fire power (e.g., Figs. 231, 247 and 254). The British augmented their musket by a sixteen- to eighteen-inch blade, rather broad and triangular in cross-section, and soon grew expert at its carnage.

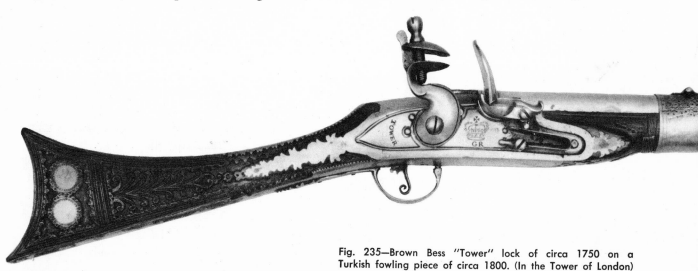

Fig. 235—Brown Bess "Tower" lock of circa 1750 on a Turkish fowling piece of circa 1800. (In the Tower of London)

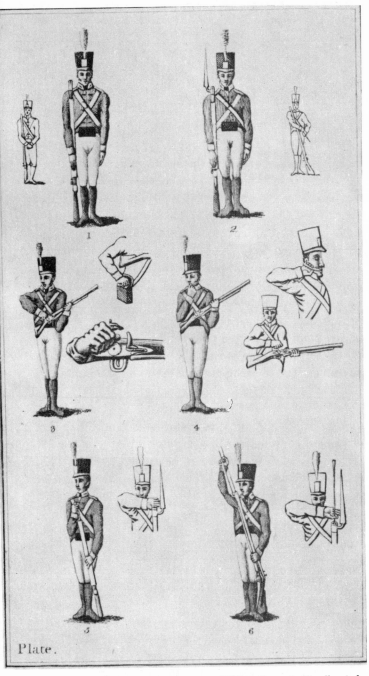

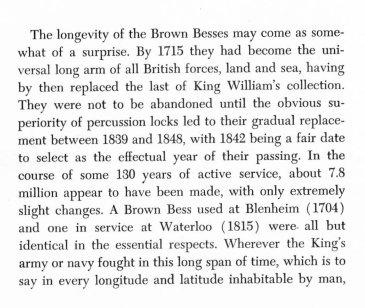

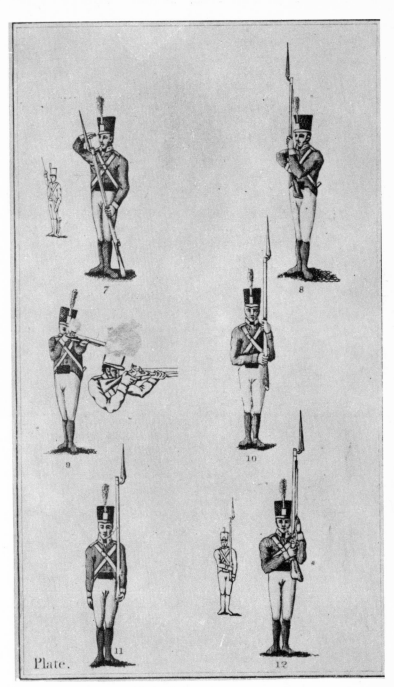

Fig. 236—Two engraved plates from William Duane's *Handbook for Infantry* (Philadelphia, 1813), showing various loading and drill exercises. Although early 19th-century American, exercises shown could apply to any army in flintlock era. For explanation, see p. 112.

The longevity of the Brown Besses may come as somewhat of a surprise. By 1715 they had become the universal long arm of all British forces, land and sea, having by then replaced the last of King William's collection. They were not to be abandoned until the obvious superiority of percussion locks led to their gradual replacement between 1839 and 1848, with 1842 being a fair date to select as the effectual year of their passing. In the course of some 130 years of active service, about 7.8 million appear to have been made, with only extremely slight changes. A Brown Bess used at Blenheim (1704) and one in service at Waterloo (1815) were all but identical in the essential respects. Wherever the King's army or navy fought in this long span of time, which is to say in every longitude and latitude inhabitable by man,

Brown Besses flashed and thundered; and as history records, rarely in vain. But this does not, in fact, constitute a monument to their enduring excellence, but rather to the enduring warmth with which the military authorities cherished the ways of their ancestors. By 1775, even before the experiences in the American War of Independence had prompted many officers to write tracts pleading for the adoption of rifles, the failings of the Brown Bess had become proverbial, the more sharply marked by comparison with the magnificent flintlock weapons which were developed for private use between 1775 and 1825. Thus, an author who preferred to be known only as A Colonel in the German Service (i.e., in the British army serving in Germany and Austria during the Napoleonic Wars), wrote a tract published in London in 1805 (after almost a century of Brown Besses!) entitled A PLAN FOR THE FORMATION OF A CORPS WHICH NEVER HAS BEEN RAISED AS YET IN ANY ARMY IN EUROPE; acidly he observed (italics in original):

A soldier's musket, if it is not exceeding badly bored, and very crooked, as many are, will strike the figure of a man at 80 yards—it *may* even at 100 yards. But a soldier must be very unfortunate indeed who shall be wounded by a common musket at 150 yards, provided his antagonist aims it at him; and as to firing at a man at 200 yards, you may just as well fire at the moon and have the same hopes of hitting your object. I do maintain, and will prove whenever called upon, that *no man was ever killed at two hundred yards* by a common soldier's musket by the person who aimed it at him . . . and in general service, an enemy fired upon by our men from 150 yards is as safe as in St. Paul's Cathedral.

Another officer, urged by prudence to be known only as An Officer of Infantry, published a booklet in 1796 entitled A SKETCH OF THE PRESENT STATE OF THE ARMY, in which he wrote:

Amongst other grievances which might easily be remedied, it may not be improper to mention the badness of the flints, and the softness of that part of the pan-cover of his firelock that the soldier calls the hammer. This is so general, that take at a venture any number of men, and after ten or twelve rounds of firing, you will find at least a fifth part of the cartridges have not been used [i.e., have failed to go off owing to insufficient sparks]; consequently one man in five would be useless as to any real effect. This we see every day at field-days and reviews; and upon service, I have seen soldiers try their pieces again and again, to no avail. Was the soldier exposed to the fire of the enemy at the same time, and the charge with the bayonet either not practical or not available, his situation is highly discouraging and very uncomfortable. . . .

But always there was the counter-argument of the withering rate of fire. If such methods were outdated by the Napoleonic era, or to prove largely ineffectual in the American War of Independence, this did not in any way tarnish the Brown Bess's record as the most efficient tool in the national abattoirs of the eighteenth century. Of all the rival muskets, only the French, the Prussian and the Russian ever proved formidable but never superior (resp. Figs. 239, 237 and 241). Of all the fortunate multitudes permitted to participate in the sport of kings, Englishmen ranked first in all but invincible musketry tactics and in the art of being blown to fragments in rhythm to inspiring music; while the French (Figs. 247 and 254) ranked second in tactics but were permitted to spill their bowels over prettier silks and laces. Of all the weapons of any period before the twentieth century, more Brown Besses survive to the present day all over the globe than any other. The flint-chipping industry—or "knapping," as this extremely difficult trade is called—packs and ships hundreds of thousands of gunflints annually from Brandon, England, into all parts of the world, and how many of these are destined for Brown Besses still used in deadly earnest in Africa and Asia will never be exactly known; reasonable conjecture puts the number somewhere near a hundred thousand.

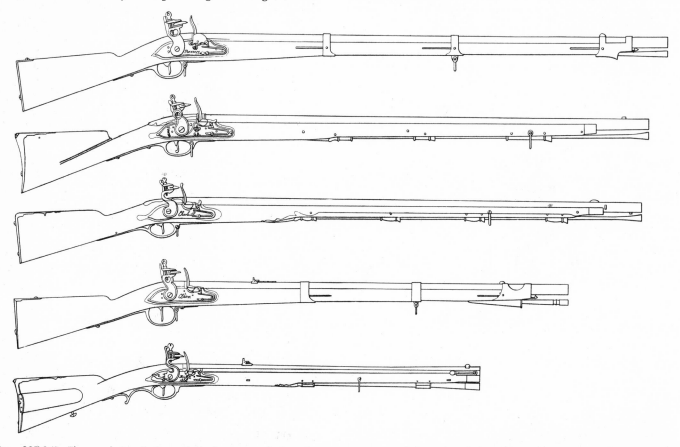

Figs. 237-241—The muskets of the principal powers during the Napoleonic Wars, circa 1795 to 1815. Not surprisingly, they were the best-designed, most effective in the world. From top to bottom: 1—Prussia's *Potzdam* or *Potsdam* musket (after Potsdam arsenal) with flash shield at side of flashpan. 2—Great Britain's *Brown Bess*. 3—France's *Charleville* musket (after Charleville arsenal and manufactory). 4—Austria's light carbine-musket stamped *Wien* (Vienna). 5—Russia's *Tula* rifle-musket (after Tula arsenal), a fairly high-quality weapon and the only rifled musket to be issued to any infantry in moderately large quantities before the 1840's; it was loaded with a patched ball, had a three-leaf rear sight adjustable for 50, 100, 150 and 200 meters; not a long-range rifle but a compromise weapon, it was probably accurate at these medium ranges if sights were set correctly, but Russian soldiers, like others, were usually unable to judge distances. Drawn after engravings in Julius Schoen, *Geschichte der Handfeuerwaffen (History of Small Arms)* Dresden, 1858.

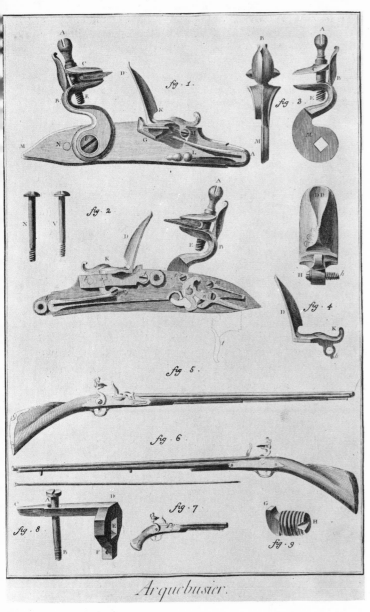

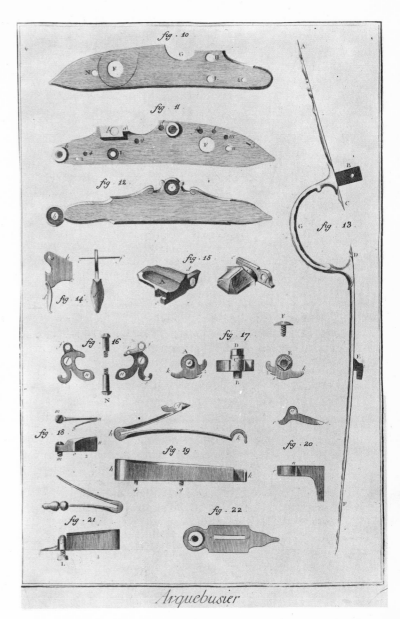

Arquebusier.

Arquebusier

Figs. 242 & 243—Two plates illustrating the article "Arquebusier" in Denis Diderot's *Encyclopédie,* Paris, 1751-65.

Left plate (by figure numbers in plate): *Fig. 1*—The complete lock. *Fig. 2*—Inside view of the lock, and the two screws which pass through stock transversely to hold it; screws thread into holes seen as ring-like sockets. *Fig. 3*—Back and side views of cock (i.e., side against lock); note shoulder which strikes top edge of lockplate to arrest snap. *Fig. 4*—Front and side views of flashpan cover. *Figs. 5 & 6*—Left and right sides of a musket, and, below lower gun, the ramrod. *Fig. 7*—A military pistol. *Fig. 8*—The "false breech" with tang and screw. *Fig. 9*—The breechplug which closes rear end of barrel and hooks into "false breech"; note powder notch—cf. Fig. 37, and Par. 3 of excerpt, p. 94.

Right plate: *Fig. 10*—Outside of stripped lockplate. *Fig. 11*—Inside of stripped lockplate. *Fig. 12*—Sideplate or screwholder (cf. Fig. 190). *Fig. 13*—

Trigger guard, with hook and pin-key which hold it to stock. *Fig. 14*—Side and front views of trigger, with pivot pin; flat internal section pushes up on sear (see dotted outline, Fig. 2, left plate). *Fig. 15*—Top and bottom views of dismounted flashpan. *Fig. 16*—Two views of the tumbler bridle, and the two screws which secure it. *Fig. 17*—Below the figure number, from left to right: left, top and right views of the tumbler; note full- and half-cock notches, and square axis which passes through round hole in lockplate and engages square socket of cock; at right of the figure number: flat-headed screw which screws into square tumbler axis to hold cock. *Fig. 18*—Side and bottom views of the sear spring. *Fig. 19*—Side and bottom views of the mainspring. *Fig. 20*—Side and bottom views of the sear. *Fig. 21*—Side and bottom views of the flashpan cover feather-spring. *Fig. 22*—The trigger plate, from underside of stock inside loop of trigger guard, through which flat section of trigger passes into the lock recess or mechanism.

The conditions in armies and navies throughout and long after the eighteenth century were such that those which prevailed throughout most of the nineteenth, hellish though these were, would have seemed like ministrations of mercy to the redcoats of Marlborough and Wellington. If the British service was in any way distinguished in this respect from those of France, Prussia and Austria, it was only in the somewhat lesser degree of sadism in high places, but to balance this, also in a greater degree of administrative incompetence which resulted in equally unbearable and tragically unnecessary

suffering of the troops. Until about 1820, 15 to 25 per cent of all the men shipped to India perished of disease in the suffocating holds of the transport ships in the course of the four months' journey around the Cape of Good Hope. Water quickly turned slimy and foul, tropical fevers and diseases were carried on board at the reprovisioning ports; exercise and play above decks was confined to two or three daily hours of killing drill in full field pack in the 100°-plus temperatures; sleeping on deck was punishable by lash and death; food consisted almost exclusively of salt pork and hardtack dispensed

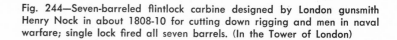

Fig. 244—Seven-barreled flintlock carbine designed by London gunsmith Henry Nock in about 1808-10 for cutting down rigging and men in naval warfare; single lock fired all seven barrels. (In the Tower of London)

once daily; and the sick and dying, if they were not forced to drill to death, rotted in their straw and hammocks. But the War Ministry greeted this happily in 1794 as the normal rate of casualties to be expected under the rules of health and sanitation prescribed by the surgeons-general, since any alteration of these, as had been urged from time to time, would have approached the conditions of passenger vessels, and would in consequence have weakened the soldiers' discipline, impaired the salubrious effects of physical hardening, and destroyed the men's wholesome sense of ever-imminent annihilation. This logic was acclaimed by all who mattered. It was the best of all possible worlds as far as the gentlemen of the weighty epaulets and forty-eight-inch waistbands were concerned, and their convictions about the excellence of the disciplinary methods were so unshakable that no material reform could be achieved until long after Waterloo. Punishments for the slightest infractions—failing to salute, failing to secure a flint firmly in the jaws of the cock, a spot on a boot when on parade—consisted of such forceful examples to future malefactors as confinement in a coffin for hours, with but a tiny airhole, or in a cell in which the soldier could neither stand nor kneel nor lie, but only

crouch until he lost consciousness. "Walking the gantlet" was a favorite: the regiment lined up in two rows facing each other, whips or cudgels in their hands; the victim was marched between, followed by solemn drummers, and beaten until he collapsed (Fig. 246). The Prussians under Frederick the Great carried this to the ultimate degree of perfection demanded by the German sense of duty and efficiency: the evildoer was tied to a rope extending from his waist to his destination at the further end of the alley, so that should he drop senseless or dead, his numb or cooling flesh might be dragged on in a widening trail of blood. Hanging by the feet over a smoke fire was not totally abolished in the French army until about 1774–78. The navy's equivalent of the gantlet was "whipping through the fleet," as readers of Nordhoff and Hall's MUTINY ON THE BOUNTY will not fail to remember; while those familiar with Herman Melville's WHITE JACKET are not likely to forget his first-hand account of equal bestialities in the American navy as late as the 1850's. But the most enlightening lessons in past martial glory may be learned from Baron von Swieten's DISEASES INCIDENT TO ARMIES (Vienna, 1762), and similar works which bare the rot beneath the gilt.

Fig. 245—Right: Punishments in an 18th-century military prison yard. Engraving by Chodowiecki, 1770.

Fig. 246—Left: The gantlet and the whipping post. Engraving by Chodowiecki, 1770.

Fig. 247—French infantry soldier. Engraving by Gravelot from *Exercise de l'Infanterie,* 1776.

men, gentlemen and the sons of even only moderately prosperous shopkeepers bought their commissions and patents as officers from the regimental colonels (Boswell spent years in his early twenties in pursuit of a good bargain), the colonels having bought theirs from lesser functionaries in the War Office (and with them, not only the lucrative business of selling lieutenancies, captaincies and majorities, but of contracting succulent graft in equipment and supply purchases), the lesser functionaries having bought their posts from the greater, the greater from the war minister, and the war minister from the king. But the classes from which the ranks and ratings were drawn could not have bought even the butchers' maggoty fat scraps or the bakers' charred oven sweepings (the "cake" in Marie Antoinette's unfortunate suggestion), for a handful of either would have postponed their enlistments for the length of hope contained in one more civilian digestive function. And so a vicious cycle turned endlessly: so long as only those abandoned wretches about whom no one cared volunteered for or were pressed into hell in a red tunic, the prevailing conditions were bound to continue, and as they continued, only the most abandoned wretches would volunteer . . . etc., etc. The slums of London, Birmingham and Liverpool showed no signs of threatening to dry up this ceaseless supply within the foreseeable future; nor did they until a time well within the memories of men still living.

Most of this is all the more surprising in the case of the British in view of the fact that torture and judicial brutality had in effect been abolished in *civilian* England by about 1700, more than a century in advance of most Continental nations (occasional lapses notwithstanding). Englishmen had perished by the hundreds of thousands in ages past for the slow evolution of those rights and principles of law and government which today form the precious bonds among the English-speaking peoples. Yet these were allowed to be summarily abrogated by the military in the eighteenth and much of nineteenth century without much public outcry. A partial answer may be found in that the army and navy, all enlistees save for men shanghaied by press gangs in times of emergency, attracted only the most poverty-stricken wretches, who were faced with the alternative of starvation and decomposition in the gutters of the slums. Usually press gangs invaded only gin mills, garbage-choked alleys and other precincts fertile with desperation. Young noble-

Fig. 248—"Recruits"—engraving by Watson & Dickson after a drawing by A. H. Bunbury, published in January, 1780. Young officers in cockerel plumage are doubtless scions of upper middle-class families whose fathers had bought them their commissions; wretches being pressed into service typified the raw-material not only of British but all other 18th-century armies.

Nor need Americans look back on their military history smug in the belief that such things went on only in the domains of "tyrants." Punishments barbaric by modern standards were introduced as necessities because circumstances in 1776 had produced not only an army which was composed of and officered by rank amateurs, none but a few dozen of whom had ever had the remotest connection with military training, but an army whose enthusiasm for being one was extremely tepid at best and conspicuously absent for the most part. A stern, experienced, professional hand was required. It arrived at Portsmouth, N. H., on December 1, 1777, attached to Baron Friedrich Wilhelm Augustus Heinrich Ferdinand von Steuben, a then forty-seven-year-old Prussian fire-breather, ex-aide-de-camp to Frederick the Great, ex-grand-marshal to the Prince of Hohenzollern-Hechingen and to the Margrave of Baden, etc., etc. In March, 1778,

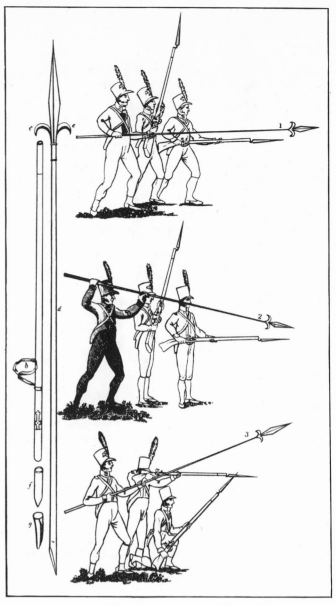

he began drilling the men at Valley Forge; in May he was made Inspector General and Drill Master; the lash whistled, the firing squads were kept busy, the straddle horses turned dark brown from blood stains, the drill fields were littered with parched, near-dead forms after the twelfth hour of punishment drill. But the desertion rate dropped from about seventy per cent to about thirty (it never dropped lower), an army took shape, and a little later, on June 28, 1778, an American army torn to pieces by Clinton's artillery at Monmouth, N. J., could be rallied and reorganized under murderous fire by sheer exercise of discipline, and by the men's greater fear of their own officers' pistol balls than of the British cannonade. In the remaining years of the war, the barbarities of Prussianism were required to keep deserters and recalcitrants in service. Sometimes to a lesser degree, sometimes to a greater, they remained fundamental to the training of American soldiers until at least a century after von Steuben's landing in New Hampshire.

Figs. 249 & 249a—Various maneuvers with pike and musket; plates from William Duane, *The American Military Library*, Philadelphia, 1808.

Fig. 250—Right: Two views of an English breech-loading flintlock musket, circa 1810. Top: Pipelike breech chamber has been withdrawn from barrel rearward and tilted up for loading with powder and ball; note touchhole, which, when chamber is reinserted, aligns with touchhole in side of barrel. Bottom: Chamber has been loaded and reinserted into breech opening, and locking levers, worked by ring visible behind battery, have secured it in place; gun is cocked and (if there were a flint in the jaws and powder in the pan) ready to fire. Simple mechanism was never put into mass production, probably because locking levers were loosened after a few hundred fires. Lock is a *Bolton* lock, an invention credited to the mathematician and amateur gunsmith George Bolton, a tutor to the children of George III, but actually thought up by the London gunsmith Henry Nock (cf. Fig. 244) in about 1795; all the components were held together by screwless joints, finally anchored by only the one broad-headed screw below the cock. Parts were said to be interchangeable, but generally were not. About 3000-plus military versions were made. (In the Tower of London)

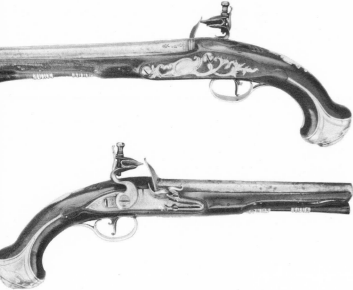

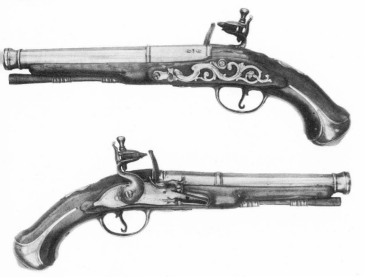

Fig. 253—Typical medium-sized mortar, late 17th to early 19th centuries. Height from bottom of base to top of barrel (when inclined as shown) about 3 feet 6 inches; diameter of ball or explosive shell 12 inches; weight of powder about 9.5 pounds. Engraving from Surirey de Saint-Rémy, *Mémoires d'Artillerie*, Paris, 1697.

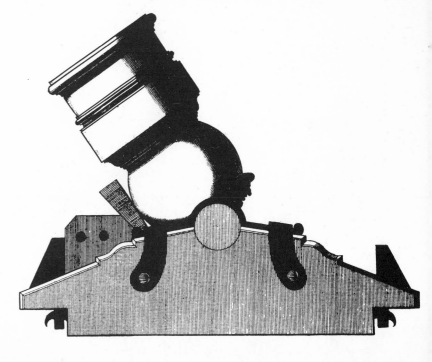

Figs. 251 & 252—Top: Pair of officer's private sidearms by Joseph Heylin of London, circa 1770-80; silver-mounted pistols have sliding safety catches on lockplates. Bottom: pair of dragoon officer's private sidearms by Cornforti of London, circa 1710-20, also silver-mounted; typical early 18th-century features are cannon barrels, curved locks with long teats at ends, absence of flashpan bridles.

In respect to military sanitation, it need only be said that the eighteenth century was an age when the Greatest and the Richest shaved their heads and wore wigs, or powdered their hair until it gave off clouds with every nod, as a preferable alternative to the perils of washing. Physicians cautioned against the injurious practice of too frequent removal of the *effluvium laudabile smegmatis naturalis*—"the laudable excretion of natural skin fat." Bathing was therefore at best a thrice-yearly occurrence, the months between creating an intimate but inescapable problem of odors which the French perfume industry rose bravely to meet; but as the seasons wore on, even the most pungent essences were defeated by superior forces. The king, Lord North, George Washington and every other *grand seigneur* of the rococo from Moscow to Williamsburg donned his winter undergarments in November and did not emerge again until the April thaws. That military standards should have fallen considerably below these civilian ones—those prevailing among the masses may be left unelaborated—goes without saying. Whatever respite the exhausted barracks soldier might have found in sleep at the end of a grueling day was claimed by a determined ambush of fleas, lice and bedbugs. The rats on warships frequently sought bits of nesting material by creeping up on sleeping sailors and biting chunks out of the lacquer-hard crust of tar which formed the sailor's hair. Frederick the Great, who was second to no man in his championing of science, liberalism and enlightenment, was perfectly serious when he crossed off an appropriation for new bathtubs for certain regiments in January, 1764, with the comment "in just five months the river will be warm enough." The old officers' manuals which required that all officers enforce "the observance of the most wholesome cleanliness" and exercise "the most stringent vigilance over the men's corporeal ablutions" must always be read through generous layers of *effluvium laudabile smegmatis naturalis.*

This is the greater context within which one must view the old uniform prints of the eighteenth—and most of the nineteenth—century; the original scene not only looked otherwise, but included more species of life than the horse and the pristine warrior in immaculately gorgeous plumage. One might suggest a thesis—if it has not been suggested—about Napoleon's celebrated pose.

Fig. 254—Two of several plates illustrating the article "Art Militaire" in Denis Diderot's *Encyclopédie,* 1751 to 1765. First three figures of center row show mounting of bayonet; others show various drills and exercises.

Art Militaire, Exercice.

CHAPTER NINE

ET US RETURN TO THE HAPPIER civilian climes in the reign of Queen Anne (1702–14). Although every year but the last of it was marked by the War of the Spanish Succession, the fighting was a million miles away in Flanders, France, Germany, Spain and other places once seen in the vicar's atlas but since forgotten. At home, peace not only reigned, it positively raged like a benevolent and slightly drunk Bacchus. The war was far from being a burden on anyone except the soldiers who were killed and maimed and their families who starved. As long as they did so quietly, no one objected (save a powerless few). The war proved the most profitable venture in British history for the London financiers, and indirectly on the trickle-down basis for every subject from duke to yeoman; its prolongation was a matter of policy. Marlborough, his wife and the Earl of Godolphin were the virtual rulers, supported by the Whig majority in Parliament as long as the lush fruits of victory continued, until in 1710 the Tories at last conspired their fall. With the elimination of French competition, the greater portion of the world's wealth flowed in English ships through English ports into English pockets, and Englishmen prospered as had never been dreamed possible for any nation of mortals. English products had no serious competition in foreign markets. Marshes, fens and bogs were reclaimed by drainage. Networks of roads were built, with the effect that distant districts and counties which had been thought barbaric twenty years before became fashionable locales for the great estates of gentry and nobility who would hitherto not have stirred from London; while the socially somewhat inferior rural gentry and nobility now visited London seasonally and maintained town houses for their cosmopolitan functions.

Fig. 255—The training and breeding of hunting dogs became extremely important and semi-scientific occupations in the sporting circles of the early 18th century. After about 1720, hardly any hunting or sporting books were published which did not devote considerable space to dogs, some with engravings such as these in Hanns Friedrich von Flemings's *Der Vollkommene Teutsche Jäger (The Complete German Hunter)*, Leipzig, 1724.

Sporting shooting inevitably soared to such a degree that the fashions of Charles II's court twenty years earlier seem like a brief prologue in comparison. The demand for fine guns was insatiable, and now that gunsmiths were busy with fat government contracts, and the supply from France had been dried up, it inflated the prices of good fowling pieces to some 500 per cent of those prevailing in the time of Charles. As yet the shooting mania had not exceeded all limits of reason as it was shortly to do in the courts of most German princelings, who did not rest happily until they had slaughtered in one day what all the people in their provinces could not have eaten in a week (cf. Fig. 256). In the reign of the first George (1714–27),

by far the greater majority of English sportsmen shot as a sport of skill, and the quarry almost invariably ended as a delicious feast. Britons went shooting alone or at most in the company of two friends; there was none of the French and German fashion of great hunting parties which ended by having the carcasses of fifty deer and several hundred birds thrown into huge limepits and covered up. Toward the end of the century, English shooting, too, was tainted by the wholesale slaughter of flying game, in defiance of the severe game laws, but this rarely or never exceeded the capacity of the game pouches, and consequently never approached the German dimensions.

Fig. 256—*"Ein kleines bestättigt Ausschiessen,"* "A small shooting party firing from cover," says superscription of this engraving in Hanns Friedrich von Fleming's *Der Vollkommene Teutsche Jäger (The Complete German Hunter)*, Leipzig, 1724. Liveried flunkies are driving deer, foxes and other game past gentlemen in shooting stand; servants behind gentlemen load guns, hand them to their masters.

Not infrequently "a small shooting party" accounted for a thousand deer in a day. Large parties, sometimes numbering five hundred or more fearless guests, often brought a day's toll to between five and ten thousand deer, boars and foxes. Von Fleming was outraged by such slaughter, agitated (naturally in vain) for strong game laws incumbent on royalty and nobility no less than on paupers.

Ein kleines bestättigt Ausschiessen.

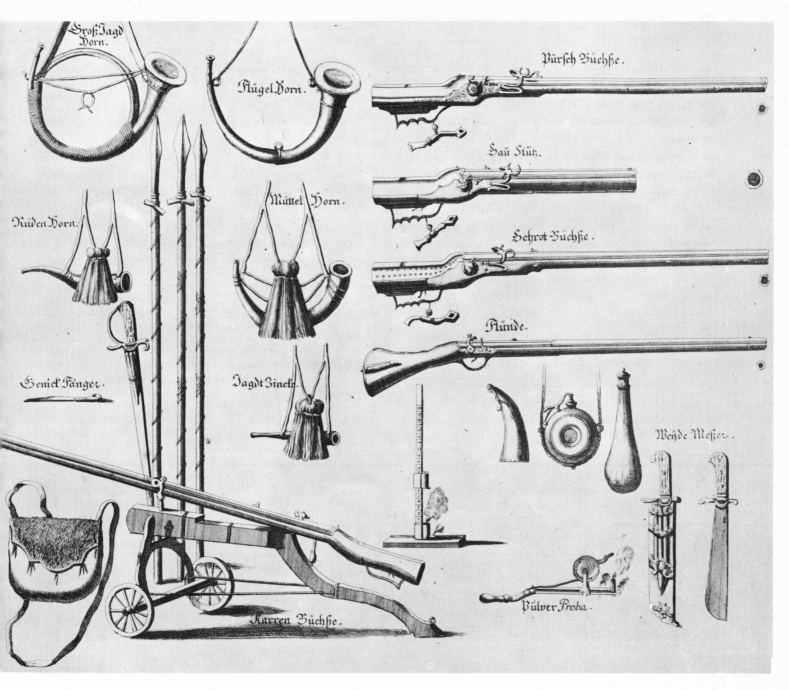

Fig. 257—17th- and early 18th-century hunting implements: five horns two knives, game pouch, three powder flasks, two powder testers. Huge gun on carriage (*Karren Büchse*) is a wheellock duck gun, wheeled up to edge of pond to fire volcanic eruption of several pounds of shot into swimming flock. Of the four horizontal guns, first three are wheellocks (note spanners tied to trigger guards), identified (top to bottom) as a stalking rifle (*Pursch Büchse*), a rifled wild-boar carbine (*Sau Stutz*), and a rifle with so slight a twist as to be useful also for shot (*Schrot Büchse*); fourth gun, a flintlock, is a *Flünde* (modern German *Flinte*), i.e., a shotgun or fowling piece. From Hans Friedrich von Fleming, *Der Vollkommene Teutsche Jäger (The Complete German Hunter)*, Leipzig, 1724.

To become expert in shooting flying even with a modern shotgun requires years of patient practice, as any reader who has ever tried it will know. It is quite different from big-game hunting with a rifle, and the best rifle shot in the county will be left gaping after the disappearing pheasant upon his first try. With the infinitesimal delay in fire of even the best flintlock, the skill required was all the greater, the more so because double-barreled guns were rare before the end of the eighteenth century. The reasons for this rarity may be noted here: barrels continued to be made long—between thirty-nine and forty-five inches—to lend greater efficiency to the powder, and even these few additional ounces at the front end made them a bit heavy for the instantaneous swing and aim required for snap shooting at an unexpectedly rising bird. *Two* such barrels could not have been brought up in time, save in the hands of the extremely few in every age and place whose co-ordination and reflexes make them what is commonly called "a natural-born shot." Thus the true-blooded English sportsman with his single-barreled gun was lured by an extremely difficult but not insuperable challenge. Furthermore, field shooting could be carried on with all the *décor* and gentility of dress and manner required by the codes of that Augustan era: one went dressed efficiently, but with one's waistcoat embroidered in good taste, not in the vulgar vestments of the English parkkeeper or Swiss mountaineer. Compared with all the other sports which pitted skill and experience against failure—tennis, football, riding to the hounds in pursuit of the fox ("the unspeakable in pursuit of the inedible," Oscar Wilde called it)—field shooting required little exertion beyond healthful walking, braving the recoil, and reloading quickly (the last often done by servants—cf. 1699 journal, p. 95, rt. col.; AIMWELL's second speech, p. 134; and Fig. 202). A good shot would invariably bring cries of "Hurrah!" "Bully!" and "Well done, sir, well done!" if accomplished in the company of friends, or, depending on the level of urbanity of those involved, a polite ripple of applause and tipping of hats. Thus it was an outdoor sport for all who could afford to indulge in it: the young for the show of supple harmony of eye and muscles, the middle aged for the same plus the opportunity of doing so without discomfort, the elderly for the eternal pursuit of youth, and all of them for the satisfaction of venting their private wraths on living creatures. By 1727 there was probably not one middle- or upper-class man or boy in England, Scotland, Ireland or Wales who had not tried his luck at least once; the greater number returned for more; and the greater number of these became addicted. It was therefore unavoidable that the occasional, semi-literate old sporting manuals which had hitherto appeared should henceforth be couched in more erudite and entertaining language—but it was not until 1727 that at last the Muse saw fit to wreathe one in verse and to perfume it with meter. For this she anointed a Britannic Vergil named Mr. Markland, who in that year composed a bucolic entitled PTERYPLEGIA: OR THE ART OF SHOOTING FLYING. Since this contains everything there is to be said about Georgian field shooting (and much that is as true today as then), including, by its very nature, the fanaticism with which the sport was hallowed, the entire prologue and 285 of the original 373 lines are here reprinted (italics in original):

PTERYPLEGIA:

OR, THE ART OF

SHOOTING-FLYING.

A

POEM

By Mr. MARKLAND, A.B., late Fellow
of St. John's College in Oxford

London, 1727
Price One Shilling

TO ALL FAIR SPORTSMEN:
GENTLEMEN,

Give me Leave to strengthen your Memories, and confirm your Experience, with a Sett of *Speculations*, newly drawn from Darkness and Confusion into the Advantage of a clear Light and *regular System*. They contain many demonstrable Truths which never before made any Figure abroad in *Terms* of *Art*, or were reduced to any *Shape* or *Expression*. On this Account I might here very reasonably plead the *Novelty* of the Subject in Defence and Excuse

of the Performance, having had no Path or Footsteps to guide me but my own long Experience; and might, with less Vanity and more Propriety than most Writers, take to myself the Title of an Author, were it not the utmost of my Ambitions only to oblige and inform my Fellow-Sportsmen, and to communicate freely and honestly what Knowledge I have treasured up in this hitherto unexplained and difficult Mystery.

Nevertheless, I am sensible, there is no becoming *Sportsmen* by Book. You may here find the Rules and proper Direction for that End; but Practice alone can make you *Masters. Bare Theory* may as soon stamp a *General* as a *Marksman*. No—You must sweat and be cold, must sweat again, and be cold again, before you can arrive at any Degree of Perfection in this Art. I have furnished you with all necessary Tools of the Trade, but it is Time and Experience must finish and accomplish the Workman; and even after seven Years Industry, you will find but too many Occasions to prove you still deficient and imperfect. It is but too true (and you must all of you bear me Witness to the Truth of this) that even the best Marksmen have their chronical Miscarriages. In some Hands, the ill Fortune of the first Shoot determines and influences the Success of all the rest: And one may take a certain Sort of Augury from the Escape and Flight of the first Mark. The natural Cause of this seems to proceed from the original Disappointment, which in some Men is irrecoverable for that whole Day. As on the contrary, a prosperous Hit shall have the very opposite Effect, and induce such an easy Serenity and steady Assurance as to carry inevitable Death with them for many Hours after.

On this Occasion I have often wondered why the *French*, of all Mankind, should alone be so expert at the GUN, I had almost said infallible. It is as rare for a professed Marksman of that Nation to miss a Bird as for one of Ours to kill. But, as I have been since informed, they owe this Excellence to their Education. They are trained up to it so very young that they are no more surprized or alarmed with a Pheasant than a Rattle-Mouse. The best Field-Philosophers living, for they are always there Masters of their Temper.

However, I have now, at last, broke the Ice, and put my young Countrymen in the Way to rival that *volatile Nation* in their peculiar Accomplishment.

I intended (according to Custom) an *Invocation* to *Apollo*, our great Exemplar in this Art, who shot *Icarus* Flying many hundred Years ago; but considering, upon second Thoughts, how many *Snites* [snipes], *Woodcocks, Partridges, Pheasants, Polts* [young guinea-fowl], &c., I had lost upon his Occasion, and how often I had been glad of the prophane Opportunity of turning my Backside on his Godship, I concluded that I had little Reason to expect his Assistance.

The *Muses* having all of them Wings, as is evident from the *sublime Flights* they take, I had less Hopes of their Inspiration. Indeed, I sensibly perceived I had disobliged them, and that they had withdrawn their Favours, upon Supposition, I suppose, of some possible Danger they might be in by my Means. However, their Ladyships were mistaken, since they were no more concerned in this Subject than Flying-Coaches, Flying-Post, Flying-Clouds, Flying-Camps, Flying-Reports or Flying-Bottles of Ale, or forty other material and immaterial Beings to which the Poets have fastened Wings, as *Time, Fame, Money, Love,* &c. In short, Gentlemen, in Consideration of the Nature of the Subject, you must not expect a very fanciful or entertaining *Poem;* but, this I will be bold to say, that as to the Matter and Substance of it, if what you find here be well read, digested and remembered, it will then prove *truly useful* and *very serviceable.*

Fig. 258—Wallcloth depicting idyllic Georgian hunting scene. Cotton and linen cloth was plate-printed in purple, then overprinted by woodblock in blue, red, yellow and brown. Inscription below urn says, "R. IONES & Co—Iany. 1st—1769" (In the Victoria & Albert Museum, London)

PTERYPLEGIA

OR, THE ART OF

SHOOTING-FLYING

SILENT and Grey the Morning's Dawn appear'd;
No Sun was promis'd, and no Wind was heard.
The Archer-God shot forth no jealous Beam
To dazzle and confound the *Marksman's* Aim,
Nor friendly Blasts conceal'd the springing Game.
My Friend and I with hopeful Prospect rose
And scorned the longer Scandal of Repose:
No dull Repast allow'd; our Tackle all
O'er Night prepared, the chearful Dogs we call;
In a close Pocket snuggs the cordial Dram—
Youth to the Old, and Crutches to the Lame!

LOW-LEATHERN-HEEL'D our lacquer'd Boots are made:
Mounted on tott'ring Stilts raw Freshmen tread;

Firm Footing an unshaken Level lends,
But Modish Heels are still the *Woodcock's* Friends.
Our Shot of sev'ral sorts, half round the Waste,
In Ticking semicircularly plac'd,
Embrac'd and poiz'd us well.[1] Silent we go,
As when *Apollo* from his Silver Bow,
Wrapped in a Cloud, the *Grecian* Camp dismay'd,
And, unperceiv'd thro' Darkness, struck 'em dead.
No flapping Sleeves our ready Arms controul;
Short Cuffs alone prove fatal to the Fowl.
Nor arm'd in warm Surtout, we vainly fear
The Sky's Inclemency, or *Jove* severe:
Active and free our Limbs and Muscles are
Whilst Excercise does glowing Warmth prepare.
To such Examples You who dare not yield,
Sneak to the Chimney-side and quit the Field!

[1] *Our Shot . . . us well:* Our shot pellets of assorted sizes we carry in a half-girth canvas pouch or belt tied around our waists.

Flugschütze.

Tireur a vol.

Fig. 259—*Flugschütze*, or as fashionable Germans preferred in an age of French elegance, a *tireur à vol*, a shooter shooting flying. Engraving from Johann Elias Ridinger, *Abbildungen der Jagtbaren Thiere (Album of Game Animals)*, Augsburg, 1740, shows scene presumably taking place in Germany but which could equally well be in England or France.

OUR SPORT almost at hand, we charge the Gun,
Whilst ev'ry well-bred Dog lies qui'tly down.
Charge not before. If over-Night the Piece
Stands loaded, in the Morn the Prime will hiss:[2]
Nor Prime too full, else you will surely blame
The hanging fire and lose the pointed Aim.
Should I of This the obvious Reason tell:
The caking Pressure does the Flame repel,
And *Vulcan's* lamed again by his own Steel.[3]
Yet cleanse the Touch-hole first: A Partridge Wing
Most to the Field for that wise Purpose bring.
In Charging, next, good Workmen never fail

To ram the Powder well, but not the Ball [shot];
One *Third* the well-turn'd Shot superior must
Arise, and overcome the nitrous Dust,
Which, dry'd and season'd in the Oven's Heat,
Has stood in close-mouthed Jarr the dampless Night.[4]
Now search for Tow, and some old Saddle pierce:
No Wadding lies so close or drives so fierce.[5]
And here be mindful constantly to Arm
With Choice of Flints, a Turn-Screw and a Worm;
The accidental Chances of the Field
Will for such Implements Occasion yield.

[2] *If over-Night . . . will hiss:* Atmospheric moisture will condense in the flashpan and spoil or at least damage the priming if the gun is left primed and loaded overnight.

[3] *The caking . . . own Steel:* The pressure of the flashpan cover will tend to cake the priming if the flashpan has been primed too full so that the sparks will not ignite the priming as certainly as if it were less and loose.

[4] *One Third . . . dampless Night:* The shot should be one and a half times the *volume measure* of the powder, which has been set out in a closed jar in the oven to dry out overnight.

[5] *Now search . . . so fierce:* Now search for tow, i.e., raw wool or flax, for the wads between powder and shot and over the shot. Nothing will more increase the gas pressure safely than the tow stuffing from an old saddle, compressed by riding into leather-like plasticity. (This was not always desirable—most shooters used plain tow or paper.)

AND NOW, our Pieces loaded, we divide
The Rows between, each takes a diff'rent Side;
Careful, yet Unconcern'd; not Idle, still
Unbent, with Dilligence enough to Kill.
Learn'd to *Take Time*, the Chief and Only Rule,
First to be practis'd in the Marksman's School.
Most Youths undisciplined the Sport confound
By random Firing on improper Ground:
For as in Flights of hasty Wit, the same
Examined, will be Parallel in Game. . . .
. . . Eager Pursuit still over-shoots Success,
And timorous Distrust will *Under*-miss.
A loit'ring Fool should no Forgiveness find,
Nor can I have scarce Pity for the Blind.
The Weak and Crazy shou'd be kept at home
And fed with Jellies till their Strength is come.
Whoever fails in any single Part
Can ne'er commence a Master of this Art.

SEE A Cock-Pheasant sprung! He mounts—he's down!
Trust to your Dogs! Quick, quick—Recharge your **Gun**
Before the Air gets in and damps the Room!
The *Chamber* hot will to the Powder give
A Benefit, and will the same receive.[6]
The open Touch-hole, too, if haste you make,
Its little fatal Train will freelier take.
Oft have I seen th' undocumented Swain
Feath'ring the Parts and cleansing off the Pan
Until the cooling Piece grew *moist* again.
The tardy Charge wiped that *cold Sweat* away—
And grew itself half *Wild-fire* by the way.[7]
Besides, suppose that Bird, but slightly touch'd
I'th' Body, mazy [8] there sits slyly couched,
When, with your Gun discharged, you come to **take**
Him up: he shall a second Effort make,
With unrecover'd Flight shall mount away
While you in vain lament th' escaping Prey.
In some close Covert he unfound shall lie,
And, subtle in his Dissolution, die.
Woodcocks and Snites and Partridge rarely run
When crippl'd in the Wing, and fairly down,
But Pheasants seldom lie: Oft'times in vain
I've sought the headlong Fowl, concluded slain.

THERE SPRUNG a single Partridge—ha! she's gone!
Oh! Sir, you'd Time enough, you shot too soon;
Scarce twenty Yards in open Sight!—for Shame!
Y'had shatter'd her to Pieces with right Aim!
Full forty Yards permit the Bird to go,
The spreading Gun [9] will surer Mischief sow;
But when too near the flying Object is,
You certainly will mangle it, or miss;
And if too far, you may too slightly wound
To kill the Bird, and yet not bring to Ground.
As Virtue 'twixt two Vices does consist,
The same in Shooting justly is confest;
But when the Trees diversify the Scene,
No Mortal there can keep the Golden Mean.
Spite of the Rules of Art he must let fly
In one of the Extremes, too far, or nigh,
Must nimbly take Advantage of what Leave
The Opens, Glades and Interstices give.
Where Woodcocks dodge, there Distance knows no Laws;
Necessity admits no room for Pause.
But in the Ersh [10] of Barley, Oats, or Wheat,

Where Quails delicious, and sweet Partridge sit,
Or in the Springs,[11] where bores the charming **Snite**,
Or where the glorious Polt [12] in open Heath
Moves sweetly in an even Line from Death:
There, if the Goodness of the Piece be prov'd,
Pursue not the fair Mark till far remov'd!
Raise the Mouth gently from below the Game
And readily let fly at the first Aim.
But without Aim admit no random Shoot—
'Tis just to judge before you execute. . . .

FIVE GENERAL sorts of *Flying Marks* there are:
The *Lineals* two, *Traverse*, and *Circular*;
The Fifth *Oblique*, which I may vainly teach
But Practice only perfectly can reach.

WHEN A BIRD comes *directly to your Face*,
Contain your Fire a while and let her pass,
Unless some Trees behind you change the Case.
If so, a little Space above her Head
Advance the Muzzle, and you strike her dead.
Ever let Shot pursue where there is room;
Marks hard before thus easy will become.

BUT WHEN the Bird *flies from you in a Line*,
With little Care I may pronounce her thine:
Observe the Rule before, and neatly raise
Your Piece til there's no *Open under-space*
Betwixt the Object and the *Silver Sight*;
Then send away, and timely stop the Flight.

TH' UNLUCKY *Cross Mark*, or the *Traverse Shoot*,
By some thought easy (yet admits Dispute,
As the most common Practice is to Fire
Before the Bird) will nicest Time require:
For, too *much* Space allow'd, the Shot will fly
All innocent and pass too nimbly by;
Too *little* Space, the Partridge, swift as Wind,
Will dart athwart and bilk her Death behind.
This makes the Point so difficult to guess,
'Cause you must be exact in Time or miss.
In other Marks there's a less desp'rate Stake,
Where the swift Shot will surely *Overtake*. . . .

FULL FORTY Yards or more to th' Left or Right
The Partridge now *Obliquely* takes her Flight.
You've there th' Advantage of a *Sideling Line*;
Be careful, nor her inward Side decline:
Else just behind the Bird the Shot will glance:
Nor have you any Hopes from *Flying Chance*.
Last is the Mark which is styl'd *Circular*
There's nothing more required but steady Care
T'attend the Motion of the Bird and gain
The best and farthest *Lineal Point* you can;
Carrying your Piece around, have Patience till
The Mark's at best Extent, then fire and kill. . . .

BUT HOLD, my Spirits fail! a Dram, a Dram,
A Sup of Vigour to pursue the Game!
Enough, enough—A Gulp too much is worse
Than none at all, like one help'd over his Horse.
Sportsmen, beware! for the superfluous Glass
Will blunt the Sight and ev'ry Object glaze,
Whilst all Things seem around one undistinguish'd **Mass**.
Th' unpointed Eye once dull'd, farewell the Game:
A Morning Sot may shoot, but never aim.
Marksmen and Rope-dancers with equal Care

---

[6] *Quick, quick . . . same receive:* Reload immediately before atmospheric moisture condenses in the breech-chamber. Loading while the barrel is still hot will further dry out the powder and give it added strength. (This is a fundamental rule of muzzle-loading shooting.)

[7] *The tardy Charge . . . the way:* Moisture having been allowed to condense in the barrel, the delayed next loading wiped it away when rammed; but the powder naturally absorbed it and the next shot became "half *Wild-fire*," i.e., a weak, sputtery shot.

[8] *Mazy:* Hidden; as in a maze.

[9] *The spreading Gun:* The spreading shot pellets.

[10] *Ersh:* Stubble field.

[11] *Springs:* Groves or copses of young trees.

[12] *Polt:* Poult; i.e., young game bird, esp. the guinea-fowl.

Th' insidious fasting Bottle shou'd forbear.
Else each who does the Glass unwisely take
E'er Noon a false and fatal Step will make;
The first will *Turkeys* slay, and make *Pigs squeak,*
The latter, ten to one, will break his Neck.

YET HOW my Blood's on fire! oh! how I hate
I' th' midst of Sport to see a Glutton eat,
When Pheasants mount, and the Gay Birds arise,
To see a Coxcomb paring of his Cheese!
Scourge, Beadle,[13] from the Field that cramming Fool,
Or pack the Mouncher back to School.
All that he chews to me proves pois'nous Food,
And does Me much more Mischief than Him Good.

HALLOO—HALLOO—See, see from yonder Furze
The Lurchers [14] have alarm'd and started Puss! [15]
Hold! What d'ye do? Sure you don't mean to Fire!
Constrain that base, ungenerous Desire,
And let the Courser and the Huntsman share
Their just and proper Title to the Hare!
Let the poor Creature pass and have fair Play,
And fight the Prize of Life out her own Way.
The tracing Hound by Nature was designed
Both for the Use and Pleasure of Mankind;
Form'd for the Hare, the Hare too for the Hound:
In Enmity each to each other bound:
Then he who dares by diff'rent Means destroy
Than Nature meant, offends 'gainst *Nature's Law.* . . .

BUT SEE, the stiffen'd Earth by Frost is bound,
The flocking Larks bestrew and peck the Ground. . . .
. . . Now let the Sportsman so dispose his Charge
As may dispense the circling Shot at large:
The Shot and Powder well proportioned be,
Neither exceeding in the Quantity;
Destruction thus shall a wide Compass take
And many little bleeding Victims make.[16]
And now proceed, not by Approach, but Storm:
Run briskly, fire amidst the rising Swarm,
And you will treble slaughter thus perform
When each Bird moves expansive in the Air,
And the whole Mark lies open, rais'd and fair!
For one o' th' Ground, you have ten Chances there.

THE WEATHER's chang'd—The Winds more briskly blow,
The Snites against the Wind will move but slow;
Thin cover'd Snites ne'er travel down the Wind,
Wise to maintain their Garments close behind.
The flirting Woodcocks now short Flights will take,
And pearching Pheasants to the Trees will make.
Turn the *wild Poultry* from the Bough—Away
For shame, ne'er let that bawling Lurcher bay,
Poachers alone surprize the gazing Prey! [17]

JOVE! LAY these ratt'ling Gusts, and smooth the Skies!
We cannot hear the whirring Partridge rise;
The flashing Prime too in our Faces drives!
And now it mizzles—the damp Powder gives—
We cannot keep our Fire-locks dry—Away,

Our sport is over, 'tis in vain to stay.

NOW THAT the pushing Winds distort the Aim,
And warp the palsy'd Barrels from the Game:
O'er Bowl of Punch suppos'd, or Tub of Ale,
Let us relate an useful *Winter-Tale:*
Matters of Fact and modern Fates my Verse
Shall with exact Integrity rehearse.
The strong Impressions may rash Youth prepare
Safely to use the dang'rous Gun with Care.
Ye Parents, let your Sons these Stories know,
And thus you may prevent the distant Woe.

A BLOOMING Youth, who had just passed the Boy,
The Father's only Child and only Joy,
As he, intent, design'd the Larks his Prey,
Himself as sweet and innocent as They,
The fatal Powder in the Porch of Death,
Having in vain discharg'd its Flash of Breath,[18]
The tender Reas'ner, curious to know,
Whether the Piece were really charg'd or no,
With Mouth to Mouth apply'd began to blow—
A dreadful Kiss! For now the silent Bane
Had bor'd a Passage thro' the whizzing Train—
The Shot all rent his Skull, and dashed around his Brain! [19]

UNGUARDED SWAINS! oh! still remember this,
And to your Shoulders close constrain the Piece,
For lurking Seeds of Death unheard may hiss!
The Gun remov'd, may in the firing fly,
Wrench from your Hands, and wound the Standers-by! [20]

ONCE MORE let me instruct th' uncaution'd Youth—
Be *Magd'line's* College Witness of the Truth. . . .
. . . As thro' the Brambles of th' intangling Brake,
The heedless *Strephon* [21] did his Passage make,
Th' unguarded Cock beneath himself he drew
Against some Sprig, and thus himself he slew!

FORGIVE ME, if I longer must detain
And tire thy Patience with this tragic Strain,
Since mine the Labour is, but thine may be the Gain.
Varied and frequent is the Accident
Which ev'ry where attends the *Hammer'd Flint.*
The neighb'ring Sparks into the Pan may fall,
And the loose Piece with Mischief may recoil.
Th' unheeded Muzzle pointed at a Friend
May instantly unthought Destruction send.
Sometimes the Cock may at half-bent go down,[22]
True Sportsmen therefore always mount the Gun.[23]
They walk with Flint by Guardian Thumb restrain'd,
With Piece well handl'd, ready at Command,
Nor need their jeopardiz'd Companions dread
Their tripping Heels, or the strain'd Ankles tread.
Such sad Events have darken'd ev'ry Scene,
That the good-natured *Muse* cou'd not forbear
T'awake your Caution, and alarm your Care.
Shepherds, farewell: Go, and her Words preserve;
The *Muse* at least will your best Thanks deserve.

FINIS

---

[13] *Beadle:* Officer.
[14] *Lurchers:* Hunting dogs.
[15] *Puss:* A hare or rabbit, *not* a cat.
[16] *The Shot . . . Victims make:* Powder and shot in equal measure by volume, which will make the shot scatter more.
[17] *Turn the . . . gazing Prey:* Flush the bird from the bough before you shoot—only poachers sneak up on perched game.
[18] *The fatal . . . of Breath:* The priming in the flashpan having flashed in vain (without firing the gun; i.e., a flash in the pan). . . .
[19] *The tender . . . his Brain:* The tender reasoner, curious to know after the flash in the pan whether or not the gun was really loaded, put the muzzle into his mouth and blew into the barrel to see whether any air would escape through the touchhole. A dreadful kiss! For meanwhile a silent spark glimmering in the carbon crust on the flashpan had bored its way into the touchhole. The gun went off fully charged while the muzzle was still in the boy's

mouth. (This horrible accident very likely happened; while possible, it would have been a once-in-a-million occurrence, by far too remote from the usual behavior of even the longest hanging fires in flintlocks to be used in a treatise of this kind as a fictional example of the weapon's perils.)
[20] *And to . . . the Standers-by:* Keep the gun close to your shoulder for a moment after you have had a flash in the pan or a misfire, for the seeds of death—sparks—may hiss unheard, and what was thought a misfire may be a hanging fire. The gun lowered untimely may fire a moment after and hit a stander-by. (Cf. the report of such an accident, p. 171).
[21] *Strephon:* Poetic name for a young shepherd or lover in pastoral verse; here a pseudonym for the unfortunate student at Magdalen College, Oxford, or Magdalene College, Cambridge, whose death is related.
[22] *Sometimes . . . down:* The cock may snap out of half cock.
[23] *Mount the Gun:* Carry it pointed harmlessly upward.

Only two regrettable circumstances marred such pleasures of Georgian gentlemen. One was the labyrinth of game-laws which Parliament and judges had erected since enactment of the 33 Hen.VIII.c.6 in 1542. To give *in extenso* all the acts, statutes and decisions of almost three centuries would require a separate volume; a few examples will serve to suggest the total picture.

In the twenty-third year of Charles II (1683), the 141-year-old qualification of £100-a-year was reinforced and raised by an act which provided that:

> Any person or persons not having lands of inheritance or freehold property, in his own or his wife's right, of the clear annual value of £100; or leasehold property for life or [for] a term of 99 years or longer, of the clear yearly value of £150, are [declared ineligible] to have or keep for themselves or any other person, guns, bows, greyhounds, setting-dogs, ferrets, lurchers, nets, hare-pipes, gins [traps], snares, or other engines for the taking or killing rabbits, hares, pheasants, partridges, or other game. . . .

By the same statute, the following were qualified from the circumstances of their birth, though they might possess no property whatever, viz., the son and heir apparent of an esquire or person of higher degree (esquires, according to law, were the Four Esquires of the King's Body); the younger sons of noblemen and their male heirs forever; and the eldest sons of baronets, Knights of the Bath and Knights Bachelors, and their male heirs in the legitimate line. Persons of higher degree than esquires were baronets and noblemen, as well as doctors in the three learned professions, officers from colonel on up, and serjeants at law. This statute was merely prohibitory and did not subject the party to any penalty, but authorized the seizure of the dogs and "engines." But by an act of the fifth year of Queen Anne (1707), any person guilty of an infraction was liable to a penalty of £5, one half of which sum was to be given to the informer, the other half to the poor of the parish, to be levied under the warrant of a justice of the peace; and in case of inability to pay, the offender might be sent to the house of correction for three months for the first offense, and four months for every subsequent offense.

Fig. 260—Young poacher and impoverished family, caught by the gamekeeper, begging the lord of the manor for clemency. Penalties could have ranged from reprimand or fine to imprisonment, transportation or hanging. Engraving by Ingouf, after a von Bénazech, 1778.

Fig. 261—Portable tree disguise. Engraving by Giuseppe Maria Mitelli (1634-1718).

Some dozen other national laws and upward of a hundred local ordinances enacted between 1683 and 1830 established the hunting seasons and the hours of the day within which this or that species of game might be hunted; the rights of and limitations on lords of manors; the penalties for poaching (imprisonment and hanging); the felonious nature of pursuing rabbits in the snow; the number of pigeons which might be shot off any one church steeple—there being no service or worshiper inside at the time—by one man in one forenoon (six); the penalties for destroying eggs of game birds; the laws of trespass, which, by an act of the fifth year of William and Mary (1694), were particularly hard on "inferior tradesmen, apprentices or other dissolute persons"; and, in short, every reasonable and unreasonable snare and pit which could possibly be constructed in the sporting paths of all the classes below the nobility, the squires and the well-to-do urbanite gentry. In any one year between 1750 and 1800, these never numbered more than 5 to 10 per cent of the population, variously about 350,000 to 800,000. Since these figures include women, children and the aged, and since not *all* gentlemen went shooting, it may be conjectured (with the aid of such statistics as the sales of guns and the manufacture of powder and shot) that between 1740 and 1840 some 75,000 to 150,000 stout-hearted men rallied annually to the banner with the

strange device *Pteryplegia!* This was more than sufficient to create the demand which by 1810 had resulted in the finest guns in the world.

The other dampening circumstance in Georgian sport was the awkward tendency of barrels to explode under certain conditions. Until about 1750, the best barrels had been the Spanish ones, which, owing to the purity, softness and enormous tensile strength of the metal obtained from the ores of Biscany, could be bored more truly and made stronger by the Spanish master craftsmen than any other in the world. Spanish makers bought old horseshoes and horseshoe-nail heads by the tons, fancying these (to an extent very correctly) to have undergone such a change in "the elastic fluid which determines the flux of the atoms"—or as we would say, the density and crystalline structure—that no tougher, more ideally suited metal for gunbarrels was conceivable. This, together with Spanish workmanship, made Spanish guns shoot farther, harder and more safely than any other. Often fifteen pounds of scrap were melted and hammered down to make one three-pound barrel. The scrap was drawn into iron wire which was wound about a rod, or *mandril,* of the desired bore diameter. Repeated heating, hammering and tempering resulted in one tube composed of thousands of turns of wire running in mutually reinforcing directions, fused into one virtually indestructible tube.

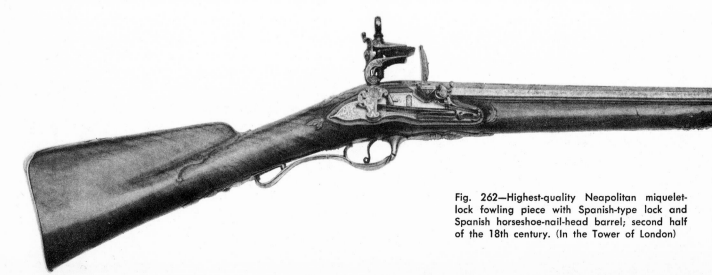

Fig. 262—Highest-quality Neapolitan miquelet-lock fowling piece with Spanish-type lock and Spanish horseshoe-nail-head barrel; second half of the 18th century. (In the Tower of London)

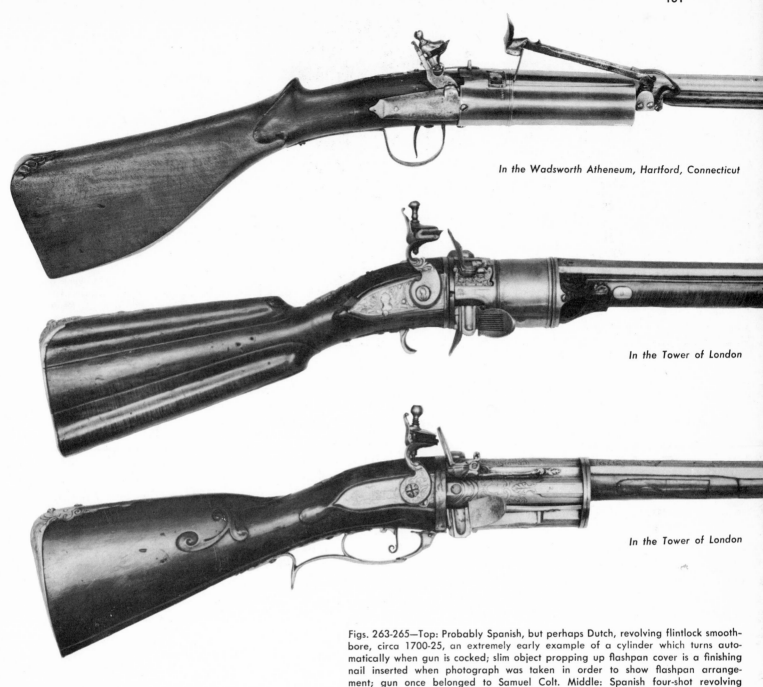

In the Wadsworth Atheneum, Hartford, Connecticut

In the Tower of London

In the Tower of London

Figs. 263-265—Top: Probably Spanish, but perhaps Dutch, revolving flintlock smooth-bore, circa 1700-25, an extremely early example of a cylinder which turns auto-matically when gun is cocked; slim object propping up flashpan cover is a finishing nail inserted when photograph was taken in order to show flashpan arrangement; gun once belonged to Samuel Colt. Middle: Spanish four-shot revolving flintlock smoothbore, circa 1760 (trigger guard missing); note typically Spanish butt (cf. Fig. 104). Bottom: German four-shot flintlock revolving smoothbore, circa 1740.

The bore was then smoothed by successively finer abrasives, the last consisting of a cylinder of talc. Such barrels could be proved with quintuple loads of powder without showing the slightest effect. Doubtless the chief ingredient was Spanish skill, for all the efforts of gunsmiths of other nations to duplicate these products, using the same scrap iron, failed miserably. According to William Round's DIRECTIONS FOR THE CHOICE OF GUNBARRELS (London, 1744), one patriotic Englishman identified only as "Mr. K——" refused to countenance such subversive slander on the genius of his countrymen, and when all experiments proved it true, he was silenced only long enough to devise the theory that the secret must lie in the peculiar nature of Spanish air. To demonstrate the in-

escapable truth of this, he sent "two of the best gun-smiths of London" to Barcelona at his own expense in 1739, who returned after two months with the fruits of their labors, including, it may be supposed, particles of Spanish air clinging to the interstices. But evidently these had been too small, or not enough air had clung, for upon being test fired with only a triple load the barrels blasted themselves and Mr. K——'s hypotheses to fragments. The number of counterfeit Spanish barrels ran to the thousands, many or most of them made in Germany, stamped with counterfeit dies of the names and identifying marks of famous Spanish workmen. Nearly all of these were death traps. Reputable gunmakers' guilds sporadically sought their suppression.

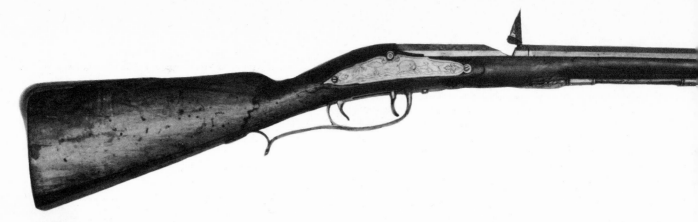

Fig. 266—German flintlock sporting gun with completely internal mechanism, signed *Stanislaus Paczel* and dated 1738. Actual barrel ends immediately in front of the hinged, wedge-shaped battery; barrel-like section extending from there backward is hollow housing containing mechanism. Touchhole is drilled into end of true barrel inside housing, immediately below hinged battery; below touchhole is small flashpan. In place of a cock, hollow housing contains horizontal bolt terminating in flint-holding jaws, activated by a coilspring. Barrel was first loaded like any muzzleloader; next, flashpan beneath battery was primed, gun was cocked or half-cocked by pulling front trigger backward (which drew back flint-holding bolt inside housing and compressed coilspring), and the battery wedge was lastly snapped shut so that the barrel became one smooth, unbroken surface. When rear trigger was pulled, bolt snapped forward horizontally, flint struck oblique underside of closed battery wedge, wedge snapped open instantly (as shown), sparks showered into the flashpan at end of barrel and the shot went off. Clever, well-made device seems sturdy, effective, and, above all, reasonably waterproof. But, like the wheellock pistol with a waterproof mechanism shown in Fig. 143 and other occasional ingenious inventions, it remained among the very rare oddties. Shooters, too, were slow to accept radical innovations. (In the Tower of London)

But in the second half of the century, English craftsmen learned to make equally good tubes, employing the *stubs* of old horseshoe nails. These they hammered and forged into wire, twisted the strands about each other like strands of rope, twisted the resulting "ropes," called *skelps,* about each other, fused the skelps together, wound them in a close coil about a mandril, heated and hammered and reheated and hammered them again for hours, and finally trimmed, bored, finished and polished the barrel which had thus been formed. This sort of work was therefore called a *stub-twist* barrel, and the quality of the skelps, in descending order, ranged from *high-skelp, skelp, sham-skelp* and *sham-damn-skelp.* Only the first two were used in good guns. The barrels were then acid-treated and covered with a thin layer of artificial rust, so that after they had been polished to mirror-smooth finishes there emerged a pattern of closely coiling ribbons of bright iron, rust browns and deep lustrous browns corresponding to the turns of the skelp around the mandril, and herringbone and whirlpool patterns within each ribbon according to the flattened twists of wire within each skelp (see barrels in Figs. 331, 342 and 353). This type of finish distinguished the *Damascus barrels* (named after similarly patterned sword steel made in that city for centuries); if well made, these were far more indestructible than any Spanish ones. Unfortunately, counterfeiting was made easy by etching the patterns into the surface of a worthless piece of trash. Many inexperienced buyers were sold suicidal instruments by criminally unscrupulous persons.

But even the *best* Damascus barrels, even the best modern shotgun barrels, to say nothing of the run of fair- to good-quality ones of the seventeenth-nineteenth centuries, would explode if allowed to rust thin in places, if allowed to become pitted by too infrequent cleaning, if the muzzle was clogged by earth or snow, or if the shooter had overcharged with unreasonable quantities of powder (this last cause being now eliminated in our age of factory-made cartridges). A fifth and common cause was an air space of an inch or more between the powder and the first wad. The reader will recall Sir Roger Williams' comment of 1590 (p. 39) that in the case of muskets "there is neither daunger nor hurt [from recoil] if the shooter have any discretion, especiallie not to overload their peeces, *and take heed that the bullets ioyne close to the powder. . . ."* Otherwise, the explosion produced a shock wave which not only made the piece recoil very forcefully, but would very likely burst it. If the air space extended a long way up the barrel—e.g., from the powder or load to the muzzle clogged with snow or earth—the bursting was, and still is, virtually inevitable. This presented an ever-present danger in the use of double-barreled guns unless the greatest care was taken to seat the shot and wads very tightly on top of the powder. If the recoil of firing the first barrel caused the shot and wad in the other to slide forward by inertia as the gun recoiled backward, the second shot could be the shooter's last.

In proof of this one need only select at random any issue of the sporting periodicals which became so popular in the wake of peace after Waterloo. For example, in various issues of THE ANNALS OF SPORTING AND FANCY GAZETTE between July, 1822, and July, 1823 (Vols. II and III), there are about two dozen news items such as these (italics in originals):

DORSET: *Shooting accident.*—As J. Ekless, Esq., of Burlesdon Bridge, was shooting wild fowl on the river, his gun unfortunately burst, carrying off part of two fingers and otherwise lacerating the left hand. Fortunately, both hands were behind the breech (a circumstance which cannot be too strongly impressed on those who are in the habit of shooting), or the arm must have been torn off, the barrel and stock having been literally blown to pieces.

White bird.—Monday, August 5 [1822], a bird of uncommon size, and perfectly white, alighted on the top of the church at Horfield, and after remaining there a considerable time, was shot at without effect. In the expectation that it would return to the same place, the gun was re-loaded with a very heavy charge; but the bird appeared no more. The same evening a labouring man discharged the piece, when it burst, and shattered his left hand so dreadfully that surgeons at our infirmary were obliged to amputate it. The unfortunate man, we understand, makes the third or fourth patient lately brought to the infirmary from accidents caused by the discharge of overloaded guns.

This latter item prompted a subscriber to write the following letter to the editor (italics his):

To the Editor of the Annals of Sporting.

SIR,— In page 185 of your last Number, I saw, with much regret, that a labouring man had been under the necessity of suffering the amputation of his left hand, in consequence of its having been wounded by the bursting of an overloaded fowling-piece. Perhaps you will allow me to trouble you with a few observations on this subject. . . . The overloading of guns . . . is seldom, if ever, the primary cause of bursting. Those lamentable accidents of which we often read, and of which we are sometimes the painful witnesses, generally arise from a *want of cleanliness.* A gun which is kept in a proper state will discharge an immense load without bursting; on the contrary . . . if the inner surface of the barrel be suffered to rust so as to form specks, after washing the barrel, wet will always lodge in these specks and thus successively facilitate the corrosion in this particular spot til the gun must ultimately burst. Among the rustics, nothing is more common than to keep a gun loaded for months, a very injudicious, as well as a very dangerous practice, unless under circumstances which I shall presently notice. Whenever a gun is fired, unless in very hot weather, the explosion is followed by a certain portion of feculent humidity, which will be plainly perceptible upon the inner surface of the barrel. If, under such circumstances, the gun remains without cleaning for any length of time, corrosion will inevitably ensue; if it be reloaded in this state, and kept so, the dampness or humidity will be communicated to the powder, which will be thus in some degree decomposed, and the corrosion greatly increased. Whenever the surface of the barrel is materially corroded, the gun is for ever afterwards rendered unsafe.

But should it be necessary to keep a gun always loaded, it may be done with perfect safety, provided the barrel be thoroughly washed with hot water, and wiped perfectly dry while the barrel is warm. If the gun be then loaded, and kept in a very dry or warm situation, it will remain for months, perhaps for years, without sustaining the least injury.

Your's, &c.

An Old Sportsman.

This letter, in turn, was probably the reason why the editors somewhat pointedly stressed the matter of cleanliness, care and long experience in the report of the next accident, which appeared six weeks later (italics mine —R.H.):

OXFORD: *Accident.*— Mr. Edward Stokes Cotterell, of Chipping-Campden, met with a very serious accident on Tuesday, October 15 [1822], by the bursting of his *double-barreled* gun, whilst shooting in the neighbourhood, whereby his left hand was lacerated in a dreadful manner. Mr. Cotterell is a careful sportsman, remarkable for keeping his gun clean and perfect, and had shot for thirty years previous without the slightest accident.

These reports stem from 1822. Needless to say, the problem was even more serious in earlier times, although not so serious as may now be the reader's impression. High-quality, well-cared-for guns did not explode, and it is more likely than not that even the experienced and sanitary Mr. Cotterell of Chipping-Camden had unwittingly clogged a muzzle by having dropped the gun, or had loaded a little carelessly so that the *second* barrel of his double-gun burst for the reasons before mentioned. Nevertheless, from whatever cause, sufficient barrels had exploded by 1794 to lead one Richard Webb to the invention of the contrivance shown in Fig. 267. He was granted a patent for it in 1795, with the somewhat optimistic description: "The Barrel being thus placed at so considerable a distance from the Trigger, and neither hand when the Gun is discharged touching any part of the Barrel, will effectually prevent those accidents which have heretofore happened from the bursting of guns, &c. This invention may be applied to Gun Barrels already made, without any alteration." This latter claim neglected to mention that while application to existing guns involved no alteration to the barrel, it required a new stock, false breech and of course the new lock itself, thus totally ruining the weight, balance and other niceties of a good gun. To shoot flying with Mr. Webb's invention must have been awkward in the extreme, and whether it was for this reason or owing to the infrequency of the bursting of really good guns, it never caught on. In fact, it seems that none was ever made save the patent model, or if any were, they are now lost from view.

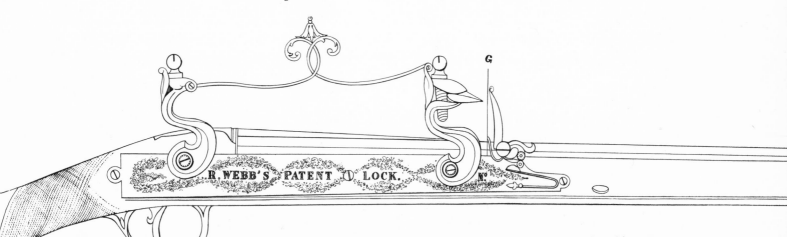

Fig. 267—Richard Webb's gunlock for saving the hands in the event of a barrel bursting; detail from patent specification drawings, February 28, 1795. Specification said: "The plan so clearly shows not only the construction but the intention of the invention that it is scarcely necessary to add anything by way of further explanation. . . ."

Figs. 268 & 269—Essentially typical copper powder flask and leather shot pouch with self-measuring release valve spouts, ca. 1810 onward. Spout of powder flask telescopes, can be pre-set for desired quantity of powder. Shooter holds flask spout-down, places index finger over end, and with his thumb works lever of the spring-valve to fill spout. Releasing valve shuts body of flask off from filled spout; shooter then tips end into muzzle of gun and takes away his finger (cf. Fig. 194). Spout of shot pouch fills as soon as pouch hangs spout-down. Shooter inserts end into muzzle and pushes see-saw valve lever, which shuts off body of pouch and simultaneously opens full spout to release shot.

Fig. 270—Above: English *eprouvette*, or powder tester, circa 1765-85. Short stubby barrel was loaded with powder to be tested, then closed up by buffer lever of the ratchet wheel. Powerful spring which held buffer pressed against oblique muzzle was also the ratchet pawl (its handle may be seen below trigger guard). When device was fired, force of explosion caused wheel to spin for a partial turn; user then counted number of notches spun. In theory, high-quality powder would account for many notches—fifteen or all seventeen—and a low-grade powder for only three or four, etc. While serviceable for discriminating between extremely good and extemely bad powder, these devices were unreliable for measuring differences of quality in middle range.

Nearly every shooter had his own best-of-all-possible refinements on the process of loading. Some swore by thick wads, some by thin; some had them cut out of cork, others of paper, others still of moss. Mr. Markland, it will be remembered, advised tough old saddle stuffing, but as powder was improved in the course of the eighteenth century, this practice fell into disuse. Some *loaded* first, *then* primed, in fear of the extremely undesirable event of a primed and half-cocked lock snapping by accident just when the last wad was being rammed in place. Others *primed* first, *then* loaded, because the act of ramming the wads on top of the powder slightly compressed the air in the barrel ahead of the wad and thus forced a few grains of powder to exit through the touchhole into the already primed pan; this ensured a connection between the priming and the main charge and thereby reduced the chances of having a flash in the pan. Many swore by steel spring chargers, i.e., small cylindrical containers divided into two sections, each with a spring lid, which had been prefilled with the desired quantity of pellets for one shot. But many more found these foolish and cumbersome, used nothing but the regular leather "pudding" shot pouch with a brass valve nozzle designed to release a certain quantity of shot with each push of the lever (Fig. 269).

By about 1770, the typical method had settled down to what it was to remain for the next hundred years, save that the question of priming was eliminated with the adoption of percussion locks instead of flintlocks between 1815 and 1835. Thus in Thomas Page's THE ART OF SHOOTING FLYING (London, 1767), which consisted of dialogues between an expert gunsmith-and-sportsman named Mr. Aimwell and a raw novice named Mr. Friendly, we find the following illuminating conversation:

DIALOGUE II

FRIENDLY
Good Morrow, Mr. Aimwell.

AIMWELL
Sir, I hope you are well. You are very punctual, to be here rather before the time appointed.

FRIENDLY
I knew you were an early riser, and am desirous you should think me diligent to receive your instructions; but I am ready to await your leisure.

AIMWELL
Sir, it gives me pleasure to see you so alert: for as to sluggards, there is nothing to be made of them. But come, Sir, I am ready. I see you have brought your servant with you, whose attendance may be useful, and I have a man who is very good hand at shooting at a dead mark; for my part, I am not fond of it, for guns seem to recoil more at a fixed mark than at a flying object; and I am apt to lay my face so close as to get a smart blow on the cheek-bone, especially if the barrel lies too straight in the stock. . . .

FRIENDLY
Pray, what is your method of loading? I have been told

that gunsmiths in general put in a large quantity of small shot, to make them fill the paper they shoot at [when demonstrating the gun to a customer in the shop].

AIMWELL

'Tis very true, indeed, they are often obliged to it, when gentlemen won't be satisfied with what is reasonable for a gun to do; and it is a common practice in this country to load with a pipe bowl of powder and a bowl and a half of shot [cf. the same proportions in PTERYPLEGIA, p. 126, right column, 2nd & 3rd lines, and fn. 4]; and when they find they can't kill often, think they don't put shot enough, and so put in more, and are obliged to lessen the quantity of powder to prevent its recoiling; not considering this axiom, "that action and re-action are equal"—that upon discharge of powder the gun is forced back, as the shot is forwards, in proportion to the weight of shot to the weight of the gun. . . . But if less of shot than powder will not carry the shot close enough for long shoots, they will certainly fly thick enough at shorter distances. To avoid the extremes, I use the best powder, and put in equal measures [in volume, not weight] of that and shot, which in weight is nearly as one to seven, but usually prime out of that quantity. To a barrel of a middle-sized bore, whose diameter is about five-eighths of an inch (which I look upon to be the best size for shooting flying) I put in two ounces of shot, No. 4, which are about 200 in an ounce, and an equal measure of powder. This is the charge I use in the field.

FRIENDLY

And what sort of wadding do you best approve of? I have heard some say that tow is best; others, cards stamped to fit the size of the bore.

AIMWELL

Tow, I think, is uncertain. If cards be used, the end of your rammer must be almost as broad as your barrel will admit of, to go down free, and quite flat at the end, to prevent the card from turning; and must be push'd down gradually, to give time for the air to pass, otherwise it will be troublesome. This is therefore not the quickest way. Old hat [i.e., felt or beaver of which hats were made, or an old hat cut up] may be used in the same manner, which is

rather better: and some say leather shreds are best. But I cannot yet find any thing better, or so ready as thin brown paper rubbed soft, and cut into pieces about one inch broad and two inches long; so that when it is once doubled, it is an inch square. I punch a small hole at the corner of each piece, put a sufficient quantity upon a key-ring, hang them into my button hole, and tear off one as I want it. This being doubled, put it into to the muzzle, and close the corners up about the rammer (the end of which ought to continue of the same bigness for at least half an inch, or rather somewhat smaller just at the end) and thrust the paper thus put into the barrel gently down upon the powder. Your rammer will come back without danger of drawing the paper back, [which would result in the dangerous air space discussed earlier], and will leave it closed against the sides of the barrel like a half cartridge. Put in another in the same manner after the shot. When your gun is quite clean, it is necessary to put in a second wad after the shot, to prevent its getting loose.

FRIENDLY

Do you ram your shot as much as your powder? I think I have heard some that pretend to experience say that they ram the powder well but not the shot [this is PTERYPLEGIA verbatim, p. 126, right column, 1st line.] What is your opinion of this?

AIMWELL

After some experience you will find, if your gun is clean, and the wad thrust but lightly down, that in walking the shot will be apt to get loose: and if you discharge the piece in that state, it will seem, by the small resistance it makes, as if there were no shot in it: and if you try one load pretty smartly rammed over the shot, and another with the wad thrust but lightly down, at a quire of paper, you will find the charge that is rammed will penetrate deepest, and that the shot will fly as regularly as the other which is not rammed.

FRIENDLY

Well, Sir, it seems rational enough; and I shall follow your counsel, and try it the first opportunity, because I think it a point necessary to be thoroughly convinced of.

Fig. 271—Wolf driving in Winter. Engraving from Hans Friedrich von Fleming, *Der Vollkommene Teutsche Jäger (The Complete German Hunter)*, Leipzig, 1724.

Nothing was more vital to the good function of a flint-lock than the rapidity and smoothness with which the cock snapped down and the flashpan cover snapped open. Although between 1675 and 1720 the use of the bridle over the tumbler, and the bridge from the flashpan to the screw, had eliminated two serious sources of friction, two more equally serious ones remained. One was the scraping contact between the mainspring and the tumbler, the other the scrape of the flashpan cover spur against the broad upper surface of the feather-spring. To eliminate these, English gunsmiths of the third quarter of the eighteenth century invented the *tumbler swivel* and the *roller-bearing feather-spring*. The first of these was a steel swivel, or link, which connected the tumbler and the mainspring as shown in Fig. 274. The latter was a small wheel at the end of the feather-spring or at times on the spur of the flashpan cover (Figs. 272 and 273). These inventions, rare before 1770, had appeared on virtually all locks of even only fair quality by 1785, and were standard equipment on all save the military and the poorest locks by 1790. Friction was thus reduced to where it was in effect negligible, and as a consequence a well-made lock not only fired many times faster, but missed fire much less frequently than any ever had before. At once the gunmakers of every nation followed the English examples, very few with English skill.

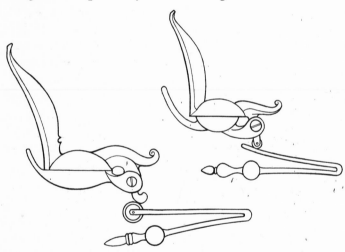

Figs. 272 & 273—"Frictionless," i.e., roller-bearing arrangements between flashpan cover spurs and feather-springs. Roller (or wheel) at end of spring was more frequent, but variations of the other method were not rare.

A further and third refinement was the "waterproof" flashpan. The first efforts toward this end had appeared in about 1760 in the form of the pierced flash shield, or lip, at the rear edge of the pan, for as has been noted in connection with the fowling pieces of the Restoration (p. 95), any drop of moisture running down the face of the battery had hitherto been guided unfailingly into the priming. With the drainage hole, however, such drops were less likely to enter the pan. After about 1770, the flashpan itself was made with a sharp, raised edge instead of the old broad, flat one, so that the cover could now fit *over* the pan and not merely rest *on* it (Fig. 274). This obviously served to keep out more water.

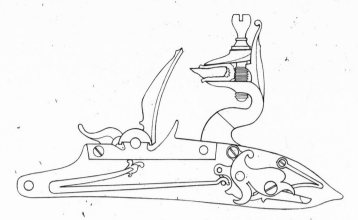

Fig. 274—Interior of a good-quality flintlock of circa 1780 to 1825. Mainspring terminates in forked claw, hooks over studs on swivel (or link) pivoted to tumbler; this reduced friction considerably. Flash shield behind pan curves down and away to allow cover to fit over raised edge of pan; drops running down battery will be guided off down the lockplate, not into the priming.

These new frictionless locks struck such fierce, hot showers of sparks, and hurled them so invariably into the direct center of the flashpan, that it had been found not only possible but extremely efficient to prime with only a few grains of finely ground powder instead of the considerably larger quantities with which flashpans had hitherto been filled. By about 1785, therefore, the flashpan had undergone a drastic change: it was thereafter (on good-quality guns) little more than an extremely small oval platform, shaped like a tiny narrow teaspoon but not nearly as deeply concave, often less than half an inch long and a quarter of an inch wide. To facilitate further the watertight fit of the cover over it, the flash shield and the bridge to the flashpan cover screw became two free-standing, separate projections of winglike shape which no longer touched the pan at all, or only joined it at its bottom (e.g., Fig. 322). Such pans were often lined with gold or platinum to resist corrosion (platinum was cheaper then), and since the priming used on them was now only a few grains, they withstood the effects of the fiery reaction throughout years of use without showing any evident signs of wear. Similarly, since about 1720 the touchholes of fine guns had been screwed-in plugs of gold, after about 1800 of platinum, with the actual touchhole drilled through them. Both the gold-lined flashpan and the gold or platinum touchhole remained the hallmarks of high workmanship until the end of the flintlock era in about 1825. Nevertheless, Thomas Johnson (whose SHOOTER'S GUIDE of 1816 [London] has already been quoted, and whose views on other matters will be called upon again) was of the opinion that:

> As to gold pans, they are more for show than utility. A steel pan will be found, with common care in cleaning it, to last longer, and to answer every purpose as well as when lined with gold. But a gold or platina touch-hole is preferable to the common one. Platina has but lately been tried for this purpose, but it is found to answer equally with gold, and at the same time is much cheaper. I have two fowling-pieces with platina touch-holes, which I have used four seasons, and they do not appear to be more worn than if they had been gold.

By 1789 the new-style locks had been so developed that the anonymous author of AN ESSAY ON SHOOTING, published in London in that year, was able to peer into his somewhat clouded crystal ball and warble contentedly:

> With regard to the locks, we have nothing material to offer, the genius and industry of the English workmen having already brought them to such a degree of elegance and perfection that we have scarcely anything farther to hope for or to require.

Still another invention must be described if we are fully to appreciate the perfection of the flintlock in its evening hours: this was the *patent breech*. Until about 1750, all guns, save perhaps a few dozen rare and experimental ones, had been fired through a simple touchhole leading through one side of the barrel. While adequate, this method ignited the charge at only one corner, with the result that not all of it burned, and efficiency was low. We have already seen that the effort to increase it had been the reason for the awkward lengths of barrels. Toward the middle of the century, there appeared what was called a *chamber-breeching* (below), in which the

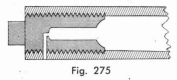

Fig. 275

touchhole was a canal in a removable breech-plug, the canal in turn leading into the direct center of the rear of the powder chamber. Ignited there, the powder burned much more completely and efficiently than when ignited at only one corner, and consequently threw the load much harder and farther. But obviously the priming now had to traverse the long distance of the canal, with the result that the time between trigger pull and shot was very perceptible (perhaps half a second). If this new invention could make the pellets reach out for a cross-flying woodcock over greater distances and send them off whistling more fiercely, they also arrived just in time to reach and whistle past it. To remedy this defect, a celebrated gunsmith in London, Henry Nock (practiced 1772–1806), invented a breech for which he was granted Patent No. 1598 in 1787. By Nock's method (Fig. 276), the breech plug was fitted with a removable, minimally thin gold or platinum touchhole through which the priming flash communicated into an antechamber (A). The powder in the antechamber was thus instantly kindled, and now the force of *its* explosion was directed through a narrow opening into the base and center of the main

powder chamber (B), so that the main charge was not only kindled, but *shot through* by a tongue of fire.

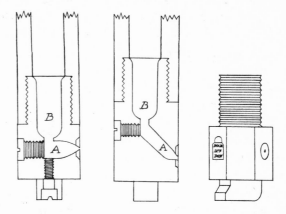

Fig. 276—Nock's patent breeches, drawn after his patent specification diagrams of April 25, 1787. Right: outside view of an octagonal breech-plug showing touchhole on right side, Nock's name stamp on top. Left and middle: cut-away views of two types of plugs screwed into rear of barrels. Powder in antechamber A is kindled instantaneously by priming in flashpan (not shown); subsequent jet of fire shoots through narrow neck in main powder chamber B. Screws at rear and left sides of plugs may be removed for cleaning antechambers.

The effect was that the gun shot so hard and so fast that the very possibility of such performance had hitherto not even been imaginable. Moreover, it was now no longer necessary to bring about the complete combustion of powder by length of barrel, and by 1790—the patent breech having caught on among sportsmen at once—the guns with barrels of twenty-six to thirty-two inches became the rule, with occasional ones of only twenty-two inches. By 1795 the old thirty-nine- to forty-eight-inch tubes were obsolete. The weight thus saved made the double-gun not only possible but highly practical, and from 1790 on the short, light, and in shape completely modern side-by-side became so ever-increasingly popular that by 1810 the single-guns were in the minority.

All these ingenuities, then, have brought us to the threshold of the nineteenth century and of the flintlock's final glory: fitted with a magnificently patterned Damascus barrel, fired by a lock finished to precision tolerances and rendered frictionless to fire instantly, lent power by the patent breech, made short, light and graceful for easy and deadly accuracy—it now lacked nothing save the last few master touches which were to come within a decade. And here we shall leave it, to return after we have taken up the history of an entirely different sort of weapon.

Fig. 277—Two partridges. German engraving, circa 1725.

CHAPTER TEN

The function of rifling—Four theories between 1475 and 1750—An experiment in 1547: demons on rifle bullets proved a fact—Problems of muzzle loading—Problems of breech loading—The opinion of Benjamin Robins—German gunsmiths in Pennsylvania in the early eighteenth century—The uselessness of the German rifle in America—The development of the "Kentucky" rifle—Its virtues and failings—The British view of the Kentucky rifle in the War of Independence—The Hessians—The Ferguson rifle—Its superiority over any other—Its rejection by myopic war lords—Its use in the War of Independence—Its demise, and the death of Ferguson—What might have been if . . . —Soldiers as judges of distance.

IFLING, AS HAS BEEN NOTED IN Chapter III, was invented, discovered or transferred from spinning arrows to guns sometime between 1450 and 1480. In simple terms, its theory and effect are as follows:

A carelessly molded ball has casting flaws—bubbles, pits, internal "cheese holes." Even the most carefully cast ones have slight imperfections, and even when these are reduced to a minimum, the lead itself varies in density so that the bullet is always slightly heavier on one side than on the other. This is true today in the case of modern conical steel- or copper-jacketed bullets, although of course to a much lesser extent. Consequently a bullet's center of gravity was and still is some distance removed from its true geometric center.

When a bullet is shot out of a smoothbore barrel, directly upon leaving the muzzle it is subjected to four main forces: the forward thrust imparted by the explosion, the impeding effect of air resistance, the downward pull of gravity, and the bullet's own turning in flight to turn its heaviest or densest side forward. The friction of this turning against the air stream creates a wobbling and deflecting effect, much like a billiard ball with "English on it." Nothing can be done about air resistance or gravity, which will ever make it the fate of a thrown object to be retarded to a halt and fall to the ground. The wobbling, however, can be eliminated or reduced to a negligible degree. If parallel spiral grooves are cut into the bore of the gunbarrel, making anywhere from one half of a turn to a turn and a half from breech to muzzle, and if the bullet is forced to "bite" into and follow them, this will impart a spinning motion to the bullet. In flight, then, the various casting imperfections and differences in density of the lead are no longer concentrated in any particular part of the bullet: instead, the spinning motion has in effect converted them into concentric rings spinning about one central axis of rotation. The centrifugal force creates an artificial equilibrium about the axis, while the gyroscopic effect prevents it from deviating from the line of the axis of the gunbarrel out of which the bullet has been shot. Thus the bullet will not turn or wobble, will create less air turbulence, and consequently will fly further and much more accurately than a non-spinning one.

There were four theories which sought to explain this phenomenon between 1475 and the middle of the eighteenth century. The first has already been mentioned (p. 36): no demon could remain astride a spinning object because rotation was the fundamental motion of God's creation—there were no demons in the spinning heavens, only on and in the stationary earth. Alternatively, other thinkers were forced by the weight of evidence to conclude that a demon could remain astride *only* on a spinning object, but the object had to be terrestrial in origin. Far from being immune to such passengers, rifle bullets could not possibly act as they did without them. To settle this matter once and for all, an experiment was conducted in Mainz in March, 1547, under the auspices of the archbishop and the *Schützenverein*, the Sharpshooters' Guild. Two riflemen were to shoot at a bull's-eye two hundred meters (219 yards) distant, one with ordinary bullets, the other with silver bullets which had been cast and loaded under innumerable demon-proofing benedictions and exorcisms, and each one deeply engraved with a crucifix. Twenty shots were fired by each man. Upon examination of the target, it was found that of the twenty plain, non-demon-proof lead balls, nineteen had hit dead on the mark and the last had come within six hands of it; while every single one of the holy silver ones, which no demon would dare to look at, had missed not only the bull's-eye but the target and backstop as well. *Ergo* (the evidence was incontrovertible), rifle bullets were demon-guided; Q.E.D. Rifles were instantly declared under anathema in Mainz, seized and burned by the dozens, and their manufacture henceforth prohibited under pain of the stake. But within a decade this decree fell into disuse, and rifles, balls and demons gradually returned. The age was innocent of any suspicion that the silver balls had not bitten into the rifling grooves as firmly as the lead, with consequent stripping of silver and much loss of compression, and that whatever spin might have been imparted to them was offset by the violent imbalance and air turbulence created by the engraved crucifixes. To this day, exorcism of rifle bullets—modern, center-fire cartridges—immediately before a hunt or a shooting match is not rare among a good many South German farmers and foresters. The Harz and Jura mountains, the Black Forest and the Tyrolean Alps are still rich in hushed, knowing tales of hunters past and present who struck their bargains with the Black Hunter in exchange for molds which cast unerring bullets. And witchcraft, black art and rifle bullets cast at midnight are the subjects of Karl Maria von Weber's opera *Der Freischütz*, in which old Samiel, the Black Hunter, almost—but happily, not quite—makes off with the soul of young Max, the enamored forester.

The two other theories on rifling were less profound. One held that the bullet simply "drilled" its way through the air. The other maintained that rifling merely exercised a resisting and retarding effect on the bullet, giving the powder behind it more time to burn more efficiently. Benjamin Robbins proved both wrong in 1747.

In order for a rifle to be effective, the bullet must *fill* the grooves to ensure its following the spiral and to prevent windage around it. In the case of a muzzle-loader, this meant hammering down an oversize ball with an iron ramrod and a mallet, a process which not only required much time and labor but which also mutilated the ball. This could be avoided by using a ball just barely *smaller* than the bore diameter between two opposite rifle *lands,* but wrapping it first in a greased patch of very thin leather or fustian which would be firmly gripped by the grooves and which in turn would firmly grip the ball. This invention has often but wrongly been attributed to the American frontiersmen of the eighteenth century, but it was known before the beginning of the seventeenth century and was described by Espinar in his ARTE DE BALLESTERIA Y MONTERIA (*The Art of Shooting & Horsemanship*) in 1644. In general, however, it did not find wide acceptance because the European shooters of the entire seventeeth and most of the eighteenth century were largely persuaded of the retarding-and-resisting theory of rifling, and consequently they thought that the harder a ball had to be hammered down the barrel, the greater the friction and retardation upon shooting and therefore the better the shot.

Fig. 278—Title-page woodcut from Joachim Rudolph Sattler's *Ausführliche Beschreibung des Gesellenschiessens in Basel (Exhaustive Description of the Shooting Match in Basel)*, Basel, Switzerland, 1605. Note musket shot from rest, arquebus shot freehand, target markers waving pointers from behind wooden walls, clown, piper, drummer, kibitzer.

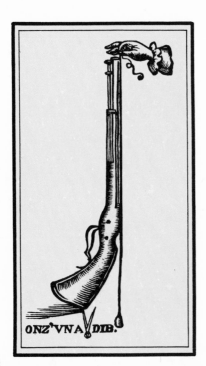

Fig. 279—Measuring the drop in the stock of an arquebus with a plumbline. Woodcut from Vita Bonfadini, *La Caccia dell'Arcobugio (Hunting with the Arquebus)*, Venice, 1691.

Fig. 280—Speed and ease of loading by a relatively effortless push with a light wooden ramrod, as in this engraving from Lucas Kilian, *Newes Soldatenbüchlein (New Book of Soldiery)*, Augsburg, 1609, made smoothbores preferable to rifles in military service.

The alternative to either of these muzzle-loading methods was to load through the breech. When the gun was fired, the oversized ball adapted itself to the rifling, and the windage was minimal. Curiously, the English gunsmiths not only excelled in these mechanisms but seem to have been the chief manufacturers of them, in spite of the fact that only a very few rich clients were able to hunt the very few deer in England. On the other hand, most breechloaders before the nineteenth century could not be made to stand up well under the constant violence of the explosions, and although many English gunmakers after about 1700 were able to make lifting and hinged breech locks which would be gas tight for a few hundred fires, eventually the parts were loosened and ultimately threatened to explode. Breech-loading rifles made on the same principle as screw-barrel pistols were not rare (Fig. 206). They seem to have served very well to fit the ball tightly and could withstand thousands of shots without danger of being loosened, but the business of unscrewing the barrel, laying it aside (or letting it dangle by its chain), loading the breech, balancing the ball and rescrewing the barrel must have been even more awkward in the case of a rifle than with a pistol. A third method, sturdy and easy to manipulate but very imperfect from the point of view of gas seepage, was the screw-plug breech, in which a vertical hole in the top, bottom or side at the rear of the barrel could be opened to admit ball and powder by the unscrewing of a stout plug, and closed again by replacing it (Figs. 281 and 282).

The rifle was naturally the gun of Germany and Switzerland, where big game abounded in the lush forests and stark mountains. By 1700 the gunmakers of Bavaria had developed short, massive, heavy wheellock and flintlock rifles which could kill bears and deer at two hundred yards with ease, while shots beyond four hundred were not unknown. These weapons were of .65 to .75 calibre, weighed thirteen to twenty pounds, and were loaded by pounding the ball down inch by inch with the iron ramrod and Herculean blows of the mallet. Usually a "false muzzle" was placed over the muzzle of the barrel when loading in order to protect the true muzzle from being marred by the ramrod, for if a rifle bore is at all nicked or scarred around the muzzle the bullet will not fly true. By 1700, too, Austrian, Bavarian and Swiss gunsmiths had developed the wheellock to such a degree of perfection that few flintlocks could ever hope to compete, and the majority of Alpine rifles were wheellocks until 1725, in spite of the enormous costs involved.

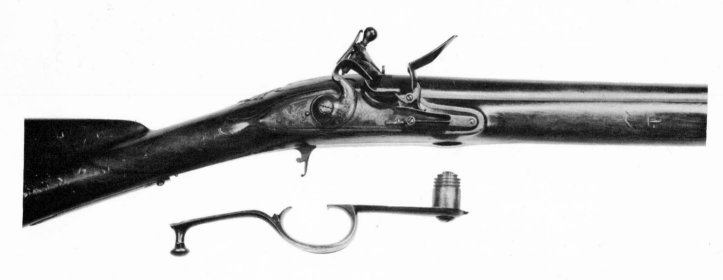

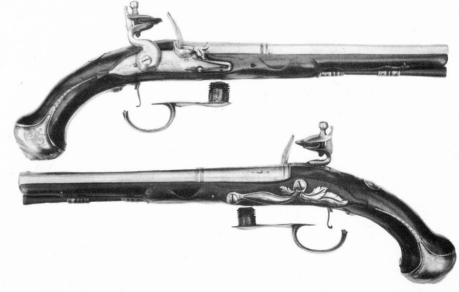

Fig. 281 & 282—Above: Breech-loading flintlock rifle by Hirst of London, circa 1750. Right: Pair of English rifled breech-loading flintlock pistols, probably the personal sidearms of an officer in about 1735–50. Both the rifle and the pistols were made with the same breech-loading mechanism. To load, breech-plug was unscrewed by its trigger guard handle; weapon was then turned bottom up and muzzle pointed upward at about 45°. Because circular loading opening on the underside led into the *front* of the breech chamber, powder was loaded first and allowed to fall backward, then ball in front of powder; plug was then replaced. Although system permitted easy loading of oversized rifle balls which would "bite" securely into the rifling grooves when fired, its great failings were that breech opening was not at rear of chamber, and that plug could easily be dropped or fumbled in heat of battle (cf. Ferguson's system, Fig. 301).

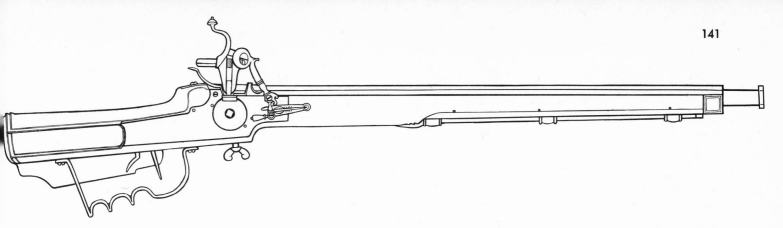

Fig. 283—Austrian wheellock rifle with interchangeable telescoping barrels, circa 1620. Small .37-calibre barrel, shown partly projecting from muzzle of large .76-calibre barrel, can be inserted in larger barrel; small barrel is locked in place by wing nut under breech; touchholes of both barrels align when small barrel is in place. Thus rifle may be used for big game hunting with .76-calibre bullets, small game or target shooting with .37-calibre. Note set-trigger and hair-trigger: after having wound the wheel, the shooter pulled the rear trigger, which "set" the mechanism; thereafter, the slightest touch on the front trigger would release the wheel to spin; this permitted taking careful aim and firing without spoiling it by a long or hard trigger pull. Set- and hair-triggers came into use about 1550-70.

Fig. 284—Wheellock by Elias Schinzel of Berlin. Circa. 1700.

Fig. 285—Below: Medium-sized German hunting rifle of the 1700-50 period, with set- and hair-triggers, carved stock and adjustable rear sight. In the 11- to 16-pound class, between .50 and .60 calibre, high-quality weapons were accurate and deadly beyond 200 yards but lacked the enormous stopping power of such monsters as Fig. 286, were consequently more often found in relatively flat forest regions rather than in Alps or other impassable mountain territories. Although occasionally loaded with patched balls, method most frequently employed was iron ramrod and mallet.

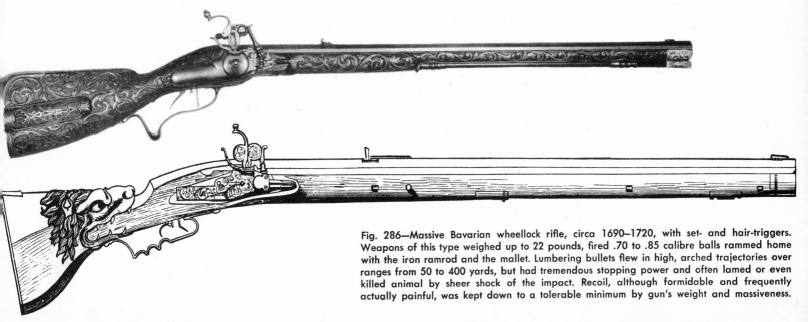

Fig. 286—Massive Bavarian wheellock rifle, circa 1690–1720, with set- and hair-triggers. Weapons of this type weighed up to 22 pounds, fired .70 to .85 calibre balls rammed home with the iron ramrod and the mallet. Lumbering bullets flew in high, arched trajectories over ranges from 50 to 400 yards, but had tremendous stopping power and often lamed or even killed animal by sheer shock of the impact. Recoil, although formidable and frequently actually painful, was kept down to a tolerable minimum by gun's weight and massiveness.

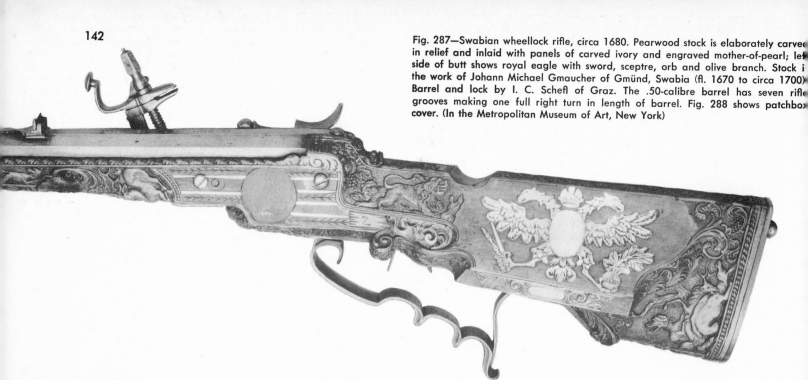

Fig. 287—Swabian wheellock rifle, circa 1680. Pearwood stock is elaborately carved in relief and inlaid with panels of carved ivory and engraved mother-of-pearl; left side of butt shows royal eagle with sword, sceptre, orb and olive branch. Stock is the work of Johann Michael Gmaucher of Gmünd, Swabia (fl. 1670 to circa 1700). Barrel and lock by I. C. Schefl of Graz. The .50-calibre barrel has seven rifle grooves making one full right turn in length of barrel. Fig. 288 shows patchbox cover. (In the Metropolitan Museum of Art, New York)

Fig. 288—"Patchbox" cover of rifle in Fig. 287; ivory panel in pearwood shows winged Venus and Eros astride winged ball in sea. Spring latch which keeps box closed is released by pressing Venus' umbilicus. "Patchbox" inletted into rifle butts of European iron-ramrod-and-mallet-loaded rifles were of course not used for storage of greased patches, but of spare flints, pyrites, touchhole pricker, screwdriver, etc.

The German immigrant gunsmiths in America who settled and opened their shops in and near Lancaster, Reading and other frontier towns in eastern Pennsylvania, introduced German rifles in the New World at the beginning of the eighteenth century. Business flourished, for good rifles were scarce; but at once problems developed. A frontiersman who often trekked through the wilderness for weeks could hardly be expected to carry along a thirteen- to twenty-pound gun, a hammer, the enormous quantity of powder required for .65- to .75-calibre barrels, a false muzzle and a pouch of bullets so large that a month's supply—say 150—weighed between eight and twelve pounds; and if the supplies had to be carried not only for a month, but as was often the case, for half a year, the weight would have come to the utterly impossible total of sixty-five to ninety pounds. Wheellocks were of course by far too complicated for American conditions, where a broken part often had to be heated, fused and re-tempered in campfires and reforged on rocks and tree stumps instead of anvils.

Further, should a German or French hunter return to his village empty-handed after a day's prowl, the consequences were usually no worse than that he would snore peacefully through the night in his warm featherbed until the next day afforded another opportunity. The European was never startled out of his sleep by the flickering light of burning cabins and the screams of his neighbor's children as tomahawks split their guts. In America, hit or miss spelled life or death, and frontiersmen could not rely on rifles whose slow, lumbering bullets and high-curving trajectories required careful estimating whether the target was 100, 150, 200, 250 or 300 yards distant, and setting the rear sight accordingly.

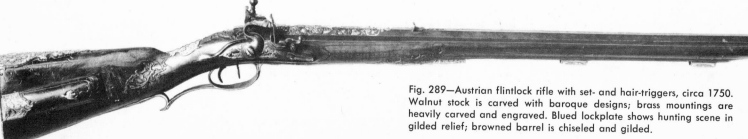

Fig. 289—Austrian flintlock rifle with set- and hair-triggers, circa 1750. Walnut stock is carved with baroque designs; brass mountings are heavily carved and engraved. Blued lockplate shows hunting scene in gilded relief; browned barrel is chiseled and gilded.

Bürg Jæger. Chasseur aux Montagnes.

Fig. 290—Left: *Bürg Jaeger* (modern German *Berg Jäger*) or *Chasseur aux Montagnes*, a mountain hunter, here specifically in the Swiss Alps. In Alpine terrain, where stalking wounded game was often impossible, hunter relied on the bullets with murderous impact and on the short, heavy, big-bore rifles described earlier in the text (here two wheellocks). Engraving from Johann Elias Ridinger, *Abbildungen der Jagtbaren Thiere* (*Album of Game Animals*), Augsburg, 1740.

Fig. 291—Below: Allegorically engraved powder horns of ox's or deer's thighbone were made in the Italian Alps or Dolomites from the late 16th to early 19th centuries; example shown dates from circa 1800.

What the Americans demanded of their gunsmiths seemed impossible: a rifle which would weigh no more than ten pounds, shoot such small bullets that a month's supply would weigh no more than three pounds at the most and preferably only one, with proportionately small quantities of powder, be easy to load, and which would shoot with such velocity and flat trajectories that *one* fixed rear sight would serve as well at fifty yards as at three hundred, the necessary but slight difference in elevation being supplied by the shooter's experience.

By about 1735 the impossible had taken shape in the form of the gun which is now groundlessly referred to as the *Kentucky rifle*. If any geographic epithet must be attached, it should be called the *Pennsylvania rifle,* for there it was born and developed. It was used in Kentucky no more than in every other state and territory of the Great Wilderness from Scranton and Raleigh to Des Moines and Fort Worth, and ultimately even to Vancouver and Monterey.

To accomplish all the desired ends, the gunsmiths had reduced the calibre to between .40 and .55, requiring bullets of which respectively 73 and 29 weighed a pound. The stocks were reduced to the minimal quantity of wood possible, while the weight saved by this expedient and by the slimming of the barrel was partially added to the length of the barrel, which might measure anywhere from forty to fifty inches, usually about forty-two to forty-eight. Loaded with a powder charge weighing between one-third and one-half the weight of the ball, the spheres were propelled with such velocity that there was no appreciable drop at the most normal shooting ranges of 50 to 150 yards, while the expert eye compensated for the drop between 150 and 300. True, such small bullets did not have the stopping power of the German high-trajectory three-quarter-inch calibres, but then, the American was very rarely faced with dangerous game which had to be stopped in its charge by sheer impact, while it had been the express purpose of the German guns to do just that to the wild boars so abundant in Europe and their distressing habit of charging suddenly from a bush with lowered razor tusks. The small, high-velocity bullets which flew out of the long American barrels were more than adequate to bring down any deer, bear or mountain lion inhabiting the American forests. Rarely, however, and then only for special purposes, were barrels and the stocks on which they fitted as inordinately long as popular fancy now portrays them, since obviously excessive length would have defeated the very object of utility for which they had been designed. Four and a half to five feet overall gun lengths were the practical maxima, and the "six-foot old-time shooting irons" of fiction did not exist save in the exceptional cases of bench-rested target rifles, or guns made to measure for giants. The slender butts were carved in a characteristic crescent, with only a little or no thumb rest on the wrists. A very common feature was the patch box inletted into the right side of the butt for the storage of the greased patches described earlier (for this method of loading was invariably used), a fixture adopted from the German rifles but now closed by a hinged brass lid, often highly decoratively cut and pierced, rather than by the German wooden sliding top which was apt to be dropped and lost.

All the innumerable perils, hardships and emergencies of frontier life in which these weapons performed their appointed duties have been often retold and may safely be left to the reader's imagination. The fact that they did so with unerring certainty is attested by the emergence of civilization out of the endless primordial and hostile continent. Until the last quarter of the eighteenth century there were no guns anywhere in the world which could shoot so far, so accurately and so efficiently. When better guns were at length constructed in the form of the Ferguson rifles, these soon withered under the neglect of the British War Office, leaving the "Kentucky" the most accurate long-range shooter in the world until about 1840. This, however, was less of a distinction than would appear on first thought if we remember that it was also the world's *only* long-range shooter, specifically designed to meet conditions which prevailed nowhere else. A Kentucky rifle would have been of as little use in Bavaria and Switzerland as the Bavarian and Swiss rifles had been in America. Quite aside from the ever-present European terror of wild boars, it was absolutely necessary that an antelope or a deer should be stopped dead or lamed by impact in the craggy Alpine regions where the hunter was often on one mountain and the quarry on another, and where tracking of a wounded animal was consequently often impossible.

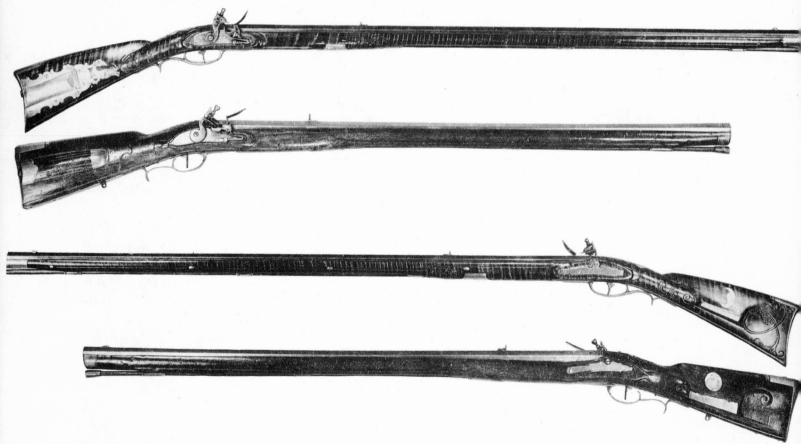

Figs. 292 & 293—Comparison of both sides of a typical American "Kentucky" rifle (upper gun) and its ancestor, a typical Bavarian flintlock rifle of circa 1700-20 (lower gun). Dimensions are:

	Kentucky rifle, 1760	Bavarian rifle, 1710
Overall length	62 in.	56 in.
Barrel length	45½ in.	40¾ in.
Weight	9 lbs. 13 oz.	10 lbs. 8 oz.
Calibre	.40	.66

Bavarian rifle has sliding patchbox cover, American hinged lid. Patchbox ornaments, buttplates, trigger guards, ramrod thimbles, side plates and forestock tips of both guns are brass; both ornaments on left sides of butts are silver; Bavarian stock is walnut, American deeply lustrous, highly contrasting so-called "tiger-flame" maple. Big, lumbering, hard-smashing bullets from Bavarian rifle flew in high, curved trajectories, requiring the use of an adjustable rear sight; small, high-velocity American bullets had low, flat trajectories permitting use of a single fixed (i.e., not adjustable) rear sight, but lacked the lethal stopping power of the German ones. Skilled, eagle-eyed marksmen with American rifles could allow for necessary long-range elevation by "feel," hit deer-sized targets at 400 yards with luck, at 300 with ease; Germans could generally do the same but only if distance was known within 25 yards, the sight set accordingly, the day windless and the shooter's judgment perfected by twenty years' experience.

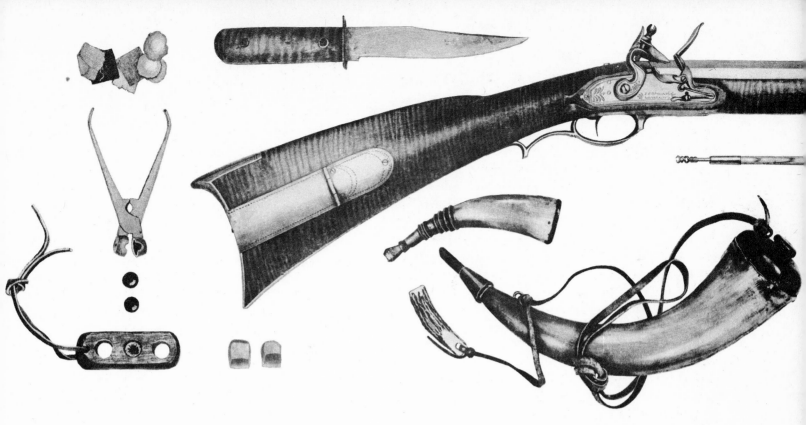

Fig. 294—The most indispensable belongings of an American frontiersman, circa 1740-1830. Splendid .50-calibre, curly-maple-stocked rifle is 62 inches long over all, weighs 9½ pounds, was evidently made for a very tall, muscular man by some unknown Pennsylvania riflesmith in about 1780. Elegant sturdiness and simple brass patchbox mark it as a real "working" rifle. Accouterments are (left, top to bottom): square and round greased patches of thin cloth or buckskin (carried in patchbox) for wrapping balls before ramming;

bullet mold; two .50 calibre balls; a "loading block" for carrying three patched balls, ready for starting into muzzle with thumb; and two spare flints. Above and below rifle: maple-handled hunting knife; rear end of ramrod fitted with corkscrewlike "worm" or "jag" for attaching bore-swabbing tow or for withdrawing a loaded charge; small powder horn for fine-grain priming; and large horn for propellent powder, with a staghorn measuring cup. (In the collection of Mr. Joel A. Gross, New York)

But however excellent the American rifles' design, the quality and workmanship of their locks were nowhere near what is now often avowed with more patriotism than objectivity. In most instances it was actually extremely crude. No experienced English sportsman would have paid a shilling for the sort of locks which most frontiersmen found adequate, and there is no comparing the workmanship of even the best makers of Pennsylvania with that of the good and better ones of London. Such late-century refinements as gold or platinum touchholes, tumbler swivels, waterproof pans and even the elementary featherspring rollers were very rare until the early nineteenth century, long after they had become standard on all competently made English locks; and when they had at last been imitated, the English precision of parts and perfection of fit and finish were always totally absent. Most Kentucky rifles still had locks at the end of the flintlock era—1820 to 1840—which would have been considered modern but third-rate by the better European gunsmiths in about 1750. In the forging, boring and rifling of barrels the Americans generally equaled but never excelled the best craftsmen of Munich, Geneva and London.

All this is not to detract from the Kentucky rifle's glory. In fact, a strong case can be made that without them the War of Independence might have been lost. The British regulars with their bayoneted Brown Besses could, and usually did, walk over the American regulars, provided the encounter fell out on open, flat ground where the infantry tactics perfected by decades of experience and implemented by years of drill could be put to use. Fortunately for the American cause, it was often possible to

draw or force the British into offering battle on an entirely different sort of terrain: sometimes hilly glens dense with high shrubbery, sometimes broken, wooded, boulderstrewn mountainsides, sometimes dark forests—but never, save in the case of effecting some special tactic, was the fighting to be done on the grounds on which the British must almost inevitably be masters. But if rugged terrain curtailed or at times even totally halted the traditional British tactics of musketry volley and bayonet charge, it also proved an impediment to the American regulars, although much less so because the self-reliant American rustics in uniform could always scatter quickly and fall back on individual firing from behind whatever natural cover—stone walls, trees—there might be. The British regulars, over-disciplined in the classical employment of the "national weapon" and deliberately trained not to aim, brought disaster on themselves whenever they attempted dispersion and individual fire over any area large enough materially to disrupt the order of rank and file. On the other hand, such muskets as had slowly been accumulated by the Americans through purchase abroad, gifts and a thin flow of native manufacture, plus the stock of captured or privately owned Brown Besses, were all but worthless for individual fire from cover. The Brown Besses, "exceeding badly bored, and very crooked" as many of them might have been, were nonetheless the best in the American array of almost unserviceable Dutch, German and French guns, many of which had been hammered together in breathtaking haste for the sole purpose of extracting as many pounds-sterling from the desperate American purchasing agents in as short a time as possible.

If then the Brown Bess (which *might* hit a man at eighty yards, with luck and a tightly fitting ball at a little above a hundred) was the best of the lot, it meant that those Americans shooting from cover with Brown Besses had clearly to approach within the British Brown Besses' effective range, while those armed with shoddier stuff had to come closer still. At this point the balance of firepower was about in equilibrium: what safety and certainty the Americans might have gained by sniping from cover was largely nullified by, say, two thousand British regulars (obscured in a smoke cloud) letting fly eight thousand or more shots a minute at random among the trees, hedges or other American places of concealment; nothing man-sized could move about in such a hail, and exposing the head in order to aim was suicide. Then fortune or tactical genius would win or lose the encounter by the maneuvers and storms which had necessarily to follow.

This had all been noted by quite a few American officers as early as Lexington (April 19, 1775) and Bunker Hill (June 17, 1775). The obvious answer would seem to have been the introduction of rifles, but this thought never crystallized in the mind of any New Englander, for rifles were all but completely unknown in these regions. Since there were no rifles to be had even if someone had wanted to have them, pressure for their adoption was not acute. Washington, Benedict Arnold, Charles Lee and a few other able officers with less parochial limitations, however, did think of the enormous and potentially decisive superiority which four or five thousand skilled riflemen would offer. Congress was prevailed upon to vote on June 14, 1776 "that six companies of expert riflemen [each to consist of sixty-eight privates and the usual officers] be immediately raised in Pennsylvania, two in Maryland and two in Virginia." The response was overwhelming. At this time about one-third of the total population was staunchly Tory, actively and bitterly opposed to what they damned as an outrageous treason; another third was undecided or indifferent; only about one-third favored independence with varying degrees of enthusiasm. But the enthusiasm of the frontiersmen from the chosen Provinces left no doubt that even if they were not all quite clear what the shooting was about, they were in favor of doing some of it anyhow. The quotas were exceeded by August 1, and by August 15 there were *fourteen* companies of about *ninety* men each on the way north—some four to eight hundred miles of marching—instead of the envisioned ten companies of sixty-eight men. Pennsylvania's nine companies, altogether about eight hundred riflemen and officers, were organized as a

battalion under Colonel William Thompson; Maryland's first company was commanded by that fabulous Indian fighter Michael Cresap, whose true adventures on the frontier pale the most lurid fiction into nursery rhymes. But the most famous of all was Daniel Morgan's company of ninety-six Virginians—destined to turn imminent disaster into victory, or at least into orderly retreat, again and again throughout the war.

They were a fierce, illiterate, cougar-like lot who arrived in the Boston area in late fall of 1776, clad in filth-encrusted buckskin moccasins, leggings, breeches, hunting shirts and fur caps or crazily cocked hats; they showed no sign of wanting to wash then or ever. Counting unenlisted lone hunters who came along, they numbered some 1,520. And with each came a long rifle. They did not fit into military life, if the roaring confusion about Boston could be called such, slept in the open, did no work, amused the unbelieving, wide-eyed New Englanders by filling ten-inch pewter plates with ten balls in ten shots at two hundred yards, bit each other's ears and noses off in brawls, set up a still and knocked down the camp prison whenever one of their over-stimulated peers had been hauled off by the provosts. Later—in 1777 and 1778—more nearly civilized, at times even literate contingents followed and were also dispersed along the battle and campaign lines from Georgia to Quebec. Though their numbers were still small, their effect was immediate. The British ranks were decimated time and again by an enemy who was not only five or six times beyond the normal reach of the Brown Bess, but who was invisible in the dense walls of forest and mountains. British Major General John Money recounted some of his experiences when he published his PARTIAL REORGANIZATION OF THE BRITISH ARMY in 1799:

> To the American War I look with a heavy heart for examples of the great use of Irregulars—for what was the army that captured General Burgoyne's but an army of Irregulars? What other appellation can be given to Militia untrained to any species of evolution and undisciplined but that of Irregulars? At Saratoga the finest army in the world . . . laid down their arms to what Mr. Rigby in the House of Commons called an "undisciplined rabble." But they were all Woodsmen—that is, marksmen. In the action on Freeman's Farm, the 62d regiment . . . charged four times with the "national weapon" [the Brown Bess and bayonet], and furiously too, quitting their position each time; [but] the conflict was grievous to behold; the contest was unequal. The rebels fled at every charge deeper still into the woods, but when the British troops returned to their positions they were slowly followed, and those who had been the most forward in the pursuit were the first to fall. Night, long wished for, at length arrived and put an end to this bloody action.

Fig. 295—The patchboxes of American long rifles, invariably brass, constitute one of the very few species of pure native American folk art. Made in a vast profusion of patterns and details, the basic form has no antecedent among European patchboxes. American designs, many of them peculiar to a definite time and region, ranged from austere, practical simplicity (e.g., Fig. 294) to fresh adaptations of the rococo, such as the late 18th century Lancaster-area box shown at left.

Fig. 296—What Europeans thought American frontiersmen looked like, but didn't. Engraving cut in about 1785 "after a drawing by a German officer" who had fought in the War of Independence. Blissfully dogmatic caption says: "Faithful representation of the soldiers of Congress in North America, after a drawing by a German officer. The cap is of leather, with the inscription 'Congress'; the entire suit is of canvas, set all over with white tassels; the trousers go down to the ankles. Most men run about barefoot. Their firelocks are fitted with very long bayonets, which they also use as a sword." Needless to say, no apparitions even remotely similar to these ever stalked abroad in America. Real-life frontiersmen wore black felt hats, cocked in any number of fashions, or at times the now famous (but actually not too frequent) coonskin caps. In summer they wore a pair of homespun leggins and a large, loose homespun hunting shirt, tied about the waist with a rawhide belt. Tassels over the seams served to guide off rain water. In winter, homespun was replaced by buckskin, augmented by fur as dictated by temperature. Buckskin clothing was often made by Indian mistresses, and accordingly decorated with Indian designs in dyes and beadwork. Non-Indian magical and totemistic symbols were at times sewed or painted on the chest and back of the shirts, e.g., dead Indians and animals, clan insignia, and hex signs to ward off witches, evil eyes and "haints" (i.e., haunts). Footgear naturally consisted of moccasins. The rifles shown here bear some resemblance to "long" German rifles such as Fig. 293 (the only "long rifles" which the engraver could find for models), but not to anything American; and of course no American hunting rifle was ever fitted with a bayonet. Depictions of this sort contributed to the European impression of America as an exotic satellite of civilization, populated by a species of grunting Moon-men.

Wahrhafte Abbildung der Soldaten des Congreßes in Nordamericka, nach der Zeichnung eines Deutschen Officiers. Die Mütze ist von Leder, mit der Aufschrift Congreß. Die gantze Kleidung von Zwillich überall mit weißen Franzen besetzt, die Beinkleider gehen bis auf die Knöchel herunter. Die Meisten laufen barfuß. Ihrre Feuer-gewehr sind mit sehr langen Payonets versehen, welche Sie auch stat eines Seiten gewehrs gebrauchen. C.D. Henning. exc. Norimberga.

Almost at once the threat of the riflemen to the British grew to critical proportions, in spite of the fact that the British not only had the perfect counter weapon—the best rifle ever made—but that about a hundred men armed with it had been in America ever since March, 1777. Unfortunately for the British cause, neither Howe nor Clinton nor any other general officers seem to have been aware of this, and if they had been, they could not have persuaded the War Office to commence at once with the manufacture of fifteen or twenty thousand of them—although probably a mere four or five thousand would have crushed all significant American forces within three month's time. Aware, however, that *some* sort of answer must be found to the American sharpshooters, the War Office and Lord North determined to see what could be had cheaply on the German soldier market. For almost a century now, Britain and other powers had been buying occasional lots of uniformed slaves from a few dozen German co-princes and colleagues of all three Georges. Notably the Landgraves of Hessen-Kassel had enthusiastically been engaged in this profitable trade ever since Karl I had sold a thousand of his subjects to Venice in 1687 and nine thousand to England in 1702. Since the rebellion in America had not been crushed within the first three weeks, as expected, and since, indeed, it was becoming distressingly evident that it might not be for another year or two, it had already been decided in the summer of 1776 to buy about twenty-five thousand more Germans here and there—regulars, with smoothbore muskets—to expedite the process. But now, in view of the rifleman menace, it would be well to see what was being offered in the line of *Chasseurs* or *Jäger*, in theory professional rifle hunters trained as soldiers. These had long been incorporated in French and German armies with astounding success.

Accordingly, when Lord North sent one Colonel William Fawcitt to buy several thousand more German regulars, Fawcitt had orders to see what could be found in the line of *Jäger*. Upon his arrival in Germany (Karlsruhe, to be exact), thirty-odd German princes dashed off in a determined sprint to undersell each other and to cheat the British by all the rules of the tradition. The dukes, kings, margraves and landgraves of Braunschweig, Hanau, Anspach, Waldeck, Anhalt-Zerbst and the Wotans of some twenty-eight other terrestrial Walhallahs scraped their bailiwicks for any man or boy tall enough to look over a musket and strong enough to lift one. Some 20,500 males—young, old, halt, deaf, blind, sound or demented, no matter— found themselves precipitated from the plough and the barnyard into barracks, out of the wedding suit or the winding sheet into uniform. Only the most long-established cattle dealer of them all, the Landgrave of Hessen-Kassel, was being edged out by the shrewd intrigues of his competitors.

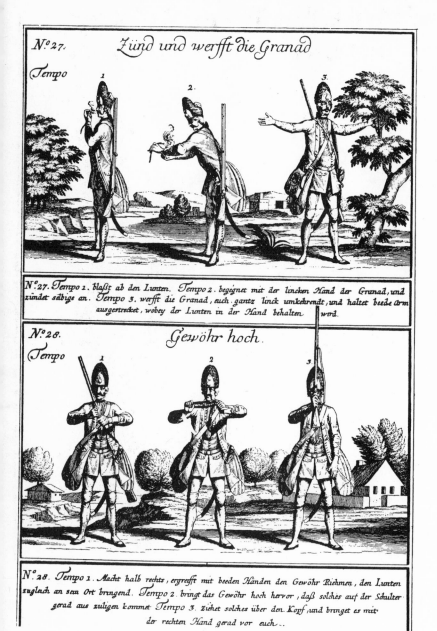

Fig. 297—Typical 18th-century German mercenaries, here Württemberger grena-diers. Shown are Commands No. 27 and 28 in *Manuale oder Handgriffe der Infan-trie nach dem Kayserlichen und Württembergischen Reglement* (*Manuals of Arms for Infantry According to the Imperial and Württemberger Regulations*), Augsburg, 1735. Command No. 27 is "Light and throw the Grenade!" Command No. 28 is "Present arms!" from starting position with gun slung across the back. Both commands were executed in three-count tempos.

Then (in early January, 1777), having procured the regulars, Fawcitt passed the word that he was also inter-ested in *Jäger*, about four thousand of them, complete with rifles. Price: double that for a regular. But the last man had just been sold—except in the Palatinate and Hessen-Kassel, whose rulers, having been squeezed out in the earlier deals, had enough stock on hand to rush off their bids by couriers with showers of sparks on the cobblestones. After about ten days it began to look as though the deal was about to go to the Palatinate. But Hessen-Kassel had prepared for such a disaster. At once he rushed an obsequious letter to Fawcitt, begging al-most tearfully to be permitted to share in the preservation

of British liberties not only by helping to suppress the rebellion in America, but by supplying four thousand Protestants instead of the Palatiners, who were all Catho-lics. For after all, might not four thousand armed Catho-lics riot upon arrival in Portsmouth, seize the throne and the Parliament, crown the Pope and undo in one bloody *coup* all that had been done since the Magna Carta? Of course, the Landgrave himself happened to be a Catho-lic, at least nominally, but for the moment this was not an insurmountable problem. Fawcitt, who seems not to have been conspicuously intelligent, gave the matter some thought and concluded that the Landgrave had done Brit-ain a double service—nay, perhaps saved her from catas-trophe. The contract for four thousand *Jäger* was placed directly. As it happened, the Landgrave had just sold 6,700 men to Louis XVI the year before and 3,886 to Maria Theresa the year before that, so that the stock was a trifle low, though available in those few hamlets and nooks of the province which the press gangs had not denuded of manhood in the past. Further, one had to be careful to leave enough manpower to support the feudal economy. But £700,000 were £700,000, and so, having set aside the minimal number of serfs which were to re-main, the creation of four thousand experienced profes-sional hunters, dead shots all and splendid veteran soldiers, was begun; about six days would suffice. What-ever criteria for selection had been observed by other rulers were quietly waived: it was no longer necessary that the prospective *Jäger* should be able to lift the gun, or even to see it distinctly, so long as he did not collapse when it was leaned against him. The minimum and maxi-mum age limits were respectively sixteen and fifty-five, but strict observance was found impractical. In six days, four thousand *Jäger* stood shivering on the barracks ex-ercise ground in the raw February wind. The extent of their experience, skill and fitness for service was left to the discovery of the purchaser after payment had been received.

Most of the other 22,500 Germans whom Fawcitt had bought wound up in America at one time or another dur-ing the war, although many were shunted on to India and only about 17,800 were used for active service in the Colonies; among them were the four thousand Hessian *Jäger* who, together with about 3,200 Hessian regulars, were the only true Hessians involved in the conflict. Owing to the universally notorious avidness with which the Landgraves of Hessen-Kassel had trafficked in human beings for ninety years, the term "Hessian" came to be generic for impressed Germans, whether they were actu-ally Württembergers, Anspachers, Hanauers or whatever. And that is how the celebrated Hessians came to perish in the American War of Independence, immortalized today on thousands of andirons. Of the total of about 37,500 Germans bought between 1776 and 1781, about 17,400—a little less than half—did not see home again.

Upon receipt of the four thousand in America, however, it was found that unfortunately most of the rifles these *Jäger* had brought along were such decrepit antiquities that any thought of restoring them to serviceable condition had to be abandoned on first inspection. Many of the passable ones were discovered to be not in the hands of seasoned *Jäger* but of ill, infirm, vacant-eyed ghosts of the Middle Ages in tall mitrelike grenadier hats who had not the foggiest notion which end of a rifle the bullet came out of, or that any came out at all. This situation did not contribute appreciably to the countering of the American riflemen, although among the four thousand there proved to be actually about fifteen hundred men who were at least semi-professional hunters, and about another four hundred children from forest regions, aged fifteen and sixteen years, who in a year or two might be made into passable riflemen. General Money continued in the previously cited work:

> No general was more beloved in an army, or more deservedly so, than was General Burgoyne; but such an army as he had was not fit to fight in woods, composed of heavy useless Germans and high-dressed British infantry—those were not the species of troops he wanted. . . .
>
> On the breaking out of the American War, I offered (being then a Captain in the service) to raise a legion, persuaded from the use I had seen made of Yagers in the woods of Westphalia in the German War, that such troops were the men wanted in America; that the Guards and high-dressed corps were not the troops, Sir, to take into woods to fight Virginia riflemen; this must now be acknowledged. I gave my proposition to Lord Barrington. It was to have consisted of two troops of *Chasseurs à Cheval* [mounted hunters with rifles] and 600 Riflemen. It was not approved of, but a corps was raised by General Tarleton in America somewhat similar to it [consisting of about one hundred loyalist Virginia militiamen]. He knew my plan, and was to have been a Captain in my legion, had it been raised. The good effect of his corps was often seen, and it would have been fortunate for us if we had raised more such legions; it would have saved the life of many a brave man who lost it in the unequal contest between high-dressed corps and corps of skillful marksmen. Seldom were the Americans' Riflemen seen—the reports of their guns you heard, but their bullets were felt. My blood ran cold in my veins for years after that unhappy war whenever it occurred to my mind the cruel situation my brave countrymen, through ignorance, had been placed in, when and where bravery was unavailing. Yet it is a doubt with me at this moment, notwithstanding the experience we have had in that war, whether we would not fight it over again in the same manner, [judging] from the cheapness with which Riflemen and Irregulars are still held.

Figs. 298 & 299—Top: Recruiting poster for "the newly created infantry regiment" of the king of Anhalt-Zerbst, circa 1778, promised that "good bonus money will be paid to each man according to his size." British purchasing commissioners thought they were buying such trim, spit-and-polish soldiers for use in American War of Independence, but when shipments were delivered in Portsmouth and New York they were found to consist largely of such hapless stalwarts as the one in the 1784 engraving by Brichet (right).

There was, as has been mentioned, one British rifle which was vastly superior in every respect to the best American specimen. This was the *Ferguson rifle*, invented by Captain (later Major) Patrick Ferguson in the early 1770's and patented in 1776. The Ferguson rifle was a plug-type breechloader. Of course, neither breech-loading nor screw breeches were new ideas, but the Ferguson rifle, besides its fine over-all design, had these radically new features:

—the opening which took the powder and ball was at the *top* of the barrel and at the *rear* of the breech chamber, instead of at the bottom of the barrel and the front of the chamber, such as the systems shown in Figs. 281 and 282; and

—the screw was so constructed that it stopped when it had reached the bottom of the bore, so that in the heat of battle it could never be accidentally lowered out of its hole to leave the tense soldier in the disastrous position of having to reinsert it with nervous, unsure fingers.

The unknown author of AN ESSAY ON SHOOTING described the loading procedure thus in 1789 (Fig. 301 will illustrate):

By far the most expeditious way of charging rifled pieces, however, is by means of an ingenious contrivance which now generally goes under the name of Ferguson's rifle barrel, from its having been employed by Major Ferguson's corps of riflemen during the last American War. In these pieces, there is a [round] opening on the upper part of the barrel, close to the breech, which is [just] large enough to admit the ball. This opening is filled by a rising screw [of which the trigger guard is the handle] which passes up from the underside of the barrel, and has its threads cut with so little obliquity that when screwed up [to close the hole], a half-turn sinks the top of it down to a level with the lower side of the calibre [i.e., flush with the bottom of the bore]. The ball is put into the opening from above [and] runs forward a little way; the powder is then poured in so as to fill up the remainder of the cavity, and a half-turn brings up the screw again, cuts off any superfluous powder, and closes up the opening through which the ball and powder were put. The chamber where the charge is lodged is without rifles [i.e., rifling], and so somewhat wider than the rest of the bore, so as to admit a ball that will not pass out of the barrel without taking on the figure of the rifles, and acquiring the rotary motion when discharged.

Ferguson's rifle was superior from every point of view to any rifle hitherto constructed. The screw breech was all but completely gas tight, and the mere one full turn of the trigger guard required to open and close it made loading extremely easy under all possible conditions. The ball, being of the diameter of the bore between two opposite grooves, was forced into the rifling by the force of the explosion. It could therefore be made to follow a sharper spiral, thereby acquiring a faster spinning motion and greater accuracy than was possible with a muzzleloaded patched ball; further, there was no windage around it, and this, together with the initial resistance which made the powder burn more completely, made a Ferguson shoot not only more accurately but much farther and harder. All these effects could be achieved in a short thirty-inch barrel, such as the officer's gun in Fig. 302 and later private sporting models, although the regulation issue ones had about thirty-six-inch barrels—still much handier than the American long rifles.

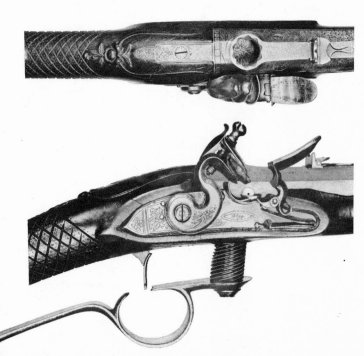

Fig. 301—Breech of a Ferguson rifle. Screw plug could not be accidentally lowered out of opening. Loading opening is on top of the barrel and at the rear of the breech chamber; ball was loaded first and rolled forward until it rested on rifling lands; cavity was then filled with powder. Closing the screw plug cut off excess powder, eliminating need to measure before loading. (Entire rifle in Fig. 302).

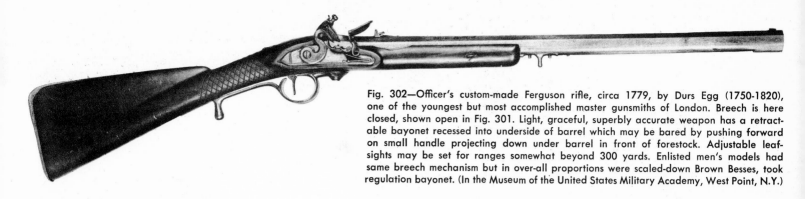

Fig. 302—Officer's custom-made Ferguson rifle, circa 1779, by Durs Egg (1750-1820), one of the youngest but most accomplished master gunsmiths of London. Breech is here closed, shown open in Fig. 301. Light, graceful, superbly accurate weapon has a retractable bayonet recessed into underside of barrel which may be bared by pushing forward on small handle projecting down under barrel in front of forestock. Adjustable leaf-sights may be set for ranges somewhat beyond 300 yards. Enlisted men's models had same breech mechanism but in over-all proportions were scaled-down Brown Besses, took regulation bayonet. (In the Museum of the United States Military Academy, West Point, N.Y.)

Ferguson's rifle was potentially invaluable even for customary tactics. But clearly it offered revolutionary possibilities the military importance of which would be difficult to exaggerate. Men armed with Fergusons could not only load and fire their weapons six to eight times a minute while standing still, but *four to six times during a full run*—with deadly two-hundred-yard accuracy and with glittering bayonets! Moreover, they could load and fire even while lying down flat on the ground behind a low cover or breastwork, without exposing themselves to the fire of the enemy. All this was of course impossible with a muzzleloader, the Americans having been obliged to stand still in the field when loading, or to rise up from behind a stone wall or other breastwork, in either instance making splendid targets of themselves; and bayonet charges with American long rifles were of course utterly out of the question and never attempted.

This new rifle, then, could have been the ultimate infantry weapon until the late 1840's; and a very strong argument can be constructed that it could have won the American War for the British within twelve weeks after its first issue of ten thousand, placed in the hands of ten thousand specially trained men. In view of this, and the fact that Britain could easily have mustered such a rifle corps within a year, it remains one of history's unilluminated enigmas why only some two hundred military Fergusons were ever made and issued, all apparently between 1776 and 1779; and considerable mystery surrounds the history of even these. One account has it that Ferguson received official permission to have them made at his own expense, then issue them to the Light Infantry (Rifle) Company of the 71st Highlanders. But Ferguson was thirty-two years old in 1776, apparently living largely or wholly on his lean pay; considering that he had enlisted as a cornet at the age of fifteen, had been on active service all his adult life, and that his father was a Scottish judge of very modest means, the possibilities of his having financed the manufacture of about two hundred fine-tolerance, close-specification precision rifles seem remote. Probably he had paid for the pilot model which he demonstrated at Woolwich in 1776

before an assemblage of Very Important People from the War Office. There, it is recorded, the "rifle gun on a new construction . . . astonished all beholders" by its incredible performance. Someone with a fair measure of authority seems to have been sufficiently impressed to order the manufacture of about two hundred, in over-all proportions smaller but unmistakable cousins of the Brown Bess. Who made these, where, when, at whose order and on what appropriation, is not known. Ferguson, at any rate, enjoyed the reputation of being the best rifle shot in the British Empire; and in 1776, his merciless, blind, raging hatred for the American rebels was new fuel for the fire of his already near-notorious ferocity in combat. He was therefore posted at once to the Colonies, where he commanded his old company in the Highlanders, reinforced there by loyalist American militiamen and riflemen. Probably there were only a hundred-odd Fergusons under his command, and these naturally formed his chosen guard. With them he rendered bloody service in several engagements throughout the summer of 1777. Then, on September 11, he and a selected handful covered the crucial advance of von Knyphausen and his Germans at the battle of Brandywine with such unerring deadliness that the attack against the American center at Chad's Ford precipitated the retreat of the entire 10,500-man American army back toward Philadelphia (this having been also one of the few successful employments of Germans). But at the climax of the action, Ferguson was shot through the right elbow by an American rifleman, and when he at last returned to duty after months of convalescence, his shooting arm had grown rigid in a right-angle bend. During his absence, his rifles had all been collected and stored in a New York cellar. Ferguson salvaged about forty, and in early 1779 received about a hundred more from England. Ordered to organize loyalist forces in North and South Carolina, where Tory sentiment ran so high that a full-scale civil war was in progress, he joined General Tarleton and the local Tories in their relentless, bitter, often barbaric suppression of the embattled Whigs. Commanding about five hundred Tory militiamen armed with muskets and bayonets, and about six hundred loyalist riflemen (130-odd may have carried his rifles), Ferguson was now free to give his fearsome wrath free rein. For almost a year he terrorized the countryside and soon earned the cognomen of "The Butcher of the Carolinas," for he spared not a Whig-owned house or crop, and at times apparently bayoneted sleeping American regulars and Whig irregulars rather than wake them and take them prisoner. On occasions he allegedly hanged as spies all Whigs captured in arms but out of uniform. In autumn of 1780 he was under orders to screen Cornwallis's flank, and in the evening of October 6 he encamped atop Kings Mountain, North Carolina. Although aware that a sizable force of Whig backwoodsmen and riflemen was gathering around him, he was over-confident and uncharacteristically foolhardy, and posted neither adequate pickets nor threw up breastworks or other defenses. On the next morning, nine hundred superbly skillful American frontiersmen poured thunder and lightning into their trapped, encircled enemy; within an hour, 225 Tories lay dead and 163 wounded and dying; many were later found slumped over protective crates and boulders with a rifle ball dead center between their eyes; the rest surrendered. And the leonine wrath of Patrick Ferguson was at last assuaged by the eight bullets which had pierced him.

After the war, the two-hundred-odd original service issue Fergusons almost all disappeared, taken home, no doubt, by Englishmen and Americans alike for private use; fewer than a dozen survive in museums and in well-known private collections in England and in the United States. Sporting versions were made by the best London gunsmiths until about 1820—many of these sighted for five hundred yards!—but their total was negligible compared to muzzle-loading rifles and the innumerable fowling pieces. Today a Ferguson is a very great rarity.

The neglect and consequent demise of Ferguson's rifle was merely another episode of bungling on the part of Lord North's tragically incompetent administration. In spite of Whig opposition and such eloquent admonitory voices as Chatham's and Burke's, North's inflated, reactionary blindness had at last succeeded in forcing a minority of the sorely exasperated Colonists to take up arms in defense of their ancient British rights and liberties, so that soon the loyalist majority was swept along by the current of events toward a rebellion they abhorred and an independence they did not favor. Yet no matter how blind, reprehensible or fatuous the North government's policies might have been, once the calamity had been precipitated it was the duty of the War Office to bring it to a victorious conclusion with all possible

haste and vigor. Instead, the paladins at Whitehall could not have labored harder to ensure first chaos, then defeat. Throughout the war, graft, corruption and brittle military vanity and traditionalism conspired to snatch defeat from the jaws of victory, and in the end succeeded in discarding an empire. The Americans did not win the War of Independence; the British lost it with iron determination. High on the roster of follies stood the neglect of Ferguson's rifle. One muses what might have happened if £5.4 million had been spent not on nearly forty thousand German peasants but on twenty thousand Ferguson riflemen—if Washington had been faced by such an army at Saratoga and Yorktown.

Notwithstanding the lessons learned at the hands of American riflemen in 1776–1783, there were still no significant rifle corps in Europe (or in the United States) throughout the Napoleonic Wars (1793-1815), save a few thousand German and Austrian *Jäger*, French *chasseurs*, and reluctantly created British rifle companies, most notably the Rifle Brigade of the 95th Infantry Regiment. These last were armed with the *Baker rifle* (after the gunsmith-inventor Ezekiel Baker of London), an iron-ramrod-and-mallet muzzleloader of no distinction, hardly more effective beyond two hundred yards than the Brown Bess beyond eighty. Only the Russians carried a rifled musket, the so-called *Tula rifle-musket* (see Fig. 241), some twenty thousand of which were issued between 1803 and 1812. True, one great obstacle stood in the way of equipping the entire army with rifles; the "Colonel in the German Service," author of the previously quoted PLAN FOR THE FORMATION OF A CORPS WHICH NEVER HAS BEEN RAISED AS YET IN EUROPE, wrote in 1805 (italics in original):

> A British soldier can *never be taught* to be a *perfect judge of different distances*. Place an object in the shape and size of a man at 150 yards distant, ask him how far that object is from him, and one will say 100 yards, another 200 yards. Place the same object at 200 yards from him, he will most likely display more ignorance. . . . Place the same object at 300 yards, you may as well not ask him the distance at all. [It] is totally beyond his judgment.

But though this lament was probably well founded, the problem had been solved by the Pennsylvania riflesmiths and better still by Patrick Ferguson. In spite of these examples, the Brown Bess remained in effect the sole arm of the British almost into the Crimea in 1854, and its counterparts in the United States and other nations prevailed just as extensively throughout their forces, and for just as long. The world's civilian hunters knew better.

Fig. 303—Fallen deer and hounds. Detail of a German sporting print, circa 1725.

CHAPTER ELEVEN

*English gunmaking compared to Spanish, German and Italian—The Brescian art of steel carving—French presentation pieces—Gunmaking spreads out of London—*THE AMERICAN SHOOTER'S MANUAL *(1827) on imported guns—The patent mania—Five extremely valuable inventions: the elevated rib; the gravitating stop; the recessed double breech; the single trigger; the water-shedding touchhole—Joseph Manton: conflicting opinions about his genius—An extraordinary example of it—Dueling and dueling pistols—The "code"—The astounding accuracy of rifled dueling pistols—Perils of principals and seconds—An unusually rational letter—The Collier revolver—The flintlock at its zenith—The coming Percussion lock.*

HE READER MAY NOW BE WONDER-
ing why the emphasis of this history has been
placed on English guns ever since we left the
era of Charles I. It may be asked fairly
whether the gunmakers of other nations do not deserve
at least as much attention, whether their products were
not as fine and fitted with as many clever refinements as
those of the English.

Now, there are two answers to this: one very prosaic
and objective, the other subtle and rooted in subjective
value judgements. To dispose of the first one quickly: a
history book of the present sort, written in English and
intended primarily for Anglo-American readers (subsequent translation into other languages notwithstanding),
must naturally train its brightest and most informative
focus on the Anglo-American past, this being surely the
most significant to the majority of readers. If the author
of these words were French, or Czech, or Portuguese, and
his readers primarily co-nationals, no doubt the tenor and
complexion of the work would be quite different. And
this is as it should be.

But does British gunsmithing *really* merit the time, space
and encomia lavished on it in this volume? Here the answer
is less facile. There is general agreement among collectors
of all nationalities that Yes, definitely, British first-line
artisan gunmaking from about the third quarter of the
eighteenth century until the generation between the two
World Wars excelled most competition of all nations . . .
provided we are speaking in terms of a mechanical precision that borders on the maniacal, of an ingenious technology and, above all, of a conscientiousness of total
craftsmanship that for over a century and a half—say 1775
to 1925—constituted the lodestar for aspirant imitators
everywhere (and to a fair extent still does to this very day).

Provided, in short, that we weigh the British claims on
a scale from which all measurements of art, fantasy and
individualism have been eliminated.

For a scale that includes these would bring us to the
other great polarity in the history of arms and armor, albeit
in its heyday in the two centuries preceding the British
ascendancy: and this was not the German, as ready tradi-

tion and 19th-century German writers would have it; nor
the French, for all the magnificence of much Gallic work;
nor the Spanish, in spite of the excellence of so many
Iberian weapons; but rather the Italian—or, better defined,
the Lombard-Venetian, the Tuscan-Emilian and the

Fig. 304—One of a pair of Spanish
miquelet pistols dated 1812. Mechanically, Spanish miquelet locks did not
change much during two centuries separating this weapon from Figs. 159 to
161.

Roman-Neapolitan, three schools very different one from
the other and yet firmly tied by a common Italic bond of
artistic maturity, by a pan-peninsular genius that subordi-
nated both superfluous mechanical precision and excessive
ornamentation to a superb, melodious marriage of grace
and fancy found only very rarely among the arms of other
places. True, technologically the Italian products were not
superior to others—but then inferior neither (comparing,
of course, with other arms on a par, class for class, cost for
cost, type for type). From the earliest Genoese matchlocks
in the 1440's to the last of the Tuscan-Emilian snaphaunces
in the 1820's, from the first Venetian wheellocks to the end
of production in the Royal Manufactury of Naples just
over a century ago, from Umbrian fowling pieces to the
fucili da guardia of Vatican officers, Italian technological
or mechanical quality was *in general* only adequate: not
really ever poor (overlooking military arms, cheap pistols
for the populace and clumsy *schioppacci* for the peasantry), not overly fitted or filed or polished internally—in
short, serviceable, durable, good-enough; the guns shot
quickly, reliably and accurately, not perhaps to the limits

of perfection but to the satisfaction of their users. But in the category of ducal, princely, regal and papal weapons, Italian technology and mechanical quality were as much international reference standards between 1550 and 1750 as were the British from about 1775 to our times.

Aesthetically, however, the Italian schools offered not only beauty and elegance without equal anywhere, but a consistency of these among—almost—all arms of all classes. It is a very subtle business, the understanding—the living-one's-self-into-the-principles—of old Italian gun design. For the master fabricators and their followers throughout the Peninsula exploited *shape* and *proportions*, the interplay of straight line and curve, in so felicitous a way that their products are lovely to the hand as well as to the eye—although rarely can this be translated into photographs. Then there is the Italian intuitive grasp of the aesthetics of materials: the use of iron and wood far more than gold, silver and ivory even in the costliest of pieces, because pierced iron and simple wood, properly exploited and joined, yield an inimitable and, to many men's minds, unsurpassable beauty. Where the decor of most other nations after the close of the seventeenth century relied more and more on rocailles cast in bronze and brass to the point of banality and tawdriness even in artistocratic pieces, Italian masters clung to and enhanced their skills in iron carving, in delicate browning and bluing, in shaping and proportioning their guns, up to a level of true artistry few others in other nations could hope to approach.

As to the German spheres—Germany, Austria, Switzerland, Bohemia—the *Jäger* rifles have been discussed. Toward the end of the eighteenth century, the Bavarians at long last conceded the passing of the wheellock, save that as late as 1750 there were two or three Munich makers—one named Kasper Alosius Hinterhirschelberger (fl. ca. 1735–65)—who would as soon have quit life as the manufacture of that time-honored excrescence of Bayovaric genius. A peculiarly German feature was the swivel-barrel over-and-under rifle in which one cock fired the flashpan of the upper barrel, the barrels being then turned to bring up the lower barrel for a second shot (Fig. 205). Three- and four-barreled revolving rifles and pistols on this principle were not rare. German flintlocks were all very competent, few excellent, none bad (save, as everywhere, the military ones), and whenever better locks were built in England, Germans built them shortly after. The heavy, lumbering, hard-hitting rifle bullets were specifically designed for service in the thick, dangerous forests and the snow-capped Alps. There was little improvement possible within the confines of this purpose. For the type of aristocratic slaughter depicted in Fig. 256, which by 1770 had so depleted the lush wildlife that many species became rarities and others extinct, liveried servants placed lighter, more gentlemanly rifles (with magnificent wood- and silverwork and less exhausting recoil) ready loaded into

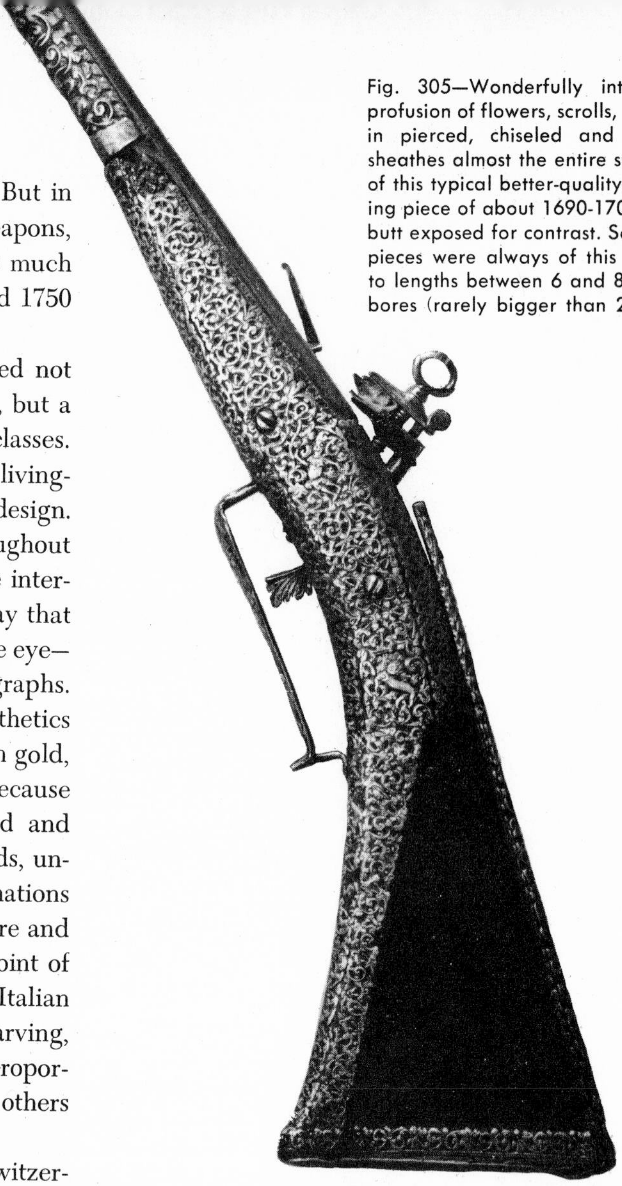

Fig. 305—Wonderfully intricate, delicate profusion of flowers, scrolls, clowns and lions in pierced, chiseled and engraved iron sheathes almost the entire stock on all sides of this typical better-quality Sardinian fowling piece of about 1690-1700, walnut in the butt exposed for contrast. Sardinian fowling pieces were always of this odd shape, ran to lengths between 6 and 8 feet, had small bores (rarely bigger than 24-gauge).

the hands of their masters. Good German civilian pistols were highly serviceable but usually enormous; fashion among the elite dictated that whoever had need of pistols must acquire an English, French or Italian pair, so that to this present day German antique shops have almost as many of these as German ones. Most German shotguns were handsome but heavy pieces with such thick-walled barrels (usually one-third octagonal and two-thirds round) that they could serve for ball as well as shot—in effect, light, unrifled rifles. Perhaps this was because shooting flying as a sport was never widely popular, practiced mainly by only a relatively small number of *Flugsschützen* who preferred to think of themselves more elegantly as *tireurs-à-vol* (Fig. 259). Their modest demands for English-type fowling pieces designed especially for shooting flying were met mostly by English and French imports. These, however, limited exclusively to shot by the thinness of their barrels, lacked the versatility useful in a fabulously game-rich nation.

The gunmakers of France—specifically, Versailles and Paris—were the only ones who could compete with the English, although not very seriously. French guns tended

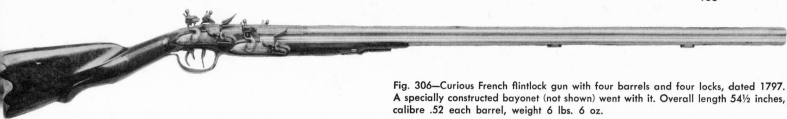

Fig. 306—Curious French flintlock gun with four barrels and four locks, dated 1797. A specially constructed bayonet (not shown) went with it. Overall length 54½ inches, calibre .52 each barrel, weight 6 lbs. 6 oz.

toward greater ornateness (but of stylized uniformity) than the English. In the test of actual performance, the typical good-quality English gun far outstripped its French parallel, while the best English guns had no parallels. But in the manufacture of presentation pieces of the $10,000-and-up class (in the 1970 equivalent) did the French excel the world, both in long arms and pistols, especially those manufactured at Versailles under the perfectionist eye of Nicolas Noël Boutet. These, however, were rarely intended for use, and performance was subordinated to the opulent adornments (Figs. 307, 335 and 337).

The only major innovation which passed across the Channel westward—dozens had traveled eastward—was the so-called "French" cock, a graceful design which was adopted by many English makers after about 1790. This seems to have originated in the Versailles manufactory, designed especially for the fabulous presentation pieces (e.g., Figs. 322, 334 and 336).

Fig. 307—Below: Details of a presentation fowling piece made in 1801 at the Versailles manufactory under the supervision of Nicolas Noël Boutet by order of Napoleon. Shield held by two lions on lockplates is inscribed BOUTET—DIRECTEUR—ARTISTE (i.e., director of the manufactory and chief designer). Materials used, in various carefully planned color contrasts, are blued steel, browned steel, polished steel, gold, silver and ebony. Barrels, for example (below), are gilded relief against blue background; lockplates gilded and silver relief of dog seizing duck, and two lions and shield; trigger guard massively sculptured in silver; nameplate on wrist gold. Typical feature found on most good- and better-grade French sporting guns is grotesque animal head carved under long curved wrist (cf. Fig. 309). (In the Metropolitan Museum of Art, New York)

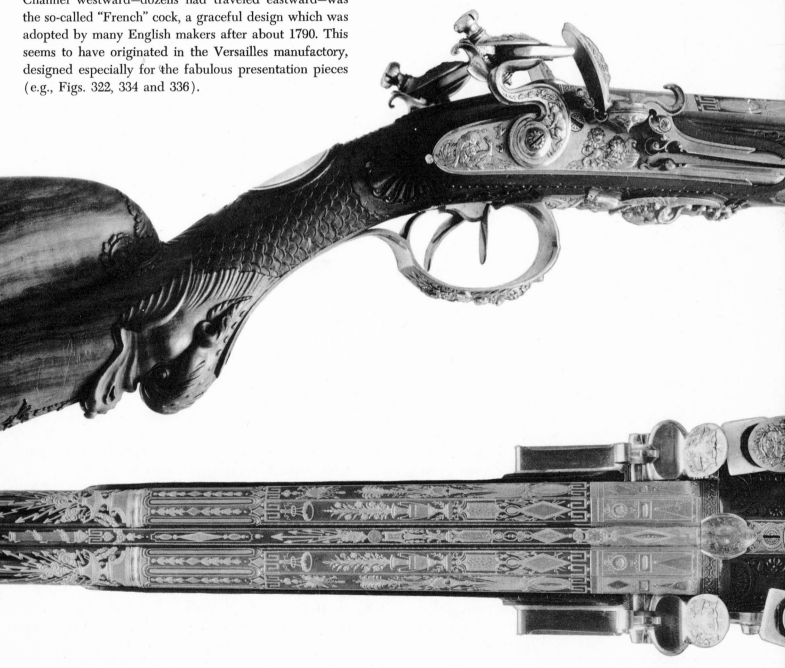

Fig. 308—Hunting horn fanfares: *La Discrette, La Fanfare de la Reine, Le Vol-ce-l'est, Le Débuché, L'Eau* and *L'Halali. La Discrette* and *La Reine* are given first for one, then for two horns. Each fanfare had specific meaning, as explained. From Jacques Lacombe, *Dictionnaire de Toutes les Espèces de Chasses (Dictionary of All the Methods of Hunting),* Paris, 1795.

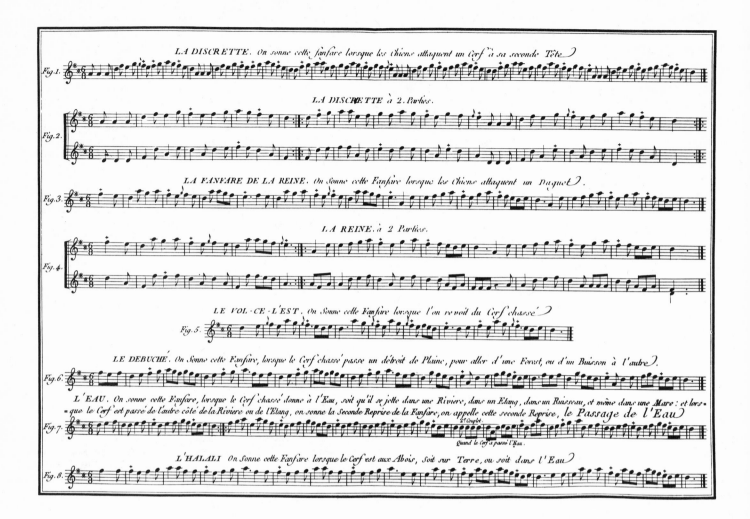

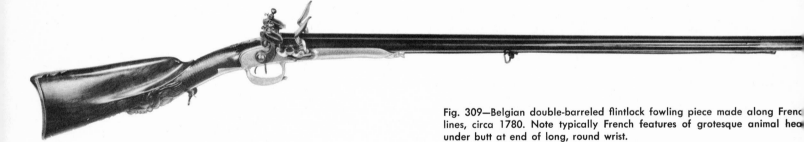

Fig. 309—Belgian double-barreled flintlock fowling piece made along French lines, circa 1780. Note typically French features of grotesque animal head under butt at end of long, round wrist.

To return, then, to London in the first few years of the nineteenth century—or rather, to Great Britain, for since about 1760 the number of provincial gunsmiths had more than doubled, and although London remained the center of the manufacture of the most expensive and the best English guns, the makers in other cities and many country villages had learned to equal the London upper-middle standards. This was important to country gentlemen not only because provincial prices were considerably lower than those fetched by comparable London items, but because repair now no longer meant shipping one's gun off to London for a three-week round trip. Moreover, the rural competition and that of other large cities soon worked itself into such a prominent share of the domestic as well as the enormous export market that the London firms were obliged to apply to good- and better-quality pieces those subtle touches of refinement which until the last decade of the eighteenth century had been reserved for the very best. By 1810 the situation had stabilized itself to a point where a buyer could find any number of makers all over Great Britain whose products were as good as would ever be necessary for normal use, while most of the London makers, like London tailors, concentrated on goods for those who could afford and would have nothing less than the very zenith of perfection. The whole matter of the relative genius of international gunsmithing was summed up by A Gentleman of Philadelphia County in THE AMERICAN SHOOTER'S MANUAL, published in 1827:

In this country we receive guns from all the manufactories in Europe, but more particularly from those in England, France, Flanders and Germany.

The French make very handsome guns, but they are too light for the shooting in this country, nor does their construction agree with our notion of fitness. The Dutch and German guns are in general low-priced and badly made, and it would be well for many could their importation be prohibited, as nineteen twentieths of all the guns which have bursted in this country were German or Dutch. They are manufactured in such quantities, and at so low prices, that great abundances of them are sold here to persons who are unable or unwilling to purchase the English guns at a higher price. Besides, they are tinselled off in such a manner as to be quite captivating; they are, however, in general nothing more than very dangerous man traps, and we should be glad to see their use entirely discontinued in this country.

The English are, without a doubt, the neatest and best gunmakers in the world. A large portion of all the guns they export are manufactured at Birmingham, and nearly all the London guns come from thence in a rough state to be filed up and fitted [with locks, furniture and breeches]. We have an idea in this country that a gun to be good must be made in London, and until a few years ago most English guns had "London" stamped or engraved upon them. We now find that many gunmakers in other parts of the kingdom are quite equal to those in London, and differ from them only in price. It may be true that the London makers are more scrupulously nice in fitting up their work, but it is very certain that much of the work for which such exorbitant charges are made is entirely superfluous. I have seen guns which were made in several of the Irish and Scottish cities quite as good as any ever made in any other place [in the kingdom].

Notwithstanding the great ingenuity and cunning of the German manufacturers, they have never been able, in all their attempts, successfully to counterfeit the English guns —the cloven foot will always be visible in some part of the work.

RAIL SHOOTING ON THE DELAWARE.

Fig. 310—"Rail Shooting on the Delaware"; engraving from *The American Shooter's Manual* (Anon., Philadelphia, 1827.)

DOWN CHARGE

. 311—"Down Charge"; both this engrav and one above were probably executed me ten years before the *Manual's* publican in 1827 and originally used in another orting book, for both guns are flintlocks, ereas the *Manual's* author says "percusn locks are now almost exclusively used."

But the fine London work "for which such exorbitant charges are made" was no more "entirely superfluous" than hand embroidery instead of power-loom patterns on a waistcoat, or six additional diamonds and a compensating balance wheel in a pocket watch. What the Gentleman of Philadelphia County doubtless had in mind was the petty patents with which choruses of gunsmiths rushed joyously and almost daily to Chancery Lane. The first quarter of the nineteenth century was an age of patent mania in which assorted intellects sought His Majesty's protection for luminous cat collars, hydraulic boot removers and burglar-proof snuffboxes, among several thousand other inspirations, many of which were of course tremendous creations destined to shake the ancient order of the planet. But it may be said that gunsmiths and their allies, the ordnance engineers, had elbowed their way to the forefront with more superfluous trivia than any other trade or industry. John Waters' patent for "pistols with a bayonet" had started the flood in 1781 by simply patenting an idea which had then been a mere half century in use (e.g., Figs. 312 and 313). Edward Thomason's 1799 "Improvements in the mechanism of the cocks of gunlocks" endeavored to obviate the half-minute operation of replacing the flint after twenty-five or thirty shots by the use of the costly gearwork shown in Fig. 314, "in which the flint is made, by the operation of cocking, to present a different angle to the hen or hammer [battery] every time the piece is fired." Patent No. 3588 was captured on July 28, 1812, by William Smith for a flashpan cover which for no discernible reason terminated "in a surface gradually rounded [instead of] an angular

edge with a flat surface beneath to cover the priming." Richard Webb's humanitarian hand-saving gunlock in the event of an explosion has already been noted (Fig. 267), but in December, 1813, the genius of one Ralph Sutton bore fruit in the form of "an effectual security to prevent the accidental discharge of fowling pieces," consisting of an automatic slide over the touchhole which suffered from only the one defect that three out of five times it also prevented the intentional discharge. For the convenience of sportsmen, John Carpenter devised "a knapsack which prevents the wet coming between it and the back, and a pouch [is] suspended in front from the shoulder straps . . . so as to counter-act its weight"; a waterproof cape and collar could be attached, which "may be rolled up in fine weather." There were many other such inventions, ranging from upside-down flashpans to steam-operated cannons; but a closing note may be struck to this paragraph by a patent granted to the great Joseph Manton (practiced 1795–1835) in 1812 for a gunlock which, when being cocked, would not subject the sportsman to the pain of a click, but instead reverberated gently with "a pleasant and musical sound."

All of these and many other "inventions" were for the most part never expected to perform any worth-while service other than to advertise the awesome brilliance of the inventor. Since a considerable number of well-heeled members of the horsy and shooting set were not particularly bright—in fact, quite noticeably stupid—it was immaterial whether the wildly boomed Great Invention was an air valve in the flashpan cover or an oval barrel; a sufficient number of the enthralled would be lured into

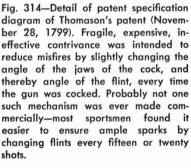

Fig. 314—Detail of patent specification diagram of Thomason's patent (November 28, 1799). Fragile, expensive, ineffective contrivance was intended to reduce misfires by slightly changing the angle of the jaws of the cock, and thereby angle of the flint, every time the gun was cocked. Probably not one such mechanism was ever made commercially—most sportsmen found it easier to ensure ample sparks by changing flints every fifteen or twenty shots.

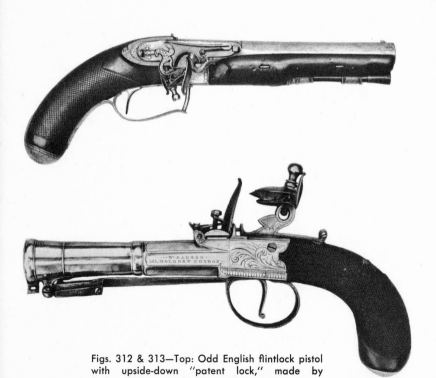
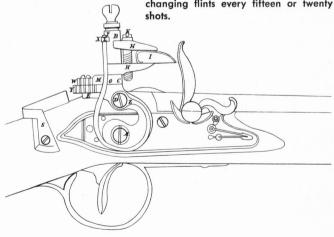

Figs. 312 & 313—Top: Odd English flintlock pistol with upside-down "patent lock," made by Tatham & Egg, London, circa 1780. Bottom: Brass-barreled blunderbuss pistol with spring-loaded bayonet, by Parker of London, circa 1810-15. Hinged bayonet snaps out when trigger guard is pulled backward; bayonet also serves as lever for unscrewing screw barrel. Sliding safety catch behind cock locks pancover shut and holds cock secure at half-cock.

the shop as curiosity seekers and leave as customers of *some* gun, usually one without the benefit of the marvelous improvement. Inevitably the "patent guns" were exposed to the scorn of intelligent sportsmen and to the fire of cartoonists such as William Maynard (Fig. 315).

Of all the patents of the 1780–1825 period which pertained to flintlocks, only five materially contributed to the guns' performances—but these so much that the Gentleman of Philadelphia County surely did not intend to include them among the "entirely superfluous" London finery. Three were developed by that unsurpassable craftsman, Joseph Manton: the *elevated rib* atop the barrels or barrel (patented in 1806 and still in use), which compensated for the universal tendency to shoot just a trifle too low when the gun was snapped to the shoulder for a fast shot at a rising bird; the 1812 invention of the *gravitating stop*, which made it absolutely impossible for

a primed lock to be snapped accidentally during loading by a too vigorous jar of the ramrod or careless jostling of the trigger; and Manton's improvement on the Nock patent breech (Fig. 276), the *recessed double breech* of 1812, which not only fired more surely and faster, but provided for a water drainage canal between the barrels so that any rain accumulating atop the barrels would be guided off through an exit on the underside of the stock immediately in front of the trigger guard, with little chance of its running down the sides and seeping into the flashpans (elevated rib, gravitating stop and recessed breech are shown in Fig. 319; cf. also Figs. 317, 322 and 334). Non-Manton touches of considerable merit were James Templeman's 1789 *single trigger*, which fired first the right, then the left barrel by two successive squeezes; and finally Thomas Noon's 1809 *water-shedding touchhole* (Fig. 316).

THE PATENT GUN that KILLS in ALL DIRECTIONS

Fig. 315—"The Patent Gun that Kills in All Directions"—a cartoon by William Maynard, published in October of 1788, satirizing the growing patent mania.

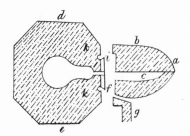

Fig. 317—Below: Part of Joseph Manton's 1792 patent specification drawings for an improved flashpan cover and patent breeches. The flashpan cover offered only slightly concave battery face, was not a significant improvement. Figs. 2 and 3 show outside view and cross section of patent breech-plug for a single-barreled gun; recessed (or "set-in") touchhole shortened path from flashpan to propellent powder, therefore resulted in faster shot. Fig. 4 shows two patent breech-plugs for a double gun.

Fig. 316—Above: Patent specification drawing of Noon's patent, May 4, 1809 (published in 1854), showing cross section of octagonal barrel, flashpan, flashpan cover and upper section of lockplate (separated from each other for purpose of diagram). Touchhole, faced with a platinum or gold platelet, is surrounded by a circular moat which guides off any moderate quantities of water which may come down from the top of the barrel. Inner edge of flashpan and flashpan cover are joined against the touchhole platelet within the area circumscribed by the drainage moat, so that water must necessarily be guided around outside of pan. Lockplate is joined against barrel below the moat; its upper edge is beveled, so that water deflected by that will run down over beveled edge and side of lock. Simple but effective invention was of great value in rendering early 19th-century flintlocks efficient and reliable, permitted firing after exposure to rain for quite some time; but flintlocks were obsolete hardly more than ten years after patent had been granted.

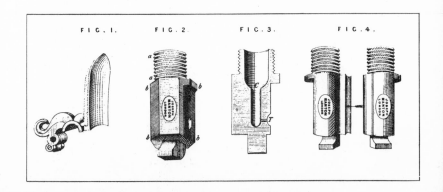

FIG. 1.   FIG. 2.   FIG. 3.   FIG. 4.

Fig. 318—English powder flask, circa 1790–1810, black lacquer with silver mountings and monogram; other side bears lion-and-unicorn device. Telescoping spout, typical of the period, could be adjusted to release desired quantity of powder when spring-valve lever was pressed (cf. Fig. 268).

quent editions), a passionate sporting gentleman, unusual among his kind and class by virtue of interests in art, music and literature, as well as of a generous philanthropy. His view was that Joseph Manton represented the ultimate pinnacle of craftsmanship to which all mankind must look with awe, and any who failed to appreciate this were clearly victims of some appalling malady and should forthwith be removed. Then there was one Colonel Charles Thornton, in whose SPORTING TOUR THROUGH FRANCE, published in 1806 (when Manton's star was bright but not yet blinding), may be found one good and quite impersonal index to the normally ruinous abuse to which Manton's guns, and especially their breeches, could be subjected with impunity:

It is generally agreed that Joseph Manton was not only a worker who rose above the standards of his London colleagues, themselves towering far above any other in the world, but that he has rarely been equaled and never surpassed in the 135 years since his death in 1835. To this the present author subscribes, with the qualification that Manton was *almost* equaled by a few of his contemporaries—perhaps eight or ten—and by fewer still in the succeeding century and a quarter. Contemporary opinions of Manton vary. There was one Colonel Peter Hawker, author of INSTRUCTIONS TO YOUNG SPORTSMEN IN ALL THAT PERTAINS TO GUNS AND SHOOTING (1814 and many subse-

Joseph Manton, the gunsmith, was of the opinion that he could make a double rifle gun sufficiently stout to carry seven balls in each barrel, and that they would do more execution than one of my seven-barreled guns. . . .

Great pains were taken in hammering the barrels of the new gun; and when it was finished, I went to witness its execution, and resigned to Manton the honour of making the first experiment, which was to take place in a passage adjoining his shop. He loaded the piece with the utmost exactness, and judging by his appearance, would cheerfully have relinquished the honour to me; but I thought it no more than justice that the inventor should be first gratified. Accordingly, he placed himself and took exact aim; but the subsequent concussion was so great, and so very different from the firing of any gun, that I thought the whole shop was blown up. . . . This, however, was not the case. It appeared that the whole force of the powder, being insufficient to drive the balls, had come out through the touch-holes, and what was very extraordinary, the gun was uninjured.

This circumstance affording an indisputable proof of the excellency of the metal, and the firmness of the touch-holes, we took out the breech and then gently forced the balls, which had moved only six inches. . . .

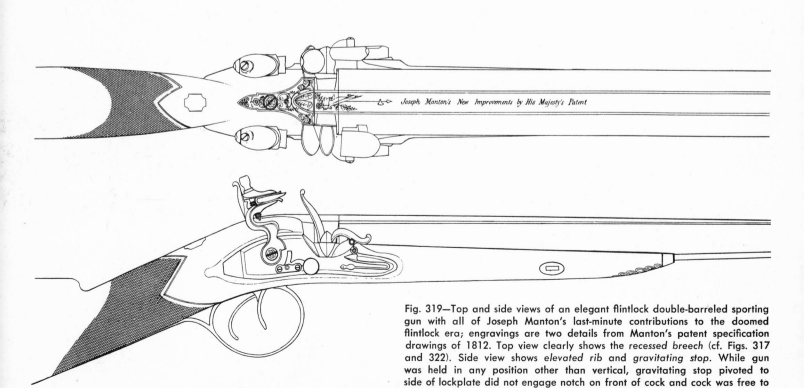

Joseph Manton's New Improvements by His Majesty's Patent

Fig. 319—Top and side views of an elegant flintlock double-barreled sporting gun with all of Joseph Manton's last-minute contributions to the doomed flintlock era; engravings are two details from Manton's patent specification drawings of 1812. Top view clearly shows the *recessed breech* (cf. Figs. 317 and 322). Side view shows *elevated rib* and *gravitating stop*. While gun was held in any position other than vertical, gravitating stop pivoted to side of lockplate did not engage notch on front of cock and cock was free to snap; when gun was turned muzzle up for loading, however, round weight at one end of the stop "gravitated" downward (i.e., toward flashpan) and thereby tripped other end to engage the notch; thus chocked, cock could not snap accidentally while shooter was ramming down loads.

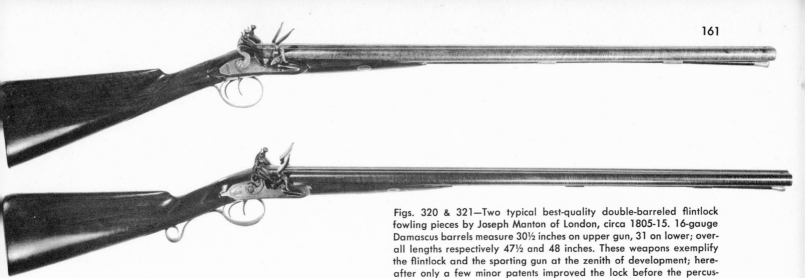

Figs. 320 & 321—Two typical best-quality double-barreled flintlock fowling pieces by Joseph Manton of London, circa 1805-15. 16-gauge Damascus barrels measure 30½ inches on upper gun, 31 on lower; overall lengths respectively 47½ and 48 inches. These weapons exemplify the flintlock and the sporting gun at the zenith of development; hereafter only a few minor patents improved the lock before the percussion system ended the age of live-spark ignition in the 1820's. The overall proportions of double guns have not changed since Manton's day.

The most objective view was probably that of Thomas Johnson in THE SHOOTER'S GUIDE of 1816, a man who was not at all a fanatic gun enthusiast and for whom shooting was only one occupation in the busy week of a moderately wealthy squire (italics in original):

As to who is the best gunsmith, it is a question, if an individual must be selected, of no easy solution. There are many country gunsmiths who make excellent fowling pieces, but the London guns are certainly turned out in the neatest manner. Manton has obtained the highest celebrity, and justly merits much of the praise bestowed upon him; but to rank him as the very pinnacle of excellence, unattainable by any other person, which has been attempted, is going too far. By this I would not be understood to be decrying the work of Manton; on the contrary, I am willing to give him his due share of praise. Assuredly, he has acquired a name of the importance of which he seems to be fully aware, for it brings him much business and enables him to charge a higher price than his fellow-labourers. However, it is not always to the name merely that merit attaches, nor should I be willing to give an extra ten guineas for that alone. *Mortimer* sounds just as well in my ears as *Manton*; *Knox* as Mortimer; *Gulley* as Knox; *Parker* as Gulley; *Stephens*, successor to *Clark*, as Parker. These are all esteemed manufacturers and have alike sent forth guns of first-rate excellence.

But it must be remembered that in addition to the five competitors named, there have never been more than half a dozen gunsmiths to equal Manton; and in the opinion of the present author no one ever really *quite* equaled him for precision of parts and elegance of finish. He lacked completely in imagination of decor, so that in an age and nation where decorative artistry on guns had been reduced to a smudge of banality die-stamped into a corner of the lockplate, he was not imaginative enough either to revive the exuberance of his ancestors, or to do away with its wilted vestiges altogether and thus arrive at what is sometimes called the beauty of pure functionalism. Manton seems to have been a slave to the obsession that he must convert raw steel and iron into a degree of precision hitherto unknown, not because it would serve any further practical purpose once the optimum had been passed, but because the goal of absolute precision, like an unclimbed mountain to others, was simply *there*. Long after he had gotten rich, old and famous, he worked molelike through the night to polish away at parts which his employees—all master craftsmen—had put aside as finished.

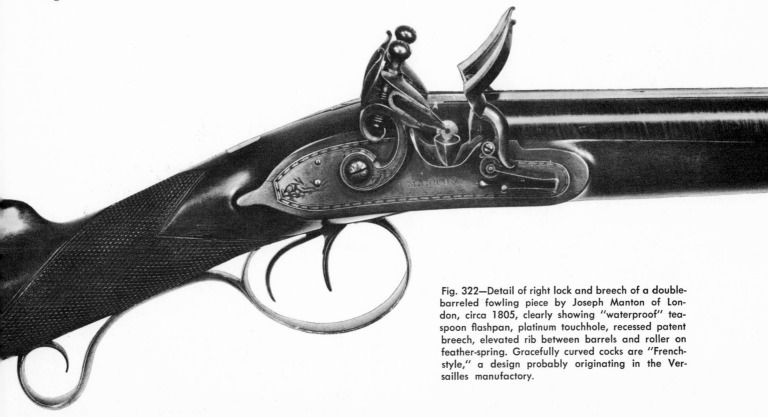

Fig. 322—Detail of right lock and breech of a double-barreled fowling piece by Joseph Manton of London, circa 1805, clearly showing "waterproof" teaspoon flashpan, platinum touchhole, recessed patent breech, elevated rib between barrels and roller on feather-spring. Gracefully curved cocks are "French-style," a design probably originating in the Versailles manufactory.

If, then, the British gunsmiths of the eighteenth century had perfected their craft to lead the world in sporting guns, they had lavished no less skill and ingenuity on the design and manufacture of pistols. Regulation issue military pistols, in England as elsewhere, were mostly on a par with or even below the very indifferent quality of muskets, and therefore in England as elsewhere (indeed, *especially* in England) officers carried their own private side arms, which, although military in shape and size, were naturally of excellent quality (e.g., Figs. 251 and 252). Between the early 1700's and the end of the flintlock era, enormous numbers of huge, massive, big-calibre semi-military "horse pistols," usually of very poor if not actually dangerous quality, poured out of the fourth-rate gunmakers' shops of all Europe, Britain included. But the many first- and second-rate British gunsmiths who were busy producing superb sporting guns naturally disdained such rubbish and instead made civilian pistols of traditional quality. These ranged from cased sets of five-inch waistcoat-pocket terrors, deadly up to twenty-five or thirty feet, to high-power, long-range rifled pistols with detachable shoulder stocks. In between came the screw-barrel and breech-loading pistols which have been discussed in earlier chapters, the fine so-called "overcoat" pistols, "traveling" pistols and "coach" pistols of well-to-do gentleman, and the many varieties of revolving and other multiple-barrel pistols which may be seen on this page and the next.

Fig. 324—Below: Small four-barreled pocket pistol by Segallas of London, circa 1750. Each barrel has own flashpan and cover. Top two barrels are fired by two cocks and two triggers, then barrels are turned manually to bring bottom two into top position. Stubby barrels unscrewed for loading. Though spiny and awkward to carry in pocket, these weapons were surprisingly effective, became popular for protection at night in dangerous, unilluminated city streets.

Fig. 323—Fine six-barreled flintlock pepperbox revolver by Twigg of London, circa 1760-80. Barrels were turned by hand, locked in place by slide on left side; all six flashpans in cylinder were primed in advance. Sliding safety catch behind cock locked gun at half-cock and locked flashpan cover shut.

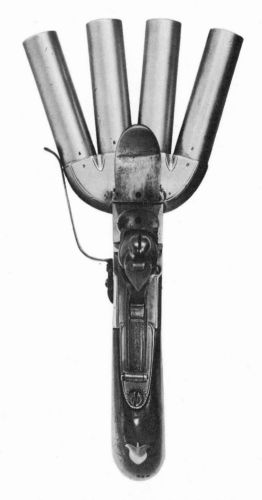

Fig. 325—Top view of an English top-hammer flintlock "duck's foot" pistol with belt hook on left side, circa 1770-1810. The four .45-calibre barrels were unscrewed individually for loading but were fired all at once by the one flashpan when trigger was pulled. "Duck's foot" pistols were used by prison guards, ship captains and others who might be called upon to defend themselves against an angry or mutinous crowd.

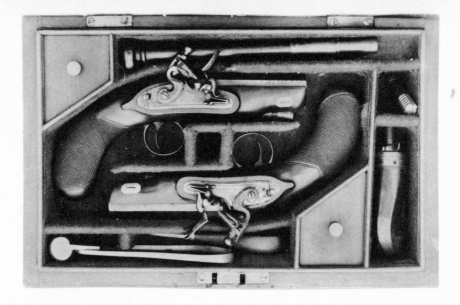

Fig. 326—Cased set of highest-quality flintlock "overcoat" pistols, i.e., stubby but powerful pistols for personal protection, by Clark of London, circa 1800-15. Accessories are: starting rod, cleaning bit, powder flask, screwdriver, bullet mold and two compartments for patches, balls and flints.

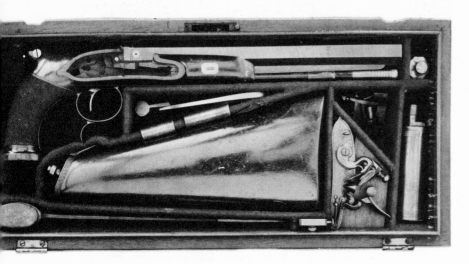

Fig. 327—Cased saw-handled rifled flintlock target pistol with detachable shoulder stock; by John Manton, Joseph's brother, circa 1810. A representative of its kind (the best), pistol could be deadly accurate at 100 yards if loaded with care. Accessories are: mallet for starting ball into muzzle (handle ends in worm); bullet mold; small oil can (in front of muzzle); powder flask; mainspring clamp (above lock); and featherspring clamp (between end of mallet handle and lock).

Fig. 328—Above: Six-barreled (two rows of three) flintlock "tap-action" pocket pistol by Brasher of London, circa 1780-1800. Six priming charges were heaped into the flashpans recessed into the "tap," a small rotary cylinder the end of which is here seen as an engraved rosette. For shooting, rotating lever on weapon's left side, and sliding selector bar on right, brought one primed pan into place beneath the battery and permitted communication of the fire through small canals in the "tap" to each individual barrel. Shooter had only to cock, close pancover, turn rotating lever (or slide selector bar), fire, repeat same operation for next shot. Barrels unscrew to load. Sliding safety catch behind cock locks flashpan cover when shut and holds cock at half-cock.

Fig. 329—Cased set of flintlock top-hammer pocket pistols by W. Parker of London, circa 1790. Each pistol is slightly more than 5½ inches long; barrels unscrew to load, and triggers, now folded up into undersides of stocks, snap out when guns are cocked. Accessories are: powder flask, bullet mold, compartment for balls and wrench for unscrewing barrels.

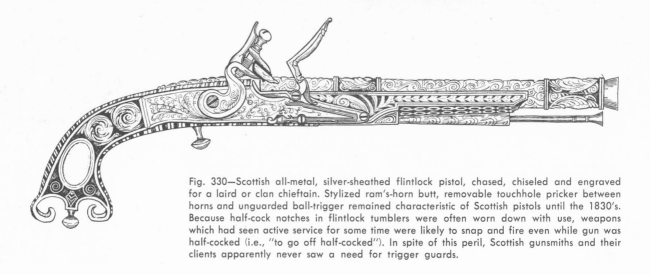

Fig. 330—Scottish all-metal, silver-sheathed flintlock pistol, chased, chiseled and engraved for a laird or clan chieftain. Stylized ram's-horn butt, removable touchhole pricker between horns and unguarded ball-trigger remained characteristic of Scottish pistols until the 1830's. Because half-cock notches in flintlock tumblers were often worn down with use, weapons which had seen active service for some time were likely to snap and fire even while gun was half-cocked (i.e., "to go off half-cocked"). In spite of this peril, Scottish gunsmiths and their clients apparently never saw a need for trigger guards.

Still another weapon which must be given a place of eminence among flintlocks is the *Collier revolver*, invented by a Bostonian boiler-making engineer, Elisha Collier, in about 1814–15. After two or three years of seeking unsuccessfully to interest American manufacturers, he went to England in 1817 and patented his design in 1818. Since Collier was himself not a gunsmith, the manufacturing was done mainly by the firm of a London engineer named Evans. After a few early trial models, the elegant form shown in Fig. 331 was settled upon. The Collier differed so radically from all its ancestors over the previous three and a half centuries that it might have had a very profound effect on the duration and conduct of the Napoleonic Wars if it had been invented fifteen years earlier. So well constructed was this ingenious device that multiple ignition was virtually impossible. The mouths of all the chambers were slightly

countersunk so that the chamber being fired was pressed over a projecting and slightly conical breech of the barrel. This also ensured perfect alignment of chamber and barrel. With the *self-priming flashpan* (Fig. 332), the shooter had only to cock the gun, fire, half cock, close the flashpan cover (which then primed the pan automatically), turn the cylinder by hand, cock and fire, etc. The 1818 patent specifications call for a coil spring around the cylinder axis which had first to be wound up by turning the cylinder counter-clockwise for several rotations, then automatically turned the cylinder clockwise one chamber at a time whenever the gun was cocked. This feature, however, seems to have been applied only to a few Collier revolving fowling pieces. In all, some 385 Collier flintlock weapons seem to have been made between 1819 and 1822, most of them pistols. For all their excellence, they came two generations too late.

Figs. 331 & 332—Above: Collier flintlock revolver with self-priming flashpan, London, circa 1819-20. One of a few dozen surviving ones, it once belonged to Samuel Colt, is now in the Wadsworth Atheneum, Hartford, Connecticut. Right: Detail of the lock and cylinder of a Collier *rifle*, mechanically identical with the pistol. Flashpan cover was actually a small hollow magazine filled with priming powder; when lowered down on small square flashpan, lever on far side turned rotary valve inside magazine and dropped required quantity of priming into pan. Collier's was the first revolver in which deadly multiple ignition was virtually impossible. Rifle shown, one of perhaps seven or ten surviving ones, is in the collection of Colt's Patent Fire Arms Company, Hartford, Connecticut.

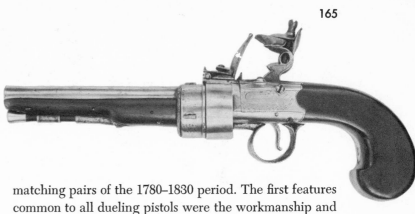

Fig. 333—Brass-barreled six-shot flintlock revolver by Powell of Dublin, circa 1775-90. Pulling back trigger guard released cylinder to be turned manually; sliding guard forward again locked it to hold top chamber aligned with barrel. All six flashpans in cylinder were primed in advance.

But doubtless the most magnificent hand-guns of the age—probably the finest single-shot pistols of any age, including ours—were the *target* and *dueling* pistols.

In the last quarter of the eighteenth century, the pistol had completely replaced the sword as the dueling weapon in England and America, and to a very large extent in France. The ritual was not so rigid or elaborate as is generally supposed. As a rule, the dueling party consisted of the principal, one or two seconds—close friends —and a physician. Usually the challenger and his party arrived at the appointed place a few minutes before the entourage of the challenged. The distance, usually twenty yards (commonly but wrongly called "paces," then and now), was measured off. The challenger's seconds brought the pistols, although the seconds of the challenged could object and insist that a favorite set belonging to their man be used instead. The principals doffed their coats, waistcoats and hats; clad in black trousers and white shirts, they took their guns from the case (held by a second), retired to the positions, held their pistols ready cocked at arm's length at their sides, turned the sides of their shooting arms toward each other (a profile presented less of a target than facing full on), and blasted away when a chosen second dropped a handkerchief or called out, "Fire!" Depending on prior agreement or on the particular "code" being followed, one round of fire might give satisfaction even though no damage had been done, or further rounds might be demanded by either side until blood was drawn. A misfire counted as a shot.

Modern fiction has transformed this barbaric rape of law and reason into a romance of heroism and honor. In Europe the popular interest is caught more by dueling pistols than by any other kind of antique firearms, while in the United States it ranks second only to the pursuit of Kentucky rifles and Colt revolvers. But even the most experienced collectors often have difficulty in distinguishing true dueling pistols from other high-quality cased and matching pairs of the 1780–1830 period. The first features common to all dueling pistols were the workmanship and materials. Both among the English and the French examples—there were practically no others—these ranged from excellent to superlative; no inferior standards were tolerable to the clientele or for the intended purpose. Therefore most dueling pistols were executed with even greater care, if such was possible, than the finest fowling pieces, for a misfire—a flash in the pan, a hanging fire or a total failure of ignition—could mean the escape of a bird who shot back. Invariably dueling pistols were cased in a velvet- or felt-lined box of richly polished wood; invariably the box was compartmentalized to hold the pistols, balls, flints, powder flask, priming powder flask, cleaning implements and so on. English boxes were almost always divided by straight partitions, French ones by contoured recesses (Figs. 342 and 350). Mechanically speaking, the French were on a par with the English, but the French put the English to shame for elegance and macabre grace.

But the final test of a dueling pistol was the elusive quality of "coming up." While most were fitted with carefully centered front and rear sights, the rules prohibited pausing for as much as an infinitesimal instant to take any deliberate aim. Combatants faced each other with pistols ready cocked at arm's length at their sides, and upon signal raised and fired instantly. It was a matter of life and death that the pistol be perfectly balanced— too light in front presented the danger of shooting too high, too heavy of shooting too low. The angle of butt and barrel had to be such that when the pistol was held in a natural, uncramped position with an extended arm, it would throw its ball precisely in the line from shoulder to index finger. A skilled marksman did not aim but "feel" his pistol dead on target merely by extending his arm toward his opponent. Many duelers found saw-handle pistols very helpful (Fig. 336).

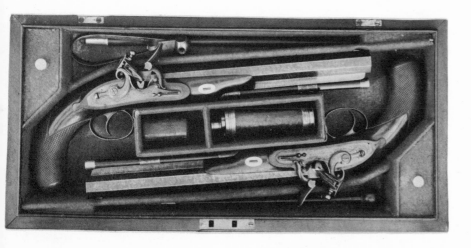

Fig. 334—Cased pair of flintlock pistols by John Manton & Sons (Joseph's brother and nephews), circa 1815, with patent V-shaped flashpans and recessed breeches. Pistols are among those which present problem whether they were made as true dueling pistols or high-quality "traveling" pistols. Inherent features weight decision in favor of dueling: most important one is that barrels are so heavy that once sighted on target their inertia will keep them from being thrown off to the right (or to the left if shooter is left-handed) when shooter's finger pulls feather-light trigger. Accessories are: bullet mold, powder flask, head of mallet in front of powder flask (detachable handle is behind bullet mold at top), cleaning rod and two compartments for patches, balls and flints.

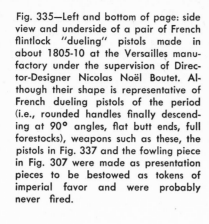

Fig. 335—Left and bottom of page: side view and underside of a pair of French flintlock "dueling" pistols made in about 1805-10 at the Versailles manufactory under the supervision of Director-Designer Nicolas Noël Boutet. Although their shape is representative of French dueling pistols of the period (i.e., rounded handles finally descending at 90° angles, flat butt ends, full forestocks), weapons such as these, the pistols in Fig. 337 and the fowling piece in Fig. 307 were made as presentation pieces to be bestowed as tokens of imperial favor and were probably never fired.

Fig. 336—Cased set of saw-handled flintlock dueling pistols by F. Innes of Edinburgh, circa 1800. Saw handles and balance leave no doubt that these are true dueling, not "traveling" pistols.

Highly ornate pistols—silver- or gold-inlaid and decoratively carved—were never intended for the duel. Obviously any shiny ornament which might catch the sun and cause a momentary glare could prove fatal; any decorative carving on the butt (other than checkering) which might in the least way impair the shooter's hold was suicidal. Thousands of magnificently decorated "dueling" pistols were made in France which were never intended to be used for anything but show and presentation to princes and retiring generals (Figs. 335, 337 and 350). Rifled pistols were never used for dueling in Britain and the United States because their accuracy was much too great at the traditional twenty yards or "paces." In France, however, they were the rule. Sets of rifled pistols of unsurpassable quality were made for target practice, and with these an expert marksman had no difficulty in hitting a common bottle cork ten out of ten times at the traditional distance. A measure of the accuracy of such guns may be learned from an advertisement by one Baron de Berenger, who operated an "Academy for Defence of Life and Property," in the May 16, 1823, issue of THE ANNALS OF SPORTING (italics in original):

The distances for pistol practice are marked at ten, fifteen, twenty-five [and] fifty yards; although occasionally I practice with *rifle pistols* at 100 yards. . . . Mechanical contrivances, with occasionally whimsical additions, serve to imitate in shooting flying, as well as at other moving or local objects. Persons desirous of possessing proof of particular feats of skill may obtain attested targets. . . .

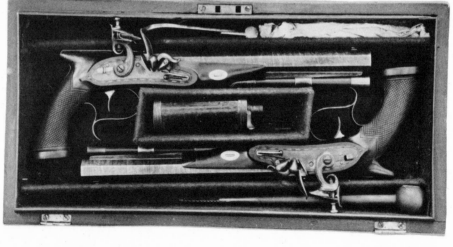

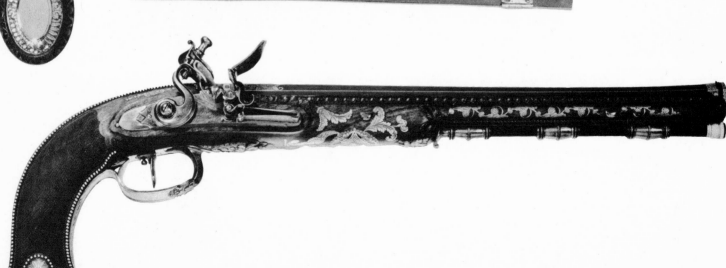

But the quality of ammunition and the care in loading were just as important as the quality of the gun. It was necessary that the quantity of powder be exactly weighed out to the grain; the balls had to be cast absolutely flawlessly of the purest lead; and the ramming had to be done with meticulous care. The task of loading (done at the scene) fell to the seconds, which at times exposed the duelers (and the seconds) to such perils as the following (reported in John Waterbury's A TREATISE ON DUELLING, published in Savannah, Georgia, 1842):

> On another occasion the Second had charged his friend's pistol so carelessly that the ball and powder had fallen out before he presented; when, but not till after receiving the opposite fire, snapping and burning prime, he discovered, on making several attempts to discharge his pistol in the air, that it was unloaded. . . .
>
> It has been known that by injudiciously over-loading, the Principal has been killed by his own pistol bursting, a part of the barrel having entered the temple; and it has frequently happened through the same cause that the pistol-hand has been shattered to pieces. I was present on an occasion when the Principal shot his own Second through the cheek, knocking in one of his double teeth, not by the ball, but by a part of the pistol barrel that was blown out near the muzzle.

Hair triggers were at times used—triggers which could be set to fire the gun upon the merest breath—but this practice involved further menaces (*ibid.*):

> A Second had given [the principal] his pistol at full cock, with a hair-trigger, which he held dangling at his side before the word was given, and in that position it went off.

. . . [The] Principal shot himself through his foot at the instep, which nearly cost him his life but put an end to further proceedings at the moment. . . .

Strictly speaking, dueling was illegal everywhere. Frenchmen, however, quite naturally considered the law a mere bagatelle, if not an actual incentive. No noteworthy efforts at enforcement were made between the death of Louis XIV in 1715 to the early twentieth century. In England, several acts of Parliament provided for death by hanging, but a tacit agreement between gentlemen and magistrates provided for the total disregard of such nonsense. All that was required was a measure of discretion—and should any meddlesome citizen ever swear out a complaint, years and decades could be spent establishing whether the alleged offense had taken place within the jurisdiction of one magistrate or another; meanwhile the plaintiff died. William, 5th Lord Byron, the poet's great-uncle, killed his man in 1765; Charles Fox "went out" in 1779; the Duke of York murdered Colonel Lennox in 1789, while the younger Pitt and the Duke of Wellington, respectively in 1798 and 1829, defended their prime-ministerial certitudes by dropping two opposition leaders. In 1809 Lord Castlereagh expressed his disapproval of certain policies by shooting Foreign Secretary Mr. Canning through the hip. The only significant instance of judicial retribution was the hanging of one Major Campbell in 1809; James, Earl (Charge-of-the-Light-Brigade) Cardigan was tried but acquitted by the House of Lords in 1840 for having wounded Captain Tuckett.

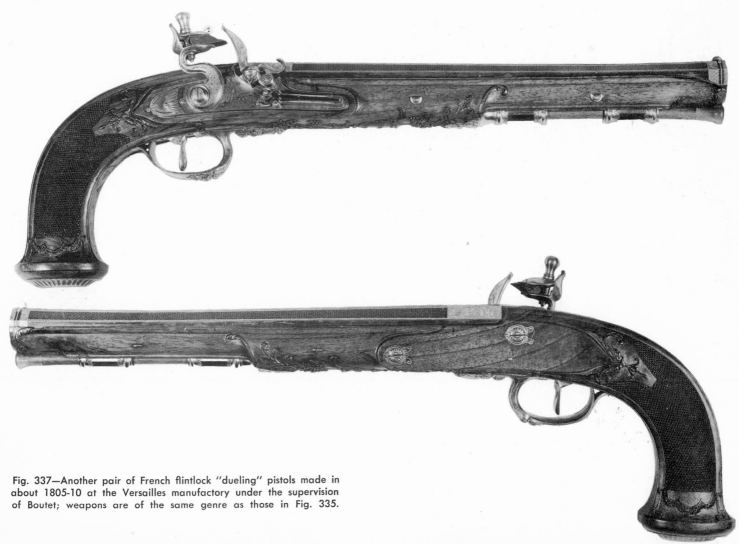

Fig. 337—Another pair of French flintlock "dueling" pistols made in about 1805-10 at the Versailles manufactory under the supervision of Boutet; weapons are of the same genre as those in Fig. 335.

It was much the same in the United States. The laws of all the states demanded fines, imprisonment or death for dueling, and in all states save the four northernmost New England ones not a soul paid the slightest attention provided the principals were gentlemen of birth and rank. In the South, the lunacy ran so wild that the author of A TREATISE ON DUELLING was able to bray out as late as 1842:

> To expect . . . that any law, now existing or hereafter to be made, can abolish duelling, is quite chimerical. It has been a custom from the earliest ages to decide differences and avenge injuries by single combat (of which more hereafter). It is a principle inherent in the breast of man, when he is aggrieved, to seek redress in the most summary way, regardless of personal danger; and in many cases the offence may be of such an aggravating and insupportable nature that no redress which the law may give can compensate the injury. I have never known a man whose heart is in the right place [to] bring an action for damages against another for seducing a beloved wife, daughter, &c. For these and such like offences the law can make no adequate retribution. The law cannot restore tranquility to the feelings of a man whilst the woman he loved is in the arms of an insidious enemy. In such a state, life is a burthen which cannot be laid down or supported till death either terminates his own existence, or that of the despoiler of his peace and honour. When a man sues for damages in such a case, it is an indubitable sign that he either did not love his wife, or did not deserve her.

The Burr-Hamilton duel on June 11, 1804, stirred considerable public resentment for a while, but in October Vice-President Burr was able to take up his job of presiding over the Senate again as though he had never murdered the one-time Secretary of the Treasury at all.

The most rational document in the history of dueling stems from the pen of Judge Breckinridge, father of John C., the Vice-President under James Buchanan from 1857 to 1861. Challenged to a duel by a British officer sometime in the late 1790's, the judge replied by letter:

> Sir;
> I have two objections to this duel matter. The one is lest I should hurt you; the other, lest you should hurt me. I do not see any good it would do me to put a bullet through any part of your body. I could make no use of you when dead for any culinary purpose, as I could a rabbit or a turkey . . . for though your flesh might be delicate and tender, yet it wants that firmness and consistency which takes and retains salt. At any rate, it would not be fit for long sea voyages. You might make a good barbacue, it is true, being of the nature of a racoon or an opossum, but people are not in the habit of barbacuing anything human now. As to your hide, it is not worth taking off, being little better than that of a two-year old colt. As to myself, I do not much like to stand in the way of anything that is harmful. I am under the apprehension you might hit me. That being the case, I think it most advisable to stay at a distance. If you want to try your pistols, take some object—a tree or a barn door—about my dimensions, and if you hit that, send me word. I shall then acknowledge that if I had been in the same place you would have killed me in a duel.
> I have the honour to be,
> Sir,
> Your hmbl. & obdt. servant,
> John Breckinridge

Arrah now, my Honey! and that Shot you!

Fig. 338—"Arrah now, my Honey! and that Shot you!" Cartoon in Mason L. Weems, *God's Revenge Against Duelling* (Philadelphia, 1821) tragi-comically satirized appalling prevalence of fashionable murders and cripplings in the name of "honor."

It was not until the 1850's that the voices of the many sane who had been outraged for generations were able to rule in the courts. Not until about 1875, however, was dueling put on a par with murder in all parts of the civilized world, except in France and the Southern states in America where the practice continued *sub rosa* for decades more, usually with the connivance of local justice.

This, then, was the flintlock at its zenith, whether in the form of a fowling piece or a Ferguson rifle by a top-flight London maker, an English or French set of target or dueling pistols, a Collier revolver or a cavernous "coaching" blunderbuss. Misfiring never if primed well and kept sharp-flinted, firing so instantaneously that trigger pull and shot were completely simultaneous as far as any human ear or eye could perceive, able to shoot even after exposure to rain—here was a mechanism in which there was no possibility of further improvement. Its imminent extinction was caused by no defect of design but by the invention of a radically and totally different mechanism which, after slightly more than three hundred years, did away with live spark ignition entirely. With it, the decline and fall of great gunmaking began.

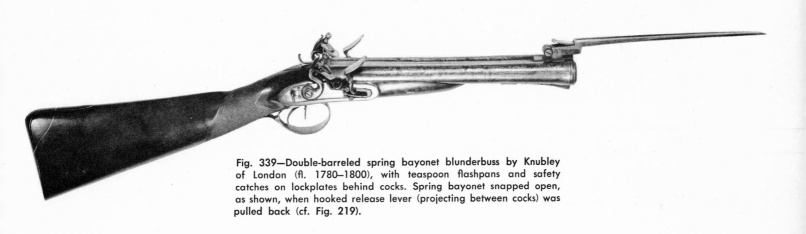

Fig. 339—Double-barreled spring bayonet blunderbuss by Knubley of London (fl. 1780–1800), with teaspoon flashpans and safety catches on lockplates behind cocks. Spring bayonet snapped open, as shown, when hooked release lever (projecting between cocks) was pulled back (cf. Fig. 219).

CHAPTER TWELVE

Inherent drawbacks of the flintlock—A terrible accident owing to a hanging fire—Detonating powders—The Rev. Forsyth's percussion lock of 1860—Forsyth & Company—Public reaction and rapid acceptance—The pill lock—Joseph Manton's percussion tubes—The percussion cap—The obvious advantages of the percussion system—The flintlock effectively obsolete in 1825—The revolver and Samuel Colt—Charles Dickens' opinion of the London Colt factory—The short step from the percussion cap to the Minié bullet (alias the "minny ball") and the breech-loading metallic cartridge—The passing of the muzzle-loader, the introduction of modern guns in the 1870's and the end of the history of firearms.

OR ALL THE PERFECTION OF THE flintlock between 1800 and 1820, there were faults in the system which no amount of skill or ingenuity could overcome. Even if rain no longer put an immediate end to days of sport, as it had a century earlier in the days of PTERYPLEGIA, no flintlock could ever be made *quite* waterproof; in time—perhaps ten minutes, perhaps ten hours—*some* water was bound to enter the flashpan, and on a very damp day the atmospheric moisture alone tended to weaken or spoil the priming. Keeping a flintlock loaded and primed for ready use at some time in the unpredictable future—days, weeks, months later—necessitated storing it in a dry, warm place to preserve the priming even from normal, non-excessive atmospheric moisture. This figured very prominently in at least one *cause célèbre*, the Wiley case of Delaware in 1815. Young Mr. Wiley, the cuckold husband, had shot seducer Dr. Theodore Wilson through the head in the presence of Governor Hall (Fig. 340). An hour later Dr. Wilson's brother got word of the murder, grabbed his long-loaded pistol, burst into the room where

Wiley was being kept, and according to Mason L. Weems in GOD'S REVENGE AGAINST ADULTERY (Philadelphia, 1818), rushed

up to the murderer, and thrusting the pistol against his heart, drew the trigger. The pistol refused to go off. He furiously cocked and tried it a second time, but with no better success; Mr. Wiley, all the time, looking at him with the dark smile of one who courted death. Discovering what young Mr. Wilson was about, governor Hall seized his arm, and crying, *"my God! what! are we all turning murderers!"* took the pistol from him, and for fear of further mischief, stepped to the window and tried it on the empty air. The pistol then went off very clear! [Italics in original.]

The fortunate Mr. Wiley, it may be added, subsequently escaped the law's revenge by dying of pneumonia in prison.

Besides the total misfire, there was also the hanging fire. It will be recalled that Mr. Markland had warned in PTERYPLEGIA not to consider a gun safe after it had flashed in the pan without a shot following, for "lurking Seeds of Death unheard may hiss" (3rd stanza, right col., p.

Fig. 340—"There! G—d d—n you, take that!" Illustration from Mason L. Weems, *God's Revenge Against Adultery* (Philadelphia, 1818), showing young Mr. Wiley murdering Dr. Wilson in the presence of Governor Hall of Delaware.

There! G—d d—n you take that!

128). Moisture and carbon in the touchhole could produce tragedies like that in the following news item from an 1817 issue of THE SPORTING MAGAZINE:

LINCOLNSHIRE

Shooting-party—On Friday, Jan. 10, Mr. Cocking of Broadholme, near Lincoln, accompanied by a friend, went out for the purpose of shooting rabbits. Whilst in pursuit of their game, a rabbit afforded a good opportunity for a shot by passing in a direction which, however, was obstructed by Mr. Cocking's friend standing in that quarter. Mr. Cocking presented his piece over the head of his friend, who accordingly crouched down a few paces off—the trigger was pulled—the powder flashed in the pan—and, as the gun did not instantly go off, the young man who stooped, conceiving that the piece had missed fire, arose from his bending position, when, shocking to relate, the contents of the gun were discharged within a few yards of his head, which was so dreadfully shattered as to cause his immediate death.

If the highest-quality locks could fire throughout a whole season's shooting with a few misses or none at all, the lower-quality ones could not, and military locks were not expected to do better than fire seven times out of ten. And lastly, no matter how hard the patent breech might fire the gun, a considerable quantity of the gases escaped through the touchhole of any flintlock or any other lock hitherto invented.

It had been learned since the 1580's that certain chemical substances, such as the fulminates of silver and mercury, and gunpowder made with potassium chlorate instead of potassium nitrate, could be made to explode if placed on some hard surface like an anvil and struck with a hammer. The great French chemist Claude Louis de Berthollet (1748–1822) experimented with these, but arrived only at explosives which were so powerful and so dangerously unstable that no practical use could be envisioned for them.

Sometime between 1800 and 1806, the Rev. Alexander Forsyth, of Belhelvie in Aberdeenshire, Scotland, a sportsman and an amateur chemist, not only envisioned but substantially developed the obvious purpose to which such substances might be put, viz., the firing of guns in place of the ancient sparks and external priming powders.

In April, 1807, Forsyth obtained a patent for a new gunlock in which a small quantity of *detonating powder* was exploded by the blow of a cock upon a plunger. This was the first and extremely clever version of the *percussion lock;* with its appearance the flintlock's days were numbered. Not only was ignition completely unfailing, regardless of wind and almost regardless of rain, but only very little gas pressure escaped through the detonating chamber. After failing to persuade the military authorities of the virtues of his system, Forsyth set up shop as a gunmaker in London in 1808 under the name of Forsyth & Company, the actual manufacturing being supervised by James Purdy, a star pupil of Joseph Manton whom Forsyth had lured from the master's domain with the avowed intention of starting out with nothing less than the best.

The lock made by Forsyth & Company was an ingenious device in which a small rotary magazine, containing enough detonating powder for twenty-five shots, was affixed to the side of the breech (Fig. 341); this was first given a half turn to allow a little detonating powder to fall into the ignition chamber, then turned back to present the plunger to the cock. Experiments in rain, fog, hail, snow and sleet proved its capability of firing some 999 out of 1,000 times, and since the flame from the detonating compound was not only guided *into* the propellent charge but shot *through* it, and since there was no open touchhole, Forsyth guns shot harder and still faster than the best flintlock ever known. Furthermore, it was extremely easy to convert existing flintlock guns to the Forsyth system by merely substituting a striker in place of the old flint cock, cutting away the flashpan, cutting a threaded hole into the barrel where the touchhole was and screwing in the plug or receptacle for the detonating magazine.

Fig. 341—Forsyth's lock, the first commercially produced percussion lock, made by Forsyth & Company between 1808 and about 1818. In place of a flashpan, Forsyth's lock had a stout cylindrical plug, the outer end of which was closed by the large screw in the center of the priming magazine, while its inner, unclosed end was screwed into the barrel at a point corresponding to flintlock touchholes. This cylindrical plug had a small aperture on its upper side directly underneath the plunger projecting from the upper end of the priming magazine. The priming magazine was fitted about the plug so that it could rotate freely. Its lower half was filled with *percussion* or *detonating powder*. To prime the gun, the shooter merely rotated the magazine through 180° so that the powder-filled lower half would come over the aperture in the cylindrical plug and deposit a small quantity of powder inside the plug. When the magazine was returned to the position shown, the inner or lower end of the plunger (kept raised by a spring) was again immediately above the aperture. When the cock or hammer struck the upper end of the plunger, the plunger in turn struck *into* the plug and ignited the powder there by *percussion;* the exploding fire shot into the barrel and instantaneously fired the main charge.

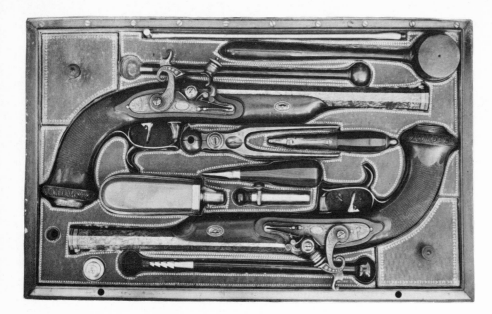

Fig. 342—Cased set of rifled percussion lock (or detonating lock) target or dueling pistols by LePage of Paris, dated 1814. The locks are adaptations of flintlocks to the new system. The flintlock flashpan has yielded to a stouter semi-cylindrical percussion powder receptacle, open at the top, which, however, is still a flashpan and not a closed detonating chamber as the plug in Forsyth's lock (Fig. 341). A flashpan cover with a detonating plunger assembly is hinged to open and close the flashpan just as the cover of flint-locks, save that instead of terminating in a bat-tery it terminates in a detonating plunger as-sembly. The flashpan cover is shown open in the upper pistol in the case, closed in the lower one and in the detail of the lock below. After the barrel had been loaded as in any muzzleloader, the shooter filled the flashpan with a little per-cussion powder and closed the cover. When the cock, or hammer, struck the plunger, the plunger in turn struck the detonating powder (just as in Forsythe's lock) and the thus ignited priming ignited the main charge through the touchhole. Virtually all sets of percussion guns made on this principle were furnished with separately carried flintlock cocks and flashpan covers. Should the shooter ever be away from a supply of detonat-ing powder (which in 1814 was still available only in a few big-city gunshops), he had merely to substitute the flintlock cock for the percussion hammer and the flintlock flashpan cover for the percussion flashpan cover; the gun could then be used as a conventional flintlock. (Courtesy of Mr. Robert Abels, New York)

The chief objection to the Forsyth lock lay in the pos-sibility of the entire magazine exploding when the gun was fired, although every effort had been made to pre-vent this by the use of tightly fitting cork gaskets around the receptacle, and by a loosely fitting cork plug in the magazine which would be blown out to release the pres-sure should the reserve priming take fire (Fig. 341). Thomas Johnson was among the middle-of-the-roaders in 1816, declaring himself open to the new (nine years old) system, although he was not yet ready to scrap his flint-locks:

While on the subject of gun locks, it would be un-pardonable not to notice, in a particular manner, the late ingenious invention of Mr. Forsyth, of Piccadilly, London. The inventor has obtained a patent for it, and thus de-scribes its properties:

"This lock is entirely different from the common gun-lock. It produces inflammation by means of percussion, and supersedes the use of flints. Its principal advantages are the following:—The rapid and complete inflammation of the whole charge of gunpowder in the chamber of the barrel—the prevention of the loss of force through the touch-hole—perfect security against rain or damp in the priming—no flash from the pan—and less risk from an ac-cidental discharge of the piece, than when the common lock is used. This being new, and different from the lock in general use, very particular printed instructions are sent with each gun to prevent any chance of mismanagement."

I have not yet used this new-invented gun-lock, but I saw it at the shop of the inventor in the month of March,

1811. It certainly appears to possess most or perhaps all the properties ascribed to it above; nor do I think there can possibly be more than one objection urged against it, and that probably not well founded—I mean on the score of danger. The cavity for holding the priming, situated in what is called the magazine, is capable of containing chemical powder sufficient for twenty-five primings, which number, I understand, is to be put into it at once. From the small space allotted for these twenty-five primings, the powder of which they consist must be consequently very strong, and it instantly struck me that it might be possible for the whole of the priming to explode at once, and thus be attended with injurious consequences. On communicat-ing this idea to the person who showed me the lock, I was informed that the possibility of such a circumstance had been anticipated, and provided for accordingly. In case the whole became inflamed, a bit of cork (fixed for the purpose) would be driven out, and thus give vent to the elastic fluid. The material for priming is what the inventor calls *chemical powder*; and when one of these locks is pur-chased, a prescription is given for making it.

That the shot may be driven with more force, I have no doubt, as none of the impelling fluid escapes by the touch-hole; and certainly it is a pleasant circumstance as to this lock, that there is no flash to blow in the shooter's face. . . . [And] if there really is no danger to be apprehended from an accidental explosion of the priming powder, I should regard the invention as a very valuable acquisition, particularly as it is applicable to military purposes also, suiting equally great guns and small.

If the sportsman should wish to try Mr. Forsyth's lock, he need not be at the expense of a new fowling-piece for the purpose, as it may be applied to any gun in the same manner as the common lock; the price for a single lock is eight guineas.

Others were less receptive, such as the correspondent who wrote to the GENTLEMAN'S MAGAZINE in 1817:

To the Editor:
Sir:
You will forgive my importunity if I take this occasion to add my views on *Mr. Forsyth's Patent Detonating Lock* to those of other recent correspondents. I cannot deny that Mr. Forsyth's invention offers many vulgar advantages, among which the most important are that the gun is made to shoot harder by consequence of the forceful kindling of the powder, and the absence of a touch-hole. Furthermore, it will doubtless fire in the most inclement weather. True sportsmen, however, do not require the new lock, for a good flint-lock will answer every conceivable purpose a

gentleman might wish. To those who say that it shoots harder, I say, the patent breech flint-lock shoots hard enough; to those who say it shoots faster, I say, if your flint-lock is good, and you have learned to use it, the difference is too trifling to merit attention by true sportsmen; to those who say it fires in violent wind and rain, I say, gentlemen do not go sporting in such weather.

If, moreover, this new system were applied to the military, war would shortly become so frightful as to exceed all bounds of imagination, and future wars would threaten, within a few years, to destroy not only armies, but civilization itself. It is to be hoped, therefore, that many men of conscience, and with a reflective turn, will militate most vehemently for the supression of this new invention.

I am, Sir, yours &c., &c.,
An English Gentleman

Fig. 343—"Le Chasseur," a mezzotint by Debucourt, circa 1820-22. Evidently a conservative, the gentleman placidly primes his flintlock, disdainful of the newfangled percussion gadgets which by this time were fast replacing the last few flintlocks on the expensive, high-quality sporting guns used by the leisure class to which the gentleman obviously belongs. His preference for flintlocks may in fact have been very well founded: having spent perhaps forty years in becoming expert with flint, he probably found that he could never recondition his reflexes to the quicker ignition and harder shot of a percussion gun.

Fig. 344 & 345—Ivory-handled lead-pouring ladle and gold-tooled leather shot pouch from a cased Dutch percussion fowling piece, circa 1835. (Courtesy of Mr. Robert Abels, New York)

The majority of English gentlemen, however—indeed the majority of Continental and American gentlemen, as well as lesser-caste shooters—had no such nostalgic or prophetic qualms and welcomed Mr. Forsyth's invention enthusiastically. By 1815, probably a quarter of all good- and best-quality guns made in England had detonating locks. By about 1814 the gunsmiths of the Continent and the United States—where the protection of royal patent did not extend—and quite a few in England, too, had made use of percussion powder in the form of small rolled pills or pellets, often enclosed in a wrapping of paper similar to the "caps" of a modern toy gun. This was placed into a small hollow receptacle on the top or the side of the barrel from which a canal communicated to the propellent charge; a solid-nosed striker on the end of the cock ignited it. Again, this system was found to lend itself well to conversion from flintlock by the method shown in Fig. 342 but it was not nearly so waterproof as Forsyth's lock. To remedy this, Joseph Manton in 1816 patented a pill system in which the pill was contained in the nose of a hollow striker, but two years later, in 1818, he patented his *percussion-tube lock* in preference to any pill or loose-powder system. In the tube system, a copper tube, five-eights of an inch long and about one-sixteenth in outside diameter, open at both ends, was filled with percussion powder and inserted into the touchhole so that only about an eighth of an inch protruded. The protrusion rested on a small anvil, a part of the lockplate roughly corresponding to the old flint flashpan; there it was struck by the blunt nose of the cock, the impact ignited the powder and crimped shut the outer or protruding end of the tube, the fire shot inward from the inserted end, and the propellent charge was instantaneously ignited by a powerful jet in its center. This system worked splendidly, its only drawback being that a tiny jet of fire also issued from the outer end of the tube in spite of the fact that the blow of the striker crimped the tube shut, and at times a few sparks blew into the shooter's face (although much less than in a flintlock).

Sometime between 1814 and 1820, one or several persons in England and America hit upon the copper *percussion cap*. Some weight is carried by the claim of one Joshua Shaw of Philadelphia, who may have employed detonators similar to percussion caps as early as 1814—but the evidence is purely circumstantial, far from compelling, and at any rate Shaw saw no need to patent his idea if indeed it was his. Colonel Peter Hawker wrote in several later and revised editions (after 1825) of INSTRUCTIONS TO YOUNG SPORTSMEN that he had more or less invented the percussion cap in about 1819—a claim not explicitly stated but suggested with the subtlety of a walrus:

When Joe first brought out his detonators [percussion tubes] in Davies Street, (those which were discarded from giving so much trouble) he made the most perfect gun I ever saw; and doubting whether such another could be got, I set my wits to work in order to simplify the invention. At last the plan of a perforated nipple, and the detonating powder in the crown of a small cap, occurred to me. I made a drawing of it, which I took to Joe. After having this explained, he said that he would show me something in a few weeks time; when, Lo and behold! there was a rough gun altered precisely on my own plan! His factotum, poor old Asell, assured me that the whole job was done from my drawing.

Thus Joe, who led the fashion for all the world, sent out a few copper-cap guns, and I know with some degree of reluctance. The trade, finding that he had then deviated from his own patent, adopted this plan: and it proved to answer so well that we now see it in general circulation.

The percussion cap operated on an extremely simple principle. A small copper cap, about an eighth of an inch in depth and diameter, or more or less as required, was partially filled with a little fulminate of mercury. It was placed over a short hollow nipple which was drilled out to communicate with the propellent charge. The cock terminated in a recessed, cuplike depression which, when the trigger was pulled, descended over the cap on the nipple and so ignited the fulminate, while the cup deflected any flash or sparks which might issue from the ignition. The jet of fire was directed through the nipple into the propellent charge and the gun went off instantaneously.

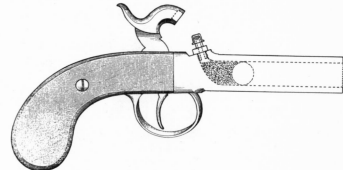

Fig. 346—Cutaway view of a typical top-hammer pocket pistol, showing principle of percussion cap system. Fulminate in crown of cap over nipple is detonated by blow of cup-nosed hammer; small but powerful jet of fire flashes through nipple directly into powder charge.

None but the most die-hard conservatives could fail to be convinced of the manifest advantages of the percussion-cap system. Shooting was now completely immune to weather, misfires were so infrequent if good caps were used that even a poor-quality gun might be expected to perform without fail throughout the season, and the lapse of time between trigger pull and shot, even though reduced to virtually zero in good flintlocks, was now absolutely zero if the nipple was kept clean. The transition from flint to percussion cap was swift, almost revolutionary. By 1820, only a few sporting guns and still fewer pistols (save dueling pistols, where tradition and flint largely prevailed into the 1840's) continued to be made with flintlocks. By 1825 a flint devotee had to go to one of the few makers who still turned out the old locks on occasions, and in 1827 the Gentleman of Philadelphia County was able to write in THE AMERICAN SHOOTER'S MANUAL:

> The lock has undergone a variety of alterations until it would seem that but little room is left for further improvement; nor do I consider any further amendment necessary, as every useful purpose appears to be completely answered by the common lock, adapted to the percussion primer. . . . It is my intention to confine my remarks on this subject to the double gun and the percussion locks, the fowling piece in this form being now almost exclusively used.

By 1835 a flintlock was greeted on the field with much the same amusement as a muzzleloader would be today. If a date must be selected for the flintlock's effective demise, 1825 would do well, and the last afterglow of the 325-year history of firelocks was totally extinguished by 1840. Flintlocks by the hundreds of thousands were converted to percussion by variations of the method shown in Figs. 347 and 349 (mainly the latter). If there was undeniably much good gunsmithing in the percussion era—circa 1820 to 1870—as far as balance and barrels were concerned, the simplicity of percussion locks required none of the masterful skill of the vanished age, and consequently the manufacture lent itself well to the universally booming new factory system.

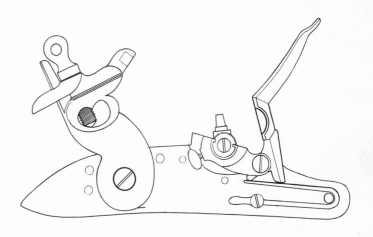

Fig. 347—Cautious experimental military modernization of the 1830's: flintlock convertible to percussion caps. For use as a percussion lock, upper flint jaw was replaced by cup-nosed striker, percussion nipple was clamped into flashpan by small set-screw on flashpan's lower left. (From Julius Schoen, *Geschichte der Handfeuerwaffen (History of Small-arms)*, Dresden, 1858.

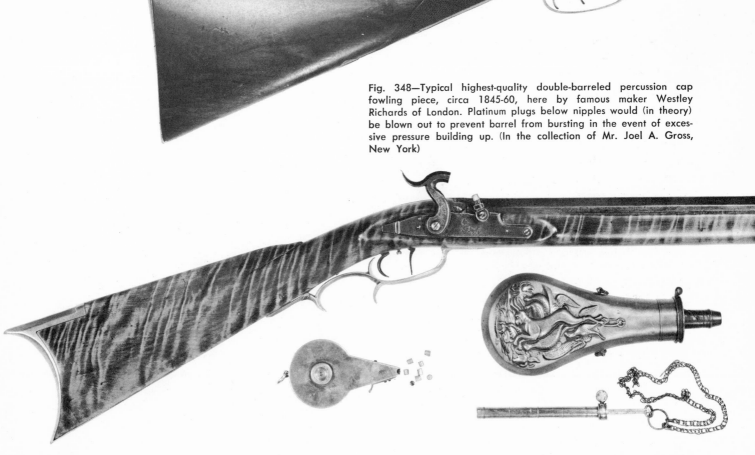

Fig. 348—Typical highest-quality double-barreled percussion cap fowling piece, circa 1845-60, here by famous maker Westley Richards of London. Platinum plugs below nipples would (in theory) be blown out to prevent barrel from bursting in the event of excessive pressure building up. (In the collection of Mr. Joel A. Gross, New York)

Fig. 349—American Kentucky rifle converted from flintlock to percussion cap by the method most frequently used both in America and in Europe between circa 1825 and 1845. The flintlock cock has been replaced by a percussion hammer, and the flintlock flashpan and feather-spring have been cut off. A cylindrical plug, closed at the outer end, from which the percussion nipple projects (nipple shown with cap), has been screwed into the greatly enlarged touchhole. Accessories are: brass powder flask embossed with still life of dead game; a percussion capper (a circular cap container with which one cap at a time can be easily fitted over the nipple from the triangular feeder); eight percussion caps (in front of capper); and a syringe-like powder measure on a chain.

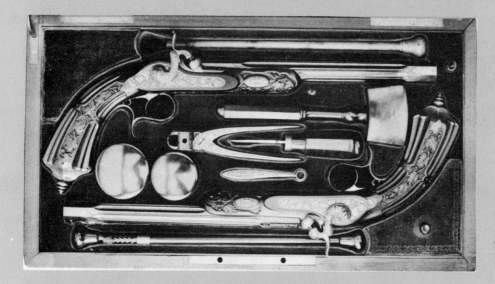

Fig. 350—Cased set of rifled percussion-cap target pistols by Firmin of Paris, circa 1855. Detail of lock below clearly shows percussion cap nipple (hammer is set at half-cock).

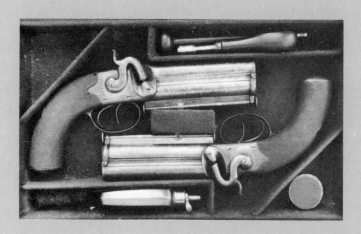

Fig. 351—Left: cased set of Irish double-barreled over-and-under percussion-cap pistols by Richardson of County Cork, circa 1840. Nearer hammer fires lower barrel.

Fig. 352—A most remarkable set of French three-system dueling or target pistols by Albert Renette of Paris, accompanied by the original bill of sale dated February 9, 1824 (not shown). By substituting cocks, nipples, bolsters, flashpans and touch-holes with various special tools provided—but always with the same locks!—it was possible to shoot with flint, percussion cap and/or detonating pill, as desired, and as caps or pills might or might not have been available. Workmanship is of the highest order. Upper pistol is shown assembled as a flintlock, lower as a cap lock; for use with a pill, nipple was removed from cap bolster, and hollow nose of cock was fitted with a special striker held by a set screw. (Palasciano Collection, Bari, Italy)

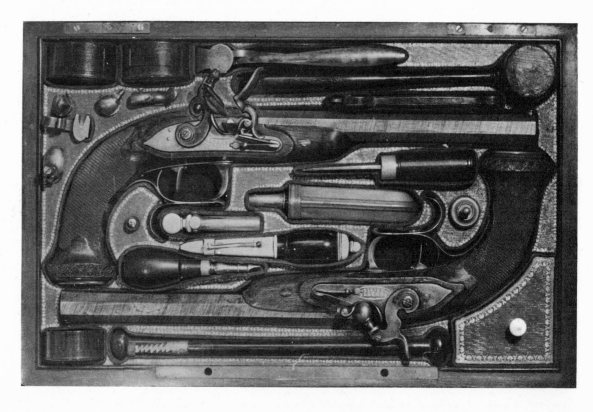

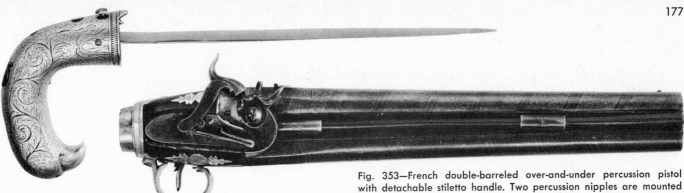

Fig. 353—French double-barreled over-and-under percussion pistol with detachable stiletto handle. Two percussion nipples are mounted on a swivel to fire first upper, then lower barrel. Mainspring is on outside of lockplate.

The most noteworthy development which followed directly upon the introduction of the percussion cap was the practical, serviceable revolver. A notion persists that Samuel Colt of Hartford, Connecticut, was the inventor of this form of weapon, the inspiration having allegedly flown to him when in 1831 the seventeen-year old apprentice seaman Colt, on a runaway voyage to India, watched the spokes of the turning steering wheel line up with a fixed point on the compass in front of it. Needless to say, the revolver was some four hundred years old when Colt obtained his first patent in 1835. There was nothing new about the *idea*, but there was something radically new about Colt's design, efficiency and mass-production system, which was among the earliest to use an assembly line and completely interchangeable parts. As has been noted, the difficulty with all revolvers prior to the percussion system was the danger of stray sparks firing all the chambers at once. The trouble with the percussion "pepperbox" revolvers of 1820–60, many of which

were made in keeping with the finest traditions of workmanship in London and Paris, was that they were muzzle heavy, clumsy and unable to withstand large-calibre charges (Figs. 354 to 356). All these and earlier revolving-principle maladies Colt corrected by (a) resorting to an extremely well-made version of the old system of having a rotating cylinder line up its top chamber with a single fixed barrel, (b) by placing the percussion nipples into spaced recesses at the end of the cylinder so that multiple ignition was impossible, and (c) by perfecting the old principle of rotating the cylinder by the action of cocking. Thus Colt stands in relation to the revolver as Henry Ford to the automobile: he did not invent it, but adapted and redesigned an idea into industrial success to such an extent that what had hitherto been achieved at great expense with only moderately satisfactory results was suddenly rendered highly functional, durable, and, owing to far-sighted engineering and manufacturing processes, remarkably cheap.

Fig. 354—Massive American four-barreled percussion-cap pepperbox revolver, circa 1835. Six-inch barrels were turned by hand, locked in place by trigger guard latch. Handle is all brass.

Fig. 355—Belgian five-barreled ring-trigger pepperbox revolver, circa 1840-45. Bar-hammer on underside fired lowest barrel. Each .47-calibre smoothbore barrel unscrewed for loading.

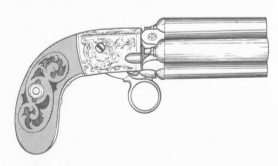

Fig. 356—English percussion-cap pepperbox revolver, circa 1845. Pulling the double-action trigger revolved barrels, raised and snapped flat bar-hammer on top. Handle is engraved silver.

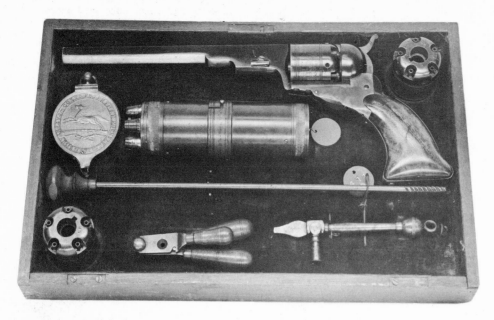

Fig. 357—Cased Colt-"Paterson" revolver with folding trigger (snaps out when pistol is cocked), 1836. Accessories are: percussion capper (cf. Fig. 349), powder flask with five nozzles to load five cylinder chambers at once, cleaning rod, wooden-handled bullet mold with sprue cutter, screwdriver-and-nipple-wrench tool, and two spare cylinders. (In the collection of the Winchester Repeating Arms Company)

In October, 1835, Colt went to England and patented his design in December. In the following February he obtained his first American patent and soon began manufacturing the now extremely rare and valuable "Paterson" models (e.g., Fig. 357) in Paterson, New Jersey. But public reaction was slow and in 1842 the factory closed in bankruptcy. Finding himself without support by the financiers who had promised it, Colt busied himself with the invention of a submarine telegraph cable—the first successful one—and supervised its laying between Manhattan, Staten Island and Governors Island in New York harbor. Things began to look up when he managed to land a government contract in 1847 for the manufacture of one thousand revolvers for the Mexican War. These, known today as the *Colt Whitney Walker Model*, were quickly manufactured in Whitneyville, Connecticut, while in the following year operations were relocated to several different shops in Hartford, where (on Pearl Street) the *Colt Dragoon Model* (Figs. 358 and 359) came

into being. Outgrowing small quarters, Colt began construction of *Colt's Patent Fire Arms Manufacturing Company* on Van Dyke Avenue in the summer of 1854, and manufacture commenced in the fall of 1855. All Colts have been made there ever since, except those manufactured in the London factory between 1853 and 1857. This branch was opened at Pimlico on the Thames in January, 1853, and for four years the *1849 Pocket Model* (Fig. 360) and the justly famous *1851 Navy Model* (Fig. 363) were made with huge success, the orders pouring in faster than the six-hundred-per-week production could meet. Charles Dickens visited the factory in early 1854 and in the May 27 issue of his magazine HOUSEHOLD WORDS published an article praising not only the efficiency of the works and the fine finish of the products, but also the high—for the time—standards of working conditions, the higher-than-prevailing pay and the short working hours (eleven a day). This account must be taken as probably true.

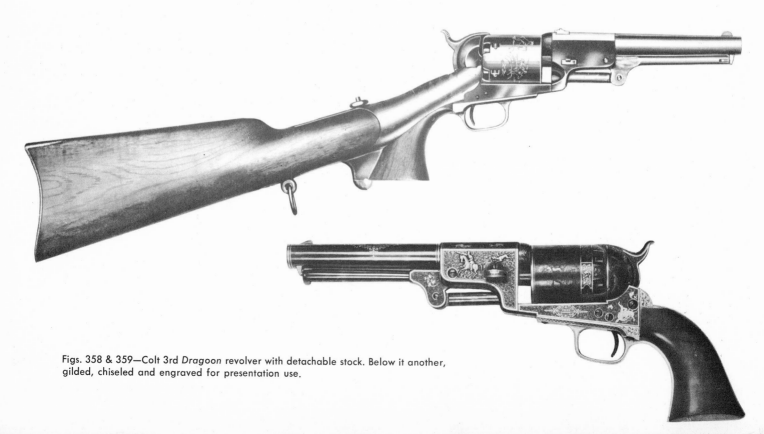

Figs. 358 & 359—Colt 3rd *Dragoon* revolver with detachable stock. Below it another, gilded, chiseled and engraved for presentation use.

Fig. 360—Below: Colt 1849 Pocket
Model, gilded, chiseled and engraved
for presentation use.

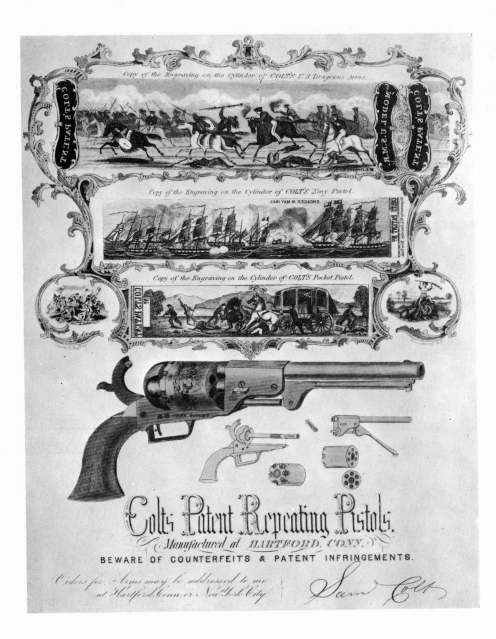

Fig. 361—Left: Colt advertisement, circa
1852-53, of the 1847 Colt-Walker
military revolver. Three narrow rectangular scenes are impressions taken
from the cylinder engravings of the
1847 Colt-Walker (top), the 1851 Navy
Model (middle), and the 1849 Pocket
Model (bottom).

In the early 1850's England issued its answer to the Colt challenge in the form of revolvers of superlative quality—but still made or at least finished by hand in the old tradition, and hence not only expensive but without the boon of interchangeable parts. Their various names (after their inventors or financial backers—most prominent among them: Adams, Tranter, Deane, Webley) are today as laden with nostalgia of Empire, sepoys, thuggee, pukkah sahibs And All That as Colt is with Forty-Niners, Gettysburg and Tall In The Saddle. There were many differences in basic gunmaking concepts between the Colt and nearly all the British revolvers. Most (not all) of the latter were solid-frame (e.g., Figs. 364 and 366), and *double-action*, meaning that pulling the trigger raised and snapped the cock, while in the *single-action* Colts it was necessary to cock with the thumb, then pull the trigger. The Colts' strong points were inexpensiveness, relatively interchangeable parts, astounding long-range accuracy and an over-all

quality that approximated the very best of British hand-crafting; their principal drawback was the lack of a solid frame, or top strap, and the consequent tendency of the barrel to work loose (but only after thousands of shots) on its mere two points of anchorage. The British weapons—new models appeared throughout the 1850's: Bentley, Dawes, Kerr, Westley-Richards, among others—tended toward heavier calibres than the Colts' .31 and .36, and were less subject to blockage of cylinder rotation owing to bits of burst cap fragments jamming the works.

Which system was better? Colt, thought the British Board of Ordnance in 1854, when it ordered 63,000 of them (41,500 1851 Navy Models alone); but then changed its mind and adopted the Adams as the official British Service Arm in 1855. The splendid Colt *Army Model* of 1860 (Fig. 362) had not been developed, for if it had it might well have proved itself the superior of the Adams for wartime duty. It served the Union army throughout the Civil War in America and no significant disadvantages are recorded. At any rate, whether owing to the British adoption of the Adams in 1855, or to the fact that the new Hartford factory was able to supply the American as well as the foreign market without the necessity of overseas factories, the Pimlico branch suspended operations in 1857 and no Colts were thereafter made anywhere but in Hartford.

There is much, much more to be said on the score, not only of Colts, but of revolvers generally. In fact, the study of these weapons is a complex discipline that lies outside the scope of the present volume and, frankly, beyond the competence of its author. Many excellent books are available on American revolvers, for the most part labors of love and noteworthy scholarship. But for the present purpose, that which has been so briefly (and, no denying it, inadequately) sketched must serve to give basic orientation; a couple of compass points, as it were, from which the reader may pursue his own course or courses according to his passions.

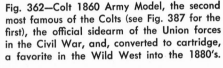

Fig. 362—Colt 1860 Army Model, the second most famous of the Colts (see Fig. 387 for the first), the official sidearm of the Union forces in the Civil War, and, converted to cartridge, a favorite in the Wild West into the 1880's.

Fig. 364—British Deane-Harding percussion revolver, circa 1854. Note top strap of solid frame and double-action trigger, typical of most British revolvers of the period. Over-all shape and proportions, too, are characteristic of British design to survive until after World War I. Gun shown here has original walnut case and accessories, was given by Carlo Collodi, author of *Pinocchio,* to *Giuseppe Verdi.* (Merli Collection, San Casciano, Fi., Italy)

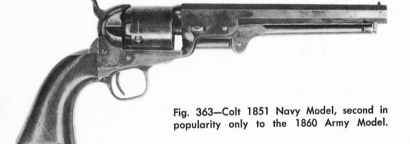

Fig. 363—Colt 1851 Navy Model, second in popularity only to the 1860 Army Model.

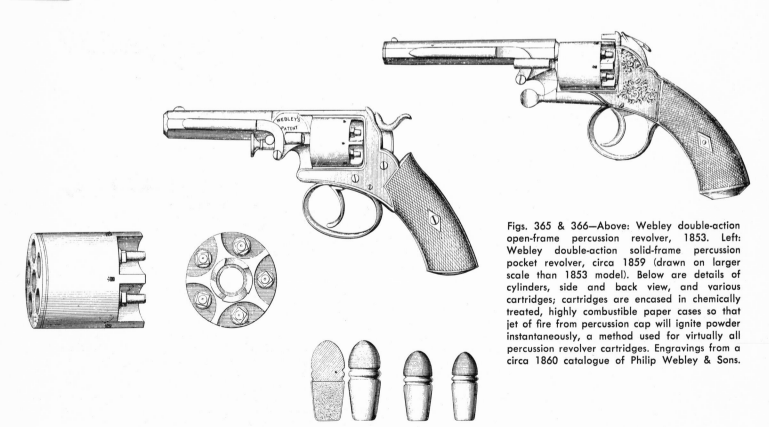

Figs. 365 & 366—Above: Webley double-action open-frame percussion revolver, 1853. Left: Webley double-action solid-frame percussion pocket revolver, circa 1859 (drawn on larger scale than 1853 model). Below are details of cylinders, side and back view, and various cartridges; cartridges are encased in chemically treated, highly combustible paper cases so that jet of fire from percussion cap will ignite powder instantaneously, a method used for virtually all percussion revolver cartridges. Engravings from a circa 1860 catalogue of Philip Webley & Sons.

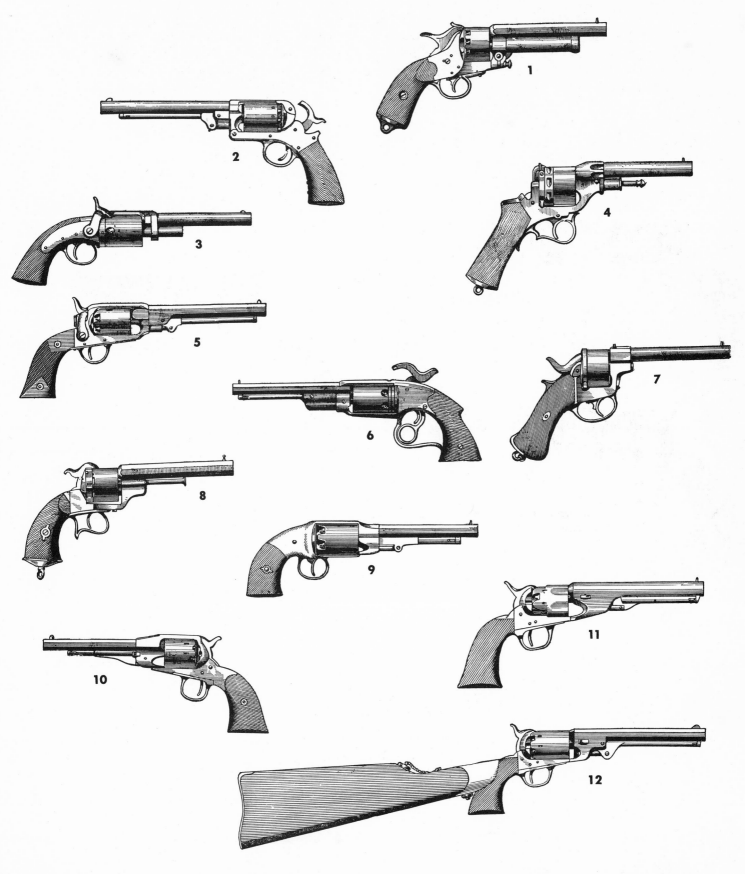

Figs. 367–378—Nearly 374,000 revolvers of about twenty different manufactures were bought by the United States government and by the Confederacy between 1861 and 1865. Prices ranged from $12 to $27 per gun (the Confederacy paying mostly in "cotton certificates"). Prominent were: (1) Le Mat (French), percussion and pinfire (q.v., left col., p. 184), with two barrels: ten shots in cylinder were fired through rifled .44 calibre upper barrel; nose of hammer could be turned down to fire one 12-gauge buckshot load in center of cylinder through lower smoothbored barrel. (2) Starr (U.S.), six shots, percussion, .44 and .36 cals.; 1856 and after. (3) Wesson & Leavitt (U.S.), five shots, percussion, .40 cal.; patented 1837. (4) Perrin (French), seven shots, .45 pinfire cartridge; 1857 and after. (5) Joslyn (U.S.), five shots, percussion, .44 cal.; 1858. (6) Savage (U.S.) Navy Model, percussion, .36 cal.; 1856 and after; ring trigger cocked gun and rotated cylinder, other trigger fired. (7) Raphael (French), .45 center-fire cartridge (q.v., right col., p. 184); 1861. (8) Lefaucheux (French), six shots, various calibres pinfire cartridges, 1858 and after. (9) Pettingill (U.S.), six shots, percussion, .44 cal., double action with internal hammer; 1856. (10) Remington (U.S.), six shots, percussion, .36 and .44 cals.; next to Colts in Figs. 362 and 363, the most widely used Civil War revolver. (11) Colt (U.S.) New Model Belt Pistol, five shots, percussion, .36 cal.; 1862. Favored by many officers as personal sidearm. (12) Colt (U.S.) 1851 Navy Model with detachable hollow shoulder stock; stock doubled as water canteen (note plug on chain).

In the 1840's, an arch-conservative sportsman, an American mountaineer in some isolated valley, a few tradition-minded dueling lunatics, might still fire the charge in their various weapons by flint, steel and flashpan—essentially an elaboration, no matter how ingeniously elaborated, of a fourteenth-century monk's gun (which the reader will recall from Fig. 97). Moreover, some thirty years and more after Forsyth's invention of 1807, the Captains Courageous who manned the most hazardous desks in the world's War Ministries defended the traditional system against all evidence and logic, so that in Britain and the United States the manufacture of military flintlocks did not cease until about 1842; the presence of Brown Besses—most of them veterans of Tourcoing and Waterloo, and a few of Yorktown—was a ridiculous but not infrequent aspect of the Crimean War in 1854–56, while in the United States a good many Union and Confederate regiments rallied to their respective causes in 1861 with their more rusty than trusty firelocks well primed. On the other hand, military modernization went on more briskly in Prussia and France (it could hardly have gone on in one and not the other), while even in Britain and the United States, flintlocks were being converted to percussion locks by the thousands, and experimental models were submitted in limitless varieties by designers everywhere. In London and Washington, most of these were tested, many proved highly effective—and nearly all rejected. A few were ordered now and then in very small quantities, and fewer still found their way into regulation issues. Figs. 379 to 385 will exemplify some mid-century martial longarms.

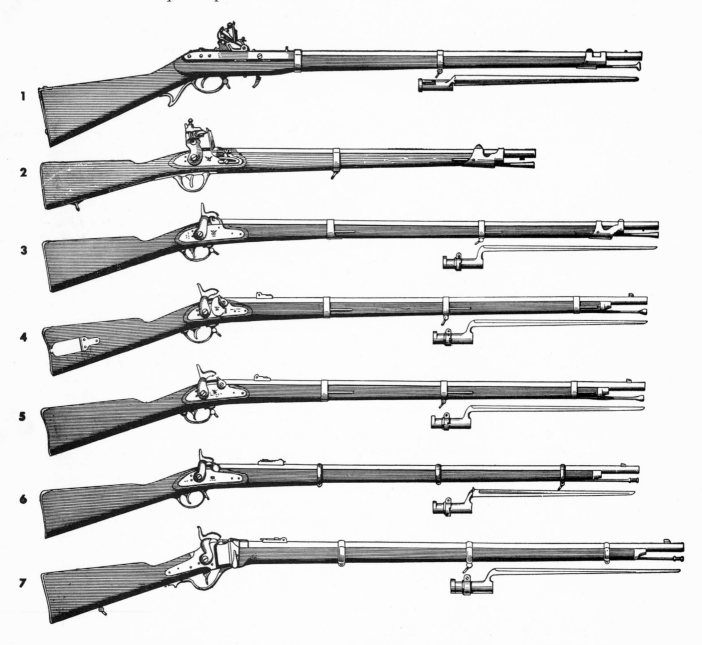

Figs. 379-385—Seven representative specimens of military long-arms, mid-19th century. (1) Hall breech-loading carbine, first official U.S. breechloader, issued from circa 1820 to the Civil War both in flintlock and percussion (after 1842 mainly in latter); .53 cal., rifled. (2) U.S. Model 1840 flintlock[!] "musketoon," a lighter and shorter version of the musket for artillerymen's use; .69 cal., smoothbore[!]. (3) U.S. Musket, Model 1841, first official percussion musket; .69 cal., rifled for use with Minié bullet, better known as the "minny ball" (see text, right col., p. 183). (4) U.S. Musket, Model 1855, percussion lock with Maynard tape primer; .58 cal., rifled for use with Minié bullet. Primer, invented by Edward Maynard of Washington in the early 1840's, consisted of small pellets of fulminate laminated at equal intervals between two thin cloth or paper tapes, like the rolls of "caps" for modern toy guns; tape was waterproofed, coiled and inserted into compartment with reniform lid at side of lockplate. Cocking automatically extended one pellet over nipple; hammer struck, detonated and cut tape. Discarded circa 1862 because of waterproofing problems. (5) U.S. Musket, Model 1861, the principal long arm of the Civil War; .58 cal., rifled (Minié bullet). (6) British Enfield Musket, Model 1853; .577 cal., rifled (Minié bullet). (7) Sharp's breech-loading system, best among dozens, here on a rifle; trigger guard operated vertical falling breech block. Made for caps, tapes and cartridges, 1848-81.

Nevertheless, although the inventors and designers generally saw their newly launched creations wrecked against the reefs of military conservatism, firearms, as every other man-made object, were now caught up in the frenetic whirl and clangor of nineteenth-century industrialism. In scarcely a generation's time, the torrential cataracts of the new order had all but swept away the placid half-millennium of shop-front manufacture and master craftsmen's guilds; now they rushed and boiled down into long-torpid strata of society; one current in particular—the newly luminous incentive of royalties and profit from the steam- and hell-fire-powered mass production system—lashed innumerable native skills and ingenuities, choked by agrarian economies since ploughs had first tilled wealth, into galvanic responsiveness. The fecund intelligences of unrecorded thousands, once faceless shepherds on village commons as old as time or shapeless bellows-pumpers in smithies older than the realm, buoyed the nascent technology and made patentees of cottage artificers. All areas of industry lay open—among them very prominently armaments production. Spurred on as never before, civilians and lower-rank military men advanced the effectiveness of firearms further in the forty years between 1830 and 1870 than it had been during the preceding three hundred, or for that matter, than it was to be in the succeeding eighty-seven.

The features which distinguish a twentieth-century small-arm from its early-nineteenth-century parallel are procedural, not principal, and consist in toto of one chemical and three mechanical contrivances, viz.: (1) the use of non-fouling, high-pressure, smokeless nitrocellulose powders which finally replaced black powder after six centuries between the early 1870's and 1900; (2) projectiles which adapt themselves to rifling grooves without an interposed patch of greased cloth or leather and without iron-rod-and-mallet ramming; (3) self-contained, self-igniting loads of powder and projectile; and (4) mechanisms for loading and igniting several such self-contained units in rapid succession with physical ease. It was the last three of these which the newly freed inventiveness of the age developed, applied and perfected between 1830 and 1870.

The first problem was the projectile. By 1830, the superiority—for military use—of rifles over smoothbores, and of oblong over spherical bullets, had been too firmly established to be ignored further. But how was an oblong to be loaded? A very fast spin was absolutely vital to stability in flight; this in turn required a far firmer seat in the grooves than had hitherto been necessary with spheres. But the area of contact, and consequently the friction, between projectile and bore was so great that only the most determined hammering could make the lead "bite" to the required depth. Some sought to solve the problem by casting projectiles with two or more lugs or studs which fitted into broad channels in the bore rather than into conventional rifling grooves; these proved unsuccessful. In the 1850's, Sir James Whitworth developed a hexagonal oblong which fitted into a hexagonal bore spiraling on itself; it was enormously successful, but almost at once another system, as will be seen further on, superseded it. In 1828, Captain Delvigne of France employed a bullet which would fall down the bore freely until it came to rest on the shoulders of a narrow breech-chamber; there it was hammered upon with an iron ramrod until it expanded sideways and filled the grooves. It also, alas, suffered such violent mutilation that Delvigne's theories plunked to earth as fast as his wobbling bullets. In 1848, Captain Thouvenin, also of France, invented an undersize conical projectile which, when rammed, came to rest on a sharp steel point projecting an inch or so from the breech-end of the bore, so that when hammered with the iron rod the lead would be impaled and thereby expanded itself. This actually worked—until the point became bent or corroded. The search for the perfect self-expanding bullet continued; pieces of lead and alloy metals in more than seven thousand shapes, sizes and sub-shapes—conical, elliptical, cylindrical, studded, saturnine, polyhedral —were blasted into the pulp of history, never to re-emerge. The obvious solution was ignored.

The obvious solution had, in fact, been provided in 1823 by Captain Norton of the 34th British Regiment. Norton had simply hollowed out a large conical convexity in the base of a bullet shaped like a short cylinder, flat at one end and pointed like a Gothic arch at the other—in mathematical terms, a right-truncated cylindro-ogival. It was so much smaller than the bore that it fell down the barrel freely, but when fired, the force of the expanding gases expanded its hollow base so forcefully into the rifling grooves that it "bit" with all the required firmness. Soon after, in 1836, the celebrated gunsmith William Greener proposed a similar hollow-base bullet, but fitted with a conical cup of wood or clay which would be driven into the cavity and thus expand the lead. The War Office, or rather, the Board of Ordnance, tested both Norton's and Greener's systems, found them to be near-perfect answers to the four-hundred-year-old problem—and rejected both.

At last, in 1848, Captain C. E. Minié of France combined the aerodynamically most stable cylindro-ogival bullet with an improvement on Norton's hollow base. It was small enough to be loaded, complete with powder and paper wrap, into the most fouled barrel by an effortless push (the paper wiping the bore clean on the way down), but would invariably expand into the rifling when fired. Minié's system was at once universally accepted. Immortalized as the "minny ball," it remained in use well into the modern breech-loading era.

Now the step to the self-igniting metallic cartridge was short. The earliest more or less successful one was for von Dreyse's *needle gun*, patented in Prussia in 1836 and adopted by the Prussian army in two slightly different versions in 1842 (Fig. 386). More successful was the *pinfire cartridge*, patented by the Parisian gunsmith Houiller in 1846. Here a small pin protruded transversely out of a copper (later brass) cylindrical powder case, closed flat at one end and holding the bullet crimped in its open other end. When the gun's flat-nosed hammer struck the pin, the pin in turn struck a small percussion cap on the opposite inside wall of the container (Figs. 391 and 392). This was the world's first self-igniting, self-contained cartridge, complete with one absolutely essential feature of modern metallic cartridges: the *expansive case*. The brass powder container expanded under the heat and physical pressure of the explosion, and thus formed a gas-tight seal against the walls of the breech-chamber. The great drawback of pinfire cartridges was that they were dangerous when dropped or otherwise mishandled, and consequently difficult to store and transport; and the aperture through which the pin projected eventually admitted atmospheric moisture.

The final solution of the cartridge problem took two forms in the late 1840's and early 1850's: the *rimfire cartridge* and the *center-fire cartridge*. In rimfire, the fulminate was contained in a hollow rim crimped around the cartridge base (Fig. 389). It worked well, but only for low-pressure or small-calibre charges; the .22 is the only practical use of it today. Several experimenters in Britain, France and the United States, but primarily Berdan and Morse in the United States, developed center-fire in the 1850's. Here a percussion cap was seated in the center of the cartridge base (Fig. 390). It had become the universal system for most high-pressure cartridges by 1870, and for virtually all cartridges since then. By 1858, rimfire revolvers and repeating rifles were being manufactured in all industrialized nations. Center-fire weapons went into production at about the same time, although at first at a more leisurely pace. By 1860, the varieties of cartridges had come to number thousands, among them the curious *Volcanic* cartridge developed in the United States in the 1850's for the rifles and pistols bearing the same patent name (incidentally, the first tubular lever-action repeaters). Its propellent charge was contained in a hollow base and consisted of pure detonating fulminate, not gunpowder. It was far too weak to be serviceable, and vanished within a few years.

Bullet and cartridge having been perfected, it now

Fig. 386—Diagram of a detail of the bolt, the coiled mainspring and the firing needle of the Prussian needle gun of 1844, and, at the right, the paper-wrapped cartridge. When trigger was pulled, needle pierced cartridge base, passed though powder, struck and ignited cap at base of bullet. Reliable for a few hundred rounds, needle thereafter began to corrode as a result of being constantly at center of explosion. System was world's first military cartridge breechloader. From A. Mattenheimer, *Die Rückladungsgewehre.* Leipzig[?], 1852.

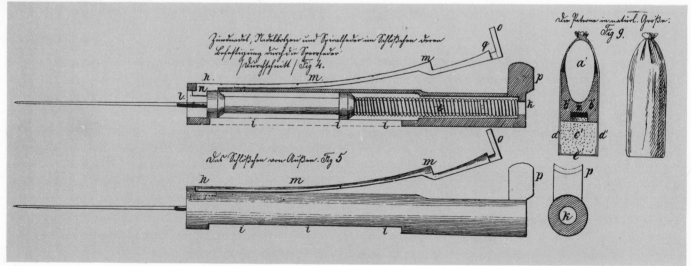

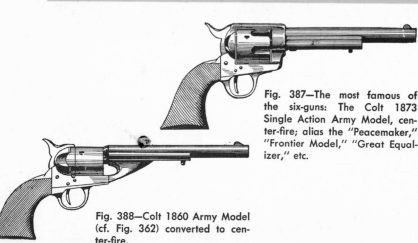

Fig. 387—The most famous of the six-guns: The Colt 1873 Single Action Army Model, center-fire; alias the "Peacemaker," "Frontier Model," "Great Equalizer," etc.

Fig. 388—Colt 1860 Army Model (cf. Fig. 362) converted to center-fire.

Figs. 389 & 390—Right: Simple diagrams of rimfire and center-fire cartridges. Rimfire cartridge has detonating fulminate in crimped ring around base; gun's striker or firing pin hits any part of crimp. Center-fire cartridge has percussion cap seated in center of base, where gun's firing pin strikes it.

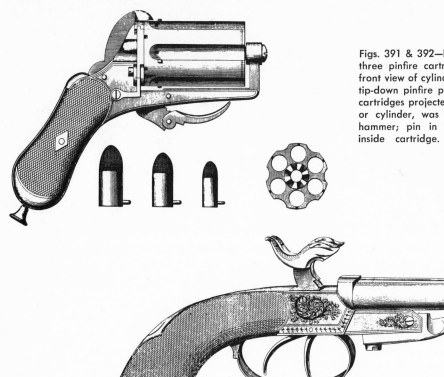

Figs. 391 & 392—Pinfire pepperbox revolver with three pinfire cartridges of various calibres, and front view of cylinder; below it, a double-barreled tip-down pinfire pistol. Small pin projecting from cartridges projected through slot at end of barrel or cylinder, was struck vertically by flat-nosed hammer; pin in turn struck percussion primer inside cartridge.

remained to perfect mechanisms to load and fire them. There is no complete catalogue of all the devices made between 1850 and 1870 for opening and closing breeches to admit one manually inserted cartridge at a time; but these had all yielded to repeaters by about 1880. Hundreds of repeating-mechanisms were developed between about 1855 and 1880, but all were variations of only three basic types, all of which have survived essentially unchanged: (1) the lever action (Figs. 393 and 394); (2) the bolt action (Figs. 395 and 396); and (3) the rotating cylinder (which of course antedates 1855 by four centuries). To this day, these basic mechanisms underlie all "modern" small arms, at times in combination with the almost equally old automatic systems of Maxim and Orbea (which will be noted in a moment). Almost every bolt-action rifle the world over, civil or military, is

essentially a German Mauser *Gewehr 98* ("Rifle, Model 1898") and its 1880's antecedents, though it may be slightly modified and called an American Springfield, or a British Enfield, or any of dozens of others. Any bolt-action rifle which is *not* essentially a Mauser *Gewehr 98* is essentially a Mannlicher of the 1880's. All lever-action rifles are at heart Henrys of the early 1860's (or even Volcanics of the 1850's). Automatic and semi-automatic weapons of whatever sort are nothing new; recoil-operated ones descend from Hiram Maxim's machine gun of 1884 (U.S.), gas-operated ones from Orbea's semi-automatic revolver of 1883 (Spanish) and from Paulson's of 1886 (British). Automatic and semi-automatic rifles and pistols have been used for seventy years, actively for sixty.

To return briefly to the muzzleloader. By 1865 it had

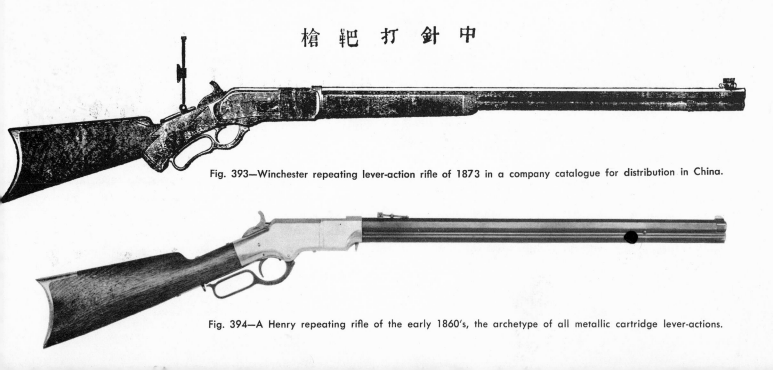

中針打靶槍

Fig. 393—Winchester repeating lever-action rifle of 1873 in a company catalogue for distribution in China.

Fig. 394—A Henry repeating rifle of the early 1860's, the archetype of all metallic cartridge lever-actions.

Figs. 395 & 396—All bolt-action rifles find their archetype in the German Gewehr 98 ("Rifle, Model 1898"). The standard infantry rifle (top) is shown with the action open and the bolt drawn back, permitting one cartridge to feed up from the magazine; pushing the bolt forward and turning down the bolt handle slides the cartridge into the breech chamber; pulling the trigger releases the firing pin, longitudinally coaxial inside the bolt, to snap forward against the center-fire cap in the base of the cartridge. Rifle is here fitted with extra-long magazine to hold twenty .31-calibre cartridges; regular service-issue magazine holds five. The carbine or short rifle (bottom), mechanically identical to the long version above it, is shown with the bolt slid forward and the handle turned down, ready for firing. Well upward of sixty Mauser designs, all essentially alike, were made and issued between 1888 and 1945; actual Mauser actions or imitations are in use on hundreds of thousands of civilian rifles. (Reproduced by permission of Francis Bannerman Sons, N. Y.)

vanished, or was on the verge of vanishing, from the military scene of all the Western powers. Millions were scrapped; millions more, muskets and pistols, were converted to center-fire breechloaders, usually single-shot. An enormous outpouring of repeaters usurped their place, and these in turn spawned their descendants and demised. Concerning muzzleloading fowling pieces, no more were being made for sporting use by 1870; pinfire and, after about 1880, center-fire double and single guns became the rule, although the thousands of fine old stub-twist-barreled guns vanished slowly, and quite a few are still in active and gentlemanly service today. One species of muzzleloader is far from extinct: the crudely-made flint and percussion general-purpose guns which Belgian factories still disgorge for use by poverty-stricken peoples in underdeveloped regions.

Although the *age* of firearms today thrives with ten thousand species in the fullest heat of its summer, the *history* of firearms ended between seventy and eighty years ago. There has been nothing new since, and almost certainly nothing new will come hereafter. To prophesy thus is not to gaze into the well-known clouded crystal ball and to opine that human ingenuity can go no further. It can, and it has—on the drawing board and in the laboratory. But in daily practice, the existing types of small arms answer their purpose with maximum effectiveness at minimum cost to make for the optimum utility. Even if science should in time devise fission-powered police pistols and thermonuclear shotguns, it is improbable that these could do the job as effectively with as little complexity for as low a cost as the conventional models now in use. And since these have now been in use for three generations, the cycle of the argument returns one to the proposition that the history of

firearms—meaning the history of their evolution—has long been a closed volume. Such "history" as has followed the demise of the muzzleloader—or, more correctly, the advent of nitrocellulose powders and metallic cartridge breechloaders—has been an interminable flow of statistics, manuals and catalogues of makes, models, serials, issues, calibres, bores, gauges, metals, muzzle velocities, foot-pounds, screw sizes, magazine capacities, etc., etc.—all very complicated and technical but fearsomely pallid and ashen and as pertinent to the history of firearms as recent developments in the chemistry of paint manufacture are to the history of art. The skill and craftsmanship —one may say, the art—of gunmaking has vanished. Machinery begets machinery, and like all machine-made machines, modern guns are inexpensive and precise; they shoot well, their barrels are good, their moving parts fit well—but, save on very expensive models, the barrels are not as good as a set of London stub-twist tubes of six generations ago—metallurgically tougher, certainly, but not as well made—nor are the parts as finely finished as those, say, of a Knox or Egg or Manton flintlock or a Purdy or Westley Richards percussion lock. In all Britain there are not two dozen men today who could make a gun by hand, let alone as well as was demanded of any eighteen-year-old apprentice in the days of Twigg or Mortimer; nor two dozen in the United States who could build a rifle out of a maple tree and two bars of pig iron, as was expected of any Pennsylvania riflesmith about the time of Bunker Hill; nor probably four dozen on all the Continent of Europe who could even approximate the craftsmanship of their wheellock- and flintlock-making ancestors. The so-called "gunsmiths" of today, with a handful of exceptions, are like our "watchmakers" who cannot make watches and our "shoemakers" whose craft consists of glueing on a new pair of rubber heels—repairmen who substitute new factory-made parts for worn ones, with an occasional bit of filing and fitting. The stock carvers, ivory inlayers, staghorn dyers, engravers, silversmiths, etchers and steel chiselers of the wheellock and part of the flintlock age have long since passed into oblivion. Their always masterful, frequently imaginative, sometimes even culturally and aesthetically creative artistry had entered its decline early in the eighteenth century; its vestiges became stereotyped in the early nineteenth, descended through the Victorian era in a triumph of lush ugliness and characteristic bad taste, and finally perished among the uniformly trite and vulgar attempts which one may buy today on "custom made" or "de luxe grade" showpieces. Resuscitation of the vanished skills and originality is of course impossible in our time, not only because it is—unfortunately—a time of die-stamps and conformity, but—fortunately—a time when firearms have passed from the household scene.

With the demise of the muzzleloader and the universal adoption of modern or essentially modern guns in the 1880's, firearms, like black Japan-lacquered phaetons and gold-and-silver moon-phase pocket watches, were swept into the insatiable furnace mouth of this industrial epoch, where they were melted down to memories and recast in the formless mold of standardized efficiency.

FINIS

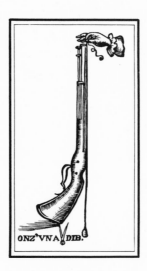

ONZ VNA DIB.

Part 1: The following is a partial list of out-of-print classics in arms and armor literature. They are available for the most part only in repositories like the New York Public Library, the British Museum, et al. They were selected for the unusual value of their pictorial contents and for their direct pertinence to the text of THE AGE OF FIREARMS.

An Account of the Life and Character of Sir Chomley Deering, Bar. &c. Anon., London, 1711.

The American Shooter's Manual. Anon., "by a Gentleman of Philadelphia County." Philadelphia, 1827.

The Annals of Sporting and Fancy Gazette; weekly magazine. London, 1820 and after.

Appier Hanzelet, Jean. *La Pyrotechnie.* Pont-à-Mousson, 1630.

———. *Recueil de Plusieurs Machines Militaires &c.* Pont-à-Mousson, 1620.

The Art of Duelling, by a Traveller. Anon., London, 1836.

Baker, Ezekiel. *Remarks on Rifle Guns.* 8th ed. London, 1825.

Beecher, Reverend Lyman. *The Remedy for Duelling (A Sermon).* New York, 1809.

Belli, Pierino. *De Re Militari et Bello Tractatus.* Venice, 1563. Translated by Herbert C. Nutting, in *The Classics of International Law,* ed. by J. B. Scott. Oxford, The Clarendon Press; London, H. Milford; 1936.

Berenger, Baron de. *Helps and Hints How to Protect Life and Property.* London, 1835.

Beaufoy, Colonel Henry. *Scloppetaria: or Considerations of the Nature and Use of Rifled Barrel Guns.* London, 1808.

Binning, Capitan Thomas. *A light to the Art of Gunnery.* London, 1676.

Bland, Humphrey. *An Abstract of Military Discipline.* Boston, 1747.

Blome, Richard (compiler, editor and partial author). *The Gentleman's Recreation.* London, 1686 (See Cox, Nicholas, below).

Bonfadini, Vita. *La Caccia dell'Arcobugio.* Venice, 1691.

Cox, Nicholas. *The Gentleman's Recreation.* London, 1677.

Daniel, Reverend William B. *Rural Sports.* London, 1801-1802.

The Dead Shot, or Sportsman's Complete Guide. Anon., London, 1866.

Diderot, Dénis. *Encyclopedie.* Paris, 1751-65.

Duane, William. *The American Military Library.* Philadelphia, 1809.

———. *A Handbook for Infantry.* Philadelphia, 1813.

An Essay on Shooting. Anon., London, 1789.

Ffoulkes, Charles John. *Arms and Armament; An Historical Survey of the Weapons of the British Army.* London, G. G. Harrap & Co., 1945.

———. *Sword, Lance and Bayonet; A Record of the Arms of the British Army and Navy.* Cambridge [England] University Press, 1939.

Firth, C. H. *Cromwell's Army.* London, 1902.

Fleming, Hanns Friedrich von. *Der Vollkommene Teutsche Jäger.* Leipzig, 1724.

Gaya, Louis de. *Traité des Armes.* Paris, 1678.

Gheyn, Jacob de. *Maniement d'armes.* Amsterdam, 1608.

Great Britain: Patent Office. *Specifications of Patents of Invention Relating to Fire-Arms, &c.* 8 vols. London, 1854.

Greener, William. *The Gun, or a Treatise on the Various Descriptions of Small Fire-Arms.* London, 1835.

———. *The Science of Gunnery.* London, 1841.

Grose, Francis. *Military Antiquities.* London, 1786-88.

Hawker, Lieutenant Colonel Peter. *Instructions to young Sportsmen in All That Pertains to Guns and Shooting.* London, 1814, &c.

Johnson, Thomas Burgeland. *The Shooter's Guide or Complete Sportman's Companion.* London, 1816.

Lacombe, Jacques. *Dictionnaire de Toutes les Espèces de Chasses.* Paris, 1795.

Markham, Gervase. *Hunger's Prevention or The Whole Arte of Fowling by Water and Land.* London, 1621.

Markland, George. *Pteryplegia: or the Art of Shooting Flying.* London, 1727.

Marolles, G. F., Magne du. *La Chasse au Fusil.* Paris, 1788.

Meyrick, Samuel Rush. *A Critical Inquiry into Antient Armour.* London, 1824.

Norton, Robert. *The Gunner, Shewing the Whole Practice of Artillery.* London, 1628.

Nye, Nathaniel. *The Art of Gunnery.* London, 1647.

A Plan for the Formation of a Corps. Anon., "by a Colonel in the German Service." London, 1805.

Quellen zur Geschichte der Feuerwaffen. Germanisches Museum (Nuremberg), Leipzig, 1872.

Ridinger, Johann Elias, *Abbildungen der Jagtbaren Thiere.* Augsburg, 1740.

Robins, Benjamin. *New Principles of Gunnery.* London, 1742.

Saint-Remy, Surirey de. *Memoires d'Artillerie.* Paris, 1697.

Schön, Julius. *Geschichte der Handfeuerwaffen.* Dresden, 1858.

Sharp, Granville. *A Tract on Duelling.* London, 1773.

The Sportsman's Companion or an Essay on Shooting. Anon., "by a Gentleman." Burlington, 1791.

Steuben, Baron von. *Regulations for the Order and Discipline of the Troops of the United States.* Albany, N.Y., 1803.

Straet (Stradanus), Jan van der. *Venationes Ferarum, Avium, Piscium &c.* Antwerp, 1566 [?].

Strictures on the Army. Anon., "by a Field Officer." Dublin, 1809.

Thornton, Col. Charles. *A Sporting Tour Through Various Parts of France.* London. 1806.

Ufano, Diego. *Artilleria, &c.* Madrid, 1621.

Valturio, Roberto. *De L'Arte Militare.* Verona, 1483.

Valturius, Robertus. *De Re Militari.* Paris, 1532.

Weems, Mason L. *God's Revenge Against Adultery.* Philadelphia, 1818.

———. *God's Revenge Against Duelling.* Philadelphia, 1821.

Weigel, Christoff. *Abbildung der Gemein-Nützlichen Haupt-Staende.* Augsburg, 1698.

Williams, Sir Roger. *A Briefe Discourse of Warre.* London, 1590.

Wilson, John Lyde. *The Code of Honor or Rules for the Government of Principals and Seconds in Duelling.* Charleston, S.C., 1845.

Part 2: A limited list of in-print books—and some readily available out-of-print ones—on firearms history. So prolific has been the flow of arms works in the decade 1960-1970 that complete bibliography would itself become a hefty volume. Hence the criteria for inclusion of a work here was (a) its interest to the general, non-specialized reader wanting to go beyond THE AGE OF FIREARMS, and (b) completion of firearms history after the chronological wind-up of THE AGE OF FIREARMS in the 1870's. Let it be heavily underlined that non-inclusion of a book in no way implies a negative judgment of its merits.

Akehurst, Richard. *Sporting Guns*. New York, 1968.

Ashdown, Chas. H. *European Arms & Armour*. New York, 1967.

Atkinson, J. A. *Duelling Pistols*. Harrisburg, Pa.

Back, D. H. L. and Neal, W. K. *The Mantons: Gunmakers*. New York, 1966.

Baird, John D. *Hawken Rifles—the Mountain Man's Choice*. Pence, Ind. 1968.

Blackmore, Howard L. *British Military Firearms 1650-1850*. New York, 1962.

————. *Firearms*. New York, 1964.

————. *Guns and Rifles of the World*. New York, 1965.

————. *Royal Sporting Guns at Windsor*. London, 1968.

Blair, Claude. *European and American Arms*. London and New York, 1962.

————. *Pistols of the World*. New York, 1968.

Carman, W. Y. *A History of Firearms*. London, 1955.

Chapel, Charles Edward. *The Complete Book of Gun Collecting*. New York, 1960.

————. *The Gun Collector's Handbook of Values*. New York, 1968.

Dillin, John G. W. *The Kentucky Rifle*. York, Pa., 1967.

Dunlap, Jack. *American, British and Continental Pepperbox Firearms*. Los Altos, Calif., 1964.

Edwards, William B. *Civil War Guns*. Harrisburg, Pa., 1962.

————. *The Story of Colt's Revolver*. Harrisburg, Pa., 1953.

Fuller, Claud E. *The Breech-Loader in the Service 1816-1917*. New Milford, Conn., 1965.

Gaibi, General Agostino. *Le Armi da Fuoco Portatili Italiane*. Milan, 1962.

Gamber, B. Thomas & H. Schedelmann. *Arms & Armour of the Western World*. New York, 1964.

George, John Nigel. *English Guns & Rifles*. Harrisburg, Pa., 1957.

————. *English Pistols and Revolvers*. New York, 1962.

Glendenning, Ian. *British Pistols and Guns 1640-1940*. New York, 1967.

Grancsay, Stephen V. *Master French Gunsmiths' Designs of the 17th Century*. New York, 1950.

————. *Sculpture in Arms and Armor*. New York, 1940.

Hayward, J. F. *The Art of the Gunmaker*. New York, 1962-64.

Hicks, James E. *French Military Weapons 1717-1938*. New Milford, Conn. 1964.

Jackson, H. J., and Whitelaw, C. *European Hand Firearms of the 16th, 17th and 18th Centuries*. London, 1959.

Kauffman, C. *The Pennsylvania-Kentucky Rifle*. New York, 1968.

Kindig, Joe (jr.). *Thoughts on the Kentucky Rifle in its Golden Age*. Wilmington, Del., 1960.

Koller, Larry. *The Fireside Book of Guns*. New York, 1959.

Lenk, Thorsten. *The Flintlock, its Origin and Development*. London, 1964.

Lindsay, Merrill. *One Hundred Great Guns*. New York, 1967.

Lister, Ronald. *Antique Firearms: Their Care and Restoration*. New York, 1964.

Merli, Alberto. *Un'Indagine sugli Armaiuoli del Contado Fiorentino nei Secoli XVI-XVIII*. Florence, Italy, 1969.

Moller, Thorsten. *Antique Danish Military Weapons*. Copenhagen, 1963.

Moore, Warren. *Weapons of the American Revolution*. New York, 1967.

Neal, W. Keith. *Spanish Guns and Pistols*. London, 1955.

Neumann, George C. *The History of the Weapons of the American Revolution*. New York, 1967.

Parsons, John E. *The First Winchester*. New York, 1955.

Partington, J. R. *A History of Greek Fire & Gunpowder*.

Peterson, Harold L. *A History of Firearms*. New York, 1961.

————. *The Pageant of the Gun*. Garden City, N.Y., 1967.

————. *The Treasury of the Gun*. New York, 1965.

————. *Arms and Armor in Colonial America*. Harrisburg, Pa., 1964 (reprint)

————. (Editor) *The Encyclopedia of Firearms*. New York, 1964.

Pope, Dudley. *Guns*. N.Y.C., 1965.

Ricketts, Howard. *Firearms*. New York, 1962.

Riling, Ray. *The Powder Flask Book*. New York, 1968.

————. *Guns & Shooting: A Bibliography*. New York, 1951.

Roberts, Ned H. *The Muzzle-Loading Cap Lock Rifle*. Harrisburg, Pa., 1958.

Serven, James E. *The Collecting of Guns*. Harrisburg, Pa., 1964.

————. *Colt Firearms from 1836*. Santa Ana, Calif., 1964.

Stone, G. C. *A Glossary of the Construction, Decoration and Use of Arms and Armour in All Countries and in All Times*. New York, 1966.

Terenzi, Marcello. *L'Arte di Michele Tattista*. Rome, 1964.

Watrous, Geo. (ed. by Hall, T. E. and Kuhlhoff, P.) *The History of Winchester Firearms 1866-1966*. New Haven, Conn., 1966.

Wilkinson, F. *Flintlock Pistols*. Harrisburg, Pa., 1968.

Williamson, F. *Winchester, the Gun that Won the West*. Washington, D.C., 1952.

INDEX

All *figure references* are in *italics*, all page references in roman. Small capital letter following page number indicates Left or Right column.